Parentheses
distinguished from dashes, **P28**

Periods, P3
with end quotation marks, **P24**

Possessive, P25

Punctuation
an introduction, **P1**

Question marks, P3
with end quotation marks, **P22**

Quotation marks
double and single, **P17**
end quotation marks with colons and
   semicolons, **P23**
end quotation marks with periods and
   commas, **P24**
end quotation marks with question
   marks and exclamation points, **P22**

op[...]
[...]
wit[...], P16
within quotes, **P17**

Quotations
altered, **P19**
in dialogue, **P16**
more than four lines long, **P18**
within quotations, **P17**

Quoting poetry, P20

Semicolons
between items in a series, **P14**
distinguished from colons, **P11**
with conjunctive adverbs, **P13**
with coordinate conjunctions, **P12**
with end quotation marks, **P23**

Titles
capital letters in, **P2**
other punctuation in, **P21**

Nouns
collective, **G40**
defined, **G14**
plurals, **G15**

Objects
of prepositions, **G26**

Participles
dangling, **G11**
defined, **G7**
irregular past, **G7, G8**
See also pp. 173–178

Parts of speech
listed, **G3**

Plurals
of nouns, **G15**

Possessive
of nouns, **P25**
of pronouns, **G20**

Prepositions
confused with conjunctions, **G31**
defined, **G26**
as final word, **G27**

Pronouns
agreement, **G17**
case, **G20, G33, G34**
defined, **G16**

possessive, **G20**
reference, **G16**
relative, **G22**
sexism, **G17**
shifts in person, **G19**
use of first person, **G18**
who/whom, **G34**
you/one, **G19**

Questions
direct and indirect, **G49**

Sentence
fragments, **G46**
fused, **G47**
See also Chapters Seven and Eight

Subjects
defined, **G35**

Verbs
be, **G12, G38, G41**
defined, **G4**
finite/nonfinite, **G9**
principal parts, **G7**
tense, **G50**

Verb Phrases
defined, **G5**
split, **G6**

Voice
active/passive, **G13**

WRITING
(Is an Unnatural Act)

WRITING
(Is an Unnatural Act)

JAMES C. RAYMOND
The University of Alabama

1817

HARPER & ROW, PUBLISHERS, New York
Cambridge, Hagerstown, Philadelphia, San Francisco,
London, Mexico City, São Paulo, Sydney

Sponsoring Editor: Phillip Leininger
Project Editor: David Nickol
Designer: Graphikann
Production Manager: Marion A. Palen
Compositor: Ruttle, Shaw & Wetherill, Inc.
Printer and Binder: The Murray Printing Company
Art Studio: Vantage Art Inc.
Cover Photo: Emily Harste

WRITING
(Is an Unnatural Act)

Library of Congress Cataloging in Publication Data

Raymond, James C   1940–
      Writing (is an unnatural act)

      Includes index.
      1.   English language — Rhetoric.   I.   Title.
PE1408.R38   808'.042   79–26767
ISBN 0–06–045342–7

Contents at a Glance

Preface   xv

CHAPTER ONE   *Introduction: What Is Writing?*   1

Rhetoric

PREWRITING

CHAPTER TWO   *Asking Questions*   15
CHAPTER THREE   *Six Questions for Critical Reading*   51

ORGANIZATION

CHAPTER FOUR   *Selecting and Arranging*   83
CHAPTER FIVE   *Paragraphs*   103

STYLE

CHAPTER SIX   *Words and Phrases: Six Problems*   137
CHAPTER SEVEN   *Assembling Sentences: Six Problems*   149
CHAPTER EIGHT   *Style: Ten Lessons*   163

The Research Paper

CHAPTER NINE   *Diary of a Term Paper*   201
CHAPTER TEN   *Library Research*   228
CHAPTER ELEVEN   *Term Paper Form*   245

Handbook

CHAPTER TWELVE   *Correctness, Dictionaries, and Spelling*   259
CHAPTER THIRTEEN   *A Do-It-Yourself Usage Guide*   280
CHAPTER FOURTEEN   *A Grammar for Writers*   287
CHAPTER FIFTEEN   *A Punctuation Guide*   378
APPENDIX   *Two Advanced Discovery Procedures*   415

Index   429

Contents

Preface   xv

CHAPTER ONE   *Introduction: What Is Writing?*   1
1. Writing Is a Way of Thinking   2
2. Writing Is an Unnatural Form of Speech   3
3. Writing Is Not "Engfish"   5
4. Writing Is Hard Work   7
   Exercises   9
   Preliminary Writing Assignments   11

Rhetoric

PREWRITING

CHAPTER TWO   *Asking Questions*   **15**
1. The Five Senses as Questions   16
   Exercise   19
   Writing Assignments   19
2. The Five Journalistic Questions   20
   Exercise   21
   Writing Assignments   22
3. An Open Set of Questions   22
   Exercises   25
   Writing Assignments   25

4. Five Traditional Angles   26
    a. Process Analysis   27
        Exercise   28
        Writing Assignment   28
    b. Division and Classification   29
        Exercise   30
        Writing Assignment   31
    c. Comparison and Contrast   32
        Exercise   34
        Writing Assignment   34
    d. Definition   35
        Exercise   37
        Writing Assignment   38
    e. Cause and Effect   39
        Exercise   43
        Writing Assignment   43
5. Interviewing   44
    Exercise   50
    Writing Assignments   50

CHAPTER THREE   *Six Questions for Critical
                     Reading*   **51**

1. Assertions and Evidence   52
2. Author and Audience   60
3. Tone and Structure   63
4. Another Essay for Critical Reading   66
5. Other Kinds of Nonscientific Evidence   71
6. Irony   73
7. Critical Readers as an Elite Group   78
    Exercises   78
    Writing Assignments   79

ORGANIZATION

CHAPTER FOUR   *Selecting and Arranging*   **83**

1. Choosing a Rhetorical Stance   84
2. The Persuasive Stance: Thesis and Outline   85
    Exercises   90
    Writing Assignment   92
    Checkpoint for Persuasive Outlines   92
3. The Expository Stance: Control Sentence and Outline   92
    a. The Plural-Noun Formula   93
    b. Outlining a Comparison and Contrast Paper   94
    c. Beyond Basic Outlines   96
    Exercises   100
    Writing Assignment   101
    Checkpoint for Expository Outlines   102

CHAPTER FIVE *Paragraphs* 103
1. First Paragraphs 104
   Exercises 111
2. Middle Paragraphs: A Basic Pattern 111
   Exercises 116
3. Middle Paragraphs: Beyond the Basic Pattern 117
   Exercises 121
4. Narrative Paragraphs 122
   Exercise 124
   Writing Assignments 124
   Checkpoint for Narrative and Process Papers 125
5. Descriptive Paragraphs 125
   Exercise 129
   Writing Assignments 129
   Checkpoint for Descriptive Papers 130
6. Concluding Paragraphs 130
   Exercises 135
   Checkpoint for Organization 136

STYLE

CHAPTER SIX *Words and Phrases: Six Problems* 137
1. Wordiness 138
   Exercise 139
2. Wrong Word 140
   Exercise 140
3. Tangled Idiom 141
   Exercise 142
4. Colloquial Diction 142
   Exercise 144
5. Pretentious Diction (Jargon) 144
   Exercise 146
6. Clichés 147
   Exercise 148

CHAPTER SEVEN *Assembling Sentences:
Six Problems* 149
1. The Verb *Be* 150
   Exercise 150
2. Passive Voice 151
   Exercise 153
3. Faulty Predication 153
   Exercise 154
4. Faulty Parallelism 154
   Exercise 156
5. Repetition 157
   Exercise 157

6. Garbles   158
   Exercise   159
   Final Checkpoint for All Papers   160

CHAPTER EIGHT *Style: Ten Lessons*   **163**
1. The Problem of Synonymy   164
   Exercises   166
2. Rhythm, Variety, and Length   167
   Exercises   171
3. Present Participles   173
   Exercises   174
4. Past Participles   175
   Exercises   177
5. Appositives   178
   Exercises   179
6. Absolutes   180
   Exercises   181
7. Combinations   182
   Exercises   183
8. Series   184
   Exercises   185
9. Balanced, Periodic, and Cumulative Sentences   188
   Exercises   193
10. Style as the Person   195
    Writing Assignment   196

The Research Paper

CHAPTER NINE *Diary of a Term Paper*   **201**
1. Finding Material   201
2. Writing the Paper   208
3. A Sample Research Paper   210
   Exercises   226

CHAPTER TEN *Library Research*   **228**
1. Preparing for Research   228
2. Preliminary Search   229
3. Focusing and Limiting   233
4. Asking Questions   234
5. Taking Notes   236
6. Paraphrase and Plagiarism   238
   Sorting It Out   241
   Exercises   242
   Writing Assignment   244

CHAPTER ELEVEN *Term Paper Form*   **245**
1. A Variety of Style Manuals   245

2. The Bibliography   246
3. Footnotes and Endnotes   249
4. Sample Notes and Bibliographic Entries   253
      Checkpoint for Research Papers   256

Handbook

CHAPTER TWELVE   *Correctness, Dictionaries,*
                        and Spelling   **259**

1. Correctness   259
     Exercises   264
2. Dictionaries   267
     Exercises   271
3. Spelling   272
     Mnemonic Devices   273
     Adding Suffixes   274
     Adding *s* to Verbs That End in *y*   275
     Ordinary Plurals   275
     Adding *s* to Nouns That End in *y*   276
     Plurals of Nouns That End in *f*   276
     Plurals of Nouns That End in *o*   277
     Plurals of Nouns Borrowed from Foreign Languages   278
     Exercises   279

CHAPTER THIRTEEN   *A Do-It-Yourself Usage*
                        Guide   **280**

CHAPTER FOURTEEN   *A Grammar for Writers*   **287**

  G1 What Is Grammar?   287
  G2 How Much Grammar Do Writers Need to Know?   288
  G3 Parts of Speech   288
  G4 Recognizing Verbs   289
     Exercise   290
  G5 Recognizing Verb Phrases   290
     Exercises   291
  G6 Splitting Verb Phrases   292
     Exercise   293
  G7 Principal Parts and Troublesome Participles   293
     Exercises   294
  G8 Verbs: Problems with Past Tense and Past Participles   295
     Exercises   296
  G9 Finite/Nonfinite Verb Forms   298
     Exercise   299
  G10 Split Infinitives   301
     Exercise   302
  G11 Dangling and Squinting Modifiers   303
     Exercise   304

G12 The Verb *Be*   305
G13 Active Voice/Passive Voice   305
     Exercise   306
G14 Nouns   306
     Exercises   307
G15 Problems with Nouns: Plurals   308
     Exercise   309
G16 Pronouns and Their Referents   309
     Exercises   311
G17 Pronouns: Agreement   312
     Exercises   316
G18 Pronouns: Use of *I/We*   317
G19 *You/One*   318
     Exercise   319
G20 Pronouns: Possessive Forms   320
G21 Contractions   321
     Exercises   321
G22 Pronouns: Relative   322
     Exercise   323
G23 Adjective and Adverbs   323
     Exercises   325
G24 Using Adjectives for Adverbs   325
     Exercise   327
G25 Comparatives and Superlatives   328
     Exercises   331
G26 Prepositions   331
     Exercises   333
G27 Prepositions at the End of a Sentence or Clause   334
G28 Conjunctions: Coordinating and Subordinating   335
     Exercise   336
G29 Coordinating Conjunctions at the Beginning of a
     Sentence   336
G30 Conjunctive Adverbs   337
G31 Prepositions and Conjunctions: *Like, As, As If, As Though*   338
G32 Interjections   339
G33 Case: *I/Me, She/Her, He/Him, They/Them*   340
     Exercise   341
G34 Case: *Who/Whom*   342
     Exercise   344
G35 Identifying Subjects and Verbs   344
     Exercises   345
G36 Agreement: Subject-Verb   346
     Exercises   347
G37 Agreement Despite Intervening Nouns   348
     Exercise   348
G38 Agreement in the Verb *Be*   349
     Exercises   350

G39 Agreement: Verbs with Multiple Subjects 351
  Exercise 353
G40 Agreement: Verbs with Collective Nouns as Subjects 353
  Exercise 356
G41 *Be* Between Singular and Plural Nouns 357
  Exercise 357
G42 Agreement: Verb with *There* as Dummy Subject 358
  Exercise 358
G43 Agreement: *Each* and *Every* 359
  Exercise 359
G44 Agreement: "One of Those (Who/That) . . ." 360
  Exercise 360
G45 Clauses: Dependent and Independent 361
  Exercise 361
G46 Fragments 362
  Exercises 364
G47 Fused Sentences 370
G48 Comma Splice 371
  Exercises 372
G49 Questions: Direct and Indirect 374
  Exercise 376
G50 Tense 376

CHAPTER FIFTEEN *A Punctuation Guide* 378

P1 Punctuation: An Introduction 378
P2 Capital Letters 382
P3 Question Marks, Exclamation Points, and Periods 383
P4 Commas 383
P5 Commas Before Coordinate Conjunctions 384
P6 Commas in a Series 385
P7 Commas in Pairs 386
P8 Commas to Set Off Material at the Beginning or End of
  a Sentence 388
P9 Comma Before *But* 390
P10 Dates and Addresses 391
P11 Colons and Semicolons 391
P12 Semicolons Before Coordinate Conjunctions 392
P13 Semicolons with Conjunctive Adverbs 393
P14 Commas and Semicolons in Series 394
P15 Open Quotation Marks and Commas 395
P16 Quotations in Dialogue 396
P17 Quotes Within Quotes: Single Quotes and Double Quotes 397
P18 Quotations More Than Four Lines Long 398
P19 Altering Quoted Material 399
P20 Quoting Poetry 400
P21 Titles 401

P22 Question Marks and Exclamation Points with End
    Quotation Marks   402
P23 Colons and Semicolons with End Quotation Marks   403
P24 Periods and Commas with End Quotation Marks   403
P25 The Apostrophe to Mark the Possessive   404
P26 The Apostrophe to Mark Plurals   406
P27 *It's/Its*   407
P28 Dashes and Parentheses   407
P29 Dashes vs. Hyphens   409
P30 Hyphens in Compound Words   410
P31 Hyphenated Words at the End of a Line   411
    Exercises   412

APPENDIX *Two Advanced Discovery Procedures*   **415**
1. Burke's Pentad: Questions for Understanding Human
  Behavior   415
    Exercises   422
    Writing Assignments   422
2. Tagmemics: Questions for Analyzing Systems   423
    Exercise   428
    Writing Assignment   428

Index   429

Preface

The title of this book is not entirely frivolous. It is intended as a corrective for some widespread misconceptions about the nature of writing. Although no one really thinks writing is a natural activity like sleeping or eating, we often think of people who cannot write as somehow deficient in the gifts of nature. The truth is that most college freshmen who cannot write are no more exceptional than most college freshmen who cannot play the violin. Either they have never been taught, or they have not practiced enough, or they have never perceived writing (or violin playing) as a skill worth learning.

The best way to write a syllabus for this book is to examine the writing assignments and choose those that are most appropriate for the objectives of the course. In addition to the preliminary assignments at the end of Chapter One, there are fifteen assignments in Chapter Two alone, each one attached to an appropriate discovery procedure discussed in that chapter (see Table of Contents). Most of these assignments lead to particular sections in the chapters on organization and style. There are also five assignments at the end of Chapter Three, on critical reading; two of these assignments (numbers 3 and 5) can be repeated indefinitely in a course that uses the critical analysis of essays as a source for writing assignments. The research paper is assigned at the end of Chapter Ten. Additional assignments are given with the advanced discovery procedures — Kenneth Burke's pentad and tagmemic invention — in the appendix.

Teachers who like to arrange a course according to the traditional modes of discourse will find suitable material in the rhetoric section of this book. The first two discovery procedures in Chapter Two are especially suited to narrative and descriptive writing; the others are especially suited to persuasive and expository writing. All of these discussions end with assignments that guide the students to appropriate sections in the chapters on organization and style.

Teachers who like to arrange a course according to the traditional patterns of development — definition, division and classification, cause and effect, comparison and contrast, and process analysis — will find a detailed treatment under "Five Traditional Angles" in Chapter Two.

Teachers who like to arrange a course from small units to large can begin with the three chapters on word choice and sentence structure (Chapters Six, Seven, and Eight), followed by Chapter Four, on paragraph structure. It would be unwise, however, to assign papers without teaching some of the prewriting techniques in Chapters Two and Three.

Teachers who like to begin with experience as a source of ideas and proceed to secondary sources later can teach the book as it is. The first few discovery procedures lead to an analysis of experience. The others lead the students progressively further from their experience, first through an interview, then through short exercises in critical reading, and finally through rudimentary library research.

The lessons on style in Chapter Eight work best if they are done occasionally — say once a week — as warm-up exercises in class. They are useless, however, if assigned as homework. These ten lessons are designed to help ordinary students produce outstanding sentences. Some teachers even use them to have best-sentence contests in class, so that students can experience for themselves the pleasure of having their work appreciated by their peers.

Peer instruction is encouraged in this book by periodic checkpoints—lists of questions students can answer as they examine the work of their classmates before it is turned in for a grade. Some teachers use these checkpoints to conduct rough-draft workshops in one or two classes preceding the due date for any given assignment.

The exercises throughout are designed to provide teachers with ideas for discussion or in-class writing assignments. There are two ways to use these exercises. One is to discuss them after the students have read the section to which the exercises are attached; in this way, the instructor avoids repeating in class what the students have already read for themselves. Another use of the exercises, however, is as a pre-reading device. Doing the exercises in class before the students have read the material may enable them to read it with more understanding.

Except for the Do-It-Yourself Usage Guide, the Handbook (Chapters Twelve through Fifteen) is largely self-explanatory. The Usage Guide, however, will require a teacher who knows how to discuss questions of disputed usage or is willing to consult the reference texts mentioned in that section. Usage, by the way, is treated in this form because most students don't know in advance when they should consult a guide. Consider working on ten or twelve usage problems a day as warm-up exercises in class, perhaps on days when the sentence exercises in Chapter Eight are not being used.

There are two good ways to use the Handbook. One is to use it as a reference text that students and teachers can consult as the need arises. On the inside covers, front and back, you will find symbols and other devices to lead you to rules of punctuation and grammar. The punctuation rules are given "P" numbers, and the grammar rules "G" numbers. These numbers are clearly marked in blocks in the margins of the second half of the book.

The other good way to use the Handbook is to divide it into manageable units and work with it for ten minutes at a time in class. An ineffective use of the Handbook, however, would be to assume that it is somehow more basic than the rest of the text and that students should master grammar and punctuation before they can begin to learn to write. It isn't, and they won't.

Correction symbols are provided — with some reluctance on the part of the author. They can be useful as a supplement to explanations, written or oral, provided by the teacher in response to a student's work. As a substitute for the teacher's explanation, however, they are at best inefficient and at worst inhumane.

No man has ever felt less like an island than the author of this book. Perhaps the largest debt is owed to the people who have made composition a serious discipline. In addition to the writers and rhetoricians mentioned at various points in the text — Aristotle, Alton Becker, Kenneth Burke, Ken Macrorie, Kenneth Pike, and Richard Young — I am consciously aware of debts to scholars as diverse as Wayne Booth, Kenneth Bruffee, Francis Christensen, Edward P. J. Corbett, Frank D'Angelo, Janet Emig, Robert Gorrell, Maxine Hairston, E. D. Hirsch, Kellogg W. Hunt, James Kinneavy, John C. Mellon, James Moffett, Walter Ong, S.J., Frank O'Hare, Paul Roberts, Mina P. Shaughnessy, James Sledd, Ross Winterowd, and Robert Zoellner. I do not mean to suggest that any of these people has approved or endorsed the contents of this book — most of them have not even seen it — but simply to acknowledge that each of them has taught me something that I would not otherwise have learned.

Closer to home, I am grateful to the University of Alabama and to the English Department for encouragement and support. I am particularly grateful to a number of graduate students and colleagues who have taught various drafts of this work over the past five years and contributed to its improvement. Among these, Robert W. Halli, Jr., Maridith Letzer, Carole Swanay, Nancy Allen, Rodney Allen, Exir Brennan, Martha Edwards, Carlanda Green, Ellen Keever, and Sandra Sockwell have made specific contributions for which I am grateful.

Not the least of my debts is to the best group of readers an author in this field could hope for: Deborah Arfken, Richard Beal, Richard Larson, Elisabeth McPherson, and Bill Smith. In addition to their comments and suggestions, which I tried my best to follow, I received invaluable help from two of my colleagues here at the University of Alabama, John P. Burke and Nancy Moss. This book would have been much the worse without the revisions they suggested.

Susan Mulligan deserves special mention for patiently typing draft after draft and for making suggestions that have materially improved the text.

Finally, I am indebted to my wife, Ginny, who in addition to pursuing a career of her own while caring for our two children, made it possible for me to have the huge blocks of uninterrupted time that every author needs. It is to her that this book is dedicated, for without her it could not have been written.

James C. Raymond

WRITING
(Is an Unnatural Act)

Chapter One

---◆---

Introduction:
What Is Writing?

When television first became popular, lovers of the written word began to worry that writing might become obsolete. In more recent years, their worry has turned into alarm as verbal skills among entering college freshmen have been steadily declining.

Writing, however, is no more threatened by the invention of television than speech was threatened by the invention of writing. Writing will survive, as speech has survived, because it can do some things better than any other medium. In general, a new medium threatens an old one only in those specific areas in which the new medium can do a better job. Speech has survived the invention of writing because it is a handier medium for most ordinary communication. And writing will survive the invention of television because writing can do things that television cannot begin to compete with.

1. Writing Is a Way of Thinking

Writing is more than a medium of communication. It is a way of remembering and a way of thinking as well. Writing makes words permanent, and thus expands the collective memory of human beings from the relatively small store that we can remember and pass on orally to the infinite capacity of a modern library. What is stored in writing can also be retrieved more easily than what is stored in any other medium. Written matter can be indexed and cataloged with a precision and economy that is still unrivaled by computers.

Apart from its importance as the collective memory of our culture, writing has a private importance as a tool for clear thinking, for sharpening our awareness of the realities around us, for solving problems and shaping arguments, for developing that sort of knowledge — clear, specific, detailed — that makes human consciousness different from every other form of consciousness on earth. When speaking, we can get away with all sorts of ill-formed opinions. If our friends agree with us, they simply nod or reinforce our prejudices with prejudices of their own. And if they disagree, they may change the subject rather than argue. But writing is a way of arguing with ourselves, a way of keeping ourselves honest by discovering precisely what we believe and finding out whether we are justified in believing it.

Writing is also a way of finding out what we know and what we need to learn. Spoken words disappear as soon as they are spoken; but writing freezes our thoughts, makes them visible and permanent so we can examine and test their quality. This is one of the unnatural advantages of writing, as well as one of its challenges.

Writing is also a way of learning. None of us can write much of interest without first thinking, probing, observing, asking questions, experimenting, and reading. We need to admit this before we can exploit the unnatural advantages of writing. Speech requires very little preparation. We open our mouths and out flow the words. Good writing, on the other hand, is like any other art — never really as spontaneous or as easy as the artist likes to make it seem.

2. *Writing Is an Unnatural Form of Speech*

Good writing is much more than speech written down. In speech, you make your meaning clear with gestures and inflections, raising your voice to indicate questions, stressing certain words for emphasis, pausing to make distinctions or to create special effects. In writing, you have to give up all these natural devices. In speech you might use the same words—for example, "The governor has been reelected"—to indicate surprise, disappointment, delight, doubt, disgust, or to ask a question. The way you say it makes the meaning. In writing, however, you need other ways to signal your meaning: punctuation, attention to word order, even the use of blank space. These devices don't come naturally.

Speech is natural. All people can talk even if they have no way of recording their language. Writing, however, is an invention as artificial as the radio and the tape recorder. Writing does not come naturally. Each generation has to teach it to the next. We have to learn not only the physical activities of forming letters and words on paper, but also a host of traditions that writers and readers have become accustomed to.

Once you realize that the traditions are artificial and to some extent arbitrary, you have a better chance of learning them. Many conventions in writing are logical: they are designed to make the meaning of written passages clear, just as pauses, gestures, and inflections are used to make spoken sentences unambiguous. Other conventions, however, are not logical: rules about spelling and usage often fall into this category. Writers obey them mainly because other writers obey them.

In some ways writing has unnatural advantages over speech. In speech, we can think only seven seconds ahead—hardly enough time to consider alternative arrangements for each sentence and each sequence of sentences. As a result, even accomplished speakers are often dismayed when they read their words copied verbatim. Trial proceedings, for example, can seem like illiterate babble when written down:

Defense Attorney: And what is your education?

Defendant: Eighth grade.

Defense Attorney: Ah—Now you say eighth grade—can you—ah—what is your effective education?

Defendant: Third grade.

Defense Attorney: How do you arrive at that?

Defendant: Well—ah—they kicked me from—I passed out—up to the third grade, and they just kicked me from one grade to the next, straight through.

Prosecuting Attorney: Judge, that's hearsay.

Judge: —ah—

Defense Attorney: Well—

Prosecuting Attorney: First, I can't see where it's relevant to start with.

In this passage, the speech of the judge and the attorneys is no more polished than the speech of the eighth-grade dropout. None of them is speaking prose destined for immortality. The frequent changes of direction in mid-sentence, the groping about for words, the incomplete sentences are all typical of the spoken language of ordinary business.

But writers have the unnatural advantage of time. They plan their words hours in advance, sometimes weeks and months in advance. A spoken word can never be retrieved; but written words can be recalled, replaced, rearranged, or rejected a thousand times before being turned over to readers.

Another unnatural aspect of writing is the range of its vocabulary. Before the invention of writing, there was a limit to the number of words that could be remembered and used by any society. Since human memory was the only medium for storing words, the only words that were likely to survive were those that were useful in everyday life and those that were preserved by specialists in one craft or another, including the craft of poetry.

But writing gives words a permanence that they could never have in an oral culture. Even rare words are preserved on paper so that they no longer depend upon the frail human memory for survival. When printing was invented, and writers turned their attention to more diverse and more specialized subjects, the vocabulary of writing grew beyond the ability of any human mind to master. A new kind of book was invented—the dictionary—so that readers and writers could keep up with the explosion of words in their own language.

The vocabulary of writing, then, is much broader than the vocabulary of speech, and part of learning to write is learning how to use the words that writers use. The vocabulary of speech comes naturally. We absorb it without effort from people around us. But much of the vocabulary of writing does not occur often in speech, and it can be mastered only through conscious effort, the sort of effort it takes to learn a foreign language.

If you hope to improve your skill as a writer, you need to improve your vocabulary. You need to learn new words of all sizes, not just the big ones that will impress the folks back home, but even little ones, words that will make your writing more precise, accurate, and economical. *Dregs*, for example, is a little word; but as one eminent writing teacher observed, a writer who doesn't know the word *dregs* has to say "what's left in the cup after you get finished drinking." Ten words to do the work of one.

Perhaps the best way to improve your vocabulary is to buy a good desk dictionary and keep it right next to the chair in which you do most of your reading and writing. If the dictionary is more than a few feet away, chances are you will not use it when you need it. Learn new words as you read. Look up the definitions and then observe how the word is used in context. If the dictionary definition makes no sense to you, ask an instructor or a fellow student for help. Sometimes off-the-cuff definitions are more helpful than dictionary definitions. Don't try to memorize every word you look up—you'll soon be discouraged. But do keep a notebook in which you collect words you think you might be able to use. Write your own definitions of these words. Use them in sentences. Return to the notebook often and study your collection as you add to it.

3. Writing Is Not "Engfish"

Some students and many experienced writers make writing more unnatural than it should be. They abandon the clarity of the spoken word altogether and invent a totally new language that scarcely anybody can read with ease.

Example

In resolving the question whether, and how, to count ballots not marked by voters in accordance with instructions, so that the intent of the voter is unclear, we have said that "if the intent of the voter can be determined with reasonable certainty from an inspection of the ballot, in the light of the generally known conditions attendant upon the election, effect must be given to that intent and the vote counted in accordance therewith."

Granted, this is unnatural English — *too* unnatural. Unfortunately, many people write it — lawyers, sociologists, educators, business people, even English teachers on occasion. The meaning of the sentence is simple enough:

When officials can figure out what the marks on a ballot mean, they must count that ballot, even if it is not marked according to instructions.

But professional people are sometimes fearful of English that is plain, simple, and direct.

The tradition of obscurity in law is fairly old; it can be traced back to England, where short sentences and punctuation within long sentences are considered unprofessional in legal documents. In the United States, a more recent tradition of obscurity has sprung up, largely within the past thirty years: the tradition of the technical specialist. Impressed by the achievements of science, people are inclined to give a scientific and technical air to everything they say and write. This new tradition has infected the language of everyone from garbage collectors who refer to themselves as sanitation engineers to university administrators who can scarcely get from subject to verb without the help of a "parameter," a "contraindication," or a "mechanism for implementation." Even scholars who write about how human beings understand language feel compelled to write about it in language no ordinary human being could understand.

Example

We know of stimulus order effects that occur in non-speech modalities with both faster and slower presentation rates than speech: hence, it is reasonable to expect that presentation order in speech also influences the percepts that are conveyed by determining the order in which they are constructed.

Among students, writing often takes an unnatural form that Ken Macrorie, a famous writing teacher, calls "Engfish" — a term that suggests a smelly, bloated form of language.

Example

It behooves us at this point in time to examine the preponderance of evidence supportive of our initial thesis with respect to the triadic transcendentalism that links Emerson and Melville to the intellectual milieu of their contemporaries.

The problem with Engfish is that it not only is unnatural, it *seems* unnatural too. It is so impressed with itself that it cannot be bothered with making things clear for the reader. Writers of Engfish confuse big words and tangled syntax for profound thought.

The essential paradox of good writing is that, despite hours of thought and preparation, despite wastebaskets stuffed with drafts, revisions, and false starts, good writing can *seem* natural. If it is really good, really unnatural in the best sense of the word, it can be as easy to understand as ordinary speech.

4. Writing Is Hard Work

Writing is not easy. An experienced writer will often labor over a single paragraph for more than an hour — not counting the thought and research that went on before the actual writing. A well-written paragraph is often the outcome of a process that included several false starts and two or three drafts. All this work for a few sentences that can be read aloud in about forty seconds.

In other words, an hour's work produces forty seconds of performance. Many students fail to improve as writers simply because they are unwilling to accept this ratio as an ordinary fact of a writer's life. But in this respect, writing is no different from any other art: movies, plays, ballets, and concerts take hundreds of hours to prepare, but only a few hours to perform.

Writers need tools. In addition to the obvious tools — paper, pencils, pens, a dictionary, perhaps a typewriter — there are two others that most good writers find indispensable: scissors and Scotch tape. As you will soon find out, writing is a process of molding information into a shape that makes sense. If you write a paper of any length without feeling the urge to cut and paste and rearrange and rearrange again, you have probably failed to understand how writing is a medium for shaping ideas.

Another good tool is a thick, spiral-bound notebook in which you take notes, collect vocabulary words, do sentence exercises, and work on passages that may eventually become part of an assigned paper.

Good writing generally contains more information per phrase, more wit, more insight, more beauty than conversation simply because writers have time in their favor — and good writers exploit that advantage. They are tough on themselves, difficult to please. They consider alternatives to every phrase they write. They take time to tinker and rearrange, scratch out, add notes in the margins, leave blank spaces to be filled in later, read their rough drafts to critical friends and hope to be told about anything flawed, dull, or obscure. That's why good writing is good.

Beginning writers, however, tend to let time become an enemy rather than an ally. Instead of using time to perfect their work, they wait till the last minute, just before the deadline, leaving themselves little time to polish and revise.

And yet beginners are pleased with their work, amazed when others find it unclear or uninteresting. This is one of the most troublesome problems for beginners: learning to see their work as others see it. All of us, when we read our own work, know the point we're trying to make. We tend to provide logical connections that are in our heads rather than on the paper; we overlook misspelled words because they don't look misspelled to us; and we neglect stylistic niceties because we consider our ideas more important.

Before you can improve as a writer, you have to find some way to see your own work objectively. Take advantage of time. You can generally see your work better if you put it aside for at least twenty-four hours. Get help from your friends. Have them read your work and encourage them to tell you honestly how it strikes them. Listen attentively to whatever they say; if you begin defending yourself or apologizing for your errors, your readers will become less honest, less valuable as editors. This book will provide you with hints and directives you can use in the process of writing, but no book can substitute for the editorial advice that teachers give students and students give one another.

EXERCISES

1. To find out exactly how unnatural writing is, choose a few passages — anything except conversation — from a respectable book, magazine, or newspaper. Read them aloud, and try to imagine yourself speaking these sentences off the top of your head. If you find that they are different from what you normally speak — different from what anybody normally speaks — try to describe the differences as precisely as you can. As an aid, rephrase the sentences in your own words, exactly as you would normally say them. Put your own version in writing and compare it to the original in structure and vocabulary.

2. Collect several sentences from printed sources and come to class prepared to discuss exactly how these sentences differ from everyday speech.

3. Collect some examples of words, phrases, and expressions that do not occur in formal writing but do occur in the speech of your family, friends, or neighbors. Can you think of any situations in which these expressions would be useful to you as a speaker? As a writer?

4. Sometimes great works of literature are written in what is generally regarded as an uneducated dialect. Here, for example, is the opening paragraph of *Huckleberry Finn*, which is generally regarded as one of the greatest American novels ever written.

You don't know about me, without you have read a book by the name of "The Adventures of Tom Sawyer," but that ain't no matter. That book was made by Mr. Mark Twain, and he told the truth, mainly. There was things which he stretched, but mainly he told the truth. That is nothing. I never seen anybody but lied, one time or another, without it was Aunt Polly, or the widow, or maybe Mary. Aunt Polly — Tom's Aunt Polly, she is — and Mary, and the Widow Douglas, is all told about in that book — which is mostly a true book; with some stretchers, as I said before.

In what specific ways is Huck's language different from what you would ordinarily expect to see in print? Would there be any difference between Huck's language and the unedited speech of a nineteenth-century Missouri grammar school dropout? What has Twain done to ordinary speech to make it great art? Can you think of any other successful novels or short stories written in what, at first glance, appears to be ordinary, unedited speech?

5. Look over the three passages quoted below and rank them in order of excellence. If these were three entries in a writing contest, which would you give first prize to, assuming that the contestants were free to write about any topic they wished? Be ready to defend your decision in class.

When I was born sometime in Auguest I beleve it was my parents was living in Erope. I gues Dads mine had other things to wory about because he sure was'nt to anxous to come to the post hospitle until after I was more than three day's old. From the beginning of time Army hospitles were not too good of a place to be born in.

Writing a research paper can be an important part of a college education if a student takes the time and effort to do it the way it should be done. True, many students buy their papers from smart friends or from term paper companies. But this should not discourage mature students from doing their own work. The best way to profit from writing a research paper is to start as early as possible, pick a subject that you really want to learn about, and think about the point or points you want to make while you are doing your research.

L.A., well, it sounded good. Tired feet, hungry, rejected and poor. Ain't had a ride in five hours. What conceivable reason, unexplainable, insane notion compelled me to hitchhike to L.A.? Well it sounded good. I guess. Those damn cars. They come around the bend, you give them your best smile, and they drive on by as your thumb slowly comes down, replaced by your middle finger. What's this? A sound, if only it could be a God-sent freak going to California. A blue van, chrome wheels, beard, long hair, praise the Lord! Don't the rubber sound good against the asphalt.

PRELIMINARY WRITING ASSIGNMENTS

1. Find an interesting passage in any issue of *Harper's, Atlantic, The New Yorker,* or *Saturday Review.* Copy a passage of approximately one hundred and fifty words. Then write a passage of your own about a similar topic — make up facts and figures if you need them — imitating the style of the passage you copied. Try to avoid the exact words of the original. When you finish, bring both passages to class and see whether your teachers and classmates can tell which is your own writing and which is copied. If they can't tell the difference, you have succeeded. If they can tell the difference, get them to tell you exactly what gives you away.

2. After studying the differences between ordinary speech and ordinary writing, compose a short paper comparing the two. What are the advantages and disadvantages of each? Should everyone try to speak English the way writers write it?

3. Write a brief paper in which you define "good writing" and distinguish it from "bad writing." You may use the three passages quoted above as examples, as well as any other examples you can find.

4. Speak into a tape recorder for sixty seconds about any subject you know well. Then write a one-page discussion on the same subject. Compare and contrast your use of spoken and written language.

RHETORIC

Chapter Two

Asking Questions

For many students, the first stage of writing is the most worrisome. They cannot think of anything to write about. Even when instructors suggest topics, students feel hopelessly lost, not because they don't like the topics, but because they feel they don't know enough to write about them.

In this chapter you will learn five different ways to explore a topic before you begin writing your first draft:

1. The Five Senses as Questions
2. The Five Journalistic Questions
3. An Open Set of Questions
4. Five Traditional Angles
5. Interviewing

The questions from the senses are useful for imaginative writing. The journalistic questions are useful for reporting events. The open set of questions is useful for sharpening your ability to learn from observation. The five traditional angles have two uses: as questions, they lead to the discovery of information; and as angles, they serve as strategies for giving information the focus and direction it needs to become a paper topic. Interviewing is asking someone else the questions you will learn to ask yourself in the first four sections.

Asking questions can be a way of playing with material before deciding what you want to make of it, like toying with modeling clay until it takes a vague shape that suggests the final shape it ought to take. If you happen to know in advance what sort of writing you want to do, you can turn directly to the questions that are most suitable for that sort of writing. If you don't know what sort of writing you want to do, working through several sets of questions may lead you to a purpose as well as to information.

You should know in advance, however, that asking a list of questions is no substitute for creativity. You cannot make ideas the way you can make hollandaise sauce, simply by following a recipe. Questions can lead you close to insight; but the spark that makes information interesting and meaningful has to come from sources within each writer, sources that no method can control. All good writing is creative writing; all worthwhile discoveries begin as acts of the imagination.

Think of the questions you ask as paths to explore, some of which will lead to dead ends, others to new and interesting territory. As you make discoveries, start thinking of ways to map them out for the benefit of your readers. More about this in the chapter on organization.

1. The Five Senses as Questions

In most academic writing, you will be communicating information rather than experience. The professor who asks for a lab report wants to know what happened in the lab, not what it was like to watch it happen. But there are many situations in which even academic writing can be enlivened by exploring a subject through the five senses. When you want to communicate an experience, when you want to let your readers witness a scene or event for themselves rather than see a mere summary of it, ask yourself the following questions before you begin writing:

1. What does it look like?
2. What does it sound like?
3. What does it taste like?
4. What does it feel like?
5. What does it smell like?

The following passage, part of a scholarly book about jails, is almost like a passage from a novel, appealing to the senses to give an impression of what it must be like to be in a specific jail.

Example
Inside a relatively modern exterior in a modest, busy part of town, was a cramped, dark, dank interior. Large, foursided cages each held sixteen men, with disheveled beds and an open toilet. Inmates are kept inside these cages twenty-four hours a day throughout their often prolonged stays in the Atlanta Jail. There is no privacy and no activity at all, artificial air and light, and nothing at all to do day and night. A dismal atmosphere, a constant din, and a wretched stench pervade the place.
—Ronald Goldfarb, *Jails: The Ultimate Ghetto*

This passage is effective partly because it appeals to the senses: the reader can, in imagination, feel "the dank interior" and the "artificial air," smell the "wretched stench," hear the "constant din," and see the "artificial . . . light" and the "open toilet." If a meal had been being served at the time, Goldfarb might have completed the description by telling us what jail food tastes like. Obviously the writer chose not just a few impersonal facts but rather details that would communicate the experience of visiting the Atlanta Jail.

The best way to get material like this is to actually visit the scene you are writing about and observe it carefully, concentrating on one sense at a time. The scene will become clear to you in ways you can hardly anticipate, just as the world becomes almost shockingly distinct for a nearsighted person who puts on a pair of eyeglasses for the first time.

If you cannot physically observe your subject, study it in your imagination. Imitate the medieval monks who meditated on holy events by picturing as vividly as they could the details of the scene—the smell of straw in a manger, the sound of wind, the bite of cold weather, the cry of an infant, the expressions on the faces of people present. According to the meditation manuals, the monks would actually go (in imagination) to the scene, speak with people involved, and listen to their responses.

Prod your observation with questions based upon all of the senses, but especially the sense of sight.

What do you see? (Don't settle for a vague description like "a man reading a newspaper"; cut close to reality with details like those Flannery O'Connor uses: "He was sitting on the edge of his chair at the table, bent over the orange sports section of the *Journal*.")

What do the people look like? Who are the bystanders? (Again, don't settle for "nearsighted" descriptions like "a bunch of hoods"; look for the kind of detail Bernard Malamud uses when he describes "the gray-hatted, thick-soled-shoe boys, who had the spare time and the mazuma and showed it in fat, wonderful rolls down in the cellar clubs to all who would look.")

What does the scene look like? (Avoid label words—words like "beautiful," "ugly," "spectacular," "great," which communicate your reaction to things rather than the things themselves. Don't write, "It was a gorgeous sunset"; describe it, as Walter Van Tilburg Clark does: "The red sunset, with narrow black cloud stripes like threads across it, lay on the carved horizon of the prairie.")

Studying even the most familiar scene through each of the senses will produce more imaginative detail than you can use in a paper. The next step is to decide which details best suit your purpose. If you are trying to communicate an experience, you have to decide what you want the experience to mean, what mood you want it to instill in your readers. Are they supposed to be pleased, amused, disgusted, or delighted with the passage? Or are you trying to convey an impression that cannot be adequately described in a single word?

EXERCISE

When we describe, we normally use visual description. But description can appeal to the other senses as well. If you are using an essay collection along with this text, read a selection in the section on description. Then, without looking back at the text, make a list of the ten images you remember most clearly. Images are objects or scenes you can re-create in your imagination. Notice which senses they appeal to. After you have made the list, locate their sources in the text. What has the writer done to make these images memorable? Can you identify any specific techniques that you can imitate in your own descriptive writing?

WRITING ASSIGNMENTS

1. Without looking, try to remember the color of the walls of your classroom, the shape and location of the light fixtures, the geometric pattern in the floor. Now look around and sharpen your awareness of what's around you. Examine the room and its contents through each of the five senses. Make a list of at least fifty details. Then select the most telling details from the list and convert them into a descriptive paragraph that will convey the sense of what it is like to be there. Turn to pp. 125–128 for advice about organizing descriptive passages. Revise and edit (see Chapters Six and Seven).

2. Visit a place in which people are involved in an activity of some sort. A bus station. A pool hall. A cafeteria. A grocery store. Any place with people in it. Examine the scene through each of your five senses. When you have noticed a few details, jot them down. Repeat the process until you have a list of at least fifty specific details. Select the best details and convert them into a paragraph or a short paper that will allow your readers to re-create the scene in their own imaginations. Turn to pp. 122–125 for suggestions about organization. Revise and edit the paper (see Chapters Six and Seven).

3. Find a picture of an object or a landscape in a magazine. Try to convert the picture into words in two different ways. First, describe the picture in a way that will enable the reader to diagram it even without seeing it. Then describe it for the imagination, giving a sense of what it would be like to see the scene. Avoid label words ("terrific," "beautiful," "ghastly"). Sharpen your powers of observation and choose details that appeal to the sensory imagination. Turn in the picture or a copy of it with your descriptions. Revise and edit the paper (see Chapters Six and Seven).

If you have trouble organizing this paper, skip ahead to pp. 125–128 for some suggestions.

2. The Five Journalistic Questions

If you are writing about an event, the simplest questions to ask in prewriting are the ones newspaper reporters try to answer in the first few sentences of every story:

Who?
What?
When?
Where?
Why?

These are easily remembered as the five *W*s. Sometimes "How" is added to the list.

Suppose, for example, you decide to write about an event on campus—let's say a recent meeting of the student senate. Before you could write about the meeting, you would have to jot down notes that answer the questions any good newspaper reporter would answer. Who attended the meeting? Who spoke up? What did the speakers have to say? What was the purpose of the meeting? What did the meeting accomplish? How was the meeting conducted? Where? When? Why did the senate act the way it did?

Each of these questions might have a number of answers, and each of the answers might be probed by some or all of the same questions. Who will carry out the senate's resolutions? How? When?

By asking questions and jotting down answers, you should generate more than enough material for a report. The next step is to sort out the information and arrange it according to its importance, discarding anything that is trivial or unrelated. If you were writing about the student senate, *where* the senate met might be unimportant, maybe not even worth mentioning, unless it had met in some unusual place for some unusual reason. If you were writing about a crime, *where* the crime took place would be very important, since readers are always curious to know how close crime strikes to where they live and work.

Once you have decided what information would be most important or most interesting to your readers, you might start out the paper as a newspaper reporter would, with a sentence or two summarizing the most important information, followed by other sentences or paragraphs that add details.

Example

Yesterday afternoon the student senate unanimously passed a resolution commending the dean of the university library for his refusal to put bound volumes of periodicals onto microfilms. The resolution, which was introduced by A & S Senator James Dillingsworth, said that library dean Lucas Schmidt had "acted in the best interest of the scholarly community."

"Anybody who does any research at all knows that you can't flip through a microfilm like you can flip through a book," said Dillingsworth in support of the resolution. "Microfilms are about as efficient as the old parchment scrolls that were used before books were invented," Dillingsworth said.

"Less efficient," added Joe Grosso, off-campus senator, who helped write the resolution. "At least you could read those old scrolls without depending on some clumsy machine that is often broken or unavailable."

In other Senate action, a bill that would . . . .

The questions asked by newspaper reporters are handy for getting at the sort of information you would need in reporting an event. If you wanted to analyze the event, however, you would need to ask other questions, like those that are explained in the next few sections of this chapter.

EXERCISE

1. Select a recent issue of a newspaper and analyze the information given in one of the lead stories on the front page. Does the reporter answer the questions who, what, when, where, why, and how within the first few lines? If any of the questions are unan-

swered, were they important questions, or was the reporter justified in omitting them?

2. Select an essay classified under narration in an essay collection. Does the narrator answer the journalistic questions in the
course of the essay? How would you compare the writing in the
essay with the writing in the newspaper account you examined
in Exercise 1? Is description always a part of good narration?
Would a newspaper report be improved by the addition of descriptive details, or merely cluttered? Explain.

Compare the structure of the essay with the structure of the
newspaper story. Is either arranged chronologically? If the structures are different, is each suited to its purpose? Explain.

WRITING ASSIGNMENTS

1. Observe an event taking place on campus or nearby, perhaps a planned event announced in the newspaper, or else an un-
planned happening that you witness by chance. In a notebook, jot
down as many answers as you can to the questions a reporter
would ask—who, what, when, where, why, and how. Sort out the
information and write it up as it would appear in a newspaper
report. Organize this paper as you would organize a newspaper
story—important information first, additional details later. Use
the checklist on pp. 160–162 as a guide to revision.

2. Observe an event, but this time examine it not only with a
reporter's questions, but with questions pertaining to the five
senses as well. Sort out your answers and write a story that re-
creates the event in the imaginations of your readers. Turn to pp.
122–125 for advice about organizing a narrative. Use the checklist on pp. 160–162 as you revise and edit your work.

3. Choose an incident reported in this evening's paper, embel-
lish it with vivid, imaginative details, and turn it into a short story
written from the point of view of someone on the scene—either a
witness or a participant. Tell the story in chronological order (see
p. 122). Use the checklist on pp. 160–162 as you prepare your final
draft.

3. An Open Set of Questions

Some writers like to rely on fixed sets of questions like those
discussed in the chapter thus far. Without a definite list, these
writers feel they would not be able to think of anything to ask.

Other writers find the lists boring, mechanical, restrictive. They prefer to let their creative curiosity run freely, roaming wherever it will, until it comes up with something worth writing about. If you are this second sort of writer, you really don't need a list of questions. But if you would like to improve your skill at free exploration, keep reading.

The trick is to regain the curiosity you had as a small child. Somewhere between the ages of three and five, you loved to ask questions, and every answer you got only prompted another question. You were learning a lot back then, perhaps more than you will ever learn again in such a short period. In prewriting, try to recover that childlike curiosity. Ask any question that pops into your head, whether you can answer it or not. Then ask questions about your answers. Here, for example, are some random, exploratory questions about an ordinary household object — a rug.

Q   What's it called?
A   A rya rug.
Q   What does *rya* mean?
A   I don't know.
Q   What's it shaped like?
A   An octagon.
Q   Are all rya rugs shaped this way?
A   No. A friend of mine has a rectangular rya.
Q   Where is yours?
A   In the den at home.
Q   What's it made of?
A   Wool.
Q   Is it made by machine or hand woven?
A   I don't know.
Q   Are hand-woven rugs generally better than machine-woven rugs, or merely more expensive?
A   I don't know.
Q   What's it look like?
A   A medium shag, with blue, green, and yellow dyes in irregular patterns.
Q   Was the wool dyed before the rug was woven or after?
A   I don't know.
Q   Can you figure it out by observing more closely?
A   Now that I've looked at it, I can see that the individual pieces of yarn are all of a single color, even right next to pieces of

yarn of different colors. This would indicate that the yarn was dyed before the rug was woven.

Q   What does the back of the rug look like?

A   On the bottom of the rug there is a stiff grid. The wool seems to have been attached to the grid.

Q   Is that like any other rugs you've seen?

A   It is like the grids for rugs advertised on TV, the kind you weave for yourself at home. Except the rya grid does not have a geometric pattern or an American eagle printed on it.

Q   Is it different from other rugs?

A   Certainly different from Oriental rugs. On the backs of those you can see only the knots — no grid. And you can tell the quality of an Oriental rug by counting the number of knots per square inch.

Q   How can you tell the quality of a rya rug?

A   I don't know.

Q   Where are rya rugs made?

A   Denmark, I think. Maybe Sweden.

The questions could go on and on (which is why they are called an "open set"). In this particular dialogue, it is apparent that the writer could not rely on observation alone to produce a complete discussion of rugs. But the dialogue did produce some interesting information, and it did raise some questions that might be answered by an interview or by research. For this reason, a dialogue with yourself is almost always a useful way to get started on any kind of writing. It helps you figure out what you know and what you need to find out.

If the dialogue about a rug seems trivial, consider a dialogue about something that interests you or about something you would like to know more about — a person, place, historical period, variety of music; an aspect of mathematics, astronomy, psychology, anthropology; a process like banking, bricklaying, or bookbinding. Observation, sharpened by questions, is not only a good way to produce material to write about; it is an intellectual exercise that gives you control over your experience, a control that is not only potentially useful but satisfying in itself.

If you are examining a topic you already know fairly well or one that you can observe firsthand, an open-ended dialogue of questions and answers should turn up more information than you need for a short paper. If you are examining a topic that you don't know very well, the dialogue should indicate what information you should be looking for in an interview or in research.

Once you have material to work with, turn to Chapter Four for advice about choosing a rhetorical stance and a pattern of organization.

EXERCISES

1. Bring an object — any object — into class. Let the class observe the object by composing a question-and-answer dialogue about it. Notice how many of the questions can be answered by observation alone, and notice how the dialogue brings the object into sharper focus for the observers. Speculate with your classmates on how you might find the answers to the questions you cannot answer by observation alone.

2. If a genie from a magic lamp promised you all the knowledge in the world about any subject, what would your choice be? Some aspect of human affairs? Sports? Life after death? History? Astronomy? With the help of your classmates, pick out what you think would be a subject that any intelligent person should be interested in. Then, together with your classmates, ask as many questions as you can about that subject and have someone write the questions on the blackboard. After you have asked all the questions you can, look them over and try to arrange them in related groups. Assume that you can answer all the questions and that you want to publish your knowledge in a book. How would you divide it into chapters? What would your first chapter contain? What about the others?

WRITING ASSIGNMENTS

1. Find something on campus worth observing — a building, a meeting, a project, a concert, a play, an animate or inanimate object. Plant yourself nearby and observe. Jot down as many notes as you can — at least fifty separate observations. If you have trouble starting your list, begin by using the five senses as questions. Then ask the five journalistic questions, and improvise an open set of questions in a dialogue with yourself. If you can find someone who might be able to answer questions you can't answer for yourself, ask them as a newspaper reporter would.

After you have made your observations, just think about them on and off for twenty-four hours and try to see how some of your observations could be linked together in an interesting report. Then, in a brief but detailed paper, describe the object or event, explain any discoveries you may have about it simply by observing it with more than ordinary attention or by asking some knowledgeable person, explain any interesting questions for which you found no answers, and indicate how you might go about discovering the answers if you wanted them. If you can't find the angle you need to bring your observations to life, read the next section of this chapter. If you need help with organization, read Chapter Four. Use Chapters Six and Seven as a guide to revision.

2. If there is an art exhibit on campus or nearby, take a pencil and note pad to it and see how much you can learn by observation alone. Don't hesitate to ask questions, however, if there is someone around who seems willing to answer them. Make a list of at least fifty observations, using the questioning techniques discussed in this chapter so far. Give yourself a full day to think about your observations, trying to decide why you liked the items that pleased you most and why you were puzzled or put off by other items. In a brief paper, describe in detail the items that impressed you most and explain your reaction. If you choose to describe items you did not like, offer your best guesses about what the person in charge of the exhibit might have seen in them. Read Chapter Four for advice about organization. Use the checklist on pp. 160–162 as you prepare your final draft.

4. Five Traditional Angles

Questions from the senses, the journalistic questions, and open sets of questions generally lead to information. But information is not a paper. Normally information just lies there on your note pad—mute, inert, lazy, daring you to try to transform it into an essay worth reading.

To bring information to life you need a point, an angle, a plan of attack. In a general way, your purpose as a writer is almost always to make your reader familiar with a subject you know something about or with a viewpoint you would like to share. But you need a more specific purpose too. If the more specific purpose is not provided by the assignment itself, you might consider the five traditional angles discussed below.

They can be used not only as questions for further exploration of your topic, but as devices for bringing information to life, giving it a purpose, a focus, or a direction.

The five traditional angles are these:

a. Process Analysis
b. Division and Classification
c. Comparison and Contrast
d. Definition
e. Cause and Effect

As you mull over your ideas, even before you begin to write, see if one of these angles will serve as the point of your paper.

a. Process Analysis

If your subject is a process — anything that involves changes, stages, or steps — a process analysis may provide the angle for bringing the topic to life. In a process analysis, a writer explains how something takes place or took place: how the human brain evolved during the last ice age; how corporations influence political institutions; how the Constitution was written. In school, students are often asked to write about processes that may be familiar to them: how to tune up a car; how to bake a cake; how to get the courses you want. The first part of this textbook is a process analysis: how to write a paper. In the second part is another process analysis: how a particular research paper came to be written.

Whether your subject is simple or sophisticated, the process of writing a process paper is the same. First, study the process until you know its essential steps in sufficient detail to provide an analysis. Then, imagine how much your readers already know about the process — if anything — so you won't bore them by overexplaining or confuse them by underexplaining. And finally, explain the process. Normally, a process paper is the easiest of all papers to organize, since the outline of the paper can mirror the process itself.

Like several of the other angles, a process can sometimes be expressed very briefly. The key to expanding a process analysis to an entire paper is to accumulate lots of details or examples about each stage of the process before you begin writing.

Two words of caution: don't pad. Don't add trivial details just to make your paper longer. If you cannot discover enough important and interesting details to write a process analysis long enough to satisfy an assignment, you would do better to choose a different process instead of boring your readers with empty words.

Writers sometimes choose an angle before they find much information about their topic, and they sometimes choose an angle after they have developed their information. If you know in advance what angle you intend to take, you can be on the lookout for ways to develop that angle as you explore your sources of information — your experience, observation, experimentation, or research. If you choose the angle after you have explored your sources, you will probably discover that the angle requires you to find some additional information. In either case, choosing an angle helps you get an intellectual grasp of your subject and helps you explore its dark corners and hidden spots so that it becomes clearer to you as you make it clearer to your readers.

EXERCISE

Read several essays listed under process analysis in an essay collection. By noticing what terms the writer leaves unexplained, you can determine how much knowledge the writer expects the reader to have already. Do you find that any of the writers expected too much of you personally as a reader? Did some of them expect too little? Notice how the essay is organized. Would an outline of the essay be virtually the same as an outline of the process itself?

WRITING ASSIGNMENT

Write a process analysis that your classmates would find interesting and informative.

As you look over the following list of possible topics, you will notice some that you can write about from past experience and others that will require you to expand your knowledge with an experiment, an interview (see p. 44), or library research (see Chapter Ten). Topics for process papers include "how to" explanations of any sort: how to survive in the wilderness; how to live on $30.00 a week; how to read a book; how to study for an exam; how to survive in a strange city; how to fix a broken _____; how to make the world's greatest _____; how to raise _____; how to win at _____; how to get rid of _____. Process papers can also be written about how something happened: how the energy crisis (or jazz, or the Constitution) came about; how the Whigs (or dinosaurs, or the Incas) disappeared; how the Bolsheviks (or the Democrats, or the Republicans) came to power. Process papers can be written about how something might be done: how garbage might be turned into fuel; how solar energy might be made practical.

If you are using an essay collection along with this text, the section on process analysis may suggest other topics for consideration.

To write a process analysis, follow these steps.

1. Choose a process and a source of information.
2. Divide the process into its stages as they occur in chronological order.
3. Jot down notes about each stage.
4. Describe the process, using its stages as an outline and defining any technical or unusual terms as they occur.
5. Add an introduction (see p. 104) and a conclusion (see p. 130).
6. Revise and edit (see Chapters Six and Seven).

b. Division and Classification

Division and classification are two sides of the same coin. To divide is to begin with a general view of the subject and then to break it down into logical parts and subparts. Earth can be divided into continents and oceans, continents into countries, and countries into various local jurisdictions. To classify is to begin with a small part of a subject and show how it is one part of something larger. Children play a classification game when they write their home addresses, not stopping with the state and zip code, but adding the country, the continent, the name of the planet, the solar system, the Milky Way, and the universe itself.

Division and classification are good angles to use when you can divide your subject into groups and subgroups. If you wanted to write about campus politics, for example, you might begin by dividing all the political forces into logical groups: Greeks, independents, and uninvolved. How do these groups differ from one another? Each group could probably be subdivided and studied in further detail. In what ways do the various fraternities and sororities differ from one another in their political philosophies? How many different kinds of independent but politically minded students are there? What sorts of students choose to ignore campus politics altogether? By dividing a subject into its logical parts and subparts and describing or defining each category, you can often turn inert information into an interesting analysis.

When you divide or classify, make sure the categories do not overlap, and make sure that taken together they add up to the whole thing studied. A paper on campus politics that divides the subject into KD's, music majors, and off-campus senators will not provide a very useful analysis, because those categories are not complete and may very well overlap.

Classification is the opposite of division. It treats the subject like a single piece in a puzzle and tries to show how it fits in with the rest. Normally the difference between classification and division is simply the direction in which the discussion travels. Using division as an angle on campus politics, a paper would begin with an overview and then describe each logical division or subdivision; using classification as an angle, a paper would discuss individual students and show how their political interests fit in with the interests of other groups of students.

Division and classification will not of themselves fill out an essay. Dividing and classifying are normally prewriting activities, like building the frame of a house. To add to the frame, explore each division with some other angle — describing, defining, comparing, contrasting, or explaining. Any of the questions and angles discussed in this chapter may provide sources for developing your ideas about each item you classify or divide.

EXERCISE

Read several essays listed under division and classification in an essay collection. Depending on the book you choose, you may discover that division and classification are so similar that they are hardly distinguished from one another. For each essay, determine whether the writer has mapped out a number of categories (division) or whether the writer has chosen an instance of something in order to see how it fits in with larger groups (classification). In each case, draw a diagram of the categories, and determine whether they overlap and whether they cover the subject completely. Notice how the writer fleshes out each of the subparts. Are examples used? Descriptions? Other devices?

WRITING ASSIGNMENT

Write a division or classification paper that your classmates would find interesting and informative.

Anything that has a name can be divided or classified. If you cannot think of a topic, just open up a dictionary and go through all the nouns until you come to one that interests you: antiques, bats, charlatans, dates, existentialism, fetishes, and so on. If you have time to research your topic (see Chapter Ten) or to conduct an interview (see p. 44), be sure to choose something that you find interesting enough to work with for a while. If you don't have time for research, choose a topic that you already know well from personal experience.

You will find additional ideas for classification and division papers in an essay collection if you happen to be using one along with this text. Remember that the heart of this sort of paper is usually not the division or classification itself, but what you have to say about each division or what you can learn about something by seeing it as part of a class.

Follow these steps.

1. Choose a topic that will fit in either of these sentences: There are (number) kinds of (topic); *or* (Topic) can be divided into (number) parts.
2. Divide the topic into its various kinds in such a way that taken together the kinds cover all varieties of the topic without overlapping.
3. Jot down notes about how you might explain each of the kinds — either by definition (see p. 35), by description, by listing examples, by relating illustrative stories, or by some combination of methods.
4. Outline the body of the paper (see Chapter Four) and write it.
5. Add an introduction (see p. 104) and a conclusion (see p. 130).
6. Revise and edit (see Chapters Six and Seven).

c. Comparison and Contrast

Comparison and contrast can provide you with both a way of discovering material and a way of organizing what you discover. The organization of comparison-contrast papers is discussed in Chapter Four. As a discovery technique, comparison and contrast is like doing two puzzles at once, making sense of one by finding out how the other works.

Suppose, for example, you know that music composed in Western Europe between 1600 and 1750 is generally called "baroque" and that music composed between 1750 and 1820 is generally called "classical." And suppose you have heard so much of this music you can tell which period a piece belongs to just by listening to a few bars. But when friends ask you how you know which is which, you can only say, "I don't know, they just sound different."

You can make the differences clearer even to yourself by listening to a stack of records and sharpening your powers of observation in a dialogue focusing on similarities and differences.

Q Name a few things the two kinds of music have in common.
A Instruments, sometimes voices. Meticulous structure.
Q Are there any differences in the instruments used in the two kinds of music?
A I'm sure there is, but I can't name any specifics.
Q Are there any differences between the way voices are used?
A Yes, I can hear the difference in my head, but I can't describe it.
Q Are there any differences in the overall sound of the two kinds of music? Any differences in form?
A Yes on both counts. But I can't put it into words.

Now you are ready to observe. Go to the library, take out a few recordings of music from each period, and listen attentively until you can give precise answers to questions you could answer only vaguely before.

If you observe carefully, you will notice that classical music is performed with instruments much like those used by musicians today, but baroque music is often performed on older instruments. The viola da gamba, the harpsichord, the recorder, and a small high-pitched trumpet are likely to be heard in baroque music, while the cello, the piano, and the clarinet were first used by composers in the classical period.

After you listen closely for a while, you may notice a difference in the way the human voice is used. In baroque music, the voice is more likely to be used like an instrument in the orchestra. Words are stretched out almost beyond recognition, as if their sounds were more important than their meaning: "And His glory shall bee-ee ee-ee ee — ee ee ee ee — ee-ee-ee-ee-e — ee-ee re-veal-ed." In classical music, the words are generally less distorted. In baroque music, it is not unusual to have different voices singing different words at the same time, making understanding next to impossible; in classical music, the text is usually set clearly enough to be understood.

There is a difference, too, in the overall sound. For most listeners, baroque music sounds as if all the instruments were pursuing independent melodies (which they frequently are). Listening to this music is like watching the inner workings of a watch, everything moving in precise relationship with everything else, some motions fast, some slow, but no one motion dominating the others. In classical music the instruments seem to be all at the same place at the same time, either playing a melody in unison or supplying a background for a dominant melody.

The two periods also differ in characteristic forms: There is no symphony in baroque music. And they differ in their harmony: classical music is relatively free of dissonance.

After you have made a list of similarities and differences, you are ready to use comparison and contrast as an angle from which to write. To do this, look over your notes and try to discover categories in which you can classify the similarities and differences you have noticed. If you were examining classical and baroque music, a good set of categories for your observations would be these: instruments used; use of the human voice; overall sound; characteristic forms. With categories of this sort you are ready to outline your paper and begin writing. You need only arrange the categories in the order you think your readers would find most interesting and then describe the characteristics of one kind of music and then the other under each category.

For more specific details about the organization of comparison-contrast papers, see p. 94.

EXERCISE

Read several essays listed under comparison and contrast in a collection and choose one for close analysis. Identify the categories of comparison used in each essay and write them across the top of a piece of paper. Under each category, briefly indicate the similarities and differences mentioned in the essay. Then outline the essay and see if you can discover the writer's reasons for giving the essay the structure it has.

WRITING ASSIGNMENT

Write a comparison and contrast paper that your classmates would find interesting and informative. Among the topics in the following list there are some that you can compare and contrast on the basis of your past experience and others that will require interviewing (see p. 44) or library research (Chapter Ten). Topics for comparison and contrast papers include the following: two cities; two countries; two languages; two kinds of pets; two schools; two famous personalities in the same field; two jobs; two academic subjects; two impressions of the same place (a then-and-now paper); two kinds of painting or architecture (impressionism and expressionism, Romanesque and Baroque); two games (bridge and canasta, squash and racquetball); two points of view on a given issue (labor and management on safety laws, Democrats and Republicans on tax reform). If you are using an essay collection along with this text, you will probably find more topics in the section on comparison and contrast.

To write a comparison and contrast paper, follow these steps.

1. Choose a pair of subjects that have enough common characteristics and enough differences to generate a paper.
2. Study the subjects until you can find at least three categories of comparison.
3. Make notes about similarities and differences in each category.
4. Outline the body of the paper (see p. 94) and write it.
5. Add an introduction (see p. 104) and a conclusion (see p. 130).
6. Revise and edit (see Chapters Six and Seven).

d. Definition

Ordinarily writers define unusual words in passing as a courtesy to their readers. Definitions of this sort do not take up much space. Sometimes, however, the definition of terms can be the material for an entire essay. Definitions that occupy more than a line or two are called extended definitions. Whether a definition is brief or extended, it is normally one of five common types: descriptive definition, functional definition, logical definition, etymological definition, or definition by example.

In a recent *New Yorker* article, Henry S. F. Cooper, Jr., used a *descriptive definition* of an unusual word in his discussion of the surface of Mars. "The ground," Cooper wrote, "reminded many of the geologists of a type common in the Southwest called caliche — a clay that is solidified into a crust by the evaporation of water." The definition is helpful; only a few of Cooper's readers would have known the meaning of *caliche* without looking it up.

A *functional definition* is one that defines something by telling what it does. Albert Einstein once wrote a functional definition of science in a brief sentence that tells what science does: "Science searches for relations which are thought to exist independently of the searching individual."

A *logical definition* is one that explains how something is part of a group of other things of its kind and how it is different from everything else in the group. A logical definition of a university, for example, might be that it is an educational institution (like many other institutions) that specializes in advanced knowledge in a wide variety of disciplines (which makes it different from other sorts of educational institutions).

An *etymological definition* is a definition based upon the history of a word. If you were defining the word *art*, for example, a good dictionary would tell you that it comes from the Latin word *ars*, which means "skill."

And finally, you can define a word by *example*. If you were defining the word *vegetable*, you could make your point by listing a few vegetables by name.

A sixth way to define a term is to borrow a definition from someone who is an *authority* in the field. If you used Einstein's definition of science in a paper of your own, you would be defining not only by function, as Einstein did, but by authority, since most readers would be inclined to accept Einstein's definition of science as authoritative. If you were working on another topic — beauty, for example — you might quote an expert in that field. The poet Samuel Taylor Coleridge was considered something of an authority in the field of artistic beauty. His definition would be worth quoting:

> The Beautiful arises from the perceived harmony of an object, whether sight or sound, with the inborn and constitutive rules of the judgment and imagination: and it is always intuitive.

Although writers often define their terms in a phrase or two, there are ways in which definition can be used as an angle for writing an entire essay. One way is to develop a paper by defining several related terms, such as several different kinds of music, or several different kinds of fish, or several different poetic devices. Another way is to apply several different kinds of definition to the same term. Yet another way is to define a term by example after example after example.

Essays developed by definition are interesting if the terms defined are new and useful, or unusual and useful, or if their traditional definitions present some problems in specific contexts. Abstractions that may seem corny when teachers assign them as paper topics can become quite challenging when you consider them in light of particular examples. What is beauty? (Is a work of art beautiful if it depicts something grotesque, like a gargoyle on a medieval cathedral?) What is life? (Are human beings alive if they have no consciousness and no hope of surviving detached from hospital machinery?) What is art? (Is the Golden Gate bridge a work of art because it is beautiful?)

As an example of how you might expand a brief dictionary definition into an entire essay, take the etymological definition of *art* as a starting point: it comes from the Latin *ars*, meaning "skill." You already know that *art* in modern English is used to describe the sorts of things you see in a museum — some of which would seem to require no discernible skill at all. If you visit a museum, then, your knowledge of the Latin origin of *art* could give you an angle for writing a paper about what you see. Is a canvas covered with seemingly random splotches of paint a work of art? If so, what is it besides skill that we are willing to recognize as art? On the other hand, are all skills — fine cooking, for example — art? If not, what is it besides skill that we demand in a work of art? You could write an entire paper about the definition of art (or about the definition of any interesting abstraction) simply by examining a dozen examples that may or may not conform to a standard definition.

Be careful, however, not to fall into the trap of assuming that a word really means or should mean what it used to mean centuries ago, perhaps in another language. Words commonly change meaning as time goes by. But tracing the changes of meaning in a good dictionary often leads to a better understanding of what a word means now. Perhaps the best dictionary for discovering old meanings is the *Oxford English Dictionary (OED)*, which shows how any current English word has been used in different contexts over the centuries, beginning with its first known appearance in written English. The first recorded use of the word *art*, for example, was in the year 1225. Its meaning has changed considerably since that time.

EXERCISE

If you are using an essay collection along with this book, read several essays listed as definition and test the advice given in this book against the performance of good writers. For example, this book has named several specific kinds of definition: definition by description, by function, by logic, by etymology, by example, and by authority. Do you recognize any of these defining techniques in the essays in your collection? Can you identify and name any other techniques?

This chapter has also mentioned three ways to extend a definition: by defining several related terms; by applying several different kinds of definitions to the same term; and by defining a term with example after example after example. As you read the essays in your collection, determine which of these strategies the writer has employed. Can you identify and explain any other strategy for writing an extended definition?

WRITING ASSIGNMENT

Write an extended definition that your classmates would find interesting and informative.

Among the topics in the following list, there are some you can write about from your past experience and others that will require interviewing (see p. 44) or library research (see Chapter Ten). Abstractions normally make good topics for definition papers: poverty, patriotism, beauty, conservatism, liberalism, sanity, conservation, morality, honesty, crime, fidelity, courage, dance (or a particular kind of dance), art (or a particular kind of art), education (or a particular kind of education). Feel free to use division and classification along with definition: you may want to name and define three schools of art, or three kinds of education, or five kinds of fidelity. If you are using an essay collection along with this book, you can probably find more ideas for topics in the section on definition.

Before settling on a topic, make sure you can illustrate it with at least one good example and preferably with several. Don't shy away from examples that seem to slip away from your definition — like the poverty that some rich people impose upon themselves or the patriotism that seems like treason. These are the kinds of examples that make the effort to define worthwhile.

Use a dictionary definition or a definition from authority at least as a prewriting device: analyze all the examples you can think of in light of the traditional definition and see whether the definition needs to be revised or explained.

To write a definition paper, follow these steps.

1. Choose an interesting abstract word (i.e., a word that names an idea rather than a thing) or a set of closely related abstract words.
2. Review the kinds of definition discussed in the preceding section and choose the kind or kinds that would shed the most light on your topic.
3. Choose the outline that best suits your material: a series of definitions of the same term; or a series of definitions of different varieties of a single term; or a series of related terms which you will define in order. (See also Chapter Four.)
5. Write the body of the paper.
6. Add an introduction (see p. 104) and a conclusion (see p. 130).
7. Revise and edit (see Chapters Six and Seven).

e. Cause and Effect

Cause and effect is a standard thought pattern in which a given topic is considered either as a cause of some other reality or as a result of some other reality. Philosophers often prefer to speak of conditions rather than causes, and they distinguish two kinds of conditions: necessary and sufficient.

A necessary condition is one that is absolutely essential to the existence of a given effect. To use a barnyard example, fertilization of an egg is a necessary condition for the production of a baby chick. No fertilization, no chick. Fertilization, however, is not the only necessary condition in this case. The egg itself must be apt for fertilization, and the right sort of environment for incubation must be provided.

A sufficient condition is one that will bring about a given effect, though other conditions might bring about the same effect. A classic example is rain as a sufficient condition for making the ground wet. If it is raining, the ground will be wet. There are, however, other ways for the ground to be wet; so rain, in this example, is merely a sufficient condition, not a necessary condition.

Scientists study causes and effects with considerable certitude in the laboratory, where they can be controlled and limited. If scientists want to determine the effect of various diets on the growth rate of earthworms, they can raise several groups of earthworms in conditions identical except for diet. Under these conditions, any variance in growth rates can be assumed to be caused by the difference in diet. Because careful scientists are always suspicious of the possibility of some unknown causes, however, they normally do not consider any experiment conclusive until it has been duplicated a number of times with the same results.

Outside the laboratory, life is seldom so obliging as to allow for scientific experimentation, and effects cannot always be attributed to a single cause. This is especially true when human behavior is involved. If you tried, for example, to say what caused you to show up for class on any given day, you would discover that you had no single motive, but rather a tangle of motives including a mixture of habit, fear, ambition, and social considerations that have little to do with the subject matter discussed in the class. Causality in human behavior, according to Sigmund Freud, is "overdetermined"; that is, human beings rarely do anything for a single, pure motive.

When we try to examine causes of events or conditions involving many individuals, the task becomes even more challenging. Why are some people starving in parts of the world while surplus food goes unused in other parts? Why was the United States government so slow to invest in the development of solar energy? What makes college students today behave differently than college students ten years ago?

If you are using an essay collection with this text, you will probably find questions like these being explored in the section on cause and effect analysis. You will notice that evidence or proof of causal relationships in these areas can never be as final as the proof scientists might develop in a laboratory. For this reason, different standards of evidence apply. As you read a cause and effect essay, you normally evaluate the evidence by observing whether the relationship suggested is plausible and logical in itself and whether it squares with your own experience and observation. If you are reading an essay about the behavior of college students, for example, you will test the analysis against your understanding of your own behavior and the behavior you have observed in others. If you are reading about something remote from your personal experience — say, the effect of nonalphabetic writing on Oriental philosophy — you will demand not only connections that seem plausible, but also enough examples to make up for your lack of personal experience.

The most common logical error in cause-effect analysis is called the *post hoc* fallacy, from the Latin phrase *post hoc ergo propter hoc*, which means "after this, therefore because of this." Basically, this is the error of confusing a relationship in time with a causal connection. If, for example, a change in the value of the dollar occurs after a presidential press conference, we cannot necessarily conclude that the conference caused the change. The change might have occurred anyway. Or if a senator changes his position on a bill after being visited by a lobbyist, we cannot necessarily conclude that the visit caused the change. The change may have already been in the works. But as these examples show, *post hoc* fallacies can be very tempting.

Like definitions, cause and effect relationships can normally be expressed in fairly brief statements: poverty causes crime; the building of a canal will endanger wildlife; the team's victory resulted from a secret strategy. And like definitions, a cause and effect relationship can be used as an angle for an entire paper if the causes (or effects) are filled out with examples, illustrations, descriptions, anecdotes, or detailed analyses.

Because cause and effect papers require lots of evidence, it is futile to try to write one unless you have explored your subject thoroughly. The only immediate source of evidence for a cause and effect paper is personal experience. If you have witnessed an event (an accident, a strategy session, an instance of unusual behavior), you may be in a position to explain the causes or the results of the event in some detail. If some person, event, or situation has affected your personality or your attitudes, you might write a paper describing the cause and the effect. Sometimes you can use personal experience as a launching pad for a cause and effect paper that ranges considerably beyond your experience. If you were wondering why students in foreign countries seem to learn English more effectively than students in the United States learn foreign languages, you might begin searching for causes by examining your own experience with foreign languages, your own motivation and success, and what you imagine the motivation and success of students in foreign countries to be.

Besides personal experience, experimentation can be a source of evidence for a cause and effect paper if the topic is simple enough and the experiment can be completed in a reasonable time. For example, if you wanted to determine how air pressure in automobile tires affects mileage, you could develop enough evidence for a short paper by checking your mileage on two trips over the same route, once with your tires overinflated, the second time with them underinflated.

To get reliable results, of course, you would have to make sure that the only important difference between the two trips was the amount of air in the tires; you would have to travel in the same direction; you would have to keep the weight of the car constant; and you would have to travel under traffic conditions that are reasonably similar.

Another source of evidence would be a questionnaire or an interview. If you wanted to determine what causes students to attend your college, you could find out by listing a number of likely factors (cost, academic reputation, social life, athletic programs, and so on) and asking a representative sample of students to tell you how important each factor was to them.

Any of these sources of evidence can be supplemented by library research. Often the experiments, the data, the interviews that are inaccessible to ordinary students have been explored by someone in print. Chapter Ten will show you how to tap those sources.

In gathering evidence for a cause and effect paper, make sure it is sufficient, relevant, and random. Sufficiency is a matter of judgment. A questionnaire sent to ten students would hardly be convincing as a sample of the entire student body; a questionnaire sent to ten thousand students would normally be more than enough. Somewhere between is a number that is both manageable for your research and large enough to provide convincing results. To determine that number, you have to make a commonsense decision based upon the nature of the subject matter and the expectations of your readers.

Relevancy is also a matter of common sense. You should not try to determine the values of current students by asking alumni or faculty members, since the students themselves are the most direct source of evidence.

Randomness means not loading the dice. If you want to know what motivates the student body as a whole, you have to make sure your sample does not limit itself to any one group (students who live near you, Greeks, English majors, athletes) to the exclusion of others.

Evidence is the essence of a cause and effect paper. Do not try to write one until you have accumulated several pages of notes about causes or effects that you have discovered through personal observation, experimentation, interviews, or research. Without specific detail, the paper is sure to be vapid and dull.

EXERCISE

Often a cause and effect relationship can be expressed in a few words or a few sentences — except, perhaps, when human choice or human attitudes are involved. Read several essays in the section on cause and effect in an essay collection and notice how each writer expands the analysis either by studying several related causes or effects or by illustrating a single cause or effect with examples, descriptions, or other devices. Can you identify and explain any new strategies for writing an extended cause and effect analysis? For each essay, determine whether the examples and illustrations are meaningful or merely fillers. Would you have the same feeling for the subject if the examples and illustrations were omitted? Look for techniques that you can imitate in a cause and effect paper of your own.

WRITING ASSIGNMENT

Write a cause and effect paper that your classmates would find interesting and informative.

Two good topics for cause and effect papers are these: any change in the world about you; any interesting human behavior that involves attitudes or choices. Changes in the world around you would include changes in language, in the role of government, in the leadership of the government, in technology, in the environment, in weather patterns, in the economy, or in foreign policy. Causes of human behavior worth investigating would include why people become heroes, why people get divorced, why people voted for X, spend money on Y, or remain loyal to Z.

There are only two kinds of cause and effect papers you can write without research, experimentation, or interviews: a paper that explains your own attitude or behavior; a paper that explains a change in something you know a lot about. If you choose some other topic, budget time for investigation or research. A cause and effect paper is perhaps the most difficult of all papers to write from the top of your head; it is a paper that must be built on persuasive evidence and sound logic.

To write a cause and effect paper, follow these steps.

1. Choose a change that has occurred (or might occur) in the physical world or choose a particular human behavior that interests you.
2. Study its causes, either by observation (using some of the questions discussed in this chapter), experimentation, interviewing (see below), or by researching in the library (see Chapter Ten).
3. Decide whether you want to write about a number of causes (or effects) or whether you want to limit yourself to several examples of the same cause (or effect); outline your paper accordingly. (See also Chapter Four.)
4. Write the paper body of the paper, illustrating, explaining, or defining the causes or effects.
5. Add an introduction (see p. 104) and a conclusion (see p. 130).
6. Revise and edit (see Chapters Six and Seven).

5. Interviewing

If you are writing about a topic that is new to you, questions may produce nothing but a string of I-don't-know answers. When this happens, an interview can be a good source of information.

No matter where you live, there are people nearby who are worth interviewing — people who can tell you how to do something you don't know how to do, people who can tell you the inside scoop on current issues of public interest, people who are worth writing about just because they are interesting in themselves. Not all of these people are celebrities. There are plenty of noncelebrities in your life who can give you some insights worth writing about. Shopkeepers, pipefitters, railway conductors, athletes, hunters, engineers, cheerleaders, musicians, farmers, cab drivers, construction workers, old people, architects, fellow students — anyone with a little intelligence can be a source of information, if you take the trouble to ask for it.

On a campus, of course, you will find no end of candidates for interviews: deans, administrative officers, professors, advisers, other students, and the powers in the student government. All you need to do is to pick out a subject you would like to know more about, pick out a person who is likely to be an expert in that subject, and (unless you know the person very well) pick up a phone and make an appointment. Interviewing takes more time than writing from the top of your head, but it almost always produces more interesting papers for both writers and readers.

Perhaps the best way to prepare for an interview is to jot down a list of questions about the topic. Questions beginning with *who, what, when, where, why,* and *how* are often good for starters. Add the other questions discussed in this chapter, and then ask your friends to help you think of more questions.

As you prepare questions, start formulating the purpose of your paper. Are you going to write something that is primarily informative, or are you going to try to prove a point? Are you going to want to include impressions of the interview itself? Could the purpose of your investigation be expressed by one of the five traditional angles discussed in the preceding section? The clearer your purpose is at the outset, the easier it will be for you to ask the right questions and to sort out the answers.

When you have more questions than you need, choose those you are most curious to know the answers to and those that are most directly related to your purpose and put them at the head of the list. Questions that you don't know how to answer are obviously good ones for the interview, but questions you think you can answer can prove even more useful. When you are interviewing an expert, take nothing for granted. Experts often have views that run counter to popular opinion.

Suppose you were interested in finding out what sort of research is being conducted on the local environment. One likely source of information would be a professor in the biology department. Prepare for the interview with a list of questions about the research (or lack of it), its causes, and its effects.

Example

1. What sort of environmental research is the biology department doing?
2. How is it conducted?
3. Where?
4. Who is involved?

5. Do you know of any environmental research being conducted in any other department on campus?
6. What has the research turned up so far?
7. What are the causes of pollution in this area?
8. What are its effects?
9. Is it dangerous to humans? To wildlife?
10. Who pays for research?
11. Are biology professors free to conduct whatever kind of research they choose?
12. What happens to the results of the research?
13. Does anyone oppose the research?
14. Has the research caused any changes in local construction or industrial practices?
15. Would you recommend biology as a major for someone who wanted to make a career of environmental protection?

Take your list of numbered questions, a blank note pad, and something to write with. You may also take a tape recorder, but always ask permission before turning it on. Many people feel nervous in the presence of recorders, and if you detect even a hint of discomfort, you might do better to limit yourself to the pencil and note pad.

Relax. Ask your prepared questions as long as they are producing interesting answers. Jot down the answers next to corresponding numbers in your notebook. Don't hesitate to ask spontaneous questions as the conversation suggests them, and don't be afraid to let the conversation drift into unanticipated territory. The new territory might make a better paper than the one you originally intended to write.

Above all, do not hesitate to ask for clarification when you need it. When your informant uses words you don't understand, ask for definitions. When your informant mentions unfamiliar names as if you should know them, do not be afraid to admit your ignorance. Never be embarrassed by not knowing something: if you knew as much as the informant does, you would not be conducting the interview. You can usually assume that names and terms you don't understand will not be understood by your readers either. Explanations of unusual references are often the better parts of interesting and informative papers.

If the interview goes well, you may follow your first prepared question with three or four spontaneous ones. If it goes
very well, you may discover so much information that your
prepared questions become irrelevant.

Example

Q What sort of environmental research is the biology department
doing?

A Well, as a department, not much. There is very little sponsored research of any kind.

Q Excuse me, what do you mean by "sponsored" research?

A Well, research that is paid for as part of a professor's job. Big
foundations will sometimes pay part of our salaries to free us
from teaching duties while we are working on a project. Sometimes the university itself sponsors research.

Q Which foundations?

A Ford sponsored some, Lilly too. And Rockefeller.

Q And there is no sponsored research on the environment?

A None to speak of. However, a number of us have been conducting experiments on our own. Analyzing fish caught in the
river, for example, to see if they have any pesticides or industrial pollutants in them. That sort of stuff. Care for some coffee?

Interviewing is somewhat like fishing. You look for likely
places to cast your bait. Sometimes the results are good, sometimes meager. In the example above, the interviewer could
move in a number of interesting directions before going on to
the next prepared question. Why is there no sponsored research? Is someone at fault—the university, the department,
the professor, or the foundations? Or should we be grateful,
as students, that professors are spending their time in the
classroom instead of in the laboratory? How about some specifics on the private research? What kind of fish are caught?
How are they analyzed? What chemicals have been turning
up? How dangerous are they to other wildlife and to human
beings? What is the source of the pollution? Are there any
practical remedies?

Notes taken from the interview in the example above might
look something like the following.

Example

---

1. No "sponsored" research
Paid for by foundations or university.

Individual prjts. — fish analysis

The number 1 at the beginning of the note indicates that this information was elicited by the first prepared question. The spontaneous questions are not written down, but the answers are noted. Many interviewers develop a private shorthand. Letters can be left out — write "prjts" for "projects" — and other private symbols can be invented, as long as they will be clear to the interviewer.

Be sure to put quotation marks around the words you intend to quote verbatim. When you quote, copy the words accurately and remember the context in which they were spoken. People are justly annoyed when they see their words distorted or quoted in a context that changes the meaning. Use quotation marks to give credit where credit is due. Don't present someone else's words as if they were your own.

Direct quotations, strategically placed, add life to the paper.

Example

According to Professor Baker, research on the environment is being conducted by individual professors in the biology department. But, says Baker, "There is very little sponsored research of any kind."

If you change your informant's words in any way, you should follow certain conventions that let the reader know changes have been made. If you decide to add words of explanation within a quoted passage, put brackets around the added material.

Example

According to Baker, "Big foundations will sometimes pay part of [professors'] salaries."

The brackets indicate that you have somehow tampered with the original words. In this case, the word *professors'* has been substituted for the word *our*. If your typewriter has no brackets, you can either draw them in by hand or make them with a combination of the underscore key and the slash mark.

If you leave out words in the middle of a quoted passage, put three periods with single spaces between them to indicate the omission. The technical name for leaving out words is *ellipsis*.

Example

Among the projects being conducted by biology professors on their own is the analysis of "fish caught in the river . . . to see if they have any pesticides or industrial pollutants in them."

In this example, the words "for example" were omitted where the three periods appear. If the ellipsis includes the end of a sentence, an additional period is used, right next to the last word quoted in the first sentence.

Example

Asked how much research on the environment was being sponsored, Baker said, "None. . . . However, a number of us have been conducting experiments on our own."

In this example, the four periods indicate a merger of two sentences that were originally separate.

Back at your desk, you need to sort out what you learned from the interview. How much of it is relevant to your purpose? Can you support the thesis or sustain the mood you had in mind when you prepared your question list? If not, have you discovered a new approach or a different mood that the material will support? Now that you have some information at your disposal, you can begin refining the purpose of your paper, selecting the useful material and discarding the rest. Once again, resist the temptation to keep material that is interesting but unrelated.

Since writers often select their material as they are organizing it, you might read Chapter Four, on organization, before sorting out the results of your interview.

EXERCISE

Look through any newspaper or popular magazine for an article that you think was based on an interview. Bring the article or a xeroxed copy of it to class. In a discussion with your classmates, observe the article closely, and try to figure out how the actual interview must have been different from the article. Be on the lookout for techniques you might like to imitate in writing your own interview paper.

WRITING ASSIGNMENTS

1. Interview a classmate you don't know very well. Keep asking questions until you discover something the classmate knows more about than you do. It may be an academic subject (Greek, math, economics), a practical skill (carpentry, cooking, auto mechanics, gardening), a hobby (raising goldfish, hunting), or a special place (a country, a town, even a neighborhood). Once you have discovered what this classmate knows, conduct an interview. Look for the sort of information you might include in a newspaper or magazine story. Then write the story. Start out with something you think your readers will find interesting, and then arrange the rest of your material in a sequence you think will hold the readers' attention. Use the checklist on pp. 160–162 as you prepare your final draft.

2. Pick out someone who knows something you don't: a friend, neighbor, official, or celebrity. Make an appointment for an interview. Prepare a list of questions in advance and conduct the interview as explained in the previous section. Write a short paper based upon the interview. For suggestions about organization, read Chapter Four. Use the checklist on pp. 160–162 as you prepare your final draft.

Chapter Three

———⟪◆⟫———

Six Questions for Critical Reading

Critical reading is the other side of persuasive writing. Reading critically means separating statements that need proof from those that don't, and examining the quality of proof offered for statements that need it. It means taking into account the character of the implied author and the disposition of the implied audience. It means being sensitive to the essay's tone and being aware of the strategy of its structure.

In a composition course, critical reading can also be a source of ideas to write about. Your instructor is likely to assign an essay and ask you to analyze and evaluate it in a short paper. This is exactly the kind of writing you will be asked to do in other courses too. Like every other kind of writing, this one requires that you ask good questions before you begin. This chapter will explain three pairs of questions you might use to examine almost anything you read:

1. Which assertions require evidence?
   What kind of evidence is offered?
2. What is the character of the implied author?
   What is the character of the implied audience?
3. What is the author's tone?
   How are the parts of the essay related to one another?

1. Assertions and Evidence

Theoretically, nothing is ever proved. No matter how much measurement or testimony or experimentation we amass, every assertion depends upon either definition of the terms, an inductive leap, or an act of faith. In Euclidean geometry we can assert that parallel lines never meet only because we have defined parallel lines as lines that never meet. In chemistry we can say that the coking of coal produces hydrogen sulfide only because *until now* every time we have coked coal, hydrogen sulfide was produced. (The assumption that future experiments will yield the same result as past experiments is called an inductive leap.) And in economics, we can say that the scarcity and beauty of gold make it more valuable than lead only because we are accustomed to valuing what is rare and what we consider beautiful. But we all know that this custom is based on human perceptions, not on the nature of lead and gold.

Despite the fact that nothing is ever completely proved, educated people have developed standards of proof that they apply to whatever they read. These standards vary according to the subject matter. The most rigorous standards are in the field of mathematics. There an assertion is either right or wrong. No "almosts" allowed. In the physical sciences, standards are almost as rigorous. There nothing is considered true unless it has been demonstrated by what is called the inductive method, which usually involves repeated measurement, sampling, and experimentation.

Many important decisions, however, have to be based upon standards of evidence that can never be as rigorous as those required by scientists and mathematicians; they have to do with values and free choices, neither of which can be quantified by mathematicians or measured in a laboratory. Should we put a stop to the arms race? How can we do so without endangering our own safety? Should we be required to register handguns? Is the Equal Rights Amendment the best way to eradicate discrimination against women? Is the creation of artificial life forms worth the risk? Should doctors be allowed to turn off life-support systems when there is no hope of a cure? Does a human fetus have rights?

None of these questions can be answered by science or mathematics. But, for practical reasons, all of them must be answered. When intelligent people discuss questions like these, they know that they are dealing with a kind of proof that is less than certain, and yet perhaps the most important kind of proof of all, since it is all we have to go on when we ask the crucial questions of our lives.

The first pair of questions a critical reader might ask are these:

Which assertions require evidence?
What kind of evidence is offered?

The following essay was published by William F. Buckley, Jr., in *Execution Eve, and Other Contemporary Ballads* (1975).* Read the essay twice, first as you normally would, and then slowly, noticing where the assertions are and watching for evidence that supports them.

CAPITAL PUNISHMENT

There is national suspense over whether capital punishment 1 is about to be abolished, and the assumption is that when it comes it will come from the Supreme Court. Meanwhile, (a) the prestigious State Supreme Court of California has interrupted executions, giving constitutional reasons for doing so; (b) the death wings are overflowing with convicted prisoners; (c) executions are a remote memory; and — for the first time in years — (d) the opinion polls show that there is sentiment for what amounts to the restoration of capital punishment.

The case for abolition is popularly known. The other case 2 less so, and (without wholeheartedly endorsing it) I give it as

* Reprinted by the author's permission.

it was given recently to the Committee of the Judiciary of the House of Representatives by Professor Ernest van den Haag, under whose thinking cap groweth no moss. Mr. van den Haag, a professor of social philosophy at New York University, ambushed the most popular arguments of the abolitionists, taking no prisoners.

(1) The business about the poor and the black suffering excessively from capital punishment is no argument against capital punishment. It is an argument against the *administration* of justice, not against the penalty. Any punishment can be unfairly or unjustly applied. Go ahead and reform the processes by which capital punishment is inflicted, if you wish; but don't confuse maladministration with the merits of capital punishment. 3

(2) The argument that the death penalty is "unusual" is circular. Capital punishment continues on the books of a majority of states, the people continue to sanction the concept of capital punishment, and indeed capital sentences are routinely handed down. What has made capital punishment "unusual" is that the courts and, primarily, governors have intervened in the process so as to collaborate in the frustration of the execution of the law. To argue that capital punishment is unusual, when in fact it has been made unusual by extra-legislative authority, is an argument to expedite, not eliminate, executions. 4

(3) Capital punishment is cruel. That is a historical judgment. But the Constitution suggests that what must be proscribed as cruel is (a) a particularly painful way of inflicting death, or (b) a particularly undeserved death; and the death penalty, as such, offends neither of these criteria and cannot therefore be regarded as objectively "cruel." 5

Viewed the other way, the question is whether capital punishment can be regarded as useful, and the question of deterrence arises. 6

(4) Those who believe that the death penalty does not intensify the disinclination to commit certain crimes need to wrestle with statistics that, in fact, it can't be proved that *any* punishment does that to any particular crime. One would rationally suppose that two years in jail would cut the commission of a crime if not exactly by 100 percent more than a penalty of one year in jail, at least that it would further discourage crime to a certain extent. The proof is unavailing. On the other hand, the statistics, although ambiguous, do not show either (a) that capital punishment net discourages; or 7

(b) that capital punishment fails net to discourage. "The absence of proof for the additional deterrent effect of the death penalty must not be confused with the presence of proof for the absence of this effect."

The argument that most capital crimes are crimes of passion committed by irrational persons is no argument against the death penalty, because it does not reveal how many crimes might, but for the death penalty, have been committed by rational persons who are now deterred. 8

And the clincher. (5) Since we do not know for certain whether or not the death penalty adds deterrence, we have in effect the choice of two risks. 9

Risk One: If we execute convicted murderers without thereby deterring prospective murderers beyond the deterrence that could have been achieved by life imprisonment, we may have vainly sacrificed the life of the convicted murderer. 10

Risk Two: If we fail to execute a convicted murderer whose execution might have deterred an indefinite number of prospective murderers, our failure sacrifices an indefinite number of victims of future murderers. 11

"If we had certainty, we would not have risks. We do not have certainty. If we have risks — and we do — better to risk the life of the convicted man than risk the life of an indefinite number of innocent victims who might survive if he were executed." 12

The assertions in Buckley's speech may be put into two categories: statements of fact and judgments. Statements of fact are statements that might be checked by observation, measurement, or reliable testimony. Buckley makes a number of factual statements in his first paragraph: that "There is national suspense over whether capital punishment is about to be abolished"; that the "Supreme Court of California has interrupted executions, giving constitutional reasons for doing so"; that "executions are a remote memory"; and that "opinion polls [favor] the restoration of capital punishment." Although it is theoretically possible to challenge every statement of fact, reasonable readers challenge only those they have reason to disbelieve or to be suspicious of. Among the factual assertions in Buckley's first paragraph, only the one about executions being "a remote memory" would invite a challenge, and then only because Buckley wrote the essay before the execution of Gary Gilmore in Utah made capital punishment a reality of the present. As for the other assertions of fact, most critical readers would accept them, partly because they are consistent with what is generally known about the subject, partly because the author does not seem to be a person who would deliberately lie, and partly because none of the facts is essential to the argument that follows.

The second sort of assertion—judgments—are statements that cannot be entirely settled by observation, measurement, or testimony. A judgment is the sort of assertion that would make a good topic for debate or a good thesis for a persuasive paper. The major judgment in this essay is that capital punishment should be restored. Buckley supports this assertion in a general way by relying on *authority*—the testimony of an expert, Ernest van den Haag. For a critical reader, authority is persuasive only if the reader happens to respect the opinion of that particular authority in the area being discussed. In this case, Buckley makes his authority impressive by citing his credentials—he is a professor of social philosophy at New York University, important enough to testify before a Congressional Committee—and by describing him as a person "under whose thinking cap groweth no moss." Critical readers would respect those credentials without being overwhelmed by them: professors of social philosophy have no infallible methods for settling questions of this sort; people who testify in Congress may or may not know what they are talking about; and Buckley may well be praising the qualities of the professor's mind simply because he is sympathetic with the professor's conclusions.

The heart of the argument, then, is the list of assertions Buckley attributes to van den Haag and the evidence offered in support of those assertions. The assertions are paraphrased below.

1. The fact that a disproportionate number of blacks and poor people are on death row is no reason for abandoning capital punishment (paragraph 3).

2. Capital punishment is "unusual" only because we don't practice it often enough (paragraph 4).

3. Capital punishment is not "cruel" if the death is not undeserved and not particularly painful (paragraph 5).
4. Although statistics about deterrence prove nothing one way or the other, the very possibility of a deterrent effect makes execution worthwhile (paragraphs 7 and 8).
5. We have to choose between sacrificing the lives of convicted murderers or risking the lives of potential victims (paragraphs 10, 11, and 12).

The first assertion can be analyzed as a *cause and effect analysis*. People who oppose capital punishment often point out that the death penalty seems to be applied to poor people and to members of minority groups in disproportionate numbers. Professor van den Haag argues that if the numbers are disproportionate, the cause is not the nature of the punishment, but rather the system that applies the punishment (paragraph 3).

A critical reader would look at this support with some suspicion. First, a critical reader knows that cause and effect relationships do not occur in human affairs as neatly as they occur in scientific laboratories. Although logically one might assume that a better court system would produce a fairer distribution of punishment for crimes, critical readers know that those responsible for administering justice are, after all, only human beings, subject to passion and prejudice just like everyone else. The argument that a disproportionate number of executions should be tolerated by certain groups until a better system can be worked out will not be persuasive to people who have a sense of fair play, particularly among the poor, among members of minority groups, and among people who are sympathetic with these interests.

Underlying van den Haag's analysis, however, is a debatable question which neither he nor Buckley states directly: Do the disproportionate figures represent prejudicial treatment in the courts, or do they simply reflect a disproportionate number of capital crimes committed by various groups? Since most crimes go unsolved, no one can answer this question. People who feel that the criminal justice system is at fault will reject van den Haag's argument because no reasonable person could expect one segment of society to suffer disproportionately while the system awaits a reform that may never take place. People who feel that the poor and members of minority groups receive a disproportionate amount of punishment because they commit a disproportionate number of crimes may be inclined to accept van den Haag's analysis because they see no injustice in it.

The next two arguments (paragraphs 4 and 5) are questions of *definition*. The Eighth Amendment to the U.S. Constitution forbids "cruel and unusual" punishment. How then do we define "cruel" and "unusual"?

Professor van den Haag chooses to define "unusual" in a statistical sense: something is unusual if it does not occur frequently. If capital punishment occurred more frequently, it would not be unusual.

A critical reader knows that a definition is persuasive only if it is reasonable in itself or if it comes from an authority the reader is willing to acknowledge. People who support capital punishment might accept van den Haag's definition of "unusual" because it seems reasonable in itself. People who are opposed to capital punishment would point out that van den Haag's definition actually leaves "unusual" without any meaning at all in the Constitution, since even the most bizarre punishments could be considered usual if they were practiced frequently. Clearly, these people would say, the framers of the Constitution did not intend "unusual" in a purely statistical sense.

In dealing with the issue of cruelty, van den Haag, as Buckley represents him, first admits that capital punishment is cruel, but then argues that it is not cruel if the death is not particularly painful nor undeserved. This is a negative definition; van den Haag defines "cruel" by saying what isn't cruel. Eliminating the possibility of torture and injustice, van den Haag asserts that merely to have someone's life put to an end is not an act of cruelty.

Some readers will accept van den Haag's definition of cruelty because it makes sense as he presents it. Others will simply ignore the definition because they feel that the Constitution's prohibition of cruel punishment is irrelevant and sentimental when society is dealing with cruel criminals. Others, however, will reject van den Haag's definition because they consider the Constitution's prohibition to be civil and humane, and because they consider death, no matter how gentle and just, to be cruel.

The next assertion (paragraph 7) uses statistics in a cause and effect analysis of capital punishment as a deterrent to potential criminals. The statistics are inconclusive. Opponents of capital punishment would agree: some studies show that capital punishment discourages crime, others show that it doesn't. Buckley and van den Haag (paragraphs 7 and 8) argue that given no statistical evidence either way, we should assume that capital punishment has at best a healthy effect on society by discouraging criminals and at worst no effect. People who oppose capital punishment might argue that capital punishment may have an unhealthy effect on society by teaching people to use death as a way of controlling other people or as a way of getting even. Critical readers know that inconclusive statistics are stubbornly inconclusive and cannot be used to support either side of the argument.

The last assertion, which Buckley calls "the clincher," is an *argument from circumstance*. In effect, this argument says that we have only two choices, both bad, though one is even worse than the other. Choice one, as Buckley presents it, is to execute convicted murderers and run the risk that their executions will not deter other potential murderers. Choice two is not to execute convicted murderers and to run the risk that other people will be murdered whose lives might have been spared in a society in which murderers are executed. According to Buckley and van den Haag, the first choice is the lesser of two evils.

The argument from circumstance is persuasive only if the reader agrees that the choices are in fact limited and that one choice is clearly less evil than the others. In this case, there are in fact only two choices: either society imposes capital punishment on certain convicts or it doesn't. What remains debatable, however, is whether one choice is clearly superior to the other. Buckley and van den Haag opt for capital punishment because they believe it may save innocent lives. People who oppose capital punishment could argue that executions might make violence seem socially acceptable and thus result in more murders.

As we have seen, the evidence presented in this essay is not scientifically conclusive. Does this mean the essay is defective? Not necessarily. Remember that there are many important issues in human affairs that cannot be settled by scientific evidence. In this essay, the issue is beyond science. It is to Buckley's and van den Haag's credit, however, that they relied mainly on arguments based on logic rather than on emotion.

But, as Aristotle pointed out long ago, most people do not have the patience or intelligence to follow a logical argument very closely. Most people will be persuaded neither by reason nor by emotion, but by the *ethos*—the character—of the author. The next two questions deal with this aspect of persuasion, which is called the ethical appeal.

2. Author and Audience

The second pair of questions a critical reader might ask are these:

What is the character of the implied author?
What is the character of the implied audience?

These questions refer not only to the actual author and the real readers, but to the character projected by the author within the text and to the sort of audience that is implied by the values and standards of evidence it is expected to share.

In writing, the character of the author is implied in two ways: in the author's style and in the values the author approves.

In writing, just as in speaking, people say something about themselves in their style. They can portray themselves as sophisticated or simple, formal or casual, excited or serene, friendly or stuffy, tough or conciliatory. There is no limit to the kinds of personalities people might express in their language.

In "Capital Punishment," the language gives few clues about the real personality of the author. His language seems intelligent enough; there is a maturity of style and word choice that makes the author seem at home in print. But, like most published authors, Buckley gives few hints about his personal origins. He writes like an educated American, but we cannot tell from the essay that he studied at the University of New Mexico and at Yale, or that he was born in New York, or that his family is wealthy, or that he lived in Europe for a while. Nor can we tell from the essay that Buckley is famous, that he is a Republican, and that he is generally conservative. Critical readers who happen to know these facts will be careful not to allow them to prejudice their evaluation of Buckley's argument.

The author does, however, have two noticeable characteristics of style that seem to say something about his personality. One is that he is not afraid of informality. When he says "Go ahead and reform the processes . . ." he seems almost to be talking rather than writing. The second characteristic is a sense of humor despite the seriousness of the topic. When he describes van den Haag as someone "under whose thinking cap groweth no moss," he is expecting his readers to smile at the incongruous juncture of two cliches and an archaic verb form.

The more important indications of ethos, however, are the author's values. Aristotle instructed his students to project values that their audiences were likely to approve, for if an audience shares an author's values in some areas, it will be inclined to accept the author's judgment in others. These values may be expressed as approval or disapproval of certain personalities — people the audience would acknowledge as heroes or villains — or they may be expressed by approval or disapproval of certain abstractions such as political affiliation, social origins, religious beliefs, patriotism, treason, courage, cowardice, honesty, or guile.

In "Capital Punishment" Buckley portrays himself as a person who respects intellectual people (the professor he cites), who is sympathetic with the innocent (the potential victims he hopes to save), and who has little use for convicted murderers. Buckley also portrays himself as a foe of injustice: If there is injustice in the system, he seems to be saying in paragraph 3, get rid of it. And he is opposed to torture and undeserved executions, both of which he disavows in paragraph 5.

In short, the ethical appeal in "Capital Punishment" works

like this: If you are, like Buckley, a person who respects intelligence, is sympathetic with innocent victims, is unsympathetic with convicted murderers, disapproves of injustice, torture, and undeserved executions, then you should, like Buckley, approve of capital punishment. It is easy to see why this line of argument is difficult for most people to resist.

Critical readers, however, do not confuse the values projected by an author with the logic of the argument. They know that they can share some or all of an author's values and still reject the author's conclusions on other grounds; and they know that they might reject the values of a given author—might find the author's politics and personal life distasteful in every way—and still admit that the author is correct on this or that particular issue. In this case, some critical readers might agree with Buckley, not because they approve of the values he projects in the essay (who wouldn't?), but because they accept his standards of evidence. Still other readers, equally intelligent and fair, might reject Buckley's conclusion, not because they reject his values, but because they are not satisfied with his standards of evidence.

The audience implied by the essay, then, is one that is not only sympathetic with the values Buckley espouses, but satisfied with his standards of proof. It is an audience that is comfortable with the effects of capital punishment on minority groups and poor people, satisfied that capital punishment is not unusual according to the Constitution's intended meaning (or indifferent to the Constitution's prohibition of unusual punishment), satisfied that death is not in itself cruel (or indifferent to the Constitution's prohibition of cruel punishment), satisfied with the evidence that capital punishment will have a deterrent effect or at least no bad effect on the crime rate, and satisfied that capital punishment is the less risky of two choices for dealing with murderers. If this profile of the audience happens to describe you as an individual, you probably find Buckley's essay persuasive.

There is, of course, another audience, one not implied in the essay. This audience may be sympathetic with the values Buckley espouses, but uneasy with the effects of capital punishment on minority groups and poor people, unconvinced by van den Haag's definitions of "unusual" and "cruel," suspicious that capital punishment may encourage murderers rather than deter them, and doubtful that executions are the lesser of two evils. If you belong to this second group, you probably find the essay unconvincing.

Which group is right? Both. And neither. At the moment, we simply lack conclusive evidence about what the effects of capital punishment might be. And yet we must decide on the basis of arguments like those advanced by Buckley and by the abolitionists whether capital punishment is indeed the less risky alternative. Critical reading will not bring certitude to the debate. It will simply enable educated people to understand why they believe what they believe and to avoid being trapped by tactics that may be irrelevant to the issue at hand.

3. Tone and Structure

The third pair of questions a critical reader might ask are these:

What is the author's tone?
How are the parts of the essay related to one another?

Tone refers to the author's attitude toward the subject matter and toward the audience. It is expressed mainly in the emotional force of the author's language. Emotional appeal, according to Aristotle, is the second most effective approach (after ethical appeal) for persuading a mass audience. Although few words are totally devoid of emotional overtones, authors can choose language that is more or less neutral in connotation, as opposed to the charged language used by politicians who are trying to stir up the populace for better or for worse. In the examples below, both Spiro Agnew and Winston Churchill use charged language rather than evidence to stir up the feelings of audiences that probably agreed with them in advance.

Examples
We shall go on to the end, we shall fight in France, we shall fight on the seas and oceans, we shall fight with growing confidence and

growing strength in the air, we shall defend our Island, whatever the cost may be, we shall fight on the beaches, we shall fight on the landing grounds, we shall fight in the fields and in the streets, we shall fight in the hills; we shall never surrender, even if, which I do not for a moment believe, this Island or a large part of it were subjugated and starving, then our Empire beyond the seas, armed and guarded by the British Fleet, would carry on the struggle, until, in God's good time, the New World, with all its power and might, steps forth to the rescue and the liberation of the old.

—Winston Churchill

As for these deserters, malcontents, radicals, incendiaries, the civil and uncivil disobedients among our young, SDS, PLP, Weatherman I and Weatherman II, the revolutionary action movement, Yippies, Hippies, Yahoos, Black Panthers, Lions and Tigers alike—I would swap the whole damn zoo for a single platoon of the kind of young Americans I saw in Vietnam. . . .

—Spiro Agnew*

In comparison with Churchill's and Agnew's tone, Buckley's seems low keyed and calm. Buckley may have realized that charged language works best with an audience that already agrees with the author, but has the opposite effect on people of other persuasions. People who agreed with Agnew back in the 1960s thought his style was perfectly appropriate; people who disagreed considered it demagoguery. In Buckley's article, there are a few phrases with emotional overtones, the most obvious of which is the assertion that van den Haag "ambushed the most popular arguments of the abolitionists, taking no prisoners" (paragraph 2). The phrase is a metaphor, comparing van den Haag's argument with guerilla warfare and suggesting that van den Haag annihilated the opposing point of view. Metaphors are commonly used in persuasive writing to give a point more power. In this case, the metaphor is something of an exaggeration that will please people who agree with Buckley and annoy those who disagree.

Another example of charged language is Buckley's description of the courts and governors who "collaborate in the frustration of the execution of the law." The phrase suggests that

* For the two quotations and the term "charged language," I am indebted to Newman P. Birk and Genevieve B. Birk, *Understanding and Using English*, Fifth Edition (Indianapolis and New York: The Bobbs-Merrill Company, 1972).

courts and governors are somehow opposed to law and order, when in fact they are part of a complexly balanced system set up by each state's ultimate law, its constitution. Still, Buckley's phrase may have a satisfying ring for those who share his point of view and it may lure people whose point of view is uncertain.

The last paragraph — a quotation from van den Haag — is resounding because it is charged. The professor uses balance and contrasts like a good classical orator. He plays "risks" against "certainty" in the first two sentences and contrasts the "life of the convicted man" with the lives of "an indefinite number of innocent victims" in the last sentence. The contrasts give the passage an almost irresistible power; we are tempted to forget there was no evidence to show whether executions would deter future murderers or encourage them.

The use of charged language to support positions for which there are no conclusive data is neither a defect nor a virtue in persuasive writing. Charged language is simply one means of persuasion available to any author. It can be used to inspire civil and humane behavior and it can be used to incite a mob. Critical readers, however, are not persuaded by charged language. They recognize it for what it is, and they see beyond it to the values, assumptions, and evidence that are the real basis of the author's opinion.

The last question deals with the structure of the essay. Analyzing the structure means more than summarizing the essay. It means summarizing in a way that shows how the parts are related to one another.

The structure of Buckley's essay could be analyzed as follows. The first paragraph introduces the topic and indicates why there is "national suspense" about the issue. The second paragraph is a transition to the body of the essay; it introduces Professor van den Haag and establishes his credentials. The rest of the essay is a summary of van den Haag's argument. That argument begins by refuting the arguments of the abolitionists: it deals in paragraph 3 with the impact of capital punishment on minorities, in paragraph 4 with the notion that capital punishment is unusual, in paragraph 5 with the notion that it is cruel, and in paragraphs 6, 7, and 8 with the fact that no one can prove that capital punishment deters crime. Paragraphs 9, 10, and 11 conclude the argument by saying we have only two choices, one of which is less risky than the other. The

last paragraph summarizes the choices in a rhetorically powerful way.

One way to understand the persuasive power of an essay's
structure is to consider the effect of other patterns of arrangement. The essay might have begun, for example, with what is
now the final quotation from van den Haag. It might have then
explained the two choices and concluded with a refutation of
the abolitionists' arguments and a clever statement about how
van den Haag had ambushed those arguments, "taking no
prisoners." To people who agreed with Buckley in advance,
this revised arrangement might have made little difference. To
people who disagreed with Buckley, however, and to people
who were undecided about capital punishment, the revised
arrangement would probably have been less effective.
Buckley's original arrangement is more persuasive because it
states the opposing point of view fairly at the outset and
attacks it systematically before proposing a different point of
view. The original structure, like a good fish trap, is easy to
wander into and difficult (but not impossible) to escape.

4. Another Essay for Critical Reading

The following essay was written by columnist Thomas Middleton for his column "Light Refractions" in the magazine
Saturday Review (April 15, 1978, p. 99).* Before you begin
reading the essay, jot down the three pairs of questions for
critical reading and fill out answers as you read.

1. Which assertions require evidence?
   What kind of evidence is offered?
2. What is the character of the implied author?
   What is the character of the implied audience?
3. What is the author's tone?
   How are the parts of the essay related to one another?

CHOICE OF LIFE-STYLE

Harry and Charlotte Spitzer are among the leaders of an or-   1
ganization called Straight Talk, the purpose of which is to
provide speakers — most of whom are heterosexual — to talk

* Reprinted by the author's permission.

to interested groups on the subject of homosexuality. It seems that an increasing number of people are interested in hearing some straight talk on the subject, and it is high time.

Harry asked me if I'd write a column about homosexuality. 2
I told him I wasn't an authority on the subject—though that has never checked me before—and I added that Light Refractions was usually about words and usage. He reminded me that the problem of homosexuality is in large part a problem of words. He's right, of course.

I feel very strongly about what is now usually referred to as 3
"gay rights." Along with many other people, I wish "gay" were not the operative word; but it is, so I'll use it, although I still refuse to use it as a noun.

One of the problem phrases most frequently used in dis- 4
cussions of gay rights is "their choice of life-style," the implication being that one chooses to be a homosexual just as one might choose to be a doctor, a lawyer, or a cabinetmaker.

When we talk about sexuality, we're in a field in which 5
there is infinite variety and almost anything is possible, so there undoubtedly are many men and women whose androgyny is so balanced that they do indeed have a choice among heterosexuality, homosexuality, and bisexuality. And, of course, there are those who under the press of circumstances turn to homosexuality as an expedient. But for most homosexuals, choice of life-style has nothing to do with it.

I had a college classmate whose name I think, although 6
I'm not certain, was Charlie. That was a long time ago.

Charlie was bright, talented, witty, and fragile-looking. He 7
was almost stereotypically the effeminate young man. I say "almost" because he worked against it. He affected, not entirely successfully, a sort of good-ol'-boy camaraderie. The consensus about Charlie was that he was almost surely a fag but a hell of a nice guy.

One afternoon, Charlie hanged himself in his dormitory 8
room. He might have considered himself, as everyone else did, "a hell of a nice guy," but I think it's safe to say that he hanged himself because he was a "fag" and therefore loathsome to society and to himself.

I had two other good friends in my youth—both of them 9
big and muscular, excellent athletes; both of them rather quiet and not much interested in girls; both highly intelligent. Fine examples of what we called the strong, silent type. Each was the sort of boy we used to elect Most Popular Boy in the Graduating Class. And both of them were dead before the

age of twenty-five — one by carbon monoxide poisoning, the other by pistol; and both because — to everyone's amazement — they were homosexual.

In this context, the phrase "choice of life-style" is an obscenity.

I've known at least two men who in order to prove to themselves and to the world that they were "normal" married women. Considering themselves perverted, they tried to pervert what in fact was perfectly natural in them. Predictably, they messed up their own lives and the lives of the women they married.

Thanks to the gay rights movement, with its gay alliances, gay task forces, and similar groups, that sort of thing is happening seldom these days, I suspect. These tragedies are becoming relics of a benighted past.

More and more of us are learning that homosexuality is in a somewhat paradoxical sense normal. We've learned that about 10 percent of every culture in the world is homosexual, so the real abnormality would be a society in which there were no homosexuals. Homosexuality itself is no more abnormal than left-handedness.

If, in the name of morality, we enact laws — or even hold attitudes — that are specifically directed against homosexuals, we are attempting to consign them — people who are good and bad, strong and weak, bright and stupid, just as we all are — to a special sort of hell, and I think we should take a very hard look at our own morality.

Compare your answers to the six questions with those below.

Which assertions require evidence?

There are two major assertions. The first is that homosexuality is not a choice (paragraph 5). The second is that laws and attitudes hostile to homosexuality are cruel and immoral (paragraph 14).

What is the evidence?

The evidence for the first assertion — that homosexuality is not a matter of choice — is argued by way of definition (paragraphs 4 and 5). Middleton argues that "choice of life-style" is the wrong phrase to apply to sexuality, which is normally not a matter of choice at all.

Specific evidence for the second assertion is given in three sets of examples in which society's attitude toward homosexuals has had tragic consequences for seven individuals — three suicides and two ruined marriages.

Finally, statistical data is presented (paragraph 13) as evidence that a certain amount of homosexuality is normal in any culture.

What is the character of the implied author?

Heterosexual. Not an authority on the subject (paragraph 2). Paradoxically, *not* being an authority (i.e., not being homosexual) gives the author more credibility among heterosexual readers, since he is not perceived as pleading his own case. Sensitive to language, and sensitive to the ways in which language colors our perceptions (paragraphs 2, 3, and 4). Able to laugh at himself — admits that not being an authority has not prevented him from expressing opinions before (paragraph 2). Sensitive to suffering of other human beings (paragraphs 6–14).

What is the character of the implied audience?

People who are a little uneasy about the subject of homosexuality, perhaps resentful of it. People who share the author's sensitivity to language and who share his sensitivity toward human suffering. People who are willing to accept the examples as relevant to Middleton's main point and who would regard the statistical fact in paragraph 13 as evidence that the examples were representative of a much larger group of people.

What is the author's tone?

The tone varies. At first the author seems to lead the reader into the subject cautiously, as if it were something they both might find a little uncomfortable. Tells a little joke on himself (paragraph 2) to ease the tension. Tone becomes tragic mid-

way through the first example, when after telling us that
Charlie was a "nice guy" he relates abruptly that Charlie
"hanged himself in his dormitory room." Tragic tone is main-
tained throughout other examples. Play on words "natural"
and "perverted" in paragraph 11 is an example of charged
language. Other examples of charged language are "obscenity"
in paragraph 10, "relics of a benighted past" in paragraph 12,
and "good," "bad," "strong," "weak," "bright," "stupid,"
and "hell" in paragraph 14. Structure of last sentence is dramatic. Almost a classic periodic sentence with three contrasting pairs ("good and bad," etc.) in the middle. Brings the essay
to a resounding conclusion — dramatic and intense like the end
of a sermon or a political speech.

How are the parts of the essay related to one another?

   In the first part of the essay, Middleton approaches the subject cautiously so as not to frighten readers who might be disturbed by the subject matter (paragraphs 1 and 2). The author
establishes himself as heterosexual, and therefore as a disinterested party. Paragraphs 4 and 5 set up the central question:
Do homosexuals have a choice? Paragraphs 6–11 give examples of personal tragedies in the lives of homosexuals trapped
in a society that assumed they did have a choice. The examples are arranged so that the intolerant attitudes become increasingly difficult to maintain: first a lonely and effeminate
young man; second two athletes, masculine in appearance and
popular with their classmates; finally, two homosexuals who,
in attempting to live the married lives society expects of them,
end up ruining their own lives as well as the lives of other people. Paragraphs 12–14 bring the essay to a conclusion, praising
the gay rights movement, providing statistics that indicate the
"normality" of homosexuality and criticizing laws and attitudes that discriminate against homosexuals. Middleton first
expresses values he expects his audience to share and then
tries to show how other values, despite their unpopularity, are
equally respectable.
   After answering the six questions about Middleton's essay,
you are in a position to say why you find it persuasive or not
persuasive. Like Buckley's essay, Middleton's is directed

toward a certain fictional audience that is implied by the essay. To the extent that you are unable or unwilling to play the role expected of that audience, you probably feel inclined to challenge the conclusion. Among the exercises at the end of this chapter is a letter written to protest Middleton's defense of homosexuals. It should provide you with a good opportunity to practice critical reading.

5. Other Kinds of Nonscientific Evidence

Aristotle dealt with the problem of evidence more than 2300 years ago. In a book called the *Nichomachean Ethics*, he distinguished the various kinds of evidence intelligent people might expect in different situations. In dealing with scientific matters, they should demand strict, logical, and scientific evidence; but in matters that cannot be settled by strict logic or scientific evidence, they should look for other kinds of evidence, one of which is called the *enthymeme*. By enthymeme Aristotle meant a pattern of thought that human beings normally accept, even though it is not as rigorous as scientific evidence or mathematical proof.* Among the enthymemes Aristotle discussed is the notion that what is rare is valuable (which is why we value gold); the notion that if our enemies don't want us to do something, then we probably should do it; and the notion that if we have already expended a lot of money or effort trying to achieve something, we should keep on trying or else all our past efforts will be wasted.

Normally people find these lines of thought persuasive; but if you examine them closely, you can come up with lots of exceptions. A rare smallpox virus would not be considered particularly valuable, even if it were the last one on earth. Our enemies may well be mistaken in what they think will do us harm. And sometimes it is better to give up on an expensive enterprise, especially if we discover that the results were not really desirable to begin with.

---

* In this discussion I reject, as Lane Cooper does, the mistaken notion "that an enthymeme [is] a syllogism with one of the three members taken for granted and suppressed." See Cooper's introduction to *The Rhetoric of Aristotle* (Englewood Cliffs, New Jersey: Prentice-Hall, Inc., © 1932 and 1960), p. xxvi.

Other kinds of nonscientific evidence are *analogy* and *precedent*.

An analogy is a double comparison: A is to B as X is to Y.

Example

Panamanians (A) resent the U.S. presence (B) in Panama as much as North Americans (X) would resent a foreign occupation (Y) on both sides of the Mississippi.

Analogies always limp. In the debate over the Panama Canal Treaty, some members of Congress were unimpressed with this analogy because they felt that, after all, no foreign country had actually built the Mississippi and paid for the right to operate it. Other people, however, found the analogy perfectly apt, for they considered the essence of the issue to be a question of local pride and feelings, not a question of legal right and wrong. For them, the analogy helped North Americans understand how Panamanians felt about the U.S. presence in their country.

Precedent is a special kind of analogy in which we argue that one situation is analogous to a previous situation.

Examples

If a teacher allows a sick student to have a take-home final, other sick students can argue from precedent that they should be allowed to have take-home finals too.

Elected heads of state should not be allowed to succeed themselves indefinitely, because in the past heads of states who were allowed to succeed themselves indefinitely eventually became dictators.

Precedent is persuasive if the reader agrees that the present case is really analogous to the earlier case, and, in legal matters, if the reader accepts the earlier decision as just or authoritative.

Neither of these lines of argument is irrefutable, but they are still necessary in deciding issues that cannot be decided scientifically. The fact that they can always be challenged does not make them useless as lines of reasoning; they are often the only lines of reasoning that can be applied to settle issues that, for practical reasons, need to be settled.

6. Irony

Critical readers are also aware of one special sort of tone that was not illustrated in the Buckley and Middleton pieces: irony. *Irony* is a game in which the author and the reader both know that the text cannot be taken at face value. In ironic essays, writers portray themselves as characters with standards of judgment that no reasonable person could approve. Often the ironic personality will defend a position that is entirely contrary to what the real author holds; but because the standards of judgment in the text are so bizarre, the reader is expected to reject what the text asserts and to accept what the text denies.

Political columnist Art Buchwald is famous for using irony as a device for exposing the absurdities of Washington politics. The column printed below was Buchwald's reaction to a business deal in which the United States Navy bankrolled a faltering private corporation. As you read the essay, look for answers to the three pairs of questions discussed in this chapter:

1. Which assertions require evidence?
   What kind of evidence is offered?
2. What is the character of the implied author?
   What is the character of the implied audience?
3. What is the author's tone?
   How are the parts of the essay related to one another?

TRUTH IN LENDING*

The United States Navy lent $54,000,000 to the Grumman Aircraft Company. The Navy defended its role as banker on the grounds that the money was not really a loan but rather an advance on F-14 airplanes which Grumman says it cannot deliver.

When my friend Morris Stans (no relation to the former Secretary of Commerce) heard that the Navy had gone into the banking business, he immediately rushed down to the Pentagon.

He said to a Wave at the desk, "I'd like to see someone about a loan."

---

* From *I Never Danced at the White House* (G. P. Putnam's Sons, © 1978). Reprinted by the author's permission.

The Wave asked Morris to be seated and then started to make some telephone calls. Finally she said, "Go to the third floor to BuNav BOC and ask for Commander Smiley."

"What does BuNav BOC stand for?" Morris asked.

"Bureau of Navy for Bailing Out Contractors," the Wave replied.

Stans went to the third floor office of Commander Smiley, who was talking on the phone. "Yes, sir. We can lend Litton Industries one hundred million dollars at five point five percent. No, sir, there are no collateral requirements. Your name on the note is good enough for us. Yes, sir, Mr. Ash, the check will be in the mail tomorrow morning."

Commander Smiley turned to Morris. "What can I do for you?"

"I'd like to borrow five hundred dollars to make some improvements on my house."

"I'm sorry, the Navy doesn't make loans for home improvements," Commander Smiley said.

"But the house is on the water," Morris said, "on Cape Cod."

"Well why didn't you say so?" Commander Smiley asked, taking out a form. "First I must ask if you've applied for this loan from a commercial bank."

"I applied to seven banks. They all turned me down. They suggested I see the Navy because they said you'll lend money to people that no bank would touch."

"That's our business," Commander Smiley said. "Our motto in the Navy is 'Impossible loans are our business.'"

"I thought it was 'Don't give up the ship.'"

"Times have changed," Smiley said. "Now would these improvements on your house benefit the Navy in any way?"

"Well, I want to repair my dock for my sailboat, but the Navy would be free to use the facilities to tie up an aircraft carrier or something in case of war."

"We very well might," Commander Smiley said, filling out the form. "How do you propose to repay the loan?"

"Ten dollars a week," Morris replied.

"That seems fair," Smiley said. "I must tell you under the Truth in Lending Navy Act that we will have to charge you six percent interest."

"But I just heard you tell Litton Industries you would only charge them five point five percent," Stans protested.

"That's because Litton owes us so much money. Now if you wanted to make a loan of, say, more than twenty million dollars, we could give you a more favorable rate as well."

"No, I'll stick with the five hundred dollars."

"Very good. Just sign here. This booklet is your payment schedule. Just make your checks payable to the Department of Defense."

"Thank you very much. The Navy won't be sorry they trusted me."

"I'm sure we won't," Smiley said, shaking Stans' hand. "On your way out pick up a new toaster or a coffeepot or an electric blanket in the lobby."

"Free?" Morris asked.

"Of course. Why do you think Grumman Aircraft came to us instead of Bank of America? They know we give out the best premiums in the country."

Which assertions require evidence?

Since irony is a game in which the text cannot be taken at face value, the ironic writer makes assertions indirectly. It is up to the reader to participate in the game by recognizing that what is presented as normal in an ironic passage is often the exact opposite of what the writer feels should be normal. In Buchwald's piece, the Navy is depicted as doing business as if it were an ordinary bank or loan company, complete with giveaways like toasters, electric blankets, and coffeepots. What Buchwald is really saying, of course, is that it is inappropriate for the Navy to behave as if it were a bank. More specifically, Buchwald is saying that it was wrong for the Navy to finance a private corporation.

What kind of evidence is offered?

The evidence in ironic essays is often reverse evidence known technically as a *reductio ad absurdum* — a reduction to absurdity. This is a technique in which writers carry the opponent's position to its logical conclusion, which turns out to be absurd. In this essay, Buchwald is implicitly saying, "If the Navy can act like a private bank in one situation, why not in every situation?" The question is answered by showing how absurd it would be if an average citizen could rely on the Navy for a loan as Grumman had, merely by asserting that the Navy would benefit from the deal.

What is the character of the implied author?

In ironic writing, there are really two authors to consider: the real writer who composed the piece and the fictional character who is implied by the standards of judgment in the text. In the Buchwald piece, the fictional character is someone who sees nothing remarkable in a story about a private citizen who secures a home improvement loan from the U.S. Navy. The real author, of course — Buchwald himself — is the sort of person who strongly disapproves of the Navy's involvement with a private enterprise.

What is the character of the implied audience?

Just as there are two implied authors in an ironic piece, there are two implied audiences. The fictional author — the pose the real author assumes — is writing to a fictional audience that would find nothing unusual in the Navy's getting into the finance business. The real audience, however, is more like the real author — willing to laugh at the foibles of human behavior, but not willing to make peace with them.

What is the author's tone?

The tone of an ironic piece is probably best described as "straight faced" or "tongue in cheek." The author's attitude toward his subject matter is a mock seriousness, like comedians who pretend not to see the point of their own jokes.

How are the parts of the essay related to one another?

The first paragraph, which is not ironic at all, connects the essay to reality by mentioning the Navy-Grumman deal in a straightforward manner. The rest of the essay relates a story that could be the logical consequence of the incident related in the opening paragraph. The description of a visit to the Pentagon at first seems realistic enough, with a Wave at a desk directing the visitor to an appropriately named office. But gradually the details become more and more absurd, making the premise they stem from — the Navy's loan to Grumman — seem ridiculous.

To understand the purpose of irony, try to imagine what Buchwald's essay would have been like if it had been written in a serious, straightforward tone. A newspaper editor writing a column condemning the Navy for its loan to Grumman would have had to provide a moral basis for disapproving of the Navy's behavior, which was, apparently, neither illegal nor economically ineffective. In other societies, standards of public behavior were established by a shared mythology or a universally recognized authority. In the middle ages, the Church and the Bible were recognized as moral authorities in political as well as in personal behavior; a critic of public behavior could base judgments on the teachings of the Church or of the Bible.

For the Romans, a common belief in the Empire's destiny as a civilizing force in the world gave rise to a public code of morality based upon what was "fit," "appropriate," or "becoming" in the light of Rome's destiny. The Latin word for this concept was *decus*, from which we get modern words like *decent* and *indecent*, *decorous* and *indecorous* as terms applied in judgment of behavior. The Roman poet Horace was able to write, without irony, that it was "sweet and fitting *(dulce et decorum)* to give up one's life for one's country" — a value judgment that Wilfred Owen used with bitter irony in a modern war poem.

But in our present culture, there is no universally recognized authority for judging public behavior other than legality and effectiveness. If it works and it's legal, how can it be bad? And without a universally recognized basis for public ethics, it is difficult to criticize behavior that is unsavory but not illegal or ineffective — like the Navy's deal with Grumman, or the tendency of some corporations to bribe officials in foreign countries. Judgments about what is unsavory are based upon personal values that may or may not be shared by the public a newspaper editor addresses. The ironist avoids the problem altogether. Instead of facing the difficult task of establishing an ethical principle for condemning the Navy's deal with Grumman, the ironist merely pretends to approve of the deal, but criticizes it indirectly by showing how absurd that sort of behavior would be if carried out to its logical extension. Instead of trying to establish moral principles, the ironist exorcises unreasonable behavior with therapeutic laughter.

7. Critical Readers as an Elite Group

Critical reading is a sophisticated skill. Some students are discouraged by the uncertainty of it all. They long for comfortable assurances that whatever they see in print is reliable, or at least that there is some foolproof method for distinguishing between what is reliable and what isn't. Aristotle was convinced that most people will take the easy way out, relying on personalities to tell them what to believe. If Aristotle was right, critical readers are an elite in every society. And because many important issues cannot be settled by scientific evidence, persuasive writers are a necessity.

EXERCISES

1. Because everyone's personal experience is different, we differ from one another in the sorts of assertions we are willing to accept without further evidence and in the sort of evidence we find persuasive. Indicate which of the following assertions you would probably accept without further evidence. Indicate what sort of evidence you would need before you could accept the others. Indicate which assertions you would be inclined to deny no matter what sort of evidence was offered. Compare your reactions to these assertions with the reactions of your classmates.

a. The Sunbelt is prospering in spite of the energy crisis.
b. Women should be allowed abortions on demand because they have a natural right to control their own bodies.
c. The oil shortage was a fiction created by American oil companies for their own benefit.
d. Students should be allowed to drop courses without penalty even as late as the day before the final exam.
e. Federal aid to church-affiliated schools is a violation of the principle of separation of church and state.
f. Unless we are mightier than the Russians, they will not be willing to negotiate.

g. Students should be made responsible for the cost of their education since they will reap the profits from it.

h. A politician who cannot keep his family together can certainly not keep the country together.

i. Doctors should be allowed to turn off life support systems because a body that cannot survive without them is not truly alive.

j. People who find ancient Indian graves on their property should be allowed to dispose of the skeletons and artifacts in any way they choose.

2. Both the front page and the editorial page of any daily newspaper will be full of stories about issues that cannot be settled by scientific evidence. Look through your favorite newspaper and find five issues of this kind. Be prepared to report on these issues in class and to explain why they cannot be settled by scientific evidence.

WRITING ASSIGNMENTS

After reading the following assignments, turn to Chapter Four for advice about organization.

1. Below is an article published by Anthony Lewis in the *New York Times* shortly after the execution of Gary Gilmore. Analyze the article by applying the six questions discussed in this chapter. Identify the major assertions. Identify and evaluate the evidence offered in support of those assertions. Indicate specifically what values and standards of evidence a reader would have to have to be persuaded by the article. Indicate what values and standards of evidence a reader would have to have to find the article unconvincing.

LET'S DO IT*

In the early morning of Nov. 13, 1849, Charles Dickens   1
came upon a crowd outside Horsemonger Lane Jail in
London. People were waiting to see a Mr. and Mrs.
Manning hanged for the murder of their lodger. Dickens
watched through the hours until sunrise, as the crowd
screamed and laughed and sang "Oh Mrs. Manning" to
the tune of "Oh Susannah." Later that day he wrote a
letter to The Times of London.

* © 1977 by The New York Times Company. Reprinted by permission.

"A sight so inconceivably awful as the wickedness and levity of the immense crowd collected at that execution could be imagined by no man . . ." he wrote. "I am solemnly convinced that nothing that ingenuity could devise to be done in this city, in the same compass of time, could work such ruin as one public execution."

Three days later, after some other comment, Dickens wrote a second letter to the editor. He said executions attracted as spectators "the lowest, the most depraved, the most abandoned of mankind." And he said steps should be taken to limit titillation of the public by stories about a condemned person.

"I would allow no curious visitors to hold any communication with him," Dickens said. "I would place every obstacle in the way of his sayings and doings being served up in print on Sunday mornings for the perusal of families."

Not even Dickens, with his sense of the grotesque, could have imagined the spectacle enacted last week in the United States. The last sayings and doings of a murderer were retailed by the press. His picture graced the weekly journals. And the grossest details of his execution were reproduced on television, to be savored by millions of families in their homes.

Most people I know who have been physically present when the state killed a human being — prison wardens, priests, newspaper reporters — have thereafter been opposed to capital punishment. Twenty years ago, on assignment as a reporter, I watched an electrocution in the District of Columbia jail. When it was over, the room smelled of roasted flesh.

But to experience such scenes vicariously removes, for many, the nausea factor. Television drama has made blood and violence as acceptable as cherry pie. It was only a small additional step to restage an actual execution. And so we had the scene of Gary Gilmore's death on the evening news programs, and sketches of his last moment in sober newspapers.

Some press agencies wanted to hire helicopters to circle over the prison yard, but the Federal Aviation Agency vetoed that idea. Reporters were forced to rely on hourly bulletins from the prison authorities, which some complained were dull.

The great innovation in the Gilmore case was an execution literary agent. A movie producer named Lawrence

Schiller signed the condemned man and his relatives to an exclusive contract for a film to be shown on television. Schiller was allowed to interview Gilmore for many hours in prison, and then to attend the execution.

The agent gave the press the juicy details of the end. When the execution order was read out by an official, Schiller said, "Gary looked at him, holding his own, not quivering." It was Schiller who said he "believed" Gilmore's last words were "Let's do it"—a phrase that the press flashed across the land.

Later, the press learned that Gilmore in his last days had had an intense correspondence with an 11-year-old girl named Amber Hunt. Miss Hunt was interviewed, and a week later her voice was still being heard on the radio.

The slaughter of gladiators and Christians in the Circus Maximus is generally regarded as a symptom of the decadence of Rome. What does it say about a country when punishment for crime becomes a circus, to be reenacted in every home? Can a society savor such spectacles without being coarsened?

Murderers do not usually deserve sympathy. But the objection to having the state kill them in turn is not sentimental. Using the apparatus of official power to extinguish a life has corrupting consequences—the more so when capital punishment is, as it has become in this country, a spectacular occasion: an event cruel and unusual.

In the absence of convincing evidence that executions deter murderers, there must be a suspicion that the practice goes on to satisfy an atavistic public desire for dramatized vengeance. Revival of the death penalty in the United States may in fact encourage murder by persons such as Gary Gilmore—a man with suicidal impulses, who could have seen a way to assure his own spectacular death.

Dickens saw that point. In 1845, in a letter to a friend, he argued among other grounds for opposing capital punishment: "I believe it to have a horrible fascination for many of those persons who render themselves liable to it, impelling them onward to the acquisition of a frightful notoriety."

2. Below is the text of a letter written in response to Thomas Middleton's article on homosexuality. Analyze the letter by applying the three pairs of questions discussed in this chapter. Then write a brief critical analysis of the letter. Was the writer of this letter a good critical reader of Middleton's column?

> I was disturbed by your recent column . . . "Choice of Life-Style." The arguments seemed to me to be strained and unconvincing, and the conclusions incorrect. To see if I was simply confirming my preconceptions about the subject, I tried an experiment with your words. For homosexual, I substituted the word liar and for homosexuality, I inserted dishonesty. I was interested to see that the article flowed just as smoothly as before.
>
> I could just as easily have used words like: bigot, cynic, anti-Semite, thief . . . rapist, adulterer, even murderer. They exist, therefore they are good. You have a vehicle that can justify anything, therefore it justifies nothing.
>
> I feel that homosexuality is as unnatural as murder, which by the way seems to come naturally to many. Making homosexuality respectable will only cause this contagious disorder to spread and infect otherwise well-adjusted and innocent people. Those who condemn themselves because of their homosexual activities do so because the practice is unnatural and pernicious, not because it is frowned upon by their peers.
>
> I think your article has only added to the harm that is done increasingly today by those who proclaim the new permissive slogan: "If it feels good, do it." and I am deeply troubled and saddened by the trend.
>
> Homosexuality, like dishonesty, can bring only harm and heartache to those who practice it, and we do them no favor by confirming their distorted behavior. We would do infinitely better to treat the illness and to assist them in rehabilitation.

3. Find an example of persuasive writing either in your essay anthology or on the editorial page of a newspaper. Use the questions discussed in this chapter to analyze the argument. Write a brief critical analysis in which you explain the effectiveness of the piece to a reader who has never seen it. Be sure to quote from the piece at the appropriate times so your reader can follow your analysis.

4. With the help of your instructor, choose an essay that is ironic in tone. Suggestions: Swift's "A Modest Proposal," or perhaps a recent column by political columnist Art Buchwald. Analyze the essay by jotting down answers to the three pairs of questions discussed in this chapter. Explain your analysis in writing for someone who has not read the essay.

Chapter Four

———⟨◆⟩———

Selecting
and Arranging

Once you have used prewriting techniques to find material to write about, you need to sort and arrange your material so that it will make sense to your readers. This can be one of the most difficult stages of writing, so prepare yourself for some hard work. In this chapter, selecting and arranging are treated under the following headings:

1. Choosing a Rhetorical Stance
2. The Persuasive Stance: Thesis and Outline
3. The Expository Stance
   a. The Plural-Noun Formula
   b. Outlining a Comparison and Contrast Paper
   c. Beyond Basic Outlines

1. Choosing a Rhetorical Stance

The rhetorical stance is the attitude that you have toward your audience and your subject matter. Although an infinite variety of rhetorical stances is theoretically possible, college writers generally take one of two stances: the *persuasive stance* or the *expository stance*. Sometimes the stance you take is specified as part of the assignment. At other times you are free to choose the stance that best suits your conception of your audience and subject matter.

A **persuasive stance** has two components:

1. an issue or question that cannot be entirely settled by empirical or scientific evidence*
2. a writer who is committed to a position statement about the subject matter

An **expository ("explaining") stance** also has two components:

1. a subject matter that is not perceived by the audience as a debatable issue
2. a writer whose purpose is to explain or inform rather than to change the reader's mind

In a persuasive stance you think of your readers as people who need to be convinced that what you say is true. In an expository stance you think of your readers as people who are mainly interested in seeing what you have to say about your subject.

The most serious mistake you can make at this stage in composing is not to take a stance at all. If you have no stance, you have no interest in your subject matter, and neither will your reader. In the persuasive stance, the thesis statement brings your topic to life by turning it into an argument. In an exposi-

---

* **Empirical evidence.** The sort of evidence we get when we physically examine things. Since there are relatively few things we can examine for ourselves, we often have to rely on physical evidence reported by people we trust —scientists, doctors, and other experts or eyewitnesses.

tory stance there may not be a thesis statement, but there must always be an angle, a purpose, or a central point to give life to the subject matter.

The following sections will explain how to bring your subject to life by working on it as an argument or by analyzing it from one of the traditional angles.

2. The Persuasive Stance: Thesis and Outline

To take a persuasive stance, survey the ideas you developed in prewriting and formulate a position statement that your ideas will support. The position statement is a thesis. You should be aware of the difference between a thesis and a topic. A topic is the subject matter. Welfare, world hunger, the women's movement, abortion, and current theater are topics, not theses.

To make a thesis out of a topic, you need to take a position that cannot be settled by empirical or scientific evidence. The statement "iron is hard" is not a thesis. It is the sort of statement that can be tested by empirical evidence. The statement "it is 5 degrees Celsius outside at this moment" is not a thesis either. It is the sort of statement we can test scientifically with the aid of a thermometer. Even the statement "California gives welfare assistance to more families with dependent children than New York does" is not a thesis, since it can be verified by consulting documents that are themselves based on empirical evidence.

The following are thesis statements.

Examples
It is the responsibility of government to break cycles of personal poverty.

The solution to world hunger is not foreign aid but international investment.

The women's movement will eventually make business practices in America more humane.

No doctor should be allowed to abort a fetus that can survive outside the womb.

Equus should be ranked among the greatest plays ever performed in America.

Notice that each of these statements might reasonably be contested. Notice, too, that a thesis statement gives life to a topic. "Current theater" is just a topic. Inert. Not alive. The proposition that "*Equus* should be ranked among the greatest plays ever performed in America" gives life to the topic. It turns an inert subject matter into a possible argument — and good arguments are always interesting.

Notice, too, that these thesis statements cannot be entirely justified by empirical or scientific evidence. They deal with value judgments ("*Equus* is a great play"), or with judgments about right and wrong ("No doctor should be allowed . . ."), or with statements about the future ("The women's movement will . . ."), or with subjects so complex that no science could manage them all ("The solution to world hunger . . ."). Questions of this sort cannot be resolved by laboratory experiments.

In supporting a thesis, however, scientific and empirical evidence can be useful. Any of the thesis statements above could benefit from arguments based on controlled experiments, or statistics, or case studies, or any of the other sources of empirical evidence we normally have confidence in. Nonscientific evidence is also useful — reliance on known authority, arguments from analogy, arguments from precedent, from definition, and from circumstance. These arguments are discussed in Chapter Three, Six Questions for Critical Reading (see especially pp. 57–60 and 71–72). None of these methods, however, could "prove" the point, because a good thesis is essentially unprovable.

When you are writing for critical readers, one of the most persuasive kinds of evidence is specific example. The more examples the better. As examples pile up, they begin to seem like scientific evidence, since the scientific method is largely a matter of testing example after example after example.

Sometimes writers formulate a thesis before they develop evidence in prewriting. Sometimes they explore a subject through prewriting and then decide what sort of thesis the evidence will support. Often writers begin with a tentative thesis, a "hunch," and then explore the subject matter in search of evidence that will support the hunch. Whichever method you use, it is important to be honest with your evidence. If you develop the evidence first, formulate a thesis that is clearly supported by the evidence. If you develop a thesis first, be willing to change or modify or even completely reject your thesis if the evidence you turn up indicates that your original hunch was wrong. Don't be like the student who stuck to his original thesis even though he could find no evidence to prove it. He began with the hunch that "letters to the editor of *Playboy* reveal the social insecurities of the people who write them"—a reasonable enough hunch, except that when the writer actually examined letters to *Playboy*, he found no supporting examples. If this happens to you, change your thesis to one that the evidence will support.

Once you have a thesis statement, the next step is to generate an outline from it. An outline is a plan for a paper. It maps out the various parts of a paper in divisions that make sense. The easiest way to build an outline is to write topic sentences that will introduce evidence for your thesis. If your evidence consists of examples, you should be able to express the relationship between the thesis and the topic sentence by "for example."

Example

   I. Introduction, leading to the thesis statement, "The incumbent mayor has been an excellent leader."

  II. Evidence.
     A. (for example) She has attracted clean industry to the city.
     B. (for example) She kept a cool head during recent floods.
     C. (for example) Under her administration the municipal budget has been balanced for the first time in fifty years.

 III. Conclusion.

Notice that each of the topic sentences *(A, B,* and *C)* makes sense as evidence supporting the thesis about the mayor's leadership. To expand this outline into a paper, the writer could add one or several paragraphs to each of the topic sentences, giving details about the industries that have arrived, their sequence of arrival, the size of their payrolls; the flood crisis and the mayor's behavior at that time; and how the mayor managed to balance the budget by a combination of decreased spending and increased revenues.

Sometimes a thesis is supported by reasons rather than by examples, and the relationship between the thesis and the support is expressed by "because" rather than by "for example."

Example
I. Introduction, leading to the thesis statement, "The laws controlling strip-mining in our state need to be tightened and more strictly enforced."
II. Evidence.
   A. (because) Each year thousands of acres of wilderness are destroyed, with unsightly clay pits left in their place.
   B. (because) The destruction of forests has threatened the survival of some species of wildlife and forced others to roam where they are unwanted.
   C. (because) Even beyond the mines themselves, erosion and the alteration of water tables are threatening vegetation, fish, and game.
III. Conclusion.

These outlines are useful for one-sided arguments. If you have a good thesis, however, and have been honest in examining the evidence, chances are you turned up at least some evidence that works against your thesis. Your paper will be more persuasive if you find a way to acknowledge this adverse evidence, refuting it if you can, or modifying your thesis to accommodate it, or else indicating why in the long run the adverse evidence really doesn't matter. The incumbent mayor has, no doubt, made mistakes—everyone has. Probably the best way to acknowledge those mistakes is to concede them in the introduction, just before the thesis, or else to mention them in passing in the conclusion, just before a final sentence or two reminding the reader of all the mayor's virtues.

If you have investigated strip-mining, you probably found some good reasons why strip-mining laws should *not* be tightened. Some coal cannot be safely or economically mined in any other way. To forbid strip-mining would cost not only the loss of the coal itself, but the loss of livelihood for thousands of miners. And for all its ecological hazards, strip-mining threatens the environment less than nuclear power plants.

Again, you might acknowledge this adverse evidence in the introduction or the conclusion. Or you might weave it into the body of the paper itself, stating first one side of the issue and then the other. Or better yet, you might be able to formulate a thesis that accommodates both kinds of evidence: "At least for the present, strip-mining is a necessary evil, which modern techniques of forestry can make tolerable." This is a multiple thesis. It makes three assertions: (1) that strip-mining is evil; (2) that it is necessary; (3) that modern forestry can make it tolerable. The outline might provide evidence for each of those assertions.

Example

I. Introduction, leading to the thesis statement, "Strip-mining is a necessary evil, which modern techniques of forestry can make tolerable."

II. Evidence.

    A. (it is evil because) Strip-mining has damaged thousands of acres of forest and endangered hundreds of species of wildlife.

    B. (it is necessary because) Strip-mining is the only feasible way to get at coal in certain beds; it provides a livelihood for thousands of miners; it is our only available alternative to nuclear power plants.

    C. (it can be tolerable because) An extensive forestry program could temporarily relocate and care for major species of wildlife, supervise reclamation of the mined area, plan reforestation, and eventually restore the wildlife.

III. Conclusion.

Notice that *A*, *B*, and *C* might each be developed through several paragraphs.

This outline will work only if your prewriting exercises have developed the evidence to back it up. If you discover that you do not have enough evidence to support a thesis, either change your thesis or return to the prewriting section, especially Chapter Two, to ask more questions and find more answers. You cannot weave a persuasive paper out of thin air. You have to have good evidence before you can expand a thesis into an outline.

EXERCISES

1. Indicate why each of the following statements would or would not make a good thesis statement.

a.   Orleans parish had a record high rainfall last year.

b.   Hopkins was a better poet than Wordsworth.

c.   Alaska is the largest state in the union.

d.   Corporations should not be allowed to campaign for political positions not directly related to their business.

e.   George Washington died in 1799.

f.   The cost of student housing has doubled in ten years.

g.   Tolstoy was a sexist author.

h.   Arabian oil is sold for three times its production cost.

i.   In twenty years, the wild turkey will be an extinct species.

j.   The only way to curb inflation is to cut federal spending.

k.   The fertilization of human ova in test tubes is in itself a morally indifferent procedure.

l.   The Library of Congress is the largest library in the United States.

m.   The concert last night was a disgrace to the orchestra.

n.   In five o'clock traffic, you can walk to a crosstown destination faster than you can ride there in a taxi.

o.   There are no good plays on Broadway this year.

2. Assume that your prewriting exercises turned up the following facts and observations. Form a thesis that you could support with this information.

a.   In almost 2000 reactor years of experience, there has been no nuclear accident that injured the public.

b.   Reactors have safety systems that back up other safety systems.

c.   Ordinary reactors do not contain enough uranium to cause a bomblike explosion.

d.   Nuclear generators cost less to operate than conventional generators.

e.   According to the U.S. Energy Research and Development Administration (ERDA), we are running out of oil.

f. Chances of an accident among 100 reactors are less than one in two hundred a year.

g. The chances of getting a fatal cancer from reactor fallout will be only 1 percent.

3. Assume that your prewriting exercises turned up the following facts and observations. Form a thesis that you could support with this information.

a. The 2000 reactor years of experience mentioned above were acquired with reactors one-twentieth the size of modern nuclear generators, built by companies that were not competing to cut costs.

b. At the Brown's Ferry plant in Alabama, a workman using a candle to find an air leak started a fire that almost caused a meltdown.

c. According to some experts, a meltdown would result in a large explosion with radioactive fallout downwind.

d. Nuclear generators cost more to build than conventional generators, and they do not last as long.

e. Some scientists say we have enough fossil fuel to last until solar power and thermonuclear fusion (safer than fission) can be perfected.

f. There is no fail-safe way to store nuclear wastes.

g. Nuclear reactors are not immune to sabotage.

4. Combine the lists of facts and ideas in exercises 2 and 3 above. Now form a thesis that you can support with this information. Does any of the information work against your thesis? If so, how might you handle that information in a paper?

5. If you are using an essay collection along with this text, read one of the essays listed under "Persuasion" or "Argumentation." To what extent is the essay consistent with the advice given in this chapter? Does the essay have a single thesis or several? Where is the thesis announced? Is the thesis the sort of statement that can be settled by empirical evidence, or is it a judgment that can never be scientifically proved? How does the writer deal with opposing points of view and with adverse evidence? How does the structure of the essay compare with the outline suggested in this chapter? Can you discover in the essay any specific techniques for argumentation or organization that you can use in writing a persuasive paper of your own?

For a more thorough approach to studying persuasive essays, see Chapter Three.

WRITING ASSIGNMENT

With the advice of your instructor, select a topic for a persuasive paper. Current events—local, national, or international controversies—can usually be tapped for topics of this sort. After choosing a topic, formulate a tentative thesis and decide on a plan for supporting it. Unless the topic is one you already know well, you may discover that you need to supplement your information with an interview (p. 44) or with research (see Chapter Ten).

Outline a paper, revising your thesis as required by the evidence you discover. Bring the outline to the next class for discussion (see Checkpoint below). Then write the paper, consulting Chapter Five for advice about first, middle, and last paragraphs, and Chapters Six and Seven for advice about editorial revision.

CHECKPOINT FOR PERSUASIVE OUTLINES

Swap outlines with a classmate. Answer in writing the following questions about your classmate's work.

a. Is the thesis clearly stated? If not, how could it be improved?
b. Does the thesis deal with an issue that cannot be entirely proved by empirical or scientific evidence?
c. Does the evidence offered really support the thesis? Explain.
d. Can you think of any other sort of evidence that should be added? Can you think of a better way to divide the evidence? Explain.
e. Look at the sequence of the outline. Indicate in writing why you think the writer has chosen this order. If the order does not make sense, suggest some adjustments.

Swap outlines again and read what your classmate has had to say about your thesis and evidence. Take a few minutes to ask questions of each other or to explain your suggestions for improvement.

When you have your thesis and evidence in satisfactory shape, read Chapter Five for advice about writing coherent paragraphs. Your next Checkpoint is on p. 136.

3. The Expository Stance: Control Sentence and Outline

Writers take an expository stance when they are not out to prove a point, but simply to explain what they have learned or to present information they have gathered. They assume that their readers are open minded, willing to learn. In college, writing is to some extent artificial, since the professors are presumably well informed about the subjects they ask their students to write about. But in college, remember, writing is not so much a medium of communication as it is a way of understanding. Writing in college is a way of gaining intellectual mastery over topics you have studied and demonstrating that mastery to people who will be pleased to see it.

a. The Plural-Noun Formula

If you decide to take an expository stance, examine your subject from one of the traditional angles discussed in Chapter Two — definition, division and classification, cause and effect, comparison and contrast, or process analysis. Then write a sentence that foreshadows the angle and the number of divisions in the body of the paper. In other words, write a general statement about your topic that includes a plural noun, preferably one with a number before it. This technique is called the plural-noun formula.

Examples

In analyzing human personality, Freud divided the mind into *three areas.*

The American Civil War had *three* major *causes.*

There are *three* different *kinds* of nuclear reactors.

The development of public support for energy conservation took place in *five stages.*

The first example foreshadows a paper that will discuss each of the three divisions of the mind. The second foreshadows a cause and effect paper with three major divisions. The third foreshadows a paper that will both divide reactors into three categories and explain their similarities and differences. And the fourth foreshadows a process analysis with five steps. Notice, by the way, that a process analysis is probably the easiest kind of paper to organize, since it can follow the steps of the process in chronological order.

Any angle you choose can be expressed in a control sentence using the plural-noun formula. The control sentence is not necessarily used in the paper itself—though it may be. Its main purpose is to help you construct an outline. Once you have written this sort of sentence, the rest of the paper should organize itself. All you need to do is add an introduction and a conclusion (see pp. 104 and 130).

Examples

Control Sentence: In analyzing human personality, Freud divided the mind into *three areas*.

   I. Introduction.
 II. Body.
     A. Definition and description of the ego.
     B. Definition and description of the superego.
     C. Definition and description of the id.
III. Conclusion or summary.

Control Sentence: There are three different kinds of nuclear reactors.

   I. Introduction.
 II. Body.
     A. Description and definition of conventional reactors.
     B. Description and definition of breeder reactors.
     C. Description and definition of fusion reactors.
III. Conclusion or summary.

Each line in these outlines could be expanded into a single paragraph or a group of paragraphs, depending upon how much relevant material you have developed in prewriting.

b. Outlining a Comparison and Contrast Paper

If you have chosen comparison and contrast as an angle, the first step in building an outline is to establish a list of categories of comparison. What aspects of these subjects do you intend to compare? If you were comparing and contrasting baroque music and classical music, the categories of comparison might be something like this:

1. instruments used
2. use of human voice
3. typical forms

Once you have listed categories of comparison in the order you consider most interesting, you have two options for outlining the paper. You can write all you know about one subject in the first half of the paper and all you know about the other subject in the second half (Option A). Or you can switch back and forth from one subject to the other, discussing each of the categories of comparison (Option B).

With two kinds of music as an example, the two options can be outlined as follows.

COMPARISON AND CONTRAST: OPTION A

I. Introduction.
II. Body.
    A. Baroque music:
        1. instruments used
        2. use of human voice
        3. typical forms
    B. Classical music:
        1. instruments used
        2. use of human voice
        3. typical forms
III. Conclusion.

COMPARISON AND CONTRAST: OPTION B

I. Introduction.
II. Body.
    A. Instruments used:
        1. in baroque music
        2. in classical music
    B. Use of human voice:
        1. in baroque music
        2. in classical music
    C. Typical forms:
        1. in baroque music
        2. in classical music
III. Conclusion.

Which option is better? That depends on the nature of your subject matter and the number of categories of comparison. The more categories there are, the better Option B seems to work. Option A depends upon the reader's ability to remember details of one subject for a longer stretch before they are compared or contrasted with corresponding details in the other subject. Option B generally brings similarities and differences into sharper focus for the reader, since it places them right next to each other.

c. Beyond Basic Outlines

Sometimes the material you have developed in prewriting just doesn't lend itself to either of the outlines discussed above. If you have only a single subject, comparison and contrast won't work; and if you use more than one angle, the plural-noun formula won't work. In these cases, you need to develop an outline specifically for your material and for what you want to say about it. But remember, an outline is good only if the various parts of the paper are *related to one another in a way that makes sense.*

Suppose, for example, you were writing a paper about crime, organized according to the outline below.

Example
Topic: Crime

   I. Introduction.
  II. Body.
      A. Crime and its causes.
      B. Crimes with victims.
      C. Problems in the courtroom.
      D. Punishment.
      E. Victimless crimes.
      F. The cost of crime.
      G. Some ideas for prevention.
      H. Rehabilitation of criminals.
 III. Conclusion.

The defect in this outline is that the various parts simply do not make the kinds of connections we are accustomed to seeing in writing. Instead of presenting a coherent discussion of one aspect — or several clearly related aspects — of crime, the writer rambles from point to point, as if by free association. The outline looks like an appendage written after the paper itself, a map of territory already traveled rather than an itinerary planned in advance.

To make a coherent outline of this material, you would have to follow three steps.

To make a coherent paper out of this material, you need to find some angle or design and trim away all the material that doesn't fit. Think of the material as a pile of lumber out of which you want to make a piece of furniture. If you thought you had to use all the lumber, every scrap, the furniture would have an odd shape indeed. But assume that you can't use it all. Play with the material until you discover a reasonable shape for some of it and discard the rest.

Example

Topic: Crime and the Courts.

   I. Introduction.
  II. Body.
      A. Problems in bringing a suspect to trial.
      B. Problems in getting a conviction.
      C. Problems in sentencing the guilty.
 III. Conclusion.

In this outline the material is limited and given a shape. It deals with one specific aspect of crime — crime and the courts — rather than with crime in general. The angle of development in the body of the outline is chronological order: what happens before a trial, what happens during a trial, and what happens at the conclusion of a trial. This sequence seems neat and orderly, as opposed to the random sequence in the first outline. And finally, everything that does not fit in with the basic design of the paper has been discarded. Discarding good material is not something inexperienced writers find easy to do. They normally are afraid that they need every fragment of information to fill out the paper to its required length. Unless you learn to resist irrelevant material, however, no matter how interesting it is, your papers will always be poorly organized.

Save the material for other uses; often it can be worked into an introduction or a conclusion.

Another difference between this outline and the first one is that here the topics in the body make sense as divisions and as a sequence. The writer intends to examine problems in criminal courts in three chronological stages: what happens before the trial, what happens during the trial, and what happens at the conclusion of the trial. It is easy to see *why* part *A* comes first, then part *B*, and then part *C*.

Other outlines, equally useful, could have been fashioned from the same material.

Example
Topic: Crime Prevention and Cure.

   I. Introduction.
  II. Body.
      A. Two approaches to crime prevention:
         1. working with potential criminals
         2. taking precautions as potential victims
      B. Two ways to treat criminals:
         1. options in punishment
         2. possibilities for rehabilitation
 III. Conclusion.

Again, this outline, like the preceding one, sets limits on the subject ("Crime Prevention and Cure" rather than everything there is to know about crime). Relevant material is selected and arranged in a pattern that makes sense. It makes sense to divide responses to crime into prevention and cure, and the subdivisions in each category also make sense.

This outline, too, leaves out lots of interesting material about crime. Some of what has been left out may be useful in an introduction or conclusion. Some of it, no matter how interesting it is in itself, may have to be saved for another paper or discarded.

Neither of the revised outlines indicates anything about the quantity of detail the papers will have. This is not necessarily a weakness in the outlines, but it does indicate a choice writers have to make. A ten-page paper developed from one of these outlines would be analogous to a photograph of Mars taken from a telescope on earth. A hundred-page paper might be analogous to a photograph of Mars taken from a camera or a satellite in space. A book-length development would be analogous to a map of Mars pieced together from photographs taken from a satellite in orbit around the planet itself. Photographs taken close to the planet are obviously richer in detail than photographs taken from a distance, but photographs taken from a distance have their uses too. If either of the outlines were developed into a ten-page paper, the paper would necessarily be a summary and overview—the sort of treatment you would expect in a magazine article—rather than an in-depth report.

Summaries and overviews have their uses. Writers who want a closer look at the topic have two choices: either they write longer papers or they focus on a single aspect of the topic. But even if the writer were to explore only a single aspect of the topic—for example, options in punishment for criminals—the question of detail would still have to be settled. You could write a book about options in punishment as well as a ten-page paper. And you could write a book or a ten-page paper about any single option. Choosing the proper length and the proper detail in a paper is like choosing the proper magnification in a microscope. One magnification could show clearly an organism that would appear as a mere speck to the naked eye. A higher magnification would show the cells that make up the tiny organism. A still higher magnification would show individual parts of a single cell. The right degree of magnification—like the right amount of detail in a paper—depends upon what you want to see.

When do writers outline? Experienced writers outline when they feel the urge to outline—when they feel their material getting out of hand, like a hedgerow that needs to be trimmed. Sometimes they start with an outline in mind and look for material to flesh it out. Sometimes they explore first, and along the way they try one or several outlines to give shape and purpose to their discoveries. Sometimes instinct alone will guide the arrangement of a paper, and the writer will outline only after the paper is written, if at all.

Inexperienced writers tend to trust their instincts for arrangement more than they should. Writing a formal outline, even after writing the paper itself, is always a good way to check on the reasonableness of your instincts. Often inexperienced writers feel the urge to outline as they write — they sense that their material is rambling and shapeless — but they don't recognize it as an urge to outline. They just feel adrift in a sea of information. That is when they should try to draw a map of their ideas, at least a tentative outline that they may well change several times before the paper is completed.

EXERCISES

1. Write a control sentence suggesting an outline and an angle for each of the following topics.

a. The Mississippi River
b. Teachers I have known
c. Things to read
d. Football and tennis
e. Two poets
f. Quality
g. Automobiles
h. Crime in America
i. New York and Paris
j. Growing your own vegetables
k. Choosing a college
l. A liberal education
m. Persons of the opposite sex
n. Inflation
o. Charlemagne and Alfred the Great

2. The following list represents the sort of notes you might have made in prewriting about divorce. Examine the list carefully, select some related ideas, and arrange them into an outline that makes sense. Don't try to use all the ideas; some of them will have to be discarded. Add topics if you need them to fill out a pattern that is not completely represented in the list. Is it possible to make more than one good outline from this list?

a. Divorce is healthier than a bad marriage.
b. Some people experience a loss of confidence immediately after a divorce.
c. Divorce can be expensive.

d. Children need to be taken into account during a divorce.

e. After initial loss of confidence, divorced people often experiment with casual sexual relationships.

f. The most common cause of divorce is money.

g. Not all divorced people lose confidence in themselves.

h. Men are often entitled to alimony.

i. Divorced people often remarry and stay married.

j. The children of divorced couples often have to deal with pressures from society at large.

k. Children are often victims of uncertain financial support as a result of divorce.

l. Courts no longer assume that the mother is the more qualified parent.

m. Children are sometimes used as pawns by divorced parents.

n. Children of divorced parents often feel guilt and shame.

o. The second most common cause of divorce is alcohol.

3. If you are using an essay collection along with this text, look at the table of contents for essays listed under "Exposition," "Analysis," or "Explaining." Are these essays divided into the five traditional angles discussed in Chapter Two of this book? Are any other angles added? Can you tell from examining the table of contents what relationship the editor of the essay collection perceives between exposition and the traditional angles?

Choose one of the essays for a close reading. To what extent is the essay consistent with the advice given in this chapter? What techniques or devices do you notice that were not discussed in this chapter? Can you discover any methods that will help you in writing an expository paper of your own?

WRITING ASSIGNMENT

With the advice of your instructor, select a topic for an expository paper. If you have trouble finding a topic, try some of the sources discussed in the first section of Chapter Ten (pp. 229–233). After exploring your topic through one or several of the five traditional angles discussed in Chapter Two, write a control sentence and an outline and bring them to the next class for discussion (see Checkpoint, p. 102). Then write and revise the paper, consulting Chapter Five for advice about first, middle, and last paragraphs and Chapters Six and Seven for advice about editorial revision.

CHECKPOINT FOR EXPOSITORY OUTLINES

Swap outlines with a classmate. Answer in writing the following questions about your classmate's work.

a. If there is a control sentence, does it clearly foreshadow the rest of the outline? If not, what adjustments would you suggest?

b. Do the divisions make sense to you, or do they seem random and disconnected? Do they overlap in ways that they shouldn't? Do they cover the material completely, or should another division be added? Can you suggest any adjustments?

c. Look at the sequence of the outline. Indicate in your own words why you think the writer has chosen this order. If the order does not make sense, suggest some adjustments.

Swap papers again and read what your classmate has had to say about your outline. Take a few minutes to ask questions of each other or to explain your suggestions for improvement.

When you have your outline in satisfactory shape, read the next chapter for advice about writing coherent paragraphs. Your next Checkpoint is on p. 136.

Chapter Five

Paragraphs

Some writers think in paragraphs. They think in terms of topic sentences, body sentences, clincher sentences, and transitional sentences as they write. Other writers think in long sequences of related ideas. They paragraph by instinct, or they return to long stretches of unindented prose and indent wherever they sense a shift in thought. For both kinds of writers, the result is usually the same: paragraphs look like units of thought, groups of related sentences. Whether you think in paragraphs or in longer stretches of sentences, you need to understand the principles that make paragraphs seem unified and coherent.

Several different kinds of paragraphs will be treated in this chapter, each with its own rules of organization:

1. First Paragraphs
2. Middle Paragraphs: A Basic Pattern
3. Middle Paragraphs: Beyond the Basic Pattern
4. Narrative Paragraphs
5. Descriptive Paragraphs
6. Concluding Paragraphs

1. First Paragraphs

Aristotle said that good drama has to have a beginning, a middle, and an end—an observation that many students consider more obvious than it really is. What Aristotle meant, of course, was that a beginning is different from a start, an end is different from a stop, and a middle is something that relates to a beginning and an end, not to a start and a stop.

Beginnings have to have a sense of beginning. If you concealed a movie camera somewhere on your campus and let it run for a few minutes, it would make a movie. But chances are the events it photographed would not constitute drama in Aristotle's sense of the word. The start would be a random event followed by a random sequence of events: students, staff, visitors, dogs, birds, bicycles, moving this way and that across the screen. The end would be simply a cessation of action, and viewers would be left to their own devices to figure out relationships between the actors and events before them.

One of a writer's tasks, then, is to invent a beginning—one sentence or several paragraphs—that can be sensed as a beginning, so that readers do not get the feeling that they are picking up on a discussion that had already been in progress. A paper beginning "In this poem, Poe expresses his fear of . . ." is off to a bad start. "In *what* poem?" the reader wonders. And it does no good to say that the title of the poem was mentioned in the title of the paper. It is a fairly well established convention in academic writing—and in most other writing as well—that the beginnings of papers are to be written as if there were no titles before them. As a rule, then, write a beginning that gives the reader a sense of beginning, and do not allow your opening sentences to rely on your title for clarity.

In addition to seeming like a beginning, there are other things a beginning might do: it might foreshadow the substance or structure of the discussion to follow; and it might arouse the reader's interest in the topic. Beginnings that foreshadow are particularly useful in business and technical writing; beginnings that arouse interest are particularly effective in journalistic essays. Both kinds have their place in college writing.

In business and technical writing, the audience is limited and is presumed to be interested in the topic for practical reasons. Beginnings in business and technical writing, therefore, tend to be very practical. Their purpose is simply to announce the topic and perhaps to show how it will be developed.

Example

In this report I will discuss the feasibility of cogenerators as a power source in our Des Moines plant. First I will explain how cogenerators work. Then I will indicate the variety and costs of cogenerators now available on the market. And finally I will show how the use of cogenerators instead of conventional power could save us approximately $250,000 in energy costs over the next ten years.

This is not a very fancy beginning, but it is a very efficient one. It makes no effort to arouse the interest of readers because it is intended only for readers who are already interested. By announcing the purpose and the structure of the report, this beginning enables its readers to interpret the details within each section efficiently. It also enables them to skim over or skip the sections they don't care to study and concentrate on those sections that contain information they would consider new or interesting.

A second sort of beginning is one that is designed to arouse the reader's attention. Journalists refer to this beginning as a "hooker," since it is supposed to get readers hooked on the topic and keep them reading. The most common devices for writing this sort of beginning are these: begin with an interesting quotation; begin with a dramatic situation; begin with a statement that promises information the reader needs or information the reader will find disconcerting, or information the reader will consider interesting or important for its own sake; begin by asking interesting questions that you intend to answer.

All of these devices can be summed up in a few words: begin with specifics. Instead of starting off with the general statements you might use in a business report, start off with specific information that is a concrete illustration of your topic.

Here is an example from an essay by E. B. White about what it is like to come home to a place one is fond of.

Example

On the day before Thanksgiving, toward the end of the afternoon, having motored all day, I arrived home and lit a fire in the living room. The birch logs took hold briskly. About three minutes later, not to be outdone, the chimney itself caught fire. I became aware of this development rather slowly. Rocking contendedly in my chair, enjoying the stupor that follows a day on the road, I thought I heard the dull, fluttering roar of a chimney swift, a sound we who live in this house are thoroughly accustomed to. Then I realized that there would be no bird in residence in my chimney at this season of the year, and a glance up the flue made it perfectly plain that, after twenty-two years of my tenure, the place was at last afire.

— "Home-Coming," *Essays of E. B. White**

Notice that this beginning — compared with the beginning of the business memorandum discussed above — is relatively inefficient. It does not get directly to the point. It does not foreshadow the rest of the essay. But it has a dramatic quality that makes the reader want to read on. Essays do not need to be as efficient as memorandums; they are written for people who have time to explore and enjoy — not for people who need practical information in a hurry. This beginning, then, is perfectly suited to its purpose.

Beginnings in scholarly writing fall somewhere between the drama of journalistic essays and the abruptness of business memorandums. Like business and technical communications, scholarly writing is intended for a limited audience with special interests. Assuming that readers will find an article interesting if it adds something meaningful to the field, scholars often begin with a summary of previous scholarship leading up to a point that they themselves would like to add. Here is the beginning of an article by John J. Burke, Jr., about Sir Walter Scott's views of history as expressed in some of his novels.

Example†

Just what The Waverly Novels reveal about Scott's attitude towards the past usually stirs controversy. One group typically

---

* Copyright © 1977 by E. B. White. Reprinted by permission of Harper & Row, Publishers, Inc.

† Abridged and reprinted by author's permission from "Scott's Views on History in *The Fortunes of Nigel*," *CLIO*, 8 (Fall 1978), pp. 3-4.

portrays Scott as a Tory reactionary who preferred the past over the present and so escaped through his imagination into the more glamorous and heroic ages of history. Another group, more in evidence in recent times, reacts to this view by stressing a more realistic, hard-headed Scott, not only at ease in the present, but also the critic of the very escapism to which he had reputedly succumbed. While both extremes contain some truth, they nevertheless distort Scott's more complex views on history, views that combine affection for the past and the present as well as a certain amount of distaste for both. It is my argument that Scott rendered his ambivalent views by constructing historical fictions in which the past criticizes the present just as the present criticizes the past, and that such contrasts were intended to have a tonic effect on his readers.

Notice the thought pattern underlying this beginning: some critics have said X (first sentence); others have said Y (second sentence); here is what I intend to say (third and fourth sentences). In the original version, of course, Burke supported his characterizations of the X and Y positions with a footnote and other details that have been omitted here.

A beginning of this sort is designed for a reader who is already interested in the novels of Walter Scott; it makes no effort to arouse the interests of people who are not particularly interested in Scott and his critics. It is a practical beginning, establishing a context for the article's thesis and foreshadowing the substance of what is to follow. Published in a scholarly journal, this beginning is perfectly suited to its purpose.

In college writing, beginnings may be businesslike, journalistic, or scholarly, depending on the writer's purpose and the reader's expectations. Some instructors like beginnings that get right to the point without fanfares or flourishes. In short papers and in essay examinations they would like nothing better than a bare thesis sentence or control sentence as a beginning. A "plural-noun" sentence (see p. 93) makes a particularly practical beginning because it foreshadows the structure of the paper as it announces the topic.

Example
In Freudian psychology, the personality is a composite of three different forces—the ego, the superego, and the id.

In a longer paper, this practical beginning may take the form of several sentences in which you say in a general way what you intend to say more specifically in the paper itself.

Example

In this paper I will discuss the causes and effects of the Hundred Years' War. Among the causes were Edward the Third's claim to the French throne territory and England's desire for the vineyards of Bordeaux and the textile industry of Flanders. The only effects were death and devastation among the common people and the self-satisfaction of an aristocracy that valued both violence and gentleness as part of a chivalric tradition.

This may not seem like a very exciting beginning to the general reader, but to a history instructor who is mainly interested in finding out what you know about the Hundred Years' War it may seem like a gem. Some instructors like this sort of beginning, and some don't. Those who like it, like it because it is efficient and to the point. Those who don't like it would call it "wooden," "stiff," or "mechanical."

It is possible to combine the practicality of a businesslike beginning with the interest of a journalistic beginning by following these three steps:

1. Write the thesis statement or control sentence at the bottom of a piece of scratch paper, where it will eventually become the last sentence in your beginning.
2. Look through your notes or search your memory for a particular incident, dramatic situation, story, or quotation that you did not have use for in the body of the paper, even though it is relevant to your thesis, perhaps even a concrete illustration of your thesis.
3. Begin with the particular instance and connect it to the thesis or control statement, revising as many times as is necessary to make the sequence of sentences smooth and coherent.

Here is an example. Suppose your thesis is that nuclear reactors are not safe. Write the thesis at the bottom of a page. Then start writing at the top of the page. For this thesis, a few sentences recapturing the fear and uncertainty occasioned by the famous accident at the Three Mile Island plant would be a good beginning.

Example

When the governor of Pennsylvania and the director of the Nuclear Regulatory Commission had to decide whether to evacuate the area near the Three Mile Island plant, they had almost no reliable facts. They were operating, as they later admitted, "almost totally in the blind," with information that ranged from ambiguous to nonexistent. As one official put it, "We saw failure modes the likes of which have never been analyzed"—which is a technical way of saying that nobody knew what was happening or what was likely to happen next. These admissions underscore what some scientists have been telling us for decades: nuclear reactors are not safe.

This particular thesis statement announces the subject but does not foreshadow the structure of the paper. If foreshadowing the structure seems useful in a particular paper, this can often be accomplished by adjusting the original thesis, making it more specific.

Example

These admissions underscore what some scientists have been telling us for decades: the known dangers of nuclear power are frightening enough; the unknown dangers are beyond imagination.

The revised thesis would be perfectly apt for a paper that discusses first the known dangers of nuclear power and then the likelihood of unknown dangers.

Beginnings that combine journalistic interest and business-like practicality are probably most appropriate in informal papers and even in research papers that are written at an elementary level—the sort of papers you are most likely to write in your first college composition course. As you advance in your major field of study, however, you will probably do well to imitate the beginnings used by scholars who publish in your field. For this reason, a paper that begins with a quick summary of previous scholarship leading up to your own contribution is often appropriate.

The following example might have been written by an English major who had done some research on the late medieval poet John Lydgate.

Example

Previous studies of Lydgate's meter can be divided into two categories. The first category includes the work of Schick and all the other editors who think Lydgate's lines can be divided into five types. The second category includes Albert Licklider, E. P. Hammond, Fitzroy Pyle, C. S. Lewis, and others who approach Lydgate's poetry as if it were written in conventional English meters. Because both groups wrongly assume that Lydgate was trying, but failing, to imitate the meter of Chaucer, neither of them manages to appreciate Lydgate's poetry as a peculiar verse form that was possible only in the sort of English that was spoken by Lydgate's contemporaries.

Like the introduction to the article on Scott discussed earlier, this one begins with what might be called an X, Y, Z thought pattern: some critics have said X; others have said Y; what I hold is Z. Often, of course, previous scholarship cannot be divided into two neat categories, and often a writer is reacting to a single article rather than to a great body of scholarship. In either case, a good beginning for a scholarly paper is to summarize what has been said before — whether it is a single article or a hundred books — and indicate how your insight fits into that context.

Now that you have studied a few introductions, you can see why beginnings are among the *last* parts of a paper to be written, even though they are the first to be read. Because writing is a process of discovery as well as an act of communication, you need to make your discoveries — by writing — before you can introduce them.

In summary, before you write a beginning, decide what sort of beginning best suits the occasion. If your reader is merely interested in how well you have mastered your subject, a thesis statement or a straightforward announcement of your plan may be sufficient. If you are writing a scholarly paper, imitate published scholars and begin by showing how your point fits in with previous scholarship. If you are writing an informal essay, or if you want to imitate good journalists, begin with something specific — perhaps a quotation or a dramatic situation — and lead the reader to your main point, foreshadowing, perhaps, the structure of the rest of the paper.

EXERCISES

1. Choose a good magazine of general interest or a scholarly journal in your major field and examine five or six introductions. To what extent do they conform to the introductions described in this section? Can you identify any additional techniques for writing introductions? If you are using an essay collection along with this text, examine the introductions in five or six essays. Be careful, however: essays in collections are sometimes excerpted from longer works, and the first paragraph in a selection may not be the first paragraph in the original work.

2. Pretend that you were asked by the President to write a memorandum about the effects of the energy shortage on the lives of private citizens in your part of the country. What categories of information would you cover in such a memorandum? Make a brief outline based on these categories and write a practical, businesslike introduction.

3. Pretend that you were asked by a national magazine to write a journalistic essay about the effects of the energy shortage on private citizens in your part of the country. How would you characterize those effects in a single sentence? Write an introduction to the article, using the journalistic techniques discussed in this chapter to lead up to your single-sentence characterization. If possible, begin with an instance or with several instances, real or imaginary, that illustrate your point.

4. You cannot really write a scholarly introduction until you have done some scholarly research. But you can practice the form with a little imagination. Invent a thesis about some literary figure, real or imaginary, or about some aspect of the subject you intend to major in. Then write an introduction to that thesis using the X, Y, Z thought pattern discussed on p. 110. Make up the scholarly references, but do your best to make them seem real. The point of this exercise is to practice form; substance doesn't matter.

2. Middle Paragraphs: A Basic Pattern

This sense of continuity is called coherence. Once you have collected your ideas, your next step is to organize them so that your readers feel a sense of continuity as their eyes travel down the pages. We recognize it as the quality of good writing that makes the various parts fit together. Coherence in writing is difficult to account for, though rhetoricians have been working at it for years.

Did you find this last paragraph difficult to comprehend? If you didn't, you read it too quickly. It lacks what this section is about to teach: the arrangement of ideas so that readers can easily grasp the connections between them. The paragraph should have been written this way:

> Once you have collected your ideas, your next step is to organize them so that your readers feel a sense of continuity as their eyes travel down the pages. This sense of continuity is called coherence. Coherence in writing is difficult to account for, though rhetoricians have been working at it for years. We recognize it as the quality of good writing that makes the various parts fit together.

Good writing is coherent on two levels: within each paragraph and among the various parts of the essay as a whole. Almost everything that can be said about coherence on the smaller scale — the relationships among ideas in a paragraph — can be applied to coherence on a larger scale — the relationships among groups of ideas in an essay.

One of the differences between inexperienced writers and mature writers is that mature writers know how to make connections between ideas. Inexperienced writers have lots of ideas, but they jot them down as independent units, sometimes single sentences that, like items on the evening news, have little to do with what comes before and after them. Sometimes, in fact, inexperienced writers make an assertion in one sentence and contradict it in the next, as this student does in a paper about James Thurber's "Secret Life of Walter Mitty":

> Mrs. Mitty, a stylish old lady with a good mind, truly loves Walter. She constantly scolds him for his absent-mindedness until he finally defends himself by saying, "I am sometimes thinking." She passes this off as another stupid expression of her senile husband. She never gives the poor man any respect. However, in his private world, Mr. Mitty attains great respect.

The defect in this passage is the same as the defect in the

outline for a paper about crime a few pages back (pp. 96–97). The individual ideas simply do not connect. They do not make sense together. When the writer asserts in the first sentence that Mrs. Mitty "truly loves Walter," readers expect some evidence of this true love in the rest of the paragraph. Instead, they discover that Mrs. Mitty's treatment of her husband is not loving. Even within a single sentence the ideas do not seem to make sense together: the writer tells us that Walter defends himself, but his meek response — "I am sometimes thinking" — hardly deserves to be called a defense. The next sentence — "She never gives the poor man any respect" — would be a fine generality either at the beginning or at the end of a paragraph filled with specific evidence. In itself the sentence is probably an accurate observation that could have been supported with details from the story; but in this paragraph it seems to be just another idea that popped into the writer's head, more or less unrelated to the discussion before it.

Only the relationship between the last two sentences is clearly expressed. The writer perceives a contrast — the difference between the scorn Walter Mitty receives from his wife and the respect he wins in his imagination — and she expresses this contrast with "however," a signal that helps readers make the connection the writer wants them to make.

Inexperienced writers tend to assume that paragraphs are coherent as long as all the sentences within them are about roughly the same subject. Thus the writer of the example above might have felt proud of it; after all, the whole paragraph is about Walter Mitty's relationship with his wife. But common subject matter is not enough to make a sequence of sentences coherent.

Perhaps the easiest way to deal with coherence in persuasive and expository paragraphs is to compose a general assertion — a topic sentence — that you can follow up with two or more sentences of example, evidence, or explanation. Some teachers recommend "clincher" sentences at the end of each paragraph, but clinchers are used very sparingly by mature writers.

Suppose, for example, you were analyzing the behavior of someone you know, a student who seemed unhappy in college and eventually dropped out. A topic sentence for one of your developing paragraphs might be something like this:

> College life turned out to be quite different from what he had been used to.

Once you have a sentence like this, developing it into a paragraph is just a matter of adding examples, or "for instances."

Example

College life turned out to be quite different from what he had been used to. Instead of teachers who would coax him to do his best, he found professors who did not seem to care if he came to class or not. Instead of the familiar library where he was welcomed and pampered like an honored guest, he found a thirty-story building in which no undergraduates were allowed beyond the main desk. Instead of the old friends who would laugh at his classroom antics, he found serious-minded students who seemed to have mastered most college material when they were in high school.

In this paragraph, every sentence is a "for instance" of the generality expressed in the first sentence. In other words, every sentence shows specifically how "college turned out to be quite different from what he had been used to." If the paragraph is taken apart, you can see this relationship more clearly. In this case, the relationship between each sentence and the topic sentence is better expressed by "How so?" than by "Why?"

> Topic Sentence: College life turned out to be quite different from what he had been used to.
>
> (How so?) Instead of teachers who would coax him to do his best, he found professors who did not seem to care if he came to class or not.
>
> (How so?) Instead of the familiar library where he was welcomed and pampered like an honored guest, he found a thirty-story building in which no undergraduates were allowed beyond the main desk.
>
> (How so?) Instead of the old friends who would laugh at his classroom antics, he found serious-minded students who seemed to

have mastered most college material when they were in high school.

The paragraph is coherent because each sentence makes sense in context. Notice that because sentences two, three, and four refer directly back to the topic sentence, they could be rearranged in any sequence and the paragraph would still be coherent.

"Why?" also states the relationship between the topic sentence and other sentences in an "effect-to-cause" pattern.

Example

President Carter's election was a surprise to many professional observers. They found it hard to believe that a man well known only in the South could gain control of the national Democratic party. They did not realize that Carter's unpopularity among middle-class Southern whites was outweighed by his support among blacks in general and especially among the liberals and the poor of both races. They were uneasy about his religious beliefs, and they assumed that more voters would share this discomfort.

The topic sentence says that people were surprised (an effect), and the others say why they were surprised (causes). The relationships may be clearer in the version printed below.

Topic Sentence: President Carter's election was a surprise to many professional observers.

(Why?) They found it hard to believe that a man well known only in the South could gain control of the national Democratic party.

(Why?) They did not realize that Carter's unpopularity among middle-class Southern whites was outweighed by his support among blacks in general and especially among the liberals and the poor of both races.

(Why?) They were uneasy about his religious beliefs, and they assumed that more voters would share this discomfort.

Once again, because the last three sentences refer directly back to the topic sentence rather than to one another, they could be rearranged in any sequence without disturbing the coherence of the paragraph.

Sometimes the sentences in paragraphs like these cannot be rearranged because their sequence is controlled by more than one kind of pattern.

Example

Topic Sentence: He was truly one of the great musical geniuses of all time.

(How so?) As an infant, he would crawl up onto the piano bench, compose little melodies, and write them down in a notation he had invented for himself.

(How so?) By the time he had entered third grade, he could perform reasonably well on the piano, the recorder, and a violin his father had made especially for him.

(How so?) He wrote a symphony when he was twelve years old and conducted its first performance that same year.

In this paragraph, each of the last three sentences refers back to the assertion made in the topic sentence and gives evidence for it. But because the evidence is arranged in a chronological sequence — according to the child's increasing age — the sentences could not be rearranged without some loss in coherence.

According to recent research, only a small percentage of paragraphs written by professional writers conform to the basic pattern — topic sentence followed by supporting sentences. But inexperienced writers often find this pattern a useful device for getting their thoughts organized. To write paragraphs in this pattern, study the material you have developed in prewriting until you can make a general statement that you can support with specific evidence or examples. Use the general statement as a topic sentence and follow it up with several sentences that give supporting evidence.

EXERCISES

1. The first sentences of the following paragraphs have been omitted. Compose an adequate opening for each paragraph.

_____

_____

_____. Grammar is generally bound

to units no longer than the sentence. Rhetoric studies not only varieties of sentences, but extends to larger units, sequences of sentences, paragraphs, and even entire books. Grammar generally considers the sentence as a structure in itself, and it is only incidentally concerned with how the sentence affects readers or listeners — as long as they recognize it as a normal sentence. Rhetoric is primarily concerned with the way sentences are perceived by their audience, and it is concerned with strategies for making the audience react the way the writer or speaker wants it to react. Grammar — at least modern grammar — tells us how the language is used, not how it should be used. But rhetoric, without being dogmatic, makes distinctions between more and less effective ways of expressing what we want to express.

_____

_____

_____. They [obstetricians] will not allow husbands in the delivery room, not even husbands who have been prepared for the experience by competent teachers. Nor will they allow husbands in the labor room, where they might help and encourage their wives in the strenuous ordeal that precedes childbirth. One doctor has even posted a sign in the waiting room of his office declaring it off limits to husbands of expectant mothers.

2. Compose coherent paragraphs using the following sentences as openers. If you disagree with the statements, change them into statements you feel you can support with evidence.

a. The instruments in an orchestra are generally divided into four families — strings, woodwinds, brass, and percussion.

b. My classes this semester can be divided into three categories.

c. Making a _____ is a lot easier than people think it is.

d. It is easy to see why _____ (radio station) is more popular than _____.

e. If you observe them closely, you will find several important differences among _____.

3. Middle Paragraphs: Beyond the Basic Pattern

Sometimes the material you have developed in prewriting just will not fit into the basic paragraph pattern. In that case, you may have to start thinking of paragraph coherence as professional writers seem to think of it. Professionals rarely write paragraphs in which two or three sentences refer back to the opening sentences. They write them on occasion, but more often they write paragraphs in which each sentence comments on the sentence before it or anticipates a sentence that is to come.

If you were to try to name all the relationships that exist among sentences in professional writing, you would discover a list that would be more bewildering than useful. Most writers prefer to rely on their intuitive judgment about whether one sentence makes sense after another. If you are uncertain about your own intuitions, a little practice may help you develop them.

For example, what would you think about a paragraph beginning with these two sentences?

> Bear Mountain College is famous for its athletic department. You can learn your way around the library with the help of a recorded tour on a cassette player.

This is an exaggerated example, perhaps. But the second sentence does not deliver what the first sentence promises. Even though it is about the general topic of Bear Mountain College, it does not follow up on the most important assertion in the first sentence—that the athletic department is famous.

What would you think about a paragraph that began with these two sentences, assuming "Fighting Grizzlies" refers to Bear Mountain athletes?

> Bear Mountain College is famous for its athletic department. The Fighting Grizzlies have always finished near the middle of their conference in every sport.

Some readers are more satisfied with this sequence than with the first one. But should they be? The second sentence does give us some information about the athletic department. But doesn't it seem to contradict the part about its being famous? A department can be famous for excellence, and perhaps even famous for failure, but it is hard to imagine a department famous for mediocrity. Perhaps the relationship that some readers perceive between the two sentences is expressed in this version:

> Bear Mountain College is famous for its athletic department. Yet the Fighting Grizzlies have never finished above the middle of their conference in any sport.

What makes the difference? Why is the connection between the sentences clearer? The single word *yet* tells the reader that the writer knows the information in the two sentences might seem to be contradictory, but sooner or later the reader will discover how a department can be both mediocre and famous. As you consider other combinations of sentences, try to discover what kinds of relationships require transitional signals like *yet* and what kinds can do without them. Consider this next pair of sentences, for example.

> Bear Mountain College is famous for its athletic department. In virtually every sport, the Fighting Grizzlies are always contenders for regional honors, if not the national championship.

Why do these two sentences seem to fit together better than any other pair we have considered so far? Perhaps because as readers we are in the habit of expecting writers to follow assertions with specific evidence or examples. When we learn that something is famous, we expect to be told why or in what way it is famous. We are, in fact, so accustomed to this relationship between sentences that we really don't need a transitional device to show the connection.

Now consider the relationship between these two sentences:

> Bear Mountain College is famous for its athletic department. Its academic departments, however, are now becoming equally famous.

For most readers, the connection is apparent, even though the second sentence seems to be going off in a new direction from the first. The relationship between the two is clear because the writer signals the new direction with the transition word *how-*

ever. The word *equally* also helps bind the two sentences together; to see what sort of binding *equally* does, read the two sentences without it.

If you tried to make a rule about the relationships between sentences based upon the examples you have seen so far, it might be something like this: When the idea in one sentence is a proof or an example of the idea in the sentence before it, no transition word is necessary; but when a sentence sets out in a new direction from the one before it, the writer needs to signal the new direction with a transition word.

Now consider the relationship between these two sentences:

Bear Mountain College is famous for its athletic department. Everybody has heard of the Fighting Grizzlies.

The connection between the two sentences is clear enough. The second sentence merely restates the first in different words. To say that everybody has heard of something is the same as saying that it is famous. This device — repeating information in different words — is known as "variation" or "restatement," and it has been recommended to writers for centuries. When you feel you have a legitimate reason for repetition of this kind — for emphasis, perhaps — you do not need a signal word to express the relationship between the two sentences.

Finally, consider the relationship between the following sentences. Would you expect a paragraph opening this way to be coherent?

Bear Mountain College is famous for its athletic department. Blue Valley College is famous for its band.

At first there seems to be no connection between the sentences and no transition word to signal a deliberate change of direction. But there is one indication that the writer is in control of the material: the sentences are perfectly parallel in structure. This parallelism, like the *yet*, a few examples back, lets the reader know that the writer is aware of the shift. Hang on for a second, the parallelism seems to be saying, and you'll find out how these two sentences are related. You would see the relationship immediately if the third sentence said something like this: "Every fall these two famous schools combine their resources in a spectacular display of NCAA football spirit."

If all of this seems a lot to remember when you are writing, just study these two rules until you understand them:

1. Every sentence should comment on, develop, qualify, amplify, explain, or be parallel to another sentence.
2. If any sentence wanders off in a new direction or seems to contradict the sentence before it, that sentence is inappropriate unless a meaningful connection is expressed with a transition word or phrase like "but," "yet," "however," "nevertheless," "on the other hand," or with some other device.

These rules apply mainly to persuasive and expository paragraphs — paragraphs about ideas. Narrative paragraphs and descriptive paragraphs have rules of their own.

EXERCISES

1. Assume that you were beginning a paragraph with this sentence:

Jazz is a spontaneous art.

Tell why each of the following statements would or would not make sense as a second sentence in the paragraph.

a. My favorite instrument is the clarinet.
b. The underlying forms are very rigid.
c. Not even the musicians know exactly what will happen next.
d. Each solo is improvised on the spot, shaped by whim, inspiration, and audience response.
e. Yet the underlying forms are very rigid.
f. Writing is a deliberate art.

2. The sentences in the following paragraph have been jumbled. Put them back into a coherent order and try to notice all the signals that control the sequence.

Then the first shot must be true; no one gets a second shot at a turkey. Wild turkeys are not easy birds to hunt. To avoid this, hunters camouflage themselves, call once or twice to attract a gobbler, and wait, silent and immobile, until the bird walks within range. They have extremely good vision; and if they spot a human within a hundred yards, they will fly away with a few quick flaps of their enormous wings.

3. If you are using an essay collection with this text, choose a paragraph four or five sentences long from one of the expository or persuasive essays. (Avoid narrative and descriptive paragraphs, since they have their own rules for coherence.) Examine the logical relationships among the sentences in the paragraph you choose. Are most of the sentences clearly related to the topic sentence? Or are they related to the sentence immediately preceding them? If any sentences take off in a new direction, are there transition words that you can identify? Can you explain the relationship that each sentence has with some other sentences?

4. Compose a paragraph, like the one in exercise 2, that can be arranged in only one sequence. Do not use obvious cues, like "First," "Second," and "Third." Then jumble the sequence of sentences. Swap jumbled paragraphs with a classmate and try to reconstruct each other's paragraphs.

4. Narrative Paragraphs

Narrative paragraphs are the easiest of all to organize; in fact, they tend to organize themselves. Narratives — stories and processes — are sequential, organized by time, one event in the story, one step in the process happening after the other. Writing, too, is sequential — one word, one sentence, one paragraph after the other. Ordinarily, then, narrative material organizes itself. First A happens, then B, and then C, and so you write about A, B, and C in that order, adding descriptive and explanatory details wherever they are needed.

If you follow a chronological sequence, you will need few transitional words and phrases. Once you establish a narrative framework, the reader understands that the action in each sentence occurs either at the same time as the action in the previous sentence or at some later time — how much later is signaled by the context. In this way, writing narrative is much like making a home movie. Just choose your subject, aim, and shoot. Events themselves, recorded in the sequence of occurrence, will seem coherent to readers and viewers.

Chronological order makes the passage below seem coherent. The only transitional word, *then* in the third sentence, has been added more for rhythm than for coherence. Notice how you infer time relationships among the sentences even though there are no other transition words.

> Eva Marrow approached City Hall now for the first time since she had been elected mayor. Outside on the sagging brick steps she passed three of the old regime, seedy politicos in seersucker suits and straw hats, pretending to shade their eyes from the glare so they would not have to acknowledge Eva's presence. She stopped momentarily halfway up the stairs and then veered over toward the fluted column the men were leaning against. "Hello Charlie," she said, "Mumphy, Edsel." The men mumbled something barely audible.

Even structure as simple as this requires planning. Time is natural, but remembering things in a temporal sequence is not. Our memories work by association, each idea suggesting a related idea from the storehouse of our memories, sometimes an idea so remotely related to what we are thinking that only a psychoanalyst would attempt to figure out the connection. Writers occasionally get themselves into trouble by recording events in whatever sequence they think of them.

Here, for example, is some incoherent advice about establishing a lawn:

> In laying sod, make sure that you keep the ground soaked for at least two weeks after the grass has been installed; otherwise, the lawn will turn brown and die. Begin by preparing the ground adequately. Do not spread fertilizer over the sod until it is well established. The best way to prepare the ground is to till it and fertilize it so that the sod can quickly develop deep roots.

A willing reader can provide the connections needed in this passage, but a better writer would have made the connections obvious by arranging the material in the order in which the events occur, or should occur:

In laying sod, begin by preparing the ground adequately. The best way to prepare the ground is to till it and fertilize it so that the sod can quickly develop deep roots. Make sure that you keep the ground soaked for at least two weeks after the grass has been installed; otherwise, the lawn will turn brown and die. Do not spread fertilizer over the sod until it is well established.

Professional writers do not always follow chronological order in writing narrative sequences. In fact, one of the special devices of skilled writers is to recount a series of events in some order other than actual occurrence. Faulkner, among other modern writers, developed this technique in his fiction, which at its best is as beguiling as any virtuoso performance, making complex artistry seem as easy as blinking.

EXERCISE

If you are using an essay collection along with this text, choose several paragraphs from essays listed under narration. Analyze their structure. Is it chronological, or has the author used a more demanding pattern? Are there many transition words? What are they? Can these paragraphs teach you any tricks for organizing narrative passages in your own writing?

WRITING ASSIGNMENTS

1. Explain any of the following processes in a single paragraph. Try to follow chronological order. Use as few transition words as you can, and be ready to justify those you feel you need.

a. Changing a tire
b. Cooking a soufflé (or some other dish)
c. Conducting an experiment
d. Learning to type
e. Writing a composition

If none of these topics appeals to you, try one of your own.

2. Write a narrative beginning with one of the following sentences. Try to follow chronological order. Use as few transition words as you can, and be ready to justify those you feel you need.

a. As soon as Roger walked into Casey's, I knew there was going to be trouble.

b. The concert opened with a tedious piece by Bizet.

c. Spring break was one disaster after another.

d. I knew the north slope was too steep for beginners, but I decided to try it anyway.

e. The last time I wrote a composition, I began by . . .

If none of these topics appeals to you, try one of your own. For other narrative assignments, see p. 22.

CHECKPOINT FOR NARRATIVE AND PROCESS PAPERS

Swap drafts with a classmate and answer the following questions in writing.

a. Is the paper arranged in chronological order? Would any other order be effective for this particular paper? Can you make any specific suggestions for improving the organization of this draft? Is the beginning of the paper adequately developed, or is more of an introduction necessary? Is the end of the paper satisfactory as an ending?

b. If the paper is primarily a story rather than a process analysis, are you given enough information to answer the five journalistic questions (see p. 20)? Would the paper be improved by the addition or deletion of information? Does the paper seem to have a point, or is it merely a dull account written only to fulfill an assignment? Any suggestions for improvement?

c. If the paper is primarily a process analysis rather than a story, are you given enough information to understand the process? Are unfamiliar terms clearly defined? Would the paper be improved by the addition or deletion of information or definitions? Is the process an interesting one? Any suggestions?

d. Does the paper give information that appeals to the five senses (see p. 16)? Would the paper be improved by the addition or deletion of images? Which images, if any, are clichéd? Which images, if any, are particularly striking?

Use the Checkpoint on pp. 160–162 to give the draft a final editing.

5. Descriptive Paragraphs

Description has its own rules, different from those for narration. Narration has a natural continuity that can be followed step by step; description lacks this convenience. The objects in the room around you, for example, exist all at the same time. If you want to describe those objects, you have to choose a sequence for arranging them. Things will not line up for description the way events arrange themselves in time. Unless you choose a suitable sequence for the various parts of a descriptive passage, your readers will not be able to imagine the scene as clearly as you would like them to.

There are a number of ways to make descriptive passages coherent. A fairly mechanical technique, commonly recommended in textbooks, is to divide the space you are describing into a logical sequence. Begin at the top and move to the bottom, or work from bottom to top, or left to right, right to left, inside to outside, outside to inside, clockwise, or counterclockwise. The sequence you choose will depend upon the nature of what you are describing and your purpose in describing it.

The following paragraph might have been written by a city planner as part of a report about a zoning ordinance. Read it and see if you can name the artificial sequences that make nonsequential material seem sequential.

On October 14, Payne Realty Co. acquired a four-acre block in downtown Munro. The block is bordered by Melpomene Avenue on the north, by Clio Avenue on the south, by Calypso Street on the east, and by Cyclops Street on the west. The northwest quadrant of the property is occupied by a cluster of pawnshops, saloons, and low-rent houses. The northeast quadrant is occupied by the old San Andreas Hotel, now abandoned and condemned. On the southeast quadrant is a large supermarket. The southwest quadrant is vacant, used partly as a junkyard and partly as a playground.

There are two logical sequences in this example. The first part of the paragraph is arranged according to the four points of the compass in the order in which they are normally named; the second part names the four quadrants in a clockwise order, beginning in the northwest. Artificial sequences like these are especially useful when the writer wants the reader to understand what is described clearly enough to diagram it. This particular subject matter could have been presented in other sequences, perhaps just as effectively.

In some situations, it is better to write for the imagination than for the intellect, and it is not necessary for the readers to be able to diagram the scene. All they need is a general impression, not necessarily unambiguous in every detail. Often a random list of impressions without any discernible sequence will work (see Goldfarb's description of a jail on p. 17 or Fowles's description of a cell on p. 370 for examples). This is called an *associative pattern*, for it connects ideas by chance association.

Even in these situations, however, writers can make descriptive passages seem sequential. See if you can discover the pattern of organization in the following paragraph before going on to the explanation following it.

> About fifteen miles below Monterey, on the wild coast, the Torres family had their farm, a few sloping acres above a cliff that dropped to the brown reefs and to the hissing white waters of the ocean. Behind the farm the stone mountains stood up against the sky. The farm buildings huddled like little clinging aphids on the mountain skirts, crouched low to the ground as though the wind might blow them into the sea. The little shack, the rattling, rotting barn were gray-bitten with sea salt, beaten by the damp wind until they had taken on the color of the granite hills. Two horses, a red calf, half a dozen pigs and a flock of lean, multi-colored chickens stocked the place. A little corn was raised on the sterile slope, and it grew short and thick under the wind, and all the cobs formed on the landward sides of the stalks.
>
> —**John Steinbeck, "Flight"**

Notice how you seem to be viewing the farm as if you were approaching it from the ocean in an airplane. First you see the panorama, the plateau cramped between sea cliffs and mountains. Then, as if approaching for a landing, you can discern the various buildings. Finally, on the ground, you can see even the small livestock and you can determine which side of the stalk the corn is growing on.

Steinbeck probably did not have an airplane in mind when he wrote this passage, but the passage is organized *as if* he did. Sometimes it helps to organize descriptive material *as if* you were viewing it in some imaginary sequence: report what you see as if you were a visitor, walking around the place and noting whatever presents itself to you.

If you compare Steinbeck's description of the Torres farm with the description of the neighborhood in the example before it, you will notice some important differences. You may not be able to imagine the neighborhood as clearly as you can visualize the farm; on the other hand, you could draw a map of the neighborhood, but not of the farm. You don't know where the farm buildings are in relation to one another or where the corn is in relation to the buildings, the mountains, and the sea, even though you may have imagined the farm much more clearly than you imagined the neighborhood. This does not mean that one passage is better than the other; Steinbeck's description was written to communicate impressions, the other was written to communicate information, and both succeeded at what they set out to do.

Another device for organizing a descriptive paragraph is to begin with a generalization and then follow up with supporting details. In other words, write a traditional topic sentence and follow it up with examples or evidence.

Example

Topic Sentence: We inspected the school building and determined that it should be condemned.

(Why?) There is hardly any plaster left on the interior walls, and the supporting timbers are infested with termites.

(Why?) The roof is rotten and full of leaks; large sheets of plaster had fallen from the ceiling onto the classroom floors during the recent rains.

(Why?) The windows, most of which have broken panes, have been painted shut for so many years that they can no longer be opened.

This pattern brings us back to the basic paragraph pattern. If your intuitions for coherence fail you, or if you just can't think of anything to say in a paragraph, you might solve both problems by relying on the old tried-and-true formula: start out with a general assertion (a topic sentence) and write two or three sentences that support that assertion with evidence, explanation, or examples.

EXERCISE

If you are using an essay collection along with this text, choose several paragraphs from essays listed under "Description." Analyze their structure. Is it associative? Logical? Generality followed by specifics? Any other identifiable pattern? Are there any transition words? What are they? Can these paragraphs teach you any tricks for organizing descriptive passages in your own writing?

WRITING ASSIGNMENTS

1. Treat each of the following sentences as if it were the topic of a paragraph. Use your imagination to provide three sentences for each, filling out the picture in vivid detail.

a. She was not a difficult person to work for, but she did give the impression that you might get spanked if you did not live up to her expectations.

b. As soon as he stepped onto the subway, even before he said anything to anyone, you could tell that he came from a long line of very wealthy patricians.

c. He was an older man, wearing a private's uniform, and he seemed to deserve a much higher rank.

d. The apartment where the old people were found was so depressing that no one wondered why they preferred death.

If none of these sentences stimulates your imagination, think of a general descriptive statement of your own and follow it up with specifics.

2. Write two descriptions of the same place or thing—one appealing to the reader's intellect, the other to the reader's imagination. For example, you could describe a furnished apartment as if you were writing an inventory for the manager, and describe it again as a scene in a novel; or you could describe a plot of land as it would be described in a courthouse record and describe it again as the setting of an outdoor adventure or romance; or you could describe an old car as you would describe it in a classified ad and describe it again as a symbol of memories you are reluctant to part with. Before attempting the second sort or description, review "The Five Senses as Questions" in Chapter Two, pp. 16–18.

Swap drafts with a classmate and use the Checkpoint below to examine the drafts.

CHECKPOINT FOR DESCRIPTIVE PAPERS

Read the descriptive paper carefully and answer the following questions in writing.

a. Is the purpose of the description to give knowledge or to appeal to the imagination? What details, if any, are inconsistent with this purpose? What details, if any, are particularly effective? Can you make any suggestions that would improve the content of the description?

b. How would you describe the pattern of organization? Logical? Associative? Topic sentence followed by details? Is the pattern appropriate for the writer's purpose? Is the pattern inconsistent in any way? Can you make any suggestions that would improve the organization of the description.

Use the Checkpoint on pp. 160–162 to give the draft a final editing.

6. Concluding Paragraphs

Just as introductions must give a sense of beginning, conclusions must give a sense of ending. Papers that stop short when the writer runs out of material are unsettling. Good conclusions have only one thing in common with one another: they *seem* like conclusions. It is impossible to list all the ways writers go about making endings seem like endings, but a few examples, corresponding to the beginnings discussed in the previous section, may give you some ideas for bringing your own papers to an end.

Just as there are practical, businesslike beginnings, there are practical, businesslike endings. And just as a practical beginning foreshadows the substance of the discussion, a practical ending reviews it. In business or technical writing the conclusion can be signalled by an obvious phrase like: "In conclusion . . ." or "In general, then . . ." or by a heading that says *Conclusion*.

Example

In general, then, I would recommend that we order fifty TOTEM cogenerators from Fiat and have them installed as soon as possible. These machines are more efficient than our present energy sources.

They can be fueled by natural gas, which is currently being piped to the plant, and they can be fueled by methane, which may soon be the only fuel available through the pipes now supplying natural gas. In addition to assuring a stable supply of energy in the event of another embargo, the cogenerators will save approximately $250,000 in energy costs over the next ten years, in effect paying for themselves.

A practical conclusion gives what business people like to refer to as the "bottom line." It expresses the writer's judgment about the subject at hand and briefly summarizes the facts supporting that judgment.

Conclusions for journalistic essays are less pointed. They use the same devices that might be used in a journalistic beginning — quotations, specific instances, dramatic situations — but the last line is usually written with an air of finality. Here is E. B. White's conclusion to his essay on "Home-Coming," the beginning of which you saw on p. 106.

*Example**

Here in New England, each season carries a hundred foreshadowings of the season that is to follow — which is one of the things I love about it. Winter is rough and long, but spring lies all round about. Yesterday, a small white keel feather escaped from my goose and lodged in the bank boughs near the kitchen porch, where I spied it as I came home in the cold twilight. The minute I saw the feather, I was projected into May, knowing that a barn swallow would be along to claim the prize and use it to decorate the front edge of its nest. Immediately, the December air seemed full of wings of swallows and the warmth of barns. Swallows, I have noticed, never use any feather but a white one in their nest-building, and they always leave a lot of it showing, which makes me believe that they are interested not in the feather's insulating power but in its reflecting power, so that when they skim into the dark barn from the bright outdoors they will have a beacon to steer by.

At first this conclusion may not seem related to the topic at all — until you realize that the first few sentences describe the features of New England that make it nice to come home to, and that the swallows in the last line, like White himself, are coming home.

Conclusions for scholarly papers, like business conclusions, often restate the point of the article and summarize the evidence; and like the conclusions of journalistic essays, they often end with a sentence that has an air of finality. The main point of John Burke's article on Sir Walter Scott (see p. 106) was that Scott saw both good and evil in his contemporary world just as he saw them both in the world of the past. Burke's final paragraph restates this thesis, summarizes the argument, and ends with a short sentence that seems final. Some of the details are omitted in the version below, but the substance is preserved.

Example*

The plot of *The Fortunes of Nigel* is then an ambivalent rendering of historical process working itself out in the lives of individuals. With it Scott renders the passing of the feudal world critically. If it was a world with admirable ideals, it was also a world where the most outrageous violence was part of the tissue of life, a world where justice was often a matter of brute physical strength. Nevertheless, Scott also renders the coming of the new critically. He recognizes its more positive features: The new world, being more open and flexible, could provide opportunities for merit to rise; it would reward men more often for their ability and achievements rather than for their birth or their rank. Yet it would be a world without any natural ideals, with only the aftershine of religion as a barrier between it and nature red in tooth and claw. In a world where individualism is the norm and self-interest the primary motive for action, selfishness is but the logical result. That would be why, when Scott accepted the victory of the new over the old, he accepted it only reluctantly. The ultimate effect on his more sensitive readers can only be tonic: They will see not only what we have gained over the past, but also what we have lost. Both are sobering thoughts.

Notice that the word "tonic" in the second to last sentence echoes the same word in the introduction (see p. 107). Writers

---

* Abridged and reprinted by author's permission from "Scott's Views on History in *The Fortunes of Nigel*," *CLIO*, 8 (Fall 1978), p. 11.

often find ways to echo their beginnings in their conclusions; this device gives an essay a sense of coming full circle.

In college writing, conclusions, like beginnings, may be practical, journalistic, or scholarly, depending on the writer's purpose and the reader's expectations. In short papers and essay examinations, a formal ending may not be necessary at all. If your beginning announces a brief discussion of the ego, the superego, and the id, you might simply end with your discussion of the id, adding no final flourishes. But in longer papers, even papers with practical beginnings, it makes sense to provide at least a practical ending. If you had written a paper about the causes and effects of the Hundred Years' War, a good way to conclude might be to summarize the main points of the discussion.

Example

The Hundred Years' War ended in exhaustion rather than in victory or defeat for either side. England's main objective — to control land in France — was completely unrealized, except for Calais. The aristocracy finally grew weary of violence, and the age of chivalry came to an end.

You may notice that the points made in this conclusion correspond roughly with the points made in the introduction (see p. 108). Rewriting an introduction is often an effective way to make an ending.

A paper that begins with a dramatic or journalistic introduction might appropriately end with the same sort of conclusion. If you had written a journalistic introduction to a paper about the dangers of nuclear power, you might try to find another specific quotation or dramatic situation for your conclusion.

Example

If there was ever any doubt about the dangers of nuclear power, that doubt should have been removed by the accident near Three Mile Island. And yet, shortly after the accident, Energy Secretary James R. Schlesinger is reported to have said that "the possibility of future accidents would need to be accepted as the price of generating the energy on which the national economy depends." Must it? The same scientists who had warned us about the dangers of nuclear energy have also claimed that cleaner, safer sources of energy are already available, if only the government would invest in them. But the government insists on clinging to an energy policy which must lead, one way or another, to a dead end.

The first sentence in this conclusion recalls the thesis — that nuclear plants are dangerous — and leads into the quotation that illustrates the thesis. Notice that the conclusion also makes reference to the beginning (see p. 109) by mentioning the same accident and the same scientists who were referred to in the introduction. Notice, too, that the last sentence has an air of finality.

Research papers can be concluded by restating the thesis (or at least referring to it), summarizing the evidence, and closing with a sentence that seems final.

Example

Lydgate's meter, like the language of the time, is an unstable mixture of English, French, and Latin. As an Englishman, Lydgate grew up with a language that was torn between the heavy stresses of its Germanic roots and the stressless French of the aristocracy. As a monk, Lydgate was accustomed to Gregorian chants in which the musical accent often occurred without regard for the pronunciation of the words. And as a poet, Lydgate was strongly influenced by French models in which syllables were counted, not stresses. To be read properly. Lydgate's poetry should be chanted without any stresses at all, giving it the sort of musical lilt that English still has when it is spoken by people who grow up where French is spoken.

This conclusion corresponds with the beginning on p. 110. It repeats the thesis, summarizes the evidence, and ends with a sentence that seems final.

Conclusions are not easy to write. They take time, hard work, and a little luck. They are somewhat easier to write, however, when you have a particular shape or outline of a conclusion in mind before you begin writing. The conclusions discussed in this chapter have three shapes:

1. The practical conclusion
   a. State the "bottom line"
   b. Summarize the supporting facts
2. The journalistic conclusion

    a. Give a quotation or dramatic illustration appropriate to the topic
    b. End with a sentence that seems final
3. The scholarly conclusion
    a. Restate the thesis
    b. Summarize the evidence
    c. End with a sentence that seems final

A nice touch in any conclusion, of course, is to echo something in the introduction.

To write a conclusion, pick the shape that best suits the sort of paper you are writing and look for material to fill out that shape. Material for restating a thesis or summarizing evidence comes, obviously, from the paper itself. Material for journalistic conclusions — specific incidents or quotations — can usually be found among the interesting bits and pieces of information you discovered in prewriting but were unable to use in the paper itself. If you know from the outset that you are going to need a journalistic beginning or a journalistic conclusion, you can be on the lookout for appropriate tidbits as you do your prewriting or research.

After choosing the appropriate shape and finding the necessary material, write a draft of an ending. Experienced writers know that the first draft seldom works. They plan to spend half an hour or more writing and rewriting the single paragraph that will bring a good paper to a good conclusion.

EXERCISES

    1. Choose a good magazine of general interest or a scholarly journal in your major field and examine five or six conclusions. To what extent do they conform to the patterns described in this chapter? Can you identify some additional patterns or techniques that would be useful in writing conclusions of your own? If you are using an essay collection along with this text, examine the conclusions in five or six essays. Be careful, however: essays in collections are sometimes excerpted from longer works, and the last paragraph in a selection may not be the last paragraph in the original work.

    2. Write conclusions corresponding to any of the three beginnings you were asked to write in exercises 2, 3, and 4 on p. 111.

CHECKPOINT FOR ORGANIZATION

After you have fleshed out your outline with full discussion, including an introduction and a conclusion, swap papers with a classmate and answer in writing the following questions about your classmate's work.

a. Read the introduction and stop. Does it read like a practical introduction, a journalistic introduction, or a scholarly introduction? Does it suit the purpose of the paper? Does it foreshadow the substance of the paper itself? Should it? Can you make some suggestions for improvement?

b. Read the first sentence in each of the other paragraphs except for the conclusion. Indicate which ones do and which ones do not seem clearly related to the discussion the introduction leads you to expect.

c. Now read the middle paragraphs very carefully. Is each sentence clearly related to the sentence before it or to the topic sentence? Can you find any sentences that do not seem related to what precedes them? Indicate which sentences seem to wander off in a new direction without a signal or a logical connection.

d. Read the conclusion. Does it give the sense of an ending? Does it read like a practical conclusion, a journalistic conclusion, or a scholarly conclusion? Does it suit the purpose of the paper? Does it review the substance of the paper? Should it? Can you make some suggestions for improvement?

Swap papers again and read what your classmate has had to say about your draft. Take a few minutes to ask questions of each other or to explain your suggestions for improvement.

As you revise your paper, consult the next two chapters for advice about common problems in style. Next Checkpoint: pp. 160–162.

Chapter Six

Words and Phrases: Six Problems

"The difference between the almost right word and the right word is really a large matter," Mark Twain once said. "'Tis the difference between the lightning-bug and the lightning."

One of the unnatural advantages of writing is that it gives writers ample time to find the right words — words that express exactly what the writer has in mind without seeming either pretentious or pedestrian. All writers, however, even professionals, need the help of editors and teachers to get their words exactly right.

In this chapter you will study six common problems with words and phrases:

1. Wordiness
2. Wrong Word
3. Tangled Idiom
4. Colloquial Diction
5. Pretentious Diction (Jargon)
6. Clichés

1. Wordiness

Verbosity — wordiness — is tedious. Do not use words that add nothing. Be stingy. Do not write "Jack is a person who eats donuts with a fork," if you can say "Jack eats donuts with a fork." Do not write "because of the fact that" if a simple "because" will suffice. On the other hand, do not eliminate so many words that your writing reads like a telegram: DONNE'S POEM GOOD STOP STRONG IMAGERY STOP CONCEIT ABOUT COMPASS ESPECIALLY EFFECTIVE STOP. If a word adds anything worthwhile to your sentence — meaning, grace, rhythm, emphasis — let it remain. But if you can remove a word, a phrase, a sentence, a paragraph, or even an entire section and not miss it, then remove it.

Compare the effectiveness of the sentences in each of the following pairs.

Examples
You will discover the verbal power of words.
You will discover the power of words.

Mrs. Burton said that insofar as her authority was concerned she had authority to sign checks for large amounts.
Mrs. Burton said she had authority to sign checks for large amounts.

Repeated words (note the "authority . . . authority" in the example above) are often a sign of verbosity. And words repeated in adjacent sentences are often a sign that the information could be expressed more economically in a single sentence.

Example
Each author chooses to bring out his point by different stylistic methods. Using different methods makes it possible for each writer to bring out his own point more effectively.

Revision: Each author chooses the style that will make his point most effectively.

Sometimes words can be deleted because what they say is

obvious from the context. Thus, "bad" can be eliminated from "Edsel complained about the bad treatment he had received from the receptionist." What other kind of treatment would he complain about? Similarly, words that overlap in meaning with nearby words can often be omitted. Instead of "The house was round and circular in shape," write "The house was round."

Sometimes wordiness results from an inadequate vocabulary. If you don't know the word *compost,* you may have to write "a mixture of various decaying organic substances, like dead leaves, egg shells, coffee grounds, and manure, used to fertilize gardens." And if you don't know the word *hackamore,* you may have to write "a bridle that exerts pressure on the nose of a horse rather than on the lips."

EXERCISE

Trim the wordiness in the examples below.

a. In conclusion, let me end by asking you for your help.

b. Jesse returned the check back to the manager.

c. At the end, the suspense increases up to the end.

d. Her complexion was very dark in color, and her smile was royally regal.

e. The cause of the accident was two separate causes.

f. The ambulance sped rapidly to the scene of the accident.

g. After the two hoses were attached together, they were sufficiently long enough to reach the edge of the garden.

h. The extra additional building was designed for storage purposes.

i. The excusing cause which he tried to make us give credence to was the fact that he was at that particular point in time somewhere else other than at the scene of the crime.

j. She sat in mute silence, thinking inwardly to herself.

k. In my opinion, the money profited from the gambling should be taxed by the county.

l. Williams then continues by denouncing football as a money-eating program.

m. His essay on big-time athletics is a critical survey of intercollegiate athletics as it stands today in American universities. The essay is an attack on big-time intercollegiate athletics, which demands complete overhaul and not adjustment.

2. Wrong Word

Sometimes writers will use a word that does not mean what they think it means.

Examples

Looking to the right, I depicted a beautiful scene.

Commoner's argument against the abuse of chemicals afflicts his credibility for some readers.

In the first example, the writer probably did not mean to say that he "depicted"—that is, painted or described—the scene. He meant to say that he *saw* a scene. Perhaps he thought *saw* wasn't fancy enough for college writing, so he groped for something fancier, something more like *discerned* or *descried*. But *saw* would have worked quite well. And in the second example, *weakens* or *destroys* might have worked instead of "afflicts."

If your reader has marked a word with the symbol WW, look up the word you used in a dictionary to find out what it means and why it doesn't fit where you used it. To find the right word, you might consult a thesaurus *along with a dictionary*, or else ask a more experienced writer to suggest the word that might express your meaning.

A thesaurus, by the way, and similar books of synonyms should be used with extreme caution, if at all. Many writing teachers recommend them for improving vocabulary. Unfortunately, books like these sometimes give the impression that any of a long list of synonyms can be substituted for any of the other words in the list, so writers use big words or impressive words instead of right words.

EXERCISE

Identify the words that do not quite fit in the sentences below. Then either replace them with more suitable words or rewrite the sentence to express the meaning you think the writer intended.

a. Amid the hundreds of thousands who support college athletics,

there are those who think the programs have grown to super-
flous proportions.

b. His views are enhanced by remarks made by athletic directors.

c. For exemplary purposes, take the subject of housing.

d. Football, which is the major collegiate sport, has commanded
many colleges.

e. The excitement of the game is due to its highly comprised action.

f. A hint of mystery, conjectured by the use of the black glove, is
part of the photograph's appeal.

g. Extravagance, implicated by its detailed features, heightens the
attractiveness of the watches.

h. The last two lines — "Parting is all we know of heaven,/And all
we need of hell" — clearly focus Emily Dickinson's aspects of
life.

i. He may not lack the knowledge of how the game is played, but
he doesn't show any awareness of how emotions can involve an
athlete's career.

j. Beauty, a common technique used to catch the reader's attention, is the dominant feature in this ad.

3. Tangled Idiom

Sometimes inexperienced writers construct phrases that just
do not normally occur in printed English. If the normal phraseology of a language is called its "idiom," departures from it
might be called "tangled idiom." At best, tangled idiom distracts the readers, like static on a radio; at worst, it is unintelligible.

Examples
The values of educational institutions have run amiss.

One reason for why an overhaul is unrealistic is the intransigency
of university officials.

Another burr under Newsome's skin was his boss's lack of appre-
ciation.

In the first example, the writer comes so close to the common
phrase "run amuck" that "run amiss" looks like an unintended slip. In the second example, the writer blends two

common idioms ("reason for" and "reason why") into one blurred phrase ("reason for why"). In the third example, the writer puts a burr under the skin, though the burr in this expression is usually under a saddle.

Many problems with idiom have to do with the choice of prepositions after certain words. Should you write "center on," "center about," or "center around"? Should you write "different from," "different than," or "different to"? According to the *American Heritage Dictionary*, *center* should be followed by *on*, *upon*, *in* or *at*, but not by *around* or *about*. And *different* should normally be followed by *from* (with some exceptions).

When you have trouble deciding which preposition should follow a particular word, look the word up in a good dictionary and you will find some guidance about how it is used. If the dictionary does not offer the guidance you need, you can usually find a professional opinion in *The Careful Writer: A Modern Guide to English Usage* (New York: Atheneum, 1973), by Theodore M. Bernstein. Although Bernstein gives his opinion about a wide variety of problems in usage and idiom, he is particularly interested in what he considers the proper choice of prepositions.

EXERCISE

Untangle the idioms in the following sentences.

a. This scepticism and fear has no real basis of reason.
b. Gun registration may cause resentment from the sportsman and happiness from the criminal.
c. My impression of the book would be too vast to do in this relatively short paper.
d. Advertisers accustom themselves with the use of vague generalities.
e. For all intensive purposes, the two paintings are identical.
f. My writing on the final examination was inferior than anything I had written during the semester.

4. Colloquial Diction

Colloquial diction is language that reads like spoken English. In some contexts, colloquial diction is perfectly appropriate. It is used by novelists when they write conversational lines for their characters.

Example

"Polly," she said, "I could have *killed* you. You sat right in front of me, right in front of me, and during the first set of my big comeback you ate a whole basket of rolls—eight: I counted them—and you cleaned up one of those ice cream scoops of butter."

—John Cheever, *Falconer*

Colloquial diction is also used by essayists when they want to establish an informal style—style with its shoes off, not trying to put on airs.

Example

When I get mail I avert my eyes so I can't see who it's from. Then I sit down on my bed and peep at it real slowly, like a poker player peeping at his cards. I can feel when I've got a letter from you, and when I peep up on your name on the envelope I let out a big yell. It's like having four aces. But if the letter is not from you, it's like having two deuces, a three, a four, and a five, all in scrambled suits. A bum kick. Nothing.

—Eldridge Cleaver, *Soul on Ice*

Colloquial diction becomes a problem when it is mixed with reasonably formal language for no good reason:

Examples

Galbraith's recent analysis of the economy was *kind of* good, but lacking in specificity.

At first Wright's houses were hardly distinguishable from others in Oak Park, but gradually he *went and thought up new* a style of his own.

All native speakers of a language have a range of diction, which they vary according to the situation. You probably have a "public" style and a "private" style of speaking—a style you would use in addressing a group of adults at an assembly and a style you use with friends. If your reader has marked a sentence or a passage with this sign—D↓—meaning that your diction is too colloquial for the occasion, the best solution is to imagine how you would express the same ideas to a large audience at a formal gathering. In rewriting, however, be careful not to go to the other extreme (see next lesson).

EXERCISE

In the following sentences, identify phrases that are too colloquial for their context.

1. The President was apparently unaware of his appointment with this real important guy in Moscow.
2. Being as how I don't like classical music, Horowitz's performance was exceptional, even for Horowitz.
3. Much of her evidence in this essay is sort of weak.
4. The crisis could have been avoided if the diplomatic corps in Mexico City had been more sensitive to the needs of ordinary Americans abroad, instead of a bunch of snotty creeps.
5. It was apparent from the interview that the king was a very interesting type person who you could have talked to for hours.

5. Pretentious Diction (Jargon)

The opposite of colloquial diction is pretentious diction — language that calls attention to itself because it is too fancy for the occasion. Pretentious diction often occurs in patches, mixed in with good, plain English. One student, for example, wrote that she had "introduced eggs into a frying utensil and injected coffee into a chalice" because, as she later confessed, she thought that *put, pan, poured,* and *cup* were all too common for college writing.

Some kinds of pretentious diction are called "jargon." Jargon is a special language of a particular field or profession. Jargon has its legitimate uses. We cannot expect lawyers to say *habeas corpus* in English, or football players to find a synonym for a "post pattern," or psychologists to avoid "sociopathic," or musicians to abandon "*andante cantible*" just because the rest of us may not understand these terms. The jargon of any given field is often the most efficient means of communication within that field.

Jargon becomes offensive, however, when there are handy English equivalents available or when people outside the field are expected to understand what is said. There is no excuse for sociologists to write so that not even other sociologists can understand them. Here, for example, is a passage by the sociologist Talcott Parsons, quoted by Richard Lanharn in *Style: An Anti-Textbook* (New Haven: Yale University Press, 1974 pp. 69–70):

> An element of a shared symbolic system which serves as a criterion or standard for selection among the alternatives of orientation which are intrinsically open in a situation may be called a value. . . . But from this motivational orientation aspect of the totality of action it is, in view of the role of symbolic systems, necessary to distinguish a "value-orientation" aspect.

Unfortunately, writing of this kind is sometimes imitated by students who read it in textbooks and journals. It is obvious, for example, that literary critics have set a none-too-lucid example for the student who wrote this comment about one of Steinbeck's short stories:

> "Flight," a short story, begins realistically and concludes symbolically. This tendency is vividly displayed and gives the reader a sense of strong conflict but, because of indirection in the telling of the story, you must draw your own inference.

Indeed you must.

Writing of this kind reaches an absolute nadir when students combine a recently acquired vocabulary of abstractions with a desire to write prose that sounds important. Sentences like those in the examples below will make pretzels of the most willing minds.

Examples

In the poem "Musée des Beaux Arts," the speaker uses informal diction and unorthodox writing along with the tragedy theme to relate the poem to his reader.

The dramatic peripeteia is finalized in the climax which is reserved for the final sentence.

If your reader has marked a sentence or a passage with this sign — D↑ — meaning that your diction is pretentious or stuffed with unnecessary jargon, the best solution is to "talk it out." Choose a real or imagined person who has lots of common sense but no knowledge of your subject. Explain what you intended by your passage to this person in spoken words. Once you have been able to express yourself clearly in speech, write down what you have said. You will notice that when you begin writing, you will be tempted to omit linking words and transitions and to use more abstractions than you would use if you were speaking. If your problem has been pretentious diction, resist the temptation. Write the passage fully. Don't say anything you don't mean. Don't choose fancy words because they "sound good" or "look good." Good-looking words sometimes merely hide meaning, not only from the reader but sometimes from the writer as well.

EXERCISE

Discuss and remedy (if you can) the diction in the following examples. Which, if any, might be justified as jargon intended for a group of specialists?

a. The virus soon built up a tolerance for the usual drugs, so the doctors excogitated with respect to the utilization of other expedients.

b. Ethical appeal maximizes the special properties that evince the quality of the product.

c. The defendant in this case was Otis, a leader in the vertical transportation industry.

d. If total disability occurs during the grace period for payment of a premium, such premium shall not be waived, nor refunded if paid, provided that failure to pay such premium within the grace period therefor shall not of itself invalidate a claim hereunder for total disability commencing during such grace period if such premium with compound interest at the rate of 5 per cent. per annum is paid at the time due proof of the claim is furnished to the Company.

e. Thus, the various components of the base interact to generate initial phrase markers, and the transformational component converts an initial phrase marker, step by step, into a phonologically represented sentence with its phrase marker.

f. Administrative personnel were directed to prioritize their developmental input infrastructures.

g. The omniscient point of view also adds in relating the theme of jealousy.

6. Clichés cliché

If you've ever been backstage in a good school theater, you know that there is a room stuffed with costumes and props from past plays — beards, wigs, Roman togas, horned helmets, gaudy ties, fake swords, pistols without firing pins, broken telephones, and other things that would be considered junk, except that they might turn out to be useful again in another play.

That's what clichés are. They are stock expressions and stock patterns of thought that people drag out from a verbal prop room and apply to the situation at hand.

Examples

I was stopped dead in my tracks.

The ship of state is in troubled waters.

The sea was emerald green, and the sand on the shore glistened as if it were covered with diamonds.

Before writing became a pervasive part of our culture, clichés were actually valued as a way of remembering insights and passing them on from one generation to the next. Now that writing serves as our collective memory, clichés have lost their usefulness; they are what stage props would be in the real world — not props at all, but junk.

Thought patterns can be clichéd, too. There are clichéd beginnings for compositions, particularly the "Down through the ages" beginning, which sometimes takes the form of "Throughout history . . ." or "Ever since the beginning of time . . ." or "Ever since Adam and Eve . . ." There are clichéd endings, the dreariest of which is "And then I woke and realized it was all a dream." And, as every student knows, there are clichéd writing assignments, like "How I spent my summer" and "My most embarrassing moment."

Why are clichés so tempting? They are tempting because they provide the writer with something to say and sometimes with a way of thinking about a topic. In the Renaissance, clichés were actually collected in "commonplace books," books that gave students ideas about their assigned topics by telling them what had already been said about them.

No writer can be entirely free of clichés; our language is simply too full of them. But writers should avoid those that have been used so often that—what can we say? That their familiarity breeds contempt? That they have worn out their welcome? Whenever you write an expression you think you've heard before, you may be writing a cliché. Whenever you are tempted to apologize for a word or expression by putting it in quotation marks, you are probably writing a cliché.

To avoid clichéd descriptions, examine the reality itself through the five senses as discussed in Chapter Two (p. 16). To avoid clichéd patterns of thought, use the discovery procedures and techniques of arrangement discussed in Chapters Two through Five. Although some of these patterns and procedures have been used for centuries, they do not *seem* clichéd because they are not attached to any particular verbal expression. No one can teach you how to write fresh metaphors and striking comparisons; originality is a gift, not a method. But the exercise below may help you learn to recognize the difference between a good phrase and a nearly good one.

EXERCISE

Some of the lines below are fresh, original, striking, and illuminating. Others come from the great verbal prop room. Can you tell which are which? The good ones are attributed to their authors at the bottom of the page.

a. You get out of life what you put into it.
b. Education is what we're all about.
c. Quality says it all.
d. A professor must have a theory, as a dog must have fleas.
e. A glittering extravaganza for children of all ages.
f. Taking composition again would be a fate worse than death.
g. Washington is a city of southern efficiency and northern charm.
h. A man should be free to enjoy his golden years without the anchor of alimony tied around his neck.
i. The machinery of government would not work if it were not allowed a little play in its joints.
j. The rise in censorship is in part due, I believe, to the concern of the half-educated for the well-being of the quarter-educated.

d. H. L. Mencken g. J. F. Kennedy i. Oliver Wendell Holmes j. Fred B. Millett

Chapter Seven

Assembling Sentences:
Six Problems

Sometimes writing is awkward or unclear because the writer has failed to understand one of the essential differences between writing and speech: *In speech, sentences flow; in writing, sentences are assembled.*

Experienced writers know that they have to review every sentence they write to make sure all the words fit together as smoothly and efficiently as clockwork. Inexperienced writers are not inclined to review sentences they write any more than they review sentences they speak. They think the parts of written sentences will mesh as naturally and easily as the parts of spoken sentences. They're wrong. They might just as well try to assemble a clock by shaking its pieces in a paper bag.

In this chapter you will study six common problems in assembling sentences:

1. The Verb *Be*
2. Passive Voice

3. Faulty Predication
4. Faulty Parallelism
5. Repetition
6. Garbles

1. The Verb Be

Because the verb *be* is often a cause of stylistic problems, every writer should learn to recognize it in all of its eight basic forms:

am, are, is
was, were
be, being, been

Good writers generally avoid the verb *be* followed by adjectives or nouns that can be turned into strong, economical verbs.

Examples
The new policy is violative of the Civil Rights Act. (weak)
The new policy violates the Civil Rights Act. (better)

His new skateboard was the cause of an accident. (weak)
His new skateboard caused an accident. (better)

Notice that the second version in each of these examples is more direct and more economical than the first because, in replacing "is" and "was," the action is moved from an adjective or a noun into the verb, where it normally belongs.

EXERCISE

Replace the verb *be* in the following sentences with a more direct and economical verb. Discuss any changes in meaning your revision may cause.

a. The teachers are hopeful that their raises will be approved by the legislature.

b. An increase in housing starts is usually indicative of a sound economy.

c. All the major companies were in opposition to the tariffs.

d. There were thirteen senators who sponsored the bill.

e. It was predictable that the staff would be resistant to change.

f. The notes are reflections of data gathered in our research.

g. Some Latin American countries are dependent upon coffee prices.

h. Only certain mushrooms are producers of enzymes that termites need in their diet.

i. Ardvaark was a surprise to us in the sixth race.

j. Terrorism is an undermining of the very possibility of peaceful political processes.

2. Passive Voice

In the passive voice, the subject is the receiver of an action rather than the doer of it.

Examples

The weapons were being built beneath a football stadium.

The victim had been seen walking along near the zoo.

The children were being returned to Peru.

In the examples, notice how the passive voice allows the real doer of the action to be concealed. Who was building the weapons? Who was returning the children to Peru? The passive voice is often employed by writers when they want to evade or conceal the responsibility for someone's behavior.

Examples

I regret to inform you that your application has been rejected.

Women were not included in the delegate assembly.

The passive voice makes it unnecessary to say who rejected the application or who failed to include women. This sort of evasion is sometimes inappropriate or confusing.

Examples
In *Hamlet,* a pessimistic view of life is held.

Freudian analysis has been judged ineffective.

Readers of sentences like these would rightly object to their vagueness. Who is pessimistic in *Hamlet*—Shakespeare, Hamlet, or one of the other characters in the play? Who has determined that Freudian analysis is ineffective?

Another characteristic of the passive voice is that it requires more words than the active voice to communicate the same amount of information.

Examples
Roger was offered a job by the manager. (passive voice, 8 words)
The manager offered Roger a job. (active voice, 6 words)

Inspections are conducted by an agency of the federal government. (passive voice, 10 words)
An agency of the federal government conducts inspections. (active voice, 8 words)

Because the passive voice is sometimes vague and always less economical than the active voice, good writers tend to avoid it except when it is genuinely useful. The passive voice may be preferable, for example, when the real doer of an action is either unknown or, in the context of a discussion, relatively unimportant.

Examples
This pyramid was constructed around 1000 B.C.

A funnel cloud has been sighted five miles east of the airport.

Lincoln was assassinated in Ford's Theater on April 14, 1865.

If your reader marks PV in the margin of your work consider changing the passive construction to an active construction. Consult **G13** (p. 305) if you have trouble distinguishing active from passive voice.

EXERCISE

Change the following sentences from passive voice to active.

a. *The Tempest* was thought by my father to be Shakespeare's most magical play.

b. Pecking acorns in the sandy ditch beside the road, a wild turkey was seen by Joel.

c. An award that he did not particularly want was received by Lucien.

d. Relocation of the plant was considered by the board of directors to be unfeasible.

e. The lesson was understood by the class because the teacher had explained it well.

3. Faulty Predication

The subject of a sentence is whatever answers the question "who?" or "what?" before the verb. (See **G35**.) The predicate includes the verb along with any words that complete or modify its meaning. When a mismatch of meanings occurs between a subject and a predicate, the result is called "faulty predication."

Examples

Grammar is where I have most of my writing problems.

College athletics is a controversy that will not be easily resolved.

I do not believe that manslaughter, self-defense, and war tragedies constitute the death penalty.

The completion of the stadium was finished on time.

In each of these examples, the meaning of the predicate does not match up with the meaning of the subject. In the first, the predicate, beginning with "is where," treats "grammar" as if it were a place. In the second, "controversy" does not equal "college athletics" in a way that allows us to say that one is the other; the writer's intention would be better expressed by a sentence beginning "College athletics is a controversial subject." The third example might be treated partly as a problem in word choice as well as in faulty predication. The writer probably meant "merit" or "deserve" instead of "constitute"; but merely changing the verb would not solve the problem entirely, since only one of the subjects, "manslaughter," would make sense with the revised predicate. The last example represents a common problem in which the meaning of a word in the subject ("completion") overlaps with the meaning of a word in the predicate ("finished"). The solution, normally, is to delete one of the words: "The stadium was finished on time."

One of the most vexing problems with faulty predication is that writers, who know what they mean, find it difficult to see why what they have written does not convey the meaning they intend. If your reader has marked a sentence or phrase of yours with the sign FP, try to understand why the predication is faulty. Talk it out with an instructor or a friend. When you can say what you meant in words that make sense to the person listening to you, write them down. But be careful that the act of writing doesn't force you into the same mismatches that you began with. You may have to make two or three attempts before you get it right.

EXERCISE

Discuss and remedy the faulty predication in the following sentences.

a. Horses are a good activity for people of every age.
b. The source of Chaucer's *Troilus* comes from Boccacio's *Philostrato*.
c. The statement about inflation was said by the press secretary.
d. Draftsmanship and design should be painted by young artists before attempting experimental forms.
e. Playing center on a professional team is a concept I have never seriously considered.

4. Faulty Parallelism

In written English, words and phrases joined by *and* are normally similar both in grammatical form and in meaning. Violations of this convention are called "faulty parallels."

Problem: My hobbies are hunting, fishing, and to write.

Solution: My hobbies are hunting, fishing, and writing.

Problem: In the parking lot outside were students from New Jersey, Texas, and Houston.

Solution: In the parking lot outside were students from New Jersey and Texas.

Problem: The desks were covered with mathematical formulas, sorority girls, and true love.

Solution: The desks were covered with mathematical formulas, sorority symbols, and emblems of true love.

Faulty parallelism can also occur around the word *or*.

Problem: He would like a career in publishing or as a teacher.

Solution: He would like a career in publishing or in teaching.

And in more subtle ways, faulty parallelism can occur around other words.

Problem: Nobody wants wealth without being happy.

Solution: Nobody wants wealth without happiness.

Sometimes the omission or addition of a small word affects parallelism.

Problem: Galumph won the election by organizing early, choosing issues carefully, and by projecting a down-to-earth image.

Solution A: Galumph won the election by organizing early, by choosing issues carefully, and by projecting a down-to-earth image.

Solution B: Galumph won the election by organizing early, choosing issues carefully, and projecting a down-to-earth image.

Problem: His success was generally attributed to his talent, integrity, and to his insatiable appetite for work.

Solution A: His success was generally attributed to his talent, to his integrity, and to his insatiable appetite for work.

Solution B: His success was generally attributed to his talent, his integrity, and his insatiable appetite for work.

Solution C: His success was generally attributed to his talent, integrity, and insatiable appetite for work.

If your reader puts the symbol ✕ in the margin of your work, look for the connecting word (*and, or, without,* etc.) and rewrite the words or phrases it connects so that they are parallel.

EXERCISE

Correct the faulty parallelism in the following sentences.

a. The city is a place where you can fight, find women, drinking, and die.

b. New students were artistic, not athletes.

c. Hank was a leader to his teammates, the coach, and to his friends.

d. James Dean was a movie star, a racing driver, and a meeting place for the young.

e. David was equally at home hunting or with a book.

f. He assured them of their welcome, and would be honored for them to stay for dinner.

g. It was clear that the selection committee preferred intelligence to being honest.

h. Today in college athletics, too much emphasis is placed on winning and how much money is brought in by the game.

i. He said our choice was either to cook for ourselves or starvation.

j. Oddly enough, Jackie was more impressed by the rock collection than seeing the astronauts.

5. *Repetition* REP

In written English, repetition is a common device for signaling parallel ideas:

". . . that government of the people, by the people, for the people shall not perish from the earth."

Because readers are accustomed to parallel ideas in connection with repeated words and structures, repetition that does not signal parallelism is distracting.

She is twenty now, and acts twelve. Feeling numb by now, I managed to stand up as soon as she walked in.

By now my arm felt like someone was putting an electric drill through my arm.

Burning a hole in my pocket was my paycheck. Hurrying to the bank, I cashed it.

In conversation these repetitions would be scarcely noticeable; but on paper they are bothersome echoes.

EXERCISE

Look for repeated words and structures in the following sentences and determine whether they are used effectively.

a. Inmates, having only each other for companions, with little else in common but crime, have turned prisons into effective schools of crime.

b. Before long we were placed in the active role before we knew it.

c. Irma walked to the grocery, walked to school, walked to work — walked, in fact, everywhere she went.

d. Sally doesn't walk; she slides. She doesn't eat; she gobbles. And she doesn't talk; she shouts.

e. At this point in the story, Salinger shifts the point of view in the story.

f. These vivid pictures immediately create the picture that Anderson intends to put in his story.

g. They were friends, but they envied each other, even hated each other.

h. It was a nice place to forget your troubles, lose your inhibitions, and feel at ease.

i. Low on gas, we stopped at a gas station and filled up the gas tank.

j. One of the nicest things about the book was the cover of the book.

6. Garbles

A garble is a group of words that is so tangled that it doesn't make any sense.

Example
The second part of the essay, Ruskin's lecture "Of Queens' Gardens," the Victorian woman's function was to help and guide her mate in the business world.

Garbles are symptoms of one of the most difficult problems that writing students face: finding a way to say what they mean. "I know what I *want* to say," students often moan, either to themselves or to their instructors, "but I just can't get it to come out right on paper."

Why not? Well, perhaps these students have ideas that are more advanced than their vocabularies, and they need to devise a serious, long-term plan for learning new words (see p. 5). Or perhaps these students really *don't* know what they want to say. They have only vague ideas that they need to clarify, either orally or on paper.

Writing is so much slower than speech that writers sometimes forget how they began a sentence by the time they get to the end of it. Perhaps this is why the individual parts of garbles make sense, even though the garble as a whole is as twisted and disjointed as a derailed train. "The second part of the essay" makes sense; "Ruskin's lecture, 'Of Queens' Gardens,'" makes sense; and "the Victorian woman's function was to help and guide her mate in the business world" makes sense. But when the three phrases are strung together, they do not make sense as a sentence.

The student who wrote this sentence actually meant to say something like this: "The second part of the essay deals with a lecture called "Of Queens' Gardens," in which John Ruskin expressed the notion that the Victorian woman's function was to help and guide her mate in the business world."

Why didn't the student write it that way? Possibly because she did not understand the necessity of assembling a sentence so that its parts fit together, rather than tossing together two or three good phrases. Possibly because she did not understand that assembling sentences means reading them over carefully and slowly, moving parts around, adding words and deleting words until at last they all snap in place with a satisfying click.

It takes time to do that sort of work. And practice. And patience.

If your reader has marked part of your writing with a question mark, read the passage out loud slowly and try to hear it with the ears of someone who does not know in advance what you are trying to say. You might practice first on some of the garbles in the exercise below.

EXERCISE

Try to discover what the writer was trying to say in each of the following garbles. What do you think caused each garble? A lack of clear thinking? A failure of vocabulary? A failure to assemble the sentence rather than toss it together? If you can, express the writer's intention in a good sentence or two of your own.

a. In my point of view, I disagree and agree with parts of the essay.
b. There are one or two things I agree with the author.
c. The fact that the players seem to be gladiators is due to the high school scouting and other means of recruiting and have paid off in the finding and developing of the most talented subjects, not the training of what's available on the university's campus.
d. Limit the size of coaching staffs and reduce the salary of the head coach is another reduction by the author.
e. Often I am awakened by the sound of screaming teenyboppers

and the splash of cold water being childishly thrown at one another.

f. In the minds of some men just as the author of this essay women love, honor, and obey their husbands.

g. The evidence Janeway gives is that seeing the middle class before its rise and the position of women today the analogy is the same and; therefore since the bourgeoisie rose in importance and influence so will the position of women rise in importance and influence.

FINAL CHECKPOINT FOR ALL PAPERS

Every experienced writer welcomes the advice of a good editor. Editorial advice can deal with substance and organization or with matters of style and punctuation. Earlier checkpoints have encouraged you and your classmates to make suggestions to one another about style and organization. This final checkpoint focuses on style and mechanics, but you should encourage your reader to make other suggestions as well.

Professional writers usually make suggestions and corrections with a set of symbols called proofreaders' marks. Some of the marks that you and your classmates might find useful are illustrated in the passage at the top of page 161.

When you are ready to type your final copy, swap papers with a classmate and use the proofreaders' symbols to make suggestions to each other. Also use the symbols below, each of which was discussed in Chapter Six or Chapter Seven.

 This symbol can be used to indicate letters, words, or phrases that should be taken out. The long part of the symbol crosses through the unnecessary material and e-shaped tail dangles in the margin. See p. 138 for a discussion of wordiness.

 Underline words that do not mean what the writer seems to think they mean, and put this symbol in the margin to indicate "Wrong Word." See p. 140 for discussion.

 Underline expressions that seem unidiomatic and put this symbol in the margin. See p. 141 for discussion.

 Underline expressions that seem too informal for their context, and put this symbol in the margin to indicate colloquial diction. See p. 142 for discussion.

In classroom work make your suggestions lightly in pencil, preferably in the margin. Use a caret to show where words or punctuation should be added or changed and put a slash mark after each comment in the margin. If a comma should be changed into a period, circle it. three short lines under a small letter indicate that the letter should be a capital; A slash through a capital letter means that it should be small. A curved line can indicate that two letters should be transposed. A pair of half moons indicates that a space within a word should be closed up. A ticktacktoe sign shows where a space should be added. The paragraph symbol shows where you think a new paragraph should begin.

The paragraph symbol preceded by the word "no" indicates that the paragraph break is inappropriate.

Another way to say the same thing is to draw a curved line from the end of one paragraph to the beginning of the paragraph that should be joined to it.

 Underline expressions that seem too technical or too stilted for their context, and put this symbol in the margin to indicate pretentious diction. See p. 144 for discussion.

 Underline expressions that call attention to themselves because you have seen or heard them many times before. Write "Cliché" in the margin. See p. 147 for discussion.

 If you notice any form of the verb *be* followed by a noun or adjective that should be converted to a verb, underline the expression and put this symbol in the margin. See p. 150 for discussion.

If you find a passive voice form that could be better expressed in the active voice, underline the verb and put this symbol in the margin. See p. 151 for discussion.

 If the subject and predicate do not make sense together, underline them and put this symbol in the margin. See p. 153 for discussion.

 If a series of words or expressions should be made parallel in form, underline the series and put this symbol in the margin. See p. 154 for discussion.

 If words or structures are repeated for no good reason, underline the repetitions and put this symbol in the margin. See p. 157 for discussion.

 If phrases or sentences do not make sense to you at all, underline them and put this symbol in the margin. See p. 158 for discussion.

Swap papers again and examine the marks your classmate has made on your draft. Take a few minutes to ask questions of each other or to explain your suggestions for improvement. Repeat this checkpoint every time you make a new copy of your paper.

Chapter Eight

---◄◆►---

Style:
Ten Lessons

Perhaps the most precise definition of style is a statement often attributed to Ella Fitzgerald: "It ain't what you do, it's the way howdya do it." Given exactly the same material to work with and asked to put it into a few sentences, different writers will compose different works, some easier to read and more pleasing to the eye and ear than others. The difference— when the subject matter is constant—is style; not what is done, but the way it is done.

Just as professional writers normally have more words at their disposal than amateurs, they also have more ways of putting the words together. Although there is no known short-cut to acquiring the vocabulary of a professional writer, there is a fairly quick method for acquiring a professional's range of sentence structures. In fact you probably already have a command of these structures. They all occur (or at least can occur) in speech. And you have probably been exposed to most of these structures in your reading. In short, you can learn these structures quickly because you already have a passive knowledge of them (you can read them without difficulty), and you may have even used them in your conversation.

The first nine lessons in this chapter are designed to help you increase the range of sentence structures you have at your disposal. The last lesson deals with style as a projection of personality. More specifically, the topics to be covered are these:

1. The Problem of Synonymy
2. Rhythm, Variety, and Length
3. Present Participles
4. Past Participles
5. Appositives
6. Absolutes
7. Combinations
8. Series
9. Balanced, Periodic, and Cumulative Sentences
10. Style as the Person

1. The Problem of Synonymy

Study the information contained in this series of very short sentences.

There was a tree. There was a barn. The tree was scrawny. The tree was next to the barn. It was a pecan tree. Spider worms had attacked the tree. Woodpeckers had attacked the tree. There was a mower. The mower was old. The mower was rusty. The mower was abandoned. The mower was in the shade of the tree. There were some goldenrods. There were some violets. The mower was nestled in the violets. The mower was nestled in the goldenrods.

If two writers tried to express these bits of information in fewer sentences, the results might be as different as the two examples below.

There was a scrawny pecan tree that had been attacked by spider worms and woodpeckers. There was also an old and rusty mower abandoned in the shade of the tree. The mower was nestled in some goldenrods and violets.

Next to the barn was a tree, a scrawny pecan, attacked by spider worms and woodpeckers. In its shade, nestled among goldenrods and violets, was an abandoned mower. The mower was rusty and old.

If you read these two versions aloud, you will probably discern a considerable difference between them. The difference is style. More specifically, the difference is that the second version makes use of a number of grammatical structures — ways of putting words together — that the first version does not use.

Some scholars would object to the notion that style is the difference between two expressions of the same ideas. They would argue that if you change the way something is said, you change its meaning. To some extent they are right. Even changing a sentence from active voice (A snake bit Maria) to passive voice (Maria was bitten by a snake) changes the emphasis in ways that are hard to define, and thus changes the meaning. So before you learn a new range of sentence structures — as you will in the next few lessons — you should realize that tinkering with sentence structure may distort the meaning you want to express; on the other hand, tinkering with sentence structure may clarify your meaning, not only for your readers but for yourself.

Suppose, for example, you had these classic bits of information to express in a single sentence: "Socrates was old" and "Socrates was wise." You could join them with a *but*; but notice how much difference in meaning there is between these two versions.

Socrates was old, but wise.
Socrates was wise, but old.

Although the information contained in the sentences is the same, the meaning is different. The first version makes readers feel a little better about Socrates because it emphasizes his wisdom rather than his age.

The following bits of information can also be combined in a

number of ways: "The President called for wage controls" and "The wage controls are unfair to working people."

Writers who want to suggest that the President deliberately did something unfair can arrange the information this way:

The President called for wage controls that are unfavorable to working people.

Writers who want to leave open the possibility that the President was not aware of the unfairness, could arrange the information this way:

The wage controls called for by the President are unfair to working people.

Both versions contain the same information, but they have different meanings.

The point of all this is that the same ideas can be arranged differently on the page to achieve different effects. Some arrangements will suit the writer's meaning better than others. Good writers are aware of the nearly infinite possibilities for rearranging words, and they tinker until they find the arrangement that best expresses their meaning.

EXERCISES

1. Combine each of the following groups of sentences in as many different ways as you can and study the different effects of each combination on meaning.

a. The calf was born without a tail.
  The calf was stuck in a dangerous bog.
b. John Doe has been accused of tax fraud.
  John Doe has recently entered the race for commissioner.
  John Doe supports the local orphanage.
c. Cecil has few friends.
  Cecil's friends are extremely fond of him.
d. The Bullets played well.
  The Bullets lost.
e. The Art Institute is now open.
  It has a large exhibition of Monets.
  It has long lines of people waiting to get in.

2. Put the following ideas into fewer sentences. Make them read as smoothly as you can. Then compare your results with the work of your classmates. Read several versions aloud and listen carefully for differences in style and meaning.

A newspaperman observed the city. His name was Henry Villard. He remarked that it did not contain one good restaurant. He remarked that it had no end of bar rooms. Most of the bar rooms were doing business. The business was fine. He felt the city looked like an untidy overgrown village. He felt the city looked indolent. He felt the city looked unfinished. He felt the city looked crowded. He felt the city looked somehow vibrant with life. Most of the streets were unpaved. Most of the streets were muddy. The plaza east of the Capitol was open. The plaza was cluttered with castings. The plaza was cluttered with building blocks. The castings were for the dome. The building blocks were for the dome. The dome was still incomplete. A battery of regular artillery unlimbered. They unlimbered casually. They unlimbered beyond the litter. They unlimbered as day came in. They took position. The position was in full view of the platform. The platform was temporary. On the platform Abraham Lincoln would presently take the oath. The oath would be as sixteenth President of the United States.

If you are curious about how an accomplished writer would put these bits of information together, see Bruce Catton, *The Coming Fury* (New York: Doubleday & Company, 1961), p. 259.

2. Rhythm, Variety, and Length

Some writing teachers will tell you to write short, clear sentences. But if you do, other teachers will tell you that your style is too choppy, that your sentences lack maturity. They'll tell you to combine your short sentences into longer sentences. Who's right? To answer this question for yourself, examine the sentence length in published work of recognized quality. Here, to begin with, is a passage from *The Dragons of Eden*, a best-selling book by astronomer Carl Sagan.

Yet we are able to date events in the remote past. Geological stratification and radioactive dating provide information on archaeological, paleontological and geological events; and astrophysical theory provides data on the ages of planetary surfaces, stars, and the Milky Way Galaxy, as well as an estimate of the time that has elapsed since that extraordinary event called the Big Bang—an explosion that involved all of the matter and energy in the present universe. The Big Bang may be the beginning of the universe, or it may be a discontinuity in which information about the earlier history of the universe was destroyed. But it is certainly the earliest event about which we have any record.

The sentences in this paragraph range from a low of 11 words (the first sentence) to a high of 63 words (the second sentence). If you count them in order, they skip from low numbers to high and back down again like a ball bouncing on a roulette wheel: 11, 63, 28, 13. The truth, then, is that both groups of teachers are right. Good writers write long sentences. They also write short sentences. But most importantly they vary the length of their sentences over a wide range.

If you read Sagan's paragraph aloud, you will discover that one effect of the variation in sentence length is a rhythm that is pleasing because it is not monotonous. In prose, rhythm is related to pauses more than to stresses. A variety of sentence lengths means a variety of stretches between the strong pauses that periods mark, which breaks the monotony that would occur in a string of sentences of the same length.

Variety of sentence length, however, is just one way of achieving the irregularly spaced pauses that make the rhythm of a passage pleasing. Another source of rhythm is the internal structure of the sentences. Pauses within sentences— particularly pauses that occur at commas, dashes, parentheses and other punctuation that sets material off from the rest of the sentence—also contribute to the rhythmic effect. One way to study the rhythm of sentences, then, is to notice not only the variety of sentence length, but the frequency of pauses within sentences. In Sagan's paragraph, there are no pauses within the first sentence, six within the second, one within the third, and none within the fourth. If we replaced the words between punctuation marks with numbers, the pattern in Sagan's four sentences would look like this:

11.
9, 4; 11, 1, 5, 19–14.
10, 18.
13.

Since pauses account for rhythm, we can say that only the first
and fourth sentences resemble each other rhythmically, for
they are both roughly the same length and neither has any
internal pauses. But the second and third sentences are nothing like each other in rhythm, nor are they anything like the
first and fourth sentences. Sagan's prose is pleasing in rhythm
because the sentences are varied in length and because their
internal structure is marked with pauses at various intervals.

It would be wrong to think, however, that prose must always
have the sort of internal rhythm that Sagan's sentences have.
Sometimes writers will deliberately repeat the structure (and
therefore the rhythm) of consecutive sentences to emphasize
parallel or contrasting ideas.

> In London, they ate Indian food. In Paris, they ate American food.

> On the first issue, we rule that the defendants did not conspire to
> sell their land to relatives at a tax auction, because no evidence of a
> conspiracy has been presented. On the second issue, we rule that
> the complainants are not entitled to the mineral rights, because
> these rights were lost when the land was sold for taxes.

In each of these pairs of examples, the pauses occur in almost
identical places, underscoring the parallel structure and
parallel ideas.

Sometimes writers use strings of short sentences without
any internal pauses. Here is an example by Kati Marton from
an article in the *Atlantic*.

> I sense that something is wrong the minute my friend opens the
> door to receive me. We have not seen each other in twenty-two
> years. It does not seem to matter. He says I haven't changed. I tell
> him the same. We both know we are lying.

The monotony of rhythm is deliberate. Marton is writing about an emotionally charged situation in short, clipped sentences, the sort of sentences we speak when we are afraid our feelings might get away from us in more expansive sentences. The effect of the passage is to put distance between the writer and the world she is writing about, a tough objectivity in which many readers would recognize the influence of Hemingway.

> Outside it was getting dark. The street-light came on outside the window. The two men at the counter read the menu. From the other end of the counter Nick Adams watched them. He had been talking to George when they came in.
>
> — Ernest Hemingway, "The Killers"

Monotony in sentence rhythm becomes a problem when it does not serve a purpose — when it does not emphasize parallel ideas or contribute to the emotional tone of a passage. Monotony also becomes a problem when a sentence or any part of a sentence goes on for too long without any internal pauses. Here is an example written by a federal judge.

> The government's concern lest the Act be held to be a regulation of production or consumption rather than of marketing is attributable to a few dicta and decisions of this court which might be understood to lay it down that activities such as "production," "manufacturing," and "mining" are strictly "local" and, except in special circumstances which are not present here, cannot be regulated under the commerce power because their effects upon interstate commerce are, as a matter of law, only indirect. [81 words]

There are lots of pauses within this sentence, but notice how long you have to go before coming to the first pause: 44 words, or about twice as long as the longest stretch between punctuation marks in any example we have examined so far. Long stretches of words without pauses are generally difficult to read. As a rule, any stretch that gets far beyond 20 words probably needs to be trimmed and rephrased for clarity.

If pauses were the only difference between mature writing and immature writing, you could achieve maturity simply by sprinkling punctuation marks over your page. Unfortunately, adding a few punctuation marks won't make your prose any better. What you need to add in all probability is a wider variety of grammatical structures, many of which can result in the sort of pauses that make writing readable and pleasant. These structures include present participles, past participles, appositives, absolutes, combinations, and series — all of which will be examined in the next several lessons.

As you work through these lessons, keep three principles in mind. First, remember that no two ways of structuring a sentence have exactly the same meaning. In choosing between sentences that are nearly synonymous, choose the one that best expresses what you want to say.

Secondly, remember that long sentences are not necessarily better than short sentences. The purpose of these exercises is not to make you write longer sentences, but simply to give you a greater variety of sentence structures to choose from, no matter how long or short the sentences are.

Thirdly, as you try out some of these new sentence structures in your own writing, remember to choose them with their context in mind. If you have a choice, try not to write two or more consecutive sentences with the same rhythm unless you are deliberately using parallel rhythm to highlight parallel ideas or to create a particular emotional tone.

EXERCISES

1. Printed below is a seven-sentence paragraph from *The Western Intellectual Tradition* by Jacob Bronowski and Bruce Mazlish (New York: Harper Torchbooks, 1962), p. 190. Analyze the variety of length and structure of these sentences by counting the words between punctuation marks. Thus the first sentence, which has 9 words and no internal punctuation would be represented by "9." The second sentence with 8 words before a comma and 21 words after it would be represented by "8, 21." Is the rhythm of this passage any more or less varied than the rhythm of Sagan's paragraph as it was analyzed in the preceding section?

Newton was by no means lacking in practical interests. He himself made the instruments for his experiments, he invented the reflecting telescope in which the stars are seen in a parabolic mirror, and he spent the last thirty years of his life in the very practical administration and reform of the Royal Mint. In this sense, Newton is heir to the tradition of Francis Bacon and stands on the shoulders of Hooke and his inventive colleagues.

What is new in Newton is something else. He is able to use the experimental method to set up a new system of fundamental concepts—the kind of system which Aristotle had set up, and which the school of Bacon had dismissed. It had been necessary to break the hold of Aristotle and the rooted belief that nature could be explained by self-evident principles; and this the first experimenters of the Royal Society had done. But when this had been done, a new basic system was needed, founded this time not on self-evident notions but on notions which would turn out, in their consequences, to match the facts of experience. This Newton knew how to do, and this is the inductive basis of modern science.

2. Use the method explained in Exercise 1 above to analyze the variety of length and structure in these sentences from *Stilwell and the American Experience in China* by Barbara W. Tuchman (New York: Bantam Books, 1972), p. 677.

There was no support now that could have been effective. Born of the imperfect Revolution of 1911, crippled by the Japanese before it was fully established, and renegade to its origins, the Kuomintang had spent its mandate in one generation. In December 1948 the Communists took the crucial city of Hsuchow, the legendary key to control of China. In April 1949 their forces swept across the Yangtze. In ensuing weeks the Generalissimo's Government, followed by some two million adherents, decamped to Formosa where it successfully reestablished itself with American support. The Middle Kingdom was left to the ungentle reign of a new Revolution.

3. Use the same system to analyze the length and variety of sentence structures in the last paper you wrote for any class. Compare the results with the figures you developed in exercises 1 and 2 and with the figures given for Sagan's paragraph in the discussion above. Do you have a wide variety of structures or are you limited to one or two types? Do you ever mix very short sentences with long ones, or are most of your sentences within a few words of their average length?

4. A more advanced version of exercises 1 through 3 would be to use T-units instead of sentences as a basis for your analysis. A T-unit consists of an independent clause plus all the words and phrases that depend on it grammatically. Researchers prefer the T-unit to the sentence as a basis for analysis because sentence length often depends upon arbitrary habits of punctuation.

If you would like to experiment with a T-unit analysis of a prose passage, choose a passage that has no sentence fragments and no dialogue. Divide the passage into T-units and count the number of words between punctuation marks within each T-unit. Do professional writers tend to vary T-unit length as much as they vary sentence length? Do they tend to vary the number of pauses within T-units as much as they vary the number of pauses within sentences? How does your own writing compare with professional writing in an analysis of this sort?

3. Present Participles

In this lesson — and in the next several lessons in this series — you will learn a few devices professional writers use to get more information into their sentences without making the sentences hard to read. In general, these devices are called free modifiers; they are free in that they are not essential to the meaning of the rest of the sentence. For this reason, they are all set off by commas.

Example

Toasting the women at the table, Brezhnev gallantly reached into a bouquet and handed one rose to Pat Nixon.

—*Time*, 8 July 1974

In this example, "Toasting the women at the table" is a present participial phrase used as a free modifier. Present participial phrases are easy to recognize. They usually begin with an -*ing* verb form that tells what a noun elsewhere in the sentence is doing. In the example, "toasting" is the present participle; it tells what "Brezhnev" is doing.

Why don't inexperienced writers use present participles this way? Inexperienced writers tend to limit themselves to the structures they use in ordinary conversation, and nobody, not even a good writer, speaks many sentences with present participles used as free modifiers. To test this assertion, read *Time*'s sentence aloud and try to imagine yourself saying it spontaneously to a friend as you walk together to the laundromat.

It sounds artificial, doesn't it? And that's why students are afraid to write this structure. They are afraid of sounding artificial.

What they don't realize is that good writing *is* artificial, in the best sense of the word. Instead of limiting themselves to the natural and unedited structures of ordinary speech, good writers consciously or unconsciously organize these structures into pleasing and efficient patterns that would be unnatural (and perhaps impossible) in speech. One of the unnatural advantages of writing is that it gives you time to plan structures that are more elegant than those you have time to plan at the speed of ordinary conversation.

EXERCISES

1. A good way to improve your writing is to imitate professional models. To get a sense of how professionals use participial phrases, write a sentence of your own just like each of the professionally written sentences below. The examples are broken up into sense phrases, and the participial phrases are printed in color type to help you recognize them. An arrow connects each participle with the word it modifies. It may help to read both the examples and your imitations of them out loud.

She leaned forward attentively,
— listening to Saul Bird,
— trying to understand what he was saying.

—**Joyce Carol Oates**

— Ignoring his sister,
— and stepping on one of my feet,
Charles repeated his question.

—**J. D. Salinger**

2. Below are groups of simple sentences derived from longer sentences written by the authors indicated. Combine the sentences in each group into one sentence using present participles. Then try to be alert for opportunities to combine sentences in your own writing projects.

a. He felt something in his blood.
   It warmed.
   It opened.
   It came to life in arrogant protestation.

—**from Joyce Carol Oates**

b. He turned up the driveway of his own house.
He held on to the gate for support.

— from John Cheever

c. Susanna changed her clothes.
She took off her pajama bottoms.
She put on a pair of blue jeans.

— from Joyce Carol Oates

3. Add two or more present participles to each of the following sentences.

a. The bus hit the side of the bridge.
b. The actors stood behind the closed curtain.
c. Myra looked toward the door.

4. Write three original sentences using one or more present participial phrases.

5. Take two of the sentences you wrote for Exercise 3 and try to write them with the participial phrases in different places. Study the difference between these versions and the originals. Is either preferable in itself? Would context make one preferable?

CAUTION: DON'T GET HOOKED ON PRESENT PARTICIPLES. Present participles are not in themselves better than other structures, so don't start cluttering your essays with *-ings*. The present participial phrase is merely one of several possible ways to add information to a sentence; it is an option you should consider in the light of context, rhythm, and the meaning you are trying to express.

4. Past Participles

You know that highway right there, built by the Martians, is over sixteen centuries old and still in good condition.

— Ray Bradbury, "August 2002: Night Meeting"

The cluster of words "built by the Martians" is a past participial phrase. A past participle is the form of a verb that fits in the blank in "having been _____ too often." Past and present participles can and do occur in the same sentence.

Used as a free modifier, the past participle describes a noun elsewhere in the sentence. In the example above, the past participle "built" describes the noun "highway."

Inexperienced writers tend not to use this form because it does not occur in their speech. They are more comfortable with the structures like subordinate clauses:

> You know that highway right there that the Martians built is over sixteen centuries old. . . .

Or they create compound sentences:

> You know that highway right there was built by the Martians and it is over sixteen centuries old. . . .

Or they write smaller simple sentences:

> You know that highway right there was built by Martians. It is over sixteen centuries old and still in good condition.

Of course, the past participial phrase is not necessarily a better form in itself, but knowing about it and knowing how to use it will broaden your choice of constructions. Past participial phrases can come anywhere in the sentence and modify nearly any element in it. They can precede what they modify:

> Seated behind an elevated desk in the high-ceilinged courtroom, Judge Harold Rothwax does not look at all pleased.

> —Loudon Wainwright

They can come after what they modify:

> Her eyes, lost in the fatty ridges of her face, looked like two pieces of coal pressed into a lump of dough.

> —William Faulkner

They can even be separated from what they modify, if the meaning is clear:

> It vanished, sucked into invisibility like a match flame.

> —William Faulkner

Participles are said to dangle when they do not modify a noun elsewhere in the sentence or when they seem to modify the wrong noun.

Erasing the blackboards, the lights were turned off and the class-room locked.

Dazed by their own success, the game was a splendid display of school spirit.

In the first example, the structure of the sentence suggests that the lights were erasing the blackboards; in the second, "dazed" has no appropriate word to modify. Both "erasing" and "dazed" are dangling participles in these sentences. For more about dangling participles, see **G11**.

EXERCISES

1. Write sentences of your own, using past participial phrases like those in the sentences below. It may help to read both the originals and your imitations out loud.

a. She suspected that, frightened and puzzled, he contemplated alarm.

—**Mary McCarthy**

b. K., enormously moved, sat on the floor and confessed.

—**Joyce Carol Oates**

c. He started towards the East, followed by the Arab.

—**Albert Camus**

2. Below are three groups of simple sentences derived from longer sentences written by the authors indicated. Turn each group into one longer sentence, using past participial phrases.

a. Helen wrote to Jenny.
Helen was exasperated.

—**from John Irving**

b. The pool was fed by an artesian well with a high iron content.
The pool was a pale shade of green.

—**from John Cheever**

c. But there was also a great deal of optimism.
The optimism was shared by all levels of the black community.
— from James Alan McPherson

3. Below are three simple sentences. Add one or more past participial phrases to each.

a. Ralph returned to the lab.
b. The boxer finally collapsed.
c. We returned home.

4. Create three original sentences, using one or more past participial phrases in each of them.
5. If possible, rearrange the position of the participle in your original sentences and study the difference in rhythm and meaning each arrangement makes.

5. Appositives

Another common device is the appositive — a noun that renames another noun in a sentence.

Example

A neighbor, a woman, complained to the mayor, Judge Stevens.
— William Faulkner

In this example, "a woman" is in apposition to "A neighbor," and "Judge Stevens" is in apposition to "the mayor."

Notice that appositives are usually free modifiers and they are set off by commas.

Appositives add detail to the words they are in apposition to: "a woman" adds detail to "a neighbor," and "Judge Stevens" tells us, specifically, who the mayor was.

Often the appositives themselves are given more detail as they are expanded into phrases with adjectives and other modifiers. Notice how the appositive phrases in the following examples add information to the sentences without making them hard to understand. Notice, too, how these phrases interrupt the flow of the sentences when they are read aloud, giving them a pleasing and interesting rhythm.

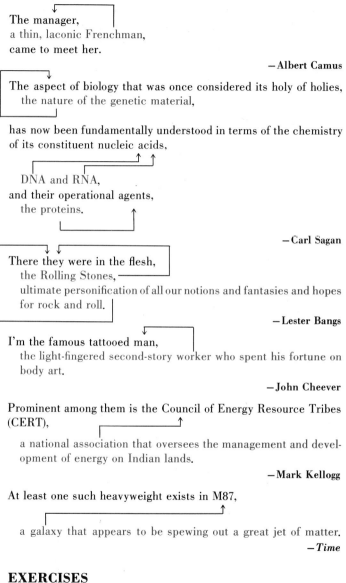

The manager,
a thin, laconic Frenchman,
came to meet her.

—**Albert Camus**

The aspect of biology that was once considered its holy of holies,
the nature of the genetic material,

has now been fundamentally understood in terms of the chemistry
of its constituent nucleic acids,

DNA and RNA,
and their operational agents,
the proteins.

—**Carl Sagan**

There they were in the flesh,
the Rolling Stones,
ultimate personification of all our notions and fantasies and hopes
for rock and roll.

—**Lester Bangs**

I'm the famous tattooed man,
the light-fingered second-story worker who spent his fortune on
body art.

—**John Cheever**

Prominent among them is the Council of Energy Resource Tribes
(CERT),
a national association that oversees the management and development of energy on Indian lands.

—**Mark Kellogg**

At least one such heavyweight exists in M87,

a galaxy that appears to be spewing out a great jet of matter.

—***Time***

EXERCISES

1. Write sentences of your own, using appositives like those in
the examples above. It may help to read both the originals and your
imitations out loud.

2. Below are three sets of short sentences derived from longer sentences written by the authors indicated. Combine each group into a single sentence with one or more appositives.

a. This was none other than Alaunia Alunosna.
This was the shopkeeper's daughter.
This was a prostitute with a look of exultation on her timid face.
— from S. J. Perelman

b. There is still in his eyes the thing you noted all morning.
There is still an extreme vulnerability to pain.
There is still an equal determination not to show the pain.
— from Tom Burke

c. That night the Board of Aldermen met.
The board consisted of three graybeards and one younger man.
The younger man was a member of the rising generation.
— from William Faulkner

3. Add one or more appositives to the following simple sentences. Vary the position of the appositives.

a. Harold brought his new girlfriend to class.
b. Mother has located the perfect house.
c. The class was astonished by the new teacher.

4. Write a few sentences of your own with subordinate clauses beginning with *who* or *which* followed by *is, are, was,* or *were.* Then rewrite each sentence, changing the subordinate clause to an appositive.

5. Take two of the sentences you wrote in Exercise 4 and practice varying the position of the appositives, as in the following example:

The general, a habitual bungler, tripped over a chair as he entered the tent.

A habitual bungler, the general tripped over a chair as he entered the tent.

6. Absolutes

An absolute phrase is a sentence modifier made up of a noun that is itself modified by an adjective or participle.

Example

"Just one kiss," she pleaded, her breath hot against my neck.

—S. J. Perelman, "Strictly from Hunger"

The phrase "her breath hot against my neck" is an absolute phrase. In this example, "breath" is the noun and "hot" the adjective modifying it.

Unlike appositives, the noun in an absolute phrase does *not* rename a noun that appears elsewhere in the sentence; in fact, it has no grammatical connection with the rest of the sentence. It is this lack of connectedness that makes absolutes "absolute."

Notice, however, how the adjective or participle in each of the examples below modifies a noun *within* the absolute phrase—not a noun elsewhere in the sentence.

Notice, too, that absolute phrases are set off by commas.

In the central parade ground sat Max Phushnuts, his chest glittering.

—S. J. Perelman

All the passengers,

heads lowered,

seemed to be listening to the voice of the wind loosened across the endless plateau.

—Albert Camus

They sat together in the classroom, when they came to class,

their arms folded,

their eyes beady and undefeated.

—Joyce Carol Oates

Jagger came down from his cloud, sitting cross legged centerstage,

his eyes placid-lake blue.

—R. Greenfield

EXERCISES

1. Write sentences with absolutes like those in the examples. Read both the examples and your imitations out loud to compare them.

2. From each group of simple sentences below, make one sentence with one or more absolutes.

a. Mary Birke sat next to the pool.
Her eyes were bloodshot.
Her feet were dangling in the water.
b. The squirrel scampered up the tree and paused on a branch just out of the dog's range.
Its eyes glowed furiously at the helpless attacker.
c. It was old Ginny, carrying her lunch in a paper sack.
Her hair was bound up in big purple curlers.
Her nylons were rolled tightly around her knees.

3. Add one or more nominative absolutes to each of the sentences below.

a. The river was swollen.
b. Cooper stormed into the saloon.
c. The defendants stood in silence.

4. Write three original sentences, each containing one or more nominative absolutes.

5. Take two of the sentences you wrote for Exercise 4 and practice varying the position of the nominative absolutes.

7. Combinations

Sometimes in professional writing, the four constructions you have just studied — present participles, past participles, appositives, and absolutes — occur in various combinations in the same sentence.

Example
Coming down early for dinner, red satin dress cut low, she attacked the silence.

— Elizabeth Bowen

In this sentence, the opening phrase, "Coming down early for dinner," is a present participial phrase, and the next phrase, "red satin dress cut low," is an absolute.

Other combinations are possible. Appositives and past participles can be used in the same sentence —

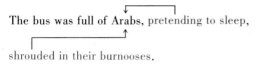

Olenka, the daughter of the retired collegiate

assessor, Pleyanniakow, was sitting on her
                    lost in thought.

— **Anton Chekhov**

— as can a past participle and a present participle:

The bus was full of Arabs, pretending to sleep,

shrouded in their burnooses.

— **Albert Camus**

And so on.

EXERCISES

1. Imitate the construction of the following sentences. Read your imitations aloud very carefully to make sure that the various word groups modify what they are supposed to modify.

a. People today are hidden away inside themselves,

alienated,   (past part.)

living in despair.   (pres. part.)

— **Donald Barthelme**

b.   The little boy,

Phillip,   (app.)

came down to visit and stood behind his father's chair,

watching everybody.   (pres. part.)

— **Joyce Carol Oates**

c. Standing barefoot in the deposits of the highway, (pres. part.)

beercans, rags, and blow-out patches,   (app.)

exposed to all kinds of ridicule,   (past part.)

he seemed pitiful.

— **John Cheever**

d.   I lay on my back a bit later,

vinegar poultice on my forehead,   (nom. abs.)

drinking a cup of steaming tea.   (pres. part.)

— **S. J. Perelman**

2. The following groups of short sentences were derived from longer sentences written by the authors indicated. Combine each group into a single sentence, using any of the constructions you have learned in these lessons.

a. She became a figure.
She existed only for the benefit of others.
She was an instrument by which the facts were communicated.
— from Joyce Carol Oates

b. And he turns and comes loping over to our table.
He is smiling.
His hands are in his pockets.
— from James Baldwin

3. Add two or more different constructions to each of the following sentences.

a. When the wind finally subsided, they returned to their home.
b. Only the gas station was left.
c. He reached inside the hollow tree.

4. Create three original sentences, using at least two constructions from the four you have learned in these lessons.
5. Take one of your original sentences and experiment with moving one of the constructions about.

8. Series

There lay the dead body of a woman, the white face turned upwards, the hands thrown out, the clothing deranged, the long hair in tangles.

— Ambrose Bierce

Another device used by professionals is the series. A series, the repetition of identical or similar structures, is a pleasing device in any art.

In writing, a series is simply a group of two or more words or word clusters with parallel grammatical functions. Don't worry if the definition eludes you; you should be able to understand what a series is by working with the examples below.

If you read Bierce's sentence out loud, with expression, you should notice that (a) it's not the kind of sentence we normally speak; (b) it differs from normal speech precisely in its formal arrangement of a series of word clusters.

Breaking the sentence up into sense phrases may make its structure clearer to you:

> There lay the dead body of a woman,
>   the white face turned upwards,
>   the hands thrown out,
>   the clothing deranged,
>   the long hair in tangles.

In this particular case, the word clusters in the series are absolutes. But almost any kind of words or word clusters can be put into series — subjects, verbs, objects, participial phrases, subordinate clauses, and even larger units.

Like all the other devices you've studied, the series is not in itself a better way of expressing ideas; it is simply an option that professional writers choose when it fits their purposes. Ordinary writers, however, rarely use the series, probably because it does not occur in ordinary speech. Ordinary writing is ordinary because it is speech-bound: it is limited to the relatively simple structures of conversation.

EXERCISES

1. The following sentences exemplify series, some more complex than others. After reading each sentence carefully, try to write a sentence of your own, following the professional model as closely as you can. It may help to read both the examples and your imitations out loud.

a. A series of two present participial phrases near the end of a sentence:

> He went on,
>   stepping happily with his new-shod feet,
>   feeling the warm sun on his back.

> —Shirley Jackson

b. A series of two present participial phrases toward the beginning of a sentence:

A car
    careening and rolling down a bank,
    battering and smashing its occupants every inch of the way,
can wrap itself so thoroughly around a tree that the front and rear
bumpers interlock.

                                —J. C. Furnas

c. A series of past participles at the beginning of a sentence:

Lost,
bewildered,
and dry-eyed,
they stood together in the middle of the room.

                                —Dan Jacobson

d. A series of past participles at the end of a sentence (and a series
of subjects at the beginning):

  "Dixie," "The Stripper," and "Potato Peel"
were the three records in greatest use for this class,
    played first at half speed,
    then blasted at full tempo.

                                —Terry Southern

e. A series of subjects:

Bricks,
rocks,
and bottles,
the weapons of the rabble, rattled around them.

                                —*Newsweek*

f. A series of verbs:

The battle-weary marshalls
    puffed cigarettes,
    sipped coffee,
    lined up for field rations of franks and sauerkraut.

                                —*Newsweek*

g. A series of direct objects:

I remember
    a few farmers,
    a woman dressed in mourning,
    a wounded and happy soldier.

                          —José Luis Borges

h. A series of appositive phrases introduced by a colon:

We must acknowledge, therefore, that a phantasmagoria of heroes
parades across our lives after all:

> Rock stars magnified by stupendous lightshows and banks of
> loudspeakers;
> athletes purified to a lean, entrancing skill made magical by the
> huge sums of money they earn
> transatlantic balloonists;
> mountain climbers;
> solitary around-the-world sailors, like Sir Francis Chichester;
> Philippe Petit, who crossed between the towers of the World
> Trade Center in New York on a wire last year.

—Paul Zweig

i. A series of subordinate clauses at the beginning of a sentence:

> Because the "serious" world is desperately unheroic;
> because we are all equal and, therefore, cramped in our mind's
> perspective;
> because failure and intimacy take up so much room in our sense
> of ourselves,

we squint sideways into a circus fairway of ballooning figures who
are free, lighter than air in their lovely futility.

—Paul Zweig

2. Where do professional writers get material for series? Sometimes they seem to go out of their way to invent it. At other times
they make series out of bits of information that inexperienced
writers might include in less formal patterns. Practice forming
series by adding elements parallel to the phrases italicized below.

a. Calvin sat on the edge of the chair, his *hand waving in the air*,
b. The fans began to arrive, *old men with green and white ties*,
c. Rastus came in late, *carrying a beer can*,

3. An important rule to remember about writing a series is that
when one member of the series is noticeably longer than the others,
it usually should be placed last. To understand this rule, all you
need to do is read an example of a sentence that violates it.

Awkward: His book dealt with muggings, inflation, the new wave
of kidnapping in Italy, and pollution.

Better: His book dealt with muggings, inflation, pollution, and
the new wave of kidnapping in Italy.

Create three original sentences with a series in each, arranging the
elements of the series from shortest to longest.

9. Balanced, Periodic, and Cumulative Sentences

Among the many varieties of sentences you encounter in good writing, three types stand out from the others clearly enough to be given names: the balanced sentence, the periodic sentence, and the cumulative sentence. Most sentences do not conform to any of these three types; most sentences, like most people, are stubbornly individual and refused to be classified. But the three exceptional types are common enough in good prose to be worth study and imitation.

A balanced sentence is like a seesaw, with roughly equal loads on either side of a central point. The central point is usually a coordinate conjunction (*and, or, but, for*) or a semicolon.

> The world is very old, and human beings are very young.
>
> — Carl Sagan

> The Renaissance is the birth of modern history, and the Italian Peninsula is its birthplace.
>
> — Jacob Bronowski and Bruce Mazlish

> What Lincoln had just said might make interesting reading in the history books some day; what he would do in the immediate future would determine what sort of history was going to be written.
>
> — Bruce Catton

A balanced sentence is more than just an ordinary sentence in which two clauses are joined by a coordinate conjunction or a semicolon. In a balanced sentence, the meaning of each half is in some way parallel or antithetical to the other, and this parallelism is often underscored by the repetition of key words, phrases, or structures. In the first example quoted above, "world" is contrasted with "human beings," "old" is contrasted with "young," "very" is repeated, and in structure each half of the sentence is identical to the other. In the second example, the notion of birth in the first half is echoed by birthplace in the second half, and the two halves are closely similar in structure and rhythm, each with "is" as a verb. And in the third example, Lincoln's words in the first half of the sentence are contrasted with his deeds in the second half; the

contrast is underscored by the repetition of the structure—
each half beginning with "what"—by the repetition of "history," and by the opposition of what would be read in the
books in the first half of the sentence with what would be
written in them in the second half.

Sometimes the balance is carried out through meanings
rather than the words themselves, as in this next example, in
which the second half of the sentence explains the meaning of
the first without actually repeating its words or structure.

> Machiavelli was a practicing politician; he knew the twists and
> turns necessary to political existence.

Like all the other devices studied in these exercises, balanced sentences are not in themselves superior to other types.
They are to be used when they serve a purpose: when the balance underscores ideas that are genuinely parallel or antithetical, and when their rhythm fits in agreeably with the rhythm
of other sentences in their context. Balance is a very old stylistic device, dating back to classical times, when people depended more than they do now on formal speeches. The balance in sentences made their meaning easier to comprehend
and remember, just as Americans today remember a phrase
like "Ask not what your country can do for you; ask what you
can do for your country" because of its balanced structure.

Another sentence type that dates back to the days of formal
oratory is the periodic sentence. A periodic sentence is one
that delays the very possibility of a period until the end of the
sentence, where a climax, anticlimax, surprise, or point of
emphasis appears.

> The player whom everyone was booing last night, the one who
> missed the final shot just as the buzzer was sounding, the one who
> had served his team well in twenty games earlier this season even
> though he was suffering from an injured rib cage and a sprained
> ankle, has just quit the team.

Two rules apply to the construction of good periodic sentences. First, the information in the last phrase must be worth
waiting for. Secondly, the sentence must begin with parallel

structures, balanced structures, or other signals that help the reader store information as it accumulates.

The following example of a periodic sentence is 107 words long. And yet, because of the neat parallelism and balance in the first part of the sentence, it is intelligible even to small children, its intended audience.

> In the loveliest town of all, where the houses were white and high and the elm trees were green and higher than the houses, where the front yards were wide and pleasant and the back yards were bushy and worth finding out about, where the streets sloped down to the stream and the stream flowed quietly under the bridge, where the lawns ended in orchards and the orchards ended in fields and the fields ended in pastures and the pastures climbed the hill and disappeared over the top toward the wonderful wide sky, in this loveliest of all towns Stuart stopped to get a drink of sarsaparilla.
>
> — E. B. White, *Stuart Little*

Periodic sentences like White's were popular in classical prose (Cicero used them to great advantage) and in Victorian prose (Cardinal Newman was fond of them), and they appear occasionally even in very modern prose; but they are not as popular as they once were. Periodic sentences make demands of both readers and writers. They demand that readers remember the information at the beginning of a sentence for a long time — until the end is reached, giving that information its significance. They demand that the writers set out their information in neat, parallel rows (notice the four parallel "where" clauses in White's sentence, and the perfect balance within each clause) and, if necessary, remind the reader of what might have been forgotten (notice White's repetition in "loveliest of all towns").

Good periodic sentences take more planning — and therefore more time to write — than ordinary sentences. And because their effect is formal and dramatic, they should be reserved for formal or dramatic situations, leading either to a surprise ending like White's anticlimax, or to a point that the writer wants to emphasize. In his recently published memoirs, Justice Earl Warren used a sentence almost identical in structure to White's:

With his popularity, if Eisenhower had said that black children were still being discriminated against long after the adoption of the Thirteenth, Fourteenth, and Fifteenth Amendments, that the Supreme Court of the land had now declared it unconstitutional to continue such cruel practices, and that it should be the duty of every good citizen to help rectify more than eighty years of wrong-doing by honoring that decision — if he had said something to this effect, I think we would have been relieved of many of the racial problems which have continued to plague us.

This kind of sentence is heavy artillery. It is to be used only in situations that require it. A periodic sentence that leads up to an insignificant point is tedious, and a periodic sentence that lacks the architectural niceties of White's and Warren's is a bore.

Not all periodic sentences are as long as those given in the examples above. Here, for example, is a periodic sentence of moderate length that appeared in *Stilwell and the American Experience in China* by Barbara Tuchman.

Withdrawn again behind its oceans, with no visible menace on the horizon, with Japan seemingly taken care of by the Washington Treaties, the United States basked in the Coolidge sun.

Relatively short for a periodic sentence — only 30 words — this one still has the essential characteristics: it delays the possibility of a period until the end, it begins with a series of parallel structures, and it closes with a phrase worth waiting for.

A cumulative sentence is one in which a comma that could be replaced by a period occurs fairly early, followed by other bits of information that are themselves separated by commas that could be replaced by periods.

The scene has changed from Florence to Rome, from the city of hard heads, sharp wits, light feet, graceful movement, to a city of weight, a city that is like a huge compost-heap of human hopes and ambitions, despoiled of its ornament, almost indecipherable, a wilderness of imperial splendour, with only one ancient emperor, Marcus Aurelius, above ground in the sunshine through the centuries. (64 words).

— **Kenneth Clark**, *Civilisation*

If you examine this sentence, you will discover that the comma after "Rome," the eighth word in the sentence, might be replaced by a period; you will also discover that the commas after "weight," "ambitions," "ornament," "indecipherable," and "splendour" could also be replaced by periods.

Cumulative sentences seem to occur more frequently in modern prose than in classical prose, and they seem to occur more frequently in narrative and descriptive writing than elsewhere. Stylists sometimes point out that Hemingway, who is generally thought of as a writer of short, tough sentences, was also a master of the long sentence with a cumulative structure. Here, for example, is a sentence from *Death in the Afternoon* with 142 words.

> Gallo, too, was a master of gracious passes made before the bull's horns, passes made with both hands, changing the muleta from one hand to the other, sometimes behind his back, passes that started as though they were to be naturals and instead, the man spinning around, the muleta wrapping itself around him and the bull following the spinning loose end of it; others in which the man turned on himself getting close to the bull's neck and winding him around him, passes made kneeling, using both hands on the muleta to swing the bull around in a curve; all passes that needed a great knowledge of the bull's mentality and great confidence to make safely, but that, with that knowledge and confidence, were beautiful to see and very satisfying to Gallo to make although they were the negation of true bullfighting.

But cumulative sentences are not necessarily long. Here, in fact, is a fairly short cumulative sentence by William Faulkner, who is generally thought of as a writer of long, convoluted sentences.

> He stood for a moment, planted stiffly on the stiff foot, looking back at the house.
>
> — **"Burn Burning"**

As you try new sentence structures in your own writing, remember that long sentences are not necessarily better than short ones, nor short ones necessarily better than long ones. Although sentences written by professionals are usually, on the average, much longer than those written by college freshmen, the *range* of sentence length in professional writing is also much greater than the range in freshman writing. A professionally written piece with an average sentence length of twenty-five words may contain some sentences of more than a hundred words and others of less than half a dozen. In ordinary freshman writing, however, the average sentence tends to be only a few words shorter than the longest sentence and a few words longer than the shortest. In other words, all the sentences are roughly the same length — which can make a monotonous style, unless it has some redeeming purpose.

To write like a professional, you need a wider range of sentence structures and you need to vary the length and rhythm of the sentences.

EXERCISES

1. In the following balanced sentence, written by Jacob Bronowski and Bruce Mazlish, the "its" refers to the Renaissance.

Some see its beginnings as early as the twelfth or thirteenth centuries; others prolong the Middle Ages until as late as the seventeenth century.

In the next example, "his" refers to Cervantes, the author of *Don Quixote*. The sentence was written by Eric Auerbach.

His representation of Spanish reality is dispersed in many individual adventures and sketches; the bases of that reality remain untouched and unmoved.

Write a balanced sentence of your own, using as a model one of the two examples above or any of the balanced sentences discussed in the preceding section.

2. Study the following sentence, which was written by historian Bruce Catton.

For a generation, Charleston had been a symbol; now it was a reality, seen for the first time, its horizons lost in the blue haze of wooded lowlands that enclosed the broad sparkling bay.

In what way is this an example of a balanced sentence? In what way is it an example of a cumulative sentence? Imitate the structure of this example with a sentence of your own.

3. Now try your hand at writing periodic sentences using E. B. White's (p. 190), Earl Warren's (p. 191), or Barbara Tuchman's as a model. Remember to delay the possibility of a period until the end. Use parallel structures at the beginning; remind the readers how the sentence began before you bring it to an end; make sure the ending is worth waiting for. Use one of the following phrases to get started, or invent a phrase of your own.

In this the greatest of all colleges,
With the money (or poverty) we have in this state,

4. Write a cumulative sentence like Kenneth Clark's. Begin with "The scene has changed from high school to college," or "The scene has changed from New York to New Orleans." Feel free to substitute other scenes you are more familiar with. Clark's sentence is broken up below to help you perceive the parallel structures within it.

The scene has changed from Florence to Rome,
> from the city of hard heads, sharp wits, light feet, graceful movement,
> to a city of weight, a city that is like a huge compost-heap of human hopes and ambitions,
>> despoiled of its ornament,
>> almost indecipherable,
>> a wilderness of imperial splendour
>>> with only one emperor,
>>>> Marcus Aurelius,
>>> above ground in the sunshine through the centuries.

5. Use one of the following cumulative sentences as a model and write a sentence of your own beginning either with "The lion raced through the city streets," or with "The teacher paced in front of the class." To keep the sentences grammatically simple, avoid using words like *because, but, or, for, that, what, when, which, while,* and *who.*

The snow fell, slowly at first, disappearing almost as soon as it touched the earth, then faster, in larger flakes, clinging in ridges along the branches of the trees and piling in deep drifts over the brown leaves.

The bull ran into the ring, head lowered, the muscles on its back taut, charging first at the picadores on their blindfolded horses and then at the spectators with their legs dangling over the fence around the edge of the arena.

10. Style as the Person

Style can be defined in a number of ways. One of the most famous definitions is by George-Louis Leclerc de Buffon, who in his *Discours sur le style (Essay on Style)* said, *"Le style c'est l'homme même"* — which may be loosely translated as "Style is the person." What Buffon seems to have meant is that all writing is a projection of a personality; in all that we read, we tend to imagine a personality behind the writing. Thus even if we did not know the authors of the passages in the examples below, we would tend to think of them as different sorts of persons not only because their subject matter is different but because they use language differently.

> Until the advent of the special theory of relativity, no one had thought that there could be any ambiguity in the statement that two events in different places happened at the same time. It might be admitted that, if the places were very far apart, there might be difficulty in finding out for certain whether the events were simultaneous, but every one thought the meaning of the question perfectly definite.
>
> — Bertrand Russell, *The ABC of Relativity*

> One April morning we were standing around in the play yard, acting as if it were a huge open-air poolhall with the firstgraders coming and going like pool balls. We were all bored with the prospect of another day's school studying Cuba.
>
> — Richard Brautigan, *Trout Fishing in America*

> No better than a fool as a father:
> the bad character which one of his sons showed from childhood. When he had grown up, far from applying himself to studies and sober habits, he had become addicted to a soft and lazy life, and as time went on to all sorts of vices, so that he became the dishonor of the entire family.
>
> — Norman O. Brown, *Closing Time*

Writers establish an image of themselves in almost everything they write. That image can be sober, witty, frivolous, profound, sloppy, businesslike, careless, or can suggest any of an infinite variety of personalities and attitudes. In part they establish their images by what they say (content), and in part by the way they say it (style).

Specifically, differences in the range of vocabulary, the kind of imagery and imagination, the treatment of conventions, the use or avoidance of conversational idiom — all these add up to what writing teachers call diction. Various kinds of diction create various personalities for the writer.

Some people have taken Buffon's statement — style is the person — to mean that style is indistinguishable from the personality of the writer. Sometimes, of course, we can recognize authors by their "voice" on a page, just as we can recognize a friend's voice on the phone. But all writers, even writers of nonfiction, use a variety of styles to project a variety of personalities. No sensitive writer uses the same style in a letter home, a letter to a lover, a letter to a prospective employer, a letter to a congressman, a letter of acceptance, and a letter of resignation.

There is, then, no single style that alone deserves to be called "good style"; there are lots of styles, and each of them can be evaluated only in the context of writer, audience, subject matter, and purpose. Writers are like actors. The better they are, the more skilled they are in projecting a number of personalities besides the one they use at home each day. Techniques for improving style, then, should be pursued, not to acquire a "one true style," but rather to acquire a broader range of stylistic options to choose from according to each occasion.

WRITING ASSIGNMENT

Write two short passages describing the same person, place, or event in two different styles from two different points of view and for two different audiences. For example, you might describe a small child as her grandmother would remember her in a diary after a visit, and then describe the child as a teacher would depict her in a formal report to her parents. Or you might describe an apartment as you would in a letter to a friend who had never seen it, and again as you would in a newspaper ad. Or you might describe a concert in the formal language of a published article, and again in the technical language of an acoustical engineer, or in the naive language of someone who had never been to a concert before. In example A below, the writer describes an automobile accident objectively, as it would be in a police report; in example B the same accident is described from the point of view of one of the drivers.

A. Police Report No. 07531-A

Vehicle A is a 1977 Mercedes. Vehicle B is a 1977 Ford pickup. Vehicle C is a late-model Chevrolet. Vehicle A was traveling at an estimated 35 mph eastward on Pelham Heights Road at the intersection of Woodridge Road. Vehicle B was traveling behind Vehicle A. Vehicle C, a noncontact vehicle, allegedly ran the stop sign controlling access to Pelham Heights Road from Woodridge Road. Vehicle A stopped to avoid collision. Vehicle B struck Vehicle A from the rear.

B. Bart was late, pushing his new Mercedes around the winding roads faster than he knew he should. There was a fork ahead, a woman in a brown Chevy waiting at the stop sign to Bart's right. Bart would take the left branch; he had the right of way. Slowly, as if she had trouble deciding to do it, the woman pulled away from the stop sign, easing across the road the way a cow would, oblivious of the danger. "I'll teach her," Bart said to himself, mashing his horn and pressing his brake just hard enough to miss her, but not by much. He raised his fist to the window, glaring in what he hoped would be an instructive manner. Then suddenly a shadow darkened Bart's rearview mirror, and he felt the impact before he heard the squeal of tires, steel bending, glass shattering. The Mercedes rolled forward, not quickly, but floating dreamlike, silently, as if the car itself were stunned. Bart got out to see what had hit him: an oversized pickup truck, its lights bent downward. It was a wrecker truck from Mo Jott's Body Shop.

THE RESEARCH
PAPER

Chapter Nine

———◆———

Diary of a Term Paper

1. Finding Material

Melanie Grubbs was a freshman at a college which she had reason to believe was about average. Her main reason was Jeff, the boy she dated. Jeff was a junior, an English major who wanted to be a Rhodes scholar. He had told Melanie the university was "about average" the same night he told her he wanted to be a Rhodes scholar.

One Monday, Melanie's composition instructor, Mr. Austern, announced that the class should write a research paper. "Working bibliography is due one week from today," he said. "Outline due the following Wednesday. Final draft due on the following Monday." The class groaned. "Any topic of your choice," the instructor said. "Ten to twelve pages should be enough. Typewritten. Double spaced. Read Chapter Nine, Ten, and Eleven for suggestions about how to get started."

Melanie was alarmed. She hated research papers. This time, she thought, she'd start early and avoid the last minute panic. So she went directly to the library and read Chapters Nine, Ten, and Eleven. That took thirty minutes. Now to find a topic.

She noticed a large old *Webster's* dictionary on a table near her. She opened the book at random half a dozen times in search of a topic.

> **Ci-pan'go** . . . A marvelous island or islands east of Asia, described in the "Voyages" of Marco Polo.

I wish I were there, thought Melanie.

> **Her'mes** . . . An Olympian god, son of Zeus and Maia.

Good picture with caption "Hermes of Praxiteles." Reminded Melanie of someone she had met during registration.

> **fire walk** . . . The ceremony or ordeal of walking through fire or upon stones heated by fire. It is performed by some of the Polynesians as a religious rite and in past ages was a recognized ordeal in Europe.

In Europe? That's surprising.

> **tide** . . . The alternate rising and falling of the surface of the ocean, and of gulfs, bays, rivers, etc., connected with the ocean.

That's an interesting subject, thought Melanie. I'll try "fire walk" first, and if that doesn't work, I'll try to learn more about tides.

Melanie walked straight to the card catalog and looked under "F" for "fire walk." She found nothing. That ends that topic, she thought. Then she looked under "T" for tide. She found three eighteenth-century books, and one recent book that dealt only with tides near Cat Island, Louisiana. This would never do. She explained her problem to a librarian.

"For 'fire walk,' the librarian said, "why not look under 'Polynesia—Social Life and Customs.'" The librarian then showed Melanie where to look, and sure enough she found six books filed under POLYNESIA—SOCIAL LIFE AND CUSTOMS.

"How should I have known to look under Polynesia for 'fire walk' material?" Melanie asked.

"You shouldn't have. That's the sort of thing librarians are trained to know. And by the way, if you need more material, try the *Social Sciences Index* in the reference room."

Melanie copied down the call numbers of the six books and rushed downstairs where she found all six in one place. One by one she opened them, checking the table of contents first and then the index in search of references to fire walks.

There were none.

I hate research papers, thought Melanie. She gathered her books and her purse and went to meet Jeff for lunch.

"What's the *Social Sciences Index?*" She asked Jeff, who, she thought, was likely to know.

"Oh, it's just an index to periodicals and magazines," Jeff said, munching on a sandwich. "Something like the *Readers' Guide*, which you probably used in high school. Only the *Readers' Guide* covers popular magazines, and the *Social Science Index* covers more serious magazines."

"How do you use it."

"Sort of like a dictionary. If you're looking for magazine articles about a certain topic, you just look up that topic in the latest volume of the *Index*. If something's been published on your topic recently, the *Index* will tell you where to find it. If you're serious, though, you'll look up the topic in all the old volumes of the *Index* too, so you can find out what has been published in the past."

"Sounds like a heck of a lot of work to me."

"It is." Then Jeff launched into one of the lectures Melanie hated. He gave her dozens of topics. He told her about bibliographies, and bibliographies of bibliographies. He suggested that she ask someone in the anthropology department about fire walking. He was, in short, a useless bore.

Melanie's composition class happened to be in the same building as the anthropology department. After class on Wednesday, she was feeling particularly desperate about not having even the beginning of a working bibliography. She couldn't even respond when the instructor asked if anyone was having problems. Hating research papers was not the sort of problem the instructor wanted to hear about.

After class she walked toward the anthropology offices. One door was open. Melanie could hear the clicking of a typewriter and the shuffling of papers within, but she could see no one. She paced in front of the door, trying to decide how foolish she would seem if she approached this perfect stranger and asked for advice about a freshman paper. Back and forth she paced. This is worse than seeing the dentist, she thought.

"You wanted to see me?"

The voice came from the open door. Inside, Melanie could see what must have been an anthropology professor standing in a dusty stream of light between his typewriter and a bright window. It looks like a cave in here, she thought. The professor's hair was wavy, gray and black, tight up against the right side of his head where he parted it, trailing off into space on the other side, as if it had been teased with static electricity. He had a thin cotton shirt over a sunken chest. His belt was tighter than his trousers, which gathered in unintended pleats around his waist. In general, he seemed harmless.

Melanie explained her problem.

"Have you tried the *Social Sciences Index* or the *Reader's Guide to Periodical Literature?*" he asked.

"I thought of that, but it seemed pointless. If there is nothing on firewalking in the card catalog, there's probably nothing in those indexes either."

The professor thought this over. "Possibly," he said. And then, "Come back tomorrow and I'll have something for you."

Melanie did not come back the next day, because she had no classes in that building. On the following day, which was Friday, she looked into the anthropology offices again. This time the professor was busy talking with two other students, but when he noticed Melanie pacing outside he motioned her in and handed her a slip of paper. On it he had written this:

Foster, George M. "The Fire Walkers of San Pedro Manique, Soria, Spain." *Journal of American Folklore*, 68 (1955), 325–332.

"One article?" Melanie asked. She has been hoping for more.

"It has notes," the professor said. "Also, you should try the *Social Sciences Index*."

"One article," Melanie said to Jeff as they ate dinner in the union that night.

"It probably has notes," Jeff said.

"It *does* have notes. So what?"

"So read the article, and copy down the titles of all the books and articles in the footnotes. They'll lead you to other books and articles with more notes. Pretty soon you'll have more than enough for a bibliography."

"I detest research papers."

Jeff started writing on a paper napkin. "Here's your schedule for tomorrow. Don't do anything about this paper till nine o'clock. I'll meet you at the library then. Work from nine to twelve. Stop at twelve no matter how the work is going. We'll picnic at the park and play some tennis from twelve to four. At four, you'll go back to the library and work till six. Quit at six no matter how well it's going."

"Why the schedule?"

"It's a psychological trick you play on yourself. You'll see how it works when you try it."

Melanie began to see how it worked when she got up the next day. She was worried about the bibliography, and not being able to get started before nine made her eager to get to work. To kill time, she studied Chapter Ten. She wanted to be sure to copy down all references in the correct form right from the start. Then she examined her topic with some of the questions in Chapter Two. Before long, she became more and more curious about who fire walkers were, why they did it, and how they managed to protect their feet. It's either a trick, she thought, or self-hypnosis.

At nine o'clock, she began reading the Foster article. It was an account of a fire walking ceremony that took place in Spain in the 1950s. She could hardly believe it. The ritual was vaguely associated with the summer solstice and with the feast of St. John the Baptist. It was a strange mixture of Christianity and paganism.

The notes lead her to a book called *The Golden Bough* by James G. Frazer, and to two books on mythology and religion by Andrew Lang. These books were full of stories about fire walking all over the world—in India, Japan, Polynesia, ancient Rome, and modern Bulgaria. There were, in fact, more stories than Melanie could summarize in her notes.

On a hunch, she looked through the books near Frazer's and Lang's on the library shelf. As it turned out, she couldn't find any references to fire walking in the tables of contents or the indexes, but she did find an interesting article about truth and science and myth by someone named Bidney. She didn't like the article, and it didn't deal directly with fire walking; but she took a few notes anyway. Somewhere else she found a reference to the three young men in the Bible who walked through a fiery furnace. She took down their names.

Another note in Foster lead to an article in *Scientific American*. The article was supposed to contain a scientific explanation of fire walking. But when Melanie asked for that volume in the science library, she was told that it was in storage, and that no one could get it for her until after lunch.

"I'll be back at four," she told the librarian. It was time to meet Jeff for the picnic anyway.

Walking in the sunlight after so much reading had a strange effect on Melanie. She felt the way she used to feel when she would sit through a double feature in midafternoon, after which daylight seemed unreal. She enjoyed the picnic and the tennis. But all the while she was curious about the article in *Scientific American*.

"I've only read five things," she told Jeff as they drove back to the library, "and it's already more information than I can handle."

At four o'clock she read the article in *Scientific American*. She wasn't sure if the explanation was sound or not. Moreover, she wasn't sure if the very attempt to provide a scientific explanation was not somehow irrelevant.

Still, she had only six references. She tried the *Encyclopaedia Britannica;* it didn't tell her anything she didn't already know. Then, out of desperation, she sat down before the *Social Sciences Index*. She counted thirty-two volumes. She did not feel like looking through thirty-two volumes, but it was only five o'clock and she was determined to work until six. At first she thought she would look under three headings: "fire walks," "St. John the Baptist," and "midsummer." Then she happened to see something about "Fiji" in the index, so she added "Fiji" to her list of headings.

Melanie looked through the most recent seventeen volumes of the index without finding a single reference. On the eighteenth try she found two articles under "fire walking." By the time she worked back to volume fourteen, she had found several more references, including a reference to the Foster article that the anthropology professor had given her. Perfect timing; it was six o'clock. Surely anything written before the Foster article must have been covered in his footnotes. Melanie was relieved. Now she wouldn't have to go all the way back to the beginning of the *Social Sciences Index*.

"It doesn't work that way," Jeff said when he found her in the reference room. "Foster's footnotes may not include all the good stuff written earlier."

"I'll stay here for another hour then and go through the rest of the index."

"You shouldn't. Five hours a day is all the research a human being can stand without brain damage. How about dinner and a movie? I'll write tomorrow's schedule on your napkin."

Later Jeff explained his schedule theory. "It's the only way to get anything done," he said. "Set yourself definite time blocks and stick to them. At the end of a time block, stop, even if you're in the middle of a sentence. Stopping in the middle of something makes it easier to get started again."

Jeff was right. The next day's schedule required three hours of compulsory research, followed by four hours of compulsory play, followed by two more hours of research. In the first hour, Melanie worked her way back to volume one of the *Social Sciences Index* (which she discovered, was originally called the *International Index,* and then was called the *Social Sciences and Humanities Index,* and then split up into the *Social Sciences Index* and the *Humanities Index*). Within the next half hour she had found the call numbers for all the periodicals in her notes — except for a few which the library did not have. By playtime, she had read more than half of the articles. In the first hour after playtime she finished reading the articles, and during the second hour she arranged the articles in alphabetical order according to author and typed out the working bibliography. She felt rather proud of herself. She had an eighteen-item bibliography on a topic that wasn't even listed in the card catalog.

2. Writing the Paper

In composition class on Monday, Mr. Austern looked over the working bibliographies. One student had a list of thirty-seven references. Everyone but the instructor seemed to know that the list came from an old paper in a fraternity file. When Mr. Austern looked at Melanie's bibliography, he seemed vaguely pleased — though Melanie thought her ten hours of work deserved a little more praise than it got.

She did get some good advice, however. Chapter Eleven did not tell her how to make a bibliographic entry for two books she had found — one, *Modern Mythology*, which she had found in a reprinted edition, the other, a book by Frazer, which seemed to be the second volume of a seventh volume of a larger work. Mr. Austern was puzzled, too, but he looked through his copy of the *MLA Handbook* and helped Melanie devise a form for handling these books.

"Now that you have something to say," the instructor droned, "your next job is to find a way to say it." Melanie tried hard to seem interested. "If you remember Chapter Four, you know that you will either write a persuasive paper or an expository paper. Do you have a point to prove?" No, thought Melanie. "If so, formulate a thesis and construct an outline with supporting information. If you just have some interesting information — no point to prove — then you are writing an expository paper." That's me, thought Melanie. "I suggest you reread Chapter Four for some advice about organization. Let's have your outlines ready by next class."

At home that night, Melanie reread Chapter Four, especially part three, "The Expository Stance: Control Sentence and Outline." I could do it chronologically, she thought, but that would be tedious. Perhaps comparison and contrast. Yes, comparison and contrast, she thought, and she jotted this down:

   I. European fire walks
  II. Indian fire walks
 III. Polynesian fire walks.

But then she decided that comparison and contrast would be tough to handle with three elements instead of two. OK, she thought, I'll start off with a classification paper, and then end up with the scientific explanation. Her revised outlined looked like this:

Control Sentence: Fire walking of various sorts has been observed among Polynesians, East Indians, and Europeans; to some extent, all of these cases can be explained by theories advanced by British scientists in the late 1930s.

I. Introduction
II. Body
    A. Classification of fire walks
        1. Polynesian
        2. East Indian
        3. European
            a. in ancient Italy
            b. in Bulgaria
            c. in Spain
    B. Scientific explanation of fire walks
III. Conclusion

Not bad, she thought. And as she read the outline, she realized that she had more material than she could use in a twelve-page paper. Instead of padding, she'd be trimming—using the outline to cut away some of the excess information she had gathered. She couldn't report all the instances of fire walking she had read about, so she would report only those that she found most interesting.

Then Melanie read through her notes with her outline in mind. She arranged her notes in five stacks—one for each of the different kinds of fire walking, one for the scientific explanation, and one for notes that didn't fit in the other four categories. She was ready to start writing, but she found that she had forgotten most of the details about the Polynesian fire walks. Back to the library. She decided that the library was, in fact, the best place to write the paper; there she could go back to her references whenever her notes were not complete enough.

On her way to campus she ran into Jeff.

"How's the paper coming?"

"Ugh!"

"Look, give me a slip of paper and I'll write you a schedule for Saturday and Sunday."

"No thanks," said Melanie. She had begun to resent Jeff's schedules.

"Well, OK. Say, listen, I'm going to have to go home this weekend anyway. See you Monday?"

"Right. See you Monday."

Back in the library, Melanie looked through her purse for a pen and found an old napkin, a souvenir of a restaurant she had gone to in New York on her senior trip. Let's see, she thought. It should take me about six hours to write this thing. Then about four hours to type it. She started writing on the napkin. Two hours writing Saturday morning, two hours Saturday afternoon, and two hours Sunday morning. That should do it. I'll type the whole thing Sunday night. Nothing else to do anyway.

She had heard the weather report on the radio: "Fair and warm through Monday." It wasn't going to be a bad weekend at all.

3. A Sample Research Paper

The research paper reproduced below is typed according to the form recommended by the *MLA Handbook for Writers of Research Papers, Theses, and Dissertations* (New York: MLA, 1977). The *MLA Handbook* does not recommend title pages for research papers. Since there is no universally recognized form for title pages, teachers who want them will explain the form they consider most appropriate.

Melanie Grubbs

Professor Austern

EH 101

October 15, 1980

Walking Through Fire

"King Nebuchadnezzar was amazed," the Bible
tells us (Daniel, 3:24). He had made a blazing
furnace seven times hotter than its usual heat,
and into it he had thrown three Hebrew dissidents
--Shadrach, Meshach, and Abednego--as punishment
for their refusal to worship the king's golden
idol. But the three men simply walked about the
furnace unharmed; "the hair of their heads had
not been singed, their trousers were untouched,
and no smell of fire lingered about them" (Daniel,
3:27). Was this a miracle? A pious exaggeration?
Or is it possible that the three Hebrew men had
discovered the secret of fire walking? Since the
close of the nineteenth century, fire walking has
been observed and studied among Polynesians, East
Indians, and Europeans; but it was not until the
late 1930s that scientists could claim to explain
how it is done.

One of the first attempts to observe fire
walking with scientific instruments was reported

by Dr. T. M. Hocken in 1898.[1] Hocken had heard about a fire walking ceremony among Fiji islanders, and he made arrangements to witness the event for himself. The ceremony took place on an island called Mbenga in Polynesia. There the natives made a huge oven in the ground to cook the sugary roots of a tree known locally as masawe. The oven was saucer shaped, twenty-five to thirty feet from rim to rim, eight feet deep in the center. At the bottom was a flat area ten feet in diameter, paved with stones.

To heat the stones, the natives covered them with a wood fire that lasted more than thirty-six hours. Before the ceremony, the burning logs were removed, leaving the stones exposed, with flames flickering up from the smoldering coals between them.

Hocken was careful to check for signs of trickery. He had heard that the feet of fire walkers were thick and leathery from continual contact with rocks and coral reefs, and he had heard that they may have been protected by a secret preparation. So Hocken obtained permission to examine the feet of two of the fire walkers before and after the ceremony. Before the ceremony, Hocken discovered, the feet were "comparatively soft and flexible—by no means leathery and insensible." Nor was there any evidence of a protective coating of any kind. "I assured myself of this," writes Hocken, "by touch, smell, and taste, not hesitating to apply my tongue as a corroborative."[2]

Hocken even attempted to measure the temperature of the oven by means of a thermometer encased in tin and suspended about five or six feet above the center of the stones. Unfortunately, the heat soon began to melt the solder on the instrument's casing, and the thermometer had to be removed when it had registered 282 degrees Fahrenheit. According to Hocken, the thermometer would have certainly exceeded its capacity of 400 degrees Fahrenheit if it had not been removed.[3]

When the oven was prepared and the stone floor spread to a white-hot circle fifteen feet in diameter, the fire walkers appeared--seven or eight of them walking in single file down one slope of the oven, and then "across and around the stones, leaving the oven at the point of entrance." The leader, according to Hocken, had spent "a second or two under half a minute"[4] in the oven. After the ceremony, Hocken once again examined the feet of the two fire walkers and found they had been in no way injured by the heat.

As for an explanation, Hocken could find none. He could discover no physical trickery. Even hypnotism, Hocken argues, which might make fire walkers not feel the pain, could not prevent the fire from blistering their feet.[5] In short, Hocken concludes, "the whole subject requires thorough scientific examination."[6]

A different style of fire walking has been observed among the Hindus, not only in India itself, but on islands nearby. One instance was vividly described by Richard D. Greenfield in 1951.[7] Greenfield was an Englishman, about to finish a tour of duty on the island of Penang in North Malaya, when a friendly native told him about a fire walking ceremony that was about to take place. Greenfield was less scientific in his observations than Hocken, but no less convincing. The ceremony took place inside a temple, where attendants had raked a red-hot charcoal pit to "a uniform thickness." Just before the fire walkers appeared, priests were fanning the pit to a red glow. "Suddenly," writes Greenfield, "the chief priest, his hands above his head, ran through the ten yards of fiery charcoal, dipping his feet into a little trough of water at the end." Then, another Indian "walked through the pit," followed by an old woman "who danced from one side of the pit to the other" and fainted when she stepped out. Finally, two Indians appeared carrying idols, apparently quite heavy, decorated with flags and flowers. The idols were supported partly by spears stuck into the Indians'

flesh. Both walked across the pit. Greenfield describes the passage vividly:

> One had his hands clasped on his stomach,
> and, with his head hanging on his chest,
> looking down at the fire, he passed
> through the pit. His feet sunk into the
> red-hot charcoal with the weight of his
> burden. The other had his hands out-
> stretched, palm downwards, as if he were
> walking a tight-rope. His face was not
> visible save for the flattened ends of
> a six-inch needle which he had stuck
> horizontally through his tongue.[8]

After the ceremony, Greenfield was invited to
examine the feet of one of the men who had carried
a decorated idol through the pit. He could find
no injury--but no explanation either:

> . . . the ash still stuck to his ankles,
> and odd pieces of charcoal adhered to
> his feet, but there was not the slight-
> est sign of a burn on those soles. I
> looked into the eyes of the Indian.
> They were expressionless, but conscious.
> This was no trance I am sure.[9]

Fire walking may seem natural enough in

exotic places like the Fiji islands or in Indian
lands where people put spears in their flesh and
needles in their tongues. What is surprising, however, is that fire walking has been practiced in
Europe, from ancient times right up to the
twentieth century. The earliest recorded occurrence was among a tribe called the "Hirpi," or
"wolf-people" who once a year "walked barefoot,
but unscathed, over the flowing embers and ashes
of a great fire of pinewood" near Mount Soracte
in Italy.[10]

A more recent ceremony dates from the thirteenth century, when, according to tradition, a
church in Kosti, in Thrace (now part of modern
Bulgaria, Turkey, and Greece) caught on fire.
Bystanders heard groans within the burning building and rushed in to discover that the groans came
from the icons—religious paintings—of Saints
Constantine and Elene. They saved the icons and
walked out of the church unharmed by the fire.
Since that incident, people who claim to be protected by those saints have danced through a fire
every year on the feast day of Saints Constantine
and Elene (May 21).

This tradition has been continued in modern
Greece, where it has been observed and described
independently by Rachel Lloyd[11] and Michael
Llewellyn Smith.[12] There the fire walkers are
called "Anastenarides," which means "sighers" or

"groaners," because of the sounds they make in
their frenzied state as they dance through the
fire.[13] According to Smith, the annual ceremony
had become something of a tourist attraction in
the Greek town of Langada, but it was more au-
thentic in another town, called Agia Elene, which
is where Smith observed it and where Lloyd had
observed it some ten years earlier. Lloyd describes the fire itself:

> Twenty feet of ground was covered with
> burning faggots and branches, the ashes
> were glowing and the heat scorched us;
> for it was the great heat of a dying
> fire, and scarlet splinters of wood
> broke off the crumbling branches and
> lay like cut rubies in the sunlight.[14]

According to Smith, the dancers were "almost in
ecstasy, crying out involuntarily," accompanied
by the music "of flute, bagpipe lyre, and
tympanum."[15] Three of the fire walkers Lloyd saw
were women, one a man. The fire walkers Smith saw
were all women, who had prepared for the event by
dancing till midnight before the feast itself. On
the day of the feast they danced through the fire:
"All five women are dancing, crossing and re-
crossing the coals, always in time to the music,
step to beat."[16] In Lloyd's account,

> a man from a neighboring village . . .
> snatched up an ikon and ran into the
> fire and jumped up and down with both
> feet together. . . . But he had had no
> time to work up his ecstasy, and the
> saint's breath was not on him, people
> said, and so he choked and fell back in
> the red ashes, and friends dragged him
> out, and he was badly burned. And every-
> one said angrily that he was a fool.[17]

Since there can be no doubt that people do
walk or dance through fire, the question remains:
how do they do it? In the late 1930s a group of
British scientists decided to answer that question. First, by advertising for a professional
fire walker, they discovered an East Indian named
Kuda Bux who was willing to walk through a charcoal pit under careful scientific observation. The
experiment has been reported, among other places,
in Scientific American.[18] The scientists set up a
charcoal pit twenty-five feet long and nine
inches deep. Its surface temperature was 806
degrees Fahrenheit—double the heat required to
bake a cake. The temperature within the coals was
2,552 degrees—hot enough to melt steel.[19] After
saying a few prayers, Bux took four steps through
the pit—covering approximately eleven feet—and
stepped out. The scientists tested Bux's feet

immediately before and after his walk and found them normal in every way--except that his feet were even cooler after than before. Persuaded that anyone could do the same thing, one of the bystanders, a man named Digby Moynagh, took off his shoes and socks and stepped onto the charcoal. He got as far as two steps and then jumped out; within thirty minutes his feet were blistered.[20] Another bystander, Maurice Chapeen, also got as far as two short quick steps, but "his feet were badly blistered and bleeding at three points."

The scientists did not give up. They developed a theory that wood, even burning wood, is a poor conductor of heat, and that if the feet of a walker came in contact with it for short periods of time, they would not receive enough heat to burn. Thus they concluded that Kuda Bux could walk across the glowing charcoal in deliberate, steady steps because each foot contacted the charcoal only twice, and remained in contact for an average of 0.40 seconds each time--not long enough to blister. Faster steps--like those taken by Moynagh and Chapeen, caused the feet to repeat contact with the embers too quickly, and thus to build up enough heat to cause blisters. Eventually, an ordinary Englishman, Reginald Adcock, was able to duplicate and even surpass the fire walking records of Kuda Bux and other Indians by imitating the style and tempo of their steps.

Adcock walked through a fire one foot longer and twice as hot as the one Bux had crossed and came out uninjured. Despite the fact that Adcock weighed more than Bux and other fire walkers whose records he broke, the scientists thought that weight was a disadvantage in fire walking.[21]

Does this scientific theory explain all the examples of fire walking described in this paper? Probably. The Fiji islanders walked on stone instead of charcoal, and seemed to remain in the oven longer than Bux and Adcock did; but scientists have already determined that stones used in Polynesian fire walking are even poorer conductors of heat than wood and that as many as twenty-five steps may be possible on heated stones.[22] The Indian walkers described by Greenfield in Malaya seemed not much different from Adcock and Bux in their performances, and the fact that the Indian woman who "danced from one side of the pit to the other" fainted would seem to confirm the British scientists' opinion that too rapid contact with the embers can be dangerous. And finally, the Anastenarides who "dance" through fire in Greece, seem to dance "through the fire" at a very steady pace—"step to beat" with the music, Smith says, so that their passage may well resemble the tempo and duration of the fire walking observed by the British scientists. The man from a neighboring Greek village who joined the Anastenarides and "jumped up and down with both feet together" was probably burned, not because "he had had no time to work up his ectasy," but because he did not walk with the steady firm pace used by successful fire walkers.

The only defect in the scientists' theory is that it is not as colorful as the explanations of the fire walkers themselves. The Anastenarides say that "in the madness of the dance we see St. Elene going before us with a jug of water, which she pours on the coals. And so the fire cools us and does not burn."[23] Kuda Bux said his immunity from burns was the result of faith, and he refused to walk on fire when his faith had been shaken.[24] The fire walkers in the Fiji Islands claim to have inherited the gift from an ancestor, Na Galita, who had once spared the life of a god he had caught in the form of an eel. The god rewarded Na Galita and all his descendants with the ability to "walk through the masawe oven unharmed."[25] The scientific explanation seems bleak compared with eel-gods and water-sprinkling saints. And though it seems reasonable enough, it does not really explain why Kuda Bux and the Anastenarides and the descendants of Na Galita and even Reglinald Adcock will walk steadily and firmly through a glowing pit while the rest of us will only watch the thermometers or read about the fire.

Notes

[1] Hocken's account is printed by Andrew Lang in Magic and Religion (London: Longman's, Green, and Co., 1901), pp. 277 to 284.

[2] Lang, p. 282.

[3] Lang, p. 281.

[4] Lang, p. 281.

[5] Lang, p. 283.

[6] Lang, p. 284.

[7] Richard D. Greenfield, "Through the Fire," Spectator, 187 (2 November 1951), 566.

[8] Greenfield, p. 566.

[9] Greenfield, p. 566.

[10] J. G. Frazer, Balder the Beautiful: The Fire—Festivals of Europe and the Doctrine of the External Soul, Part VII of The Golden Bough: A Study of Magic and Religion, 3rd ed. (London: Macmillan and Co., 1913), II, 14.

[11] Rachel Lloyd, "The Fire—Walkers," Blackwood's Magazine, 281 (April 1956), 342-8.

[12] Michael Llewellyn Smith, "Anastenaria," Spectator, 210 (21 June 1963), 802.

[13] Lloyd, p. 344.

[14] Lloyd, p. 347.

[15] Smith, p. 802.

[16] Smith, p. 802.

[17] Lloyd, pp. 347-8.

[18] Albert G. Ingalls, "Fire Walking,"
Scientific American, 160 (1939), 135–8, 173–8.

[19] Ingalls, p. 174.

[20] Ingalls, pp. 173–4.

[21] Ingalls, p. 174.

[22] Ingalls, p. 138.

[23] Smith, p. 802.

[24] Ingalls, p. 175.

[25] Lang, pp. 278–9.

Bibliography

Bidney, David. "Myth, Symbolism, and Truth." In
    Myth: A Symposium. Ed. Thomas A. Sebeok.
    Bloomington: Indiana University Press, 1958,
    pp. 1–14.

Contant, V. "Theophrastus and the Firewalk." Isis,
    45 (1954), pt. 1, 95–97.

Cronin, Grover, Jr. "John Mirk on Bonfires, Ele-
    phants and Dragons." Modern Language Notes,
    57 (1942), 113–116.

Darling, Charles R. "Firewalking." Nature, 137
    (1935), 521.

"Experimental Fire–walks." Nature, 142 (1938), 67.

"Fire walk." Encyclopaedia Britannica: Micro-
    paedia. 1978 ed.

"Fire–walking: Scientific Tests." Nature, 139
    (1937), 660. Reply by Harry Price, 928–9.

Foster, George M. "The Fire Walkers of San Pedro
    Manique, Soria, Spain." Journal of American
    Folklore, 68 (1955), 325–332.

Frazer, J. G. Balder the Beautiful: The Fire–
    Festivals of Europe and the Doctrine of the
    External Soul. Part VII of The Golden
    Bough: A Study in Magic and Religion. 2
    vols. 3rd ed. London: Macmillan and Co.,
    1913.

Greenfield, Richard D. "Through the Fire."
    Spectator, 187 (1951), 566.

Gunn, Barbara. "Firewalking Ceremony." Blackwood's
    Magazine, 291 (1962), 193–8.

Ingalls, Albert G. "Fire Walking." Scientific
    American, 160 (1939), 135–138, 173–178.

Lang, Andrew. "Walking Through Fire." Magic and
    Religion. London: Longmans, Green, and Co.,
    1901, pp. 270–294.

———. "The Fire–Walk." Modern Mythology. London:
    Longmans, Green, 1897, pp. 148–175; rpt. New
    York: AMS Press, 1968.

Lloyd, Rachel. "The Fire–Walkers." Blackwood's
    Magazine, 281 (1957), 342–8.

Price, Harry. "Kuda Bux." Spectator, 158 (1937),
    808.

Smith, Michael Llewellyn. "Anastenaria."
    Spectator, 210 (1963), 802.

Thomas, E. S. "Fire–walking." Nature, 137 (1936),
    213–15.

EXERCISES

1. Read the last sentence of the first paragraph in the research paper. Is it a thesis or merely a summary statement? Does it foreshadow the outline of the rest of the paper? Does it suggest a problem or an angle?

2. In Chapter Five you were advised to write a first paragraph by writing a control sentence first and then several sentences leading up to the control sentence, using interesting bits of information left over from your prewriting. Read the first paragraph of the research paper. Did the writer follow the advice given in Chapter Five? Why is the control sentence in the research paper slightly different from the original control sentence the writer had planned (see p. 209)?

3. The last sentence in the first paragraph of the research paper seems to foreshadow a discussion with four major divisions before the conclusion. Using this as a clue, locate the four divisions in the paper. How many paragraphs are in each division? Does the development seem balanced, or is any division longer than the others? Why are the divisions arranged the way they are? Would any other sequence have made sense?

4. Outline the paper. How does your outline differ from the preliminary outline on p. 209? Why do you think the writer did not stick to the preliminary outline in all its detail?

5. In Chapter Ten, you are advised to use quotations "only in a few special circumstances" (p. 240). Examine the use of quoted material in the sample research paper. Are all of the quotations justified by the special circumstances mentioned in Chapter Ten? Are they justified for any other reason? Why, for example, does the writer quote the detailed description of each fire walking incident instead of paraphrasing it?

6. In Chapter Eleven you are advised to avoid the "Hamlet's-father's-ghost syndrome," with quoted material drifting into the paper detached from the name of its author. Examine the quoted material in the sample paper. Do you always know who is responsible for the quoted words even before you look in the footnote?

7. You may have noticed that one of the writer's most interesting sources — the article about fire walking in Spain to which the anthropology professor had referred her — was not included in her discussion. Why do you think it was omitted? Would the paper be improved by the addition of another example, or merely lengthened?

8. In Chapter Five you were advised to write a last paragraph by writing several sentences in which you view the main points of the paper from a new angle, writing a topic sentence that will fore-shadow the rest of the paragraph and link it with the body of the paper, and writing a clincher sentence, restating the main point of the paper and perhaps recalling how the paper began. How much of this advice was followed by the writer of the sample paper? Does the last paragraph in the sample paper work as a last paragraph?

Chapter Ten

Library Research

1. Preparing for Research

Students generally shudder at the prospect of writing a research paper. They are bewildered by the forms for footnotes and bibliographies, frustrated by the complexity of the library, and uncertain how to put what they learn into their own words.

Many of these problems can be solved simply by thinking of the research as a peculiar kind of interview. Think of the books and articles you consult as people rather than objects, and you will understand how to approach them with prepared questions in mind, how to be on the lookout for interesting information you could not anticipate, and how to give them credit for words, phrases, and information just as you would give credit to someone you interviewed.

First choose a topic. If your instructor suggests a few topics, be sure to pick the one that you would most enjoy learning about. Research papers usually require several hours in the library, so why not spend the time learning about something you like?

If your instructor sets no limits on topics and you cannot think of something to write about, try the following gimmicks.

Go to the library and thumb through a recent issue of *Time*, *Newsweek*, or a similar magazine. Look at the table of contents and choose the sections that most interest you — law, education, world affairs, theater, music, business. Read the articles in that section and look for a person, place, event, system, institution, or process that you would like to know more about. If what interests you is very recent, you will probably be able to find out more about it by consulting other magazines and journals. If what interests you has been around for a while, you may be able to find more information in books.

Two other good places to browse in search of topics are dictionaries and encyclopedias. Just open them up half a dozen times and let your eye run down the page in search of something interesting. When you find it, you have a topic.

Another good source of topics is a book called *Subject Headings Used in the Dictionary Catalog of the Library of Congress*, also known as the *SHLC*. This is the book librarians use to catalog new books according to the Library of Congress system. It looks like a big dictionary. The most recent edition is in two volumes. One advantage of this book is that the subjects are listed exactly as they are used in the library's card catalog. When you find a subject that interests you, a quick look in the card catalog will tell you whether your library has any books on that topic.

If your library does not use the Library of Congress system, ask the librarian to show you the subject heading guide used there. You can search for a topic in that guide exactly as you would in the *SHLC*.

2. Preliminary Search

When you begin working on a library paper, you should choose not just one topic, but several alternatives that you might use in case the first one doesn't work out. A common mistake among beginning researchers is to assume that any college library will have information on every subject. The truth, however, is that unless you are working at one of the great college libraries, you may have to try two or three different topics before you can find one that the library can support.

Most libraries have at least three different kinds of collections—books, serials, and reference works. To find out whether the library has any material on the topics you choose, you need to learn how to find your way around these different collections.

The card catalog is the main tool for finding information in books. As soon as the library buys a book, the librarians make at least three different cards for it. One is filed alphabetically according to the name of the author. Another card is filed alphabetically according to the title. And one or more cards are filed alphabetically according to the subjects treated in the book. If you know of an author who has written about a certain topic, you might be able to find the book by looking under the author's name, even though you do not know the title of the book. If you know the title of a book, but not the author's name or even the subject heading under which it might be filed, you will find it by looking for a title card. But generally all you have in mind is a subject—no authors, no titles—and you can quickly find out whether the library has the books you need by looking for subject cards in the catalog. If you were looking for a book about Brazil, for example, you could probably find a subject card like the one below.

F   BRAZIL
2508 **Nash, Roy,** fl. 1926–
.N25   The conquest of Brazil, by Roy Nash, with eight maps and
      seventy-seven illustrations. New York, Harcourt, Brace and
      company ₁1926₎

        xvi, 438 p. front., plates, maps. 22½ cm.

        "About books on Brazil": p. 399–401.

        1. Brazil.   I. Title.

      F2508.N25 1926   26–12472
                          ᵣev **3**
      Library of Congress   ₁r73h2₎

Notice the words "About books on Brazil" near the middle of the card. This is important information for research. It tells you that the book represented by this card has a bibliography—that is, a list of books. Sometimes the word "bibliography" itself is used on a catalog card. As you conduct your preliminary search, first consult the bibliographies in all the books that have them. They will lead you to other books·on your topic.

Subject cards will *not* lead you to material in magazines and other periodicals. Why not? Think about it for a moment. Every month the library receives hundreds of periodicals, each one containing many separate articles. If the librarians tried to make cards for all these articles, they would have to make thousands and thousands of cards each month. Since this is impossible, the library buys indexes from various companies that specialize in indexing the material in selected groups of periodicals. You can consult these indexes almost exactly as you would consult the card catalog: each article is entered under the title, the author's name, and the subject matter.

If you become a specialist in some academic field, you will learn how to use the indexes that cover the journals published in your specialty. In an introductory course, however, it is sufficient to learn how to use one or two indexes of a general nature. The index most commonly used by undergraduate writers is the *Readers' Guide to Periodical Literature*, an excerpt from which you see printed on the next page. It is usually located in the reference room of the library, along with encyclopedias, dictionaries, and other works of this nature.

If you look closely at the excerpt, you can see the general topic TRAILS. This general topic happens to have one subtopic, Hawaii (i.e., trails in Hawaii). If the paper you are writing has something to do with, say, political activities on college campuses, you could find information by looking under COLLEGE in the *Readers' Guide*, and then, more specifically, under "Political activities" as a subtopic under COLLEGE.

Once you find some titles that seem likely to have the kind of information you are looking for, flip to the front of the *Readers' Guide* for the abbreviations. There you will find out

TRAILERS
Cycle tent-trailer—a box that sleeps two. S. Bronson. il Pop Sci 208:22 Je '76
Don't get caught with an illegal trailer. il Sue Farm 74:F4 N '76
  See also
Automobile boat trailers
Automobile trailers
TRAILING plants. See Hanging plants
TRAILS
Bicycle trail to guide cyclists cross country. il Parks & Rec 11:2 My '76
Bikecentennial? It's sign-up time; Trans-America trail. il Sunset 156:58 Mr '76
Bikecentennial; traveling on the Trans-America trail. J. Siple. il Am For 82:24-7+
  F '76
Celebrate '76 on the coast-to-coast bicycle route; Trans-America trail. D. Burden. il
  Pop Sci 208:104-5+ Mr '76
Hiking America's historic trails. J. Galub. bibl il Ret Liv 16:37-40 O '76
How to get trails on the ground. G. C. Bentryn and E. Hay. il Parks & Rec 11:28-9+
  Mr '76
Klondike: the trail of '98; Chilkoot trail. W. S. Home. il maps Nat Parks & Con Mag
  50:11-16 D '76
Linear recreation ways; use of rights of way for trails. R. D. Espeseth. il Parks & Rec
  11:26-7+ Ap '76
Over the mountains; emigrant trails. A. Scally. il Negro Hist Bull 38:474-7 D '75
Proposal: Emigrant Trail National Historical Monument; Applegate-Lassen trail.
  T. H. Hunt. il map Nat Parks & Con Mag 50:4-7 N '76
Road to independence; Bikecentennial. B. Gilbert. il Sports Illus 44:50+ Mr 1 '76
Weaving together the past and the present; Lincoln's old log cabin, part of Lincoln
  heritage trail. R. Chin il pors Ret Liv 16:16-19 Jl '76
What an earthquake can do: the Point Reyes earthquake trail. il Sunset 157:28 N '76
You can still hike a segment of the historic emigrant trail; California. il Sunset
  157:33 S '76
  See also
Appalachian trail
California trail
Pacific Crest national scenic trail

Hawaii
In the steps of Hawaii's explorers. . .new hiking trails along the sea. il Sunset 156:
  61-2 Mr '76
TRAIN, Michael
Building storage. E. V. Warren. il por House B 119:10+ Ja '77 *

that a reference like "il Pop Sci 208:104-5+ Mr '76" means an
illustrated article in *Popular Science*, volume 208, pp. 104,
105, and following, March 1976.

Then you need to find out where *Popular Science* (or whatever periodical you need) is located in your library. In some
libraries, a separate card catalog is kept for magazines and
journals. By consulting that catalog you can find the call number of the periodicals you need. To find the periodical itself,
you need to consult a chart called a "Location Guide" or
"Library Plan," which most libraries have posted on walls,
usually near stairwells or elevators.

Sometimes encyclopedias and other reference works can
help you find material on topics that you cannot locate directly
in the card catalog or the serials record. Encyclopedias should
be used with extreme caution. Many students have been using
encyclopedia articles as the sole source of research papers
since junior high—papers that are generally nothing more
than snippets lifted from the encyclopedia itself and re-

arranged by the writer in a way that barely evades prosecution under the copyright laws.

If you consult an encyclopedia, use it maturely. An encyclopedia can give you an overview of a topic so that you can get started on more detailed research of your own. And an encyclopedia also can give you the titles of books and articles published on your topic. Consulting an encyclopedia is just the beginning of research. If the article you read in an encyclopedia lists some books, look up those books in the card catalog.

Before you go to the library, you should be prepared for snags to develop — which is one reason for doing this sort of work long before the paper is due, allowing yourself time to solve unexpected problems. Looking for subject headings can be frustrating if you happen to guess a heading different from the one used by the catalogers. You might think the library has no material on the subject murder, for example, unless you tried looking under HOMICIDE. If you can't find subject cards related to your topic, ask a librarian for help.

3. Focusing and Limiting

Sometimes a preliminary search turns up just the amount of information you need, and sometimes it turns up more than you can reasonably be expected to handle. If you find barely enough material, read through it before trying to narrow your topic. You may discover that the material will not support the topic as you originally conceived it, but that it will support another closely related topic or some line of thought that you had not anticipated.

If it is the sort of topic that has been written about in a great many books — the French Revolution, for example — you need to limit it in some way to make your research manageable. Your library may have an entire shelf of books on the topic, and you may not have time to read them all. By selecting one aspect of the topic (e.g., the French Revolution as reflected in the poetry of Wordsworth), you can quickly glance through the tables of contents and the indexes of a large number of books and limit your reading to a relatively small number of pages.

Writing teachers sometimes say that it is impossible to write about a large topic in a short paper. This is not true. In surveys, handbooks, and encyclopedias of all kinds, you can find brief articles about the largest topics imaginable — the plays of Shakespeare, the histories of various countries, entire disciplines like physics or astronomy, and even the universe itself. The problem with writing a term paper about a topic this large is not that it is impossible: it is only too possible. You could find all you need for a short paper by consulting a single encyclopedia. You could write a paper on Shakespeare without reading any of his plays.

But then you would not have learned very much. If all you know about Shakespeare's plays is what you read in an encyclopedia, your knowledge is broad but shallow. This is why teachers insist that research topics be narrowed and focused. They prefer that you learn a lot about one of Shakespeare's plays, perhaps a lot about one *aspect* of one of Shakespeare's plays (e.g., the use of garden imagery in *Hamlet*), rather than pick up a superficial knowledge of it all.

4. Asking Questions

Once you have chosen a topic and narrowed it sufficiently, ask yourself questions that will help you decide what sort of information you should be looking for in your reading. But information in libraries is just as inert as any other form of information. To bring it to life you need to ask questions and search for angles like those discussed in Chapter Two.

For example, suppose you had browsed through a dictionary and come up with "fire walk" as a topic. In an old dictionary, the 1924 edition of *Webster's New International*, "fire walk" is defined this way: "The ceremony or ordeal of walking through fire or upon stones heated by fire. It is performed by some Polynesians as a religious rite and in past ages was a recognized ordeal in Europe."

Fire walking, like any other topic, could be explored by questions you might think of in an open-ended dialogue with yourself.

Examples

Q Do fire walks still take place?

A I think so.

Q Where?

A In Polynesia, I suppose.

Q How do we know that fire walks take place?

A I've heard that Europeans have observed fire walks, and could not find any trickery involved.

Q Can you give some examples?

A No. But I will if I can find something in the library.

Q Are you surprised that fire walks took place in Europe too?

A Yes. I thought they were limited to the South Sea Islands.

Q Where and how long ago did they take place in Europe?

A I don't know.

Q How do we know they took place in Europe?

A I don't know.

Q Are there any differences between the European ceremonies and the Polynesian ceremonies?

A I don't know.

Q In what ways are the ceremonies alike?

A I don't know.

Q Are people ever seriously burned or injured?

A I don't know.

Q How do medical experts explain the fact that some people apparently walk through fire unharmed?

A I don't know.

A dialogue like this suggests a number of approaches to the topic. You could write a paper concentrating exclusively on Polynesian fire walks or exclusively on European fire walks. Or you could write a paper comparing and contrasting the two. Or you could write a paper examining what we know about fire walks for the possibility of fraud.

Before you settle on an approach, however, you need to begin reading, taking notes, and discovering which questions your research will answer. As you read, the material you discover will help you limit and focus your approach. It may also suggest new questions and new lines of investigation. Although you cannot focus too narrowly until you have done some reading, the sooner you formulate an approach, the easier your research will be. A restricted focus enables you to skip over or skim material you know in advance will be irrelevant. If you formulate an approach too soon, however, or stick to it too rigidly, you may find that the material in the library does not support the paper you had intended to write. In reading for a research paper, maintain the same flexibility you would maintain in conducting an interview.

5. Taking Notes

If you have had unhappy experiences writing "term papers" in high school, the mention of note cards might be unwelcome. No matter how tedious these little monsters may have seemed to you back then, they can make your writing tasks in college a lot easier if you use them properly.

There is absolutely nothing sacred about note cards. The research for many fine papers has been recorded in other ways, with notes jotted in spiral binders, on the backs of mimeographed handouts that no one reads, on shirt cuffs, paper bags, laundry tickets, and whatever else happened to be within the researcher's reach.

But these methods generally prove inconvenient for the writer in the long run. When the time comes to write the paper, it is impossible to separate the notes to paste them in various parts of a rough draft. And at the last minute, when it is time to type the paper in its final form, it is difficult, if not impossible, to locate the publication data needed for footnotes and bibliographies.

The habit of using note cards efficiently at the very beginning of a research project can save much time and anxiety toward the end of the project, when energies are nearly depleted.

Choose the form you prefer best: 3″ × 5″ cards, 5″ × 7″ cards, or half sheets of paper. Nothing larger. The small format will force you to separate your notes into related bits of information that you can arrange and rearrange as the organization of your paper takes shape. Never write on the backs of note cards or note sheets: you may eventually want to put the information on the front and the information on the back in different parts of the paper.

If you are a very methodical person, you really could use

two sets of note cards: one on which you jot down information, impressions, and quotations as you read, with only a brief reference to the author and title of your source; the other on which you put the complete publication information for each item in the precise form you intend to use in the bibliography. The bibliography is a list of works consulted. It is customary to put such a list at the end of a research paper with the sources arranged alphabetically according to the last names of the authors. Although it is the last part of the paper to be typed, you will save yourself from last-minute trauma if you prepare it in standard form on note cards while your research is in progress.

Sample Bibliographic Card

Gann, Ernest K. "Thirty-three Hours that Changed the World." *Saturday Review*, 16 April 1977, pp. 7-10.

A card like this should be written out just as soon as you find a source you think you will use in your paper. Take this book with you to the library so you can jot down the information exactly as it will appear in the bibliography (Chapter Eleven). As your project nears completion, you can arrange cards like these in alphabetical order and type your bibliography directly from them. Put nothing else on your bibliographic cards. When you take notes, use separate cards like the one on the next page.

Sample Note Card

Gann, "Thirty-three Hours"
Gann very high on the significance
of Lindbergh's flight. Suggests it
could be compared "to the discovery
of fire "(p.7)." ... the more I considered
the impact of his presence on earth, the
more logical the comparison seemed "(p.7).
Strikes me as an exaggeration. What
Lind. did was inevitable. Someone
else would have if he hadn't.

The note card has an abbreviated reference to the author and title at the top. If this note were actually used in the paper, the writer could look under Gann's name in the stack of bibliographic cards and find all the information needed for a footnote.

6. Paraphrase and Plagiarism

For many students, writing a research paper is a trivial game that is played by copying (or nearly copying) material from a dozen sources, arranging it in some sequence that is at least vaguely coherent, and adding footnotes. The payoff is a paper that is supposed to satisfy the instructor, though the writer, for sure, has found no joy in it.

Actually, the result is often joyless for both student and instructor, as they spend time in conferences haggling over which phrases in the paper are sufficiently altered from their source to be claimed by students as their own work, without quotation marks or footnotes. In other words, the paper becomes a game of paraphrasing or plagiarizing. When you paraphrase—that is, express someone else's ideas in your own words and add a footnote—you win. But when you plagiarize—

that is, express someone else's ideas in someone else's words without giving credit—you lose.

The best way to beat this game is to avoid it. You can do this by playing a simple psychological trick on yourself. Don't treat the books and articles you read as books and articles. Treat them as people. Pretend that you are interviewing rather than reading, dealing with the spoken word rather than with the written word.

If you would pretend that words in books and periodicals disappeared shortly after you read them, just as spoken words do, you would have no trouble with paraphrasing. Read the material you have found, *put it aside*, and write notes from what you remember. If you ever find yourself taking notes by glancing back and forth from what you are writing to what you are reading, then you should put quotation marks around the notes and copy exactly what is in the book. In general, however, it is better to read what you want to read, *put it aside*, and jot down what you have learned on note cards.

When do you use quotation marks? You use quotation marks in a research paper in exactly the same situations that would require them in writing a paper from an interview. You use them when you quote your source word for word. But since a paper is supposed to represent what you think about a subject as well as what your sources say, quotations should be fairly infrequent. A paper that is nothing but a string of one quoted passage after another is not really a research paper. It does not demonstrate the sort of mastery you would have over material if you could express it in your own words.

Of course, it takes time to gain this mastery, particularly if you are exploring a subject that is new to you. So your first step in writing a research paper is to get started early. Give yourself lots of time to digest new information well enough to express it orally without referring to notes. As you read through your material, keep playing with it in your mind, looking for a problem, an angle, a thesis to support, a rhetorical stance (see Chapter Four). You are not ready to begin writing the paper until you have mastered the material well enough to tell a friend, without looking at your notes, what your topic is and (if you take a persuasive stance) what your thesis is, or (if you take an expository stance) what your angle is. (If you haven't dealt with these terms in writing other papers, they are all explained in Chapter Four.) When you can talk your paper out in your own words, then you are ready to write it.

Not that the paper will be exactly what you would talk. On the contrary, as soon as you begin writing, you will notice that writing forces you to be more precise in your thinking, that it suggests patterns of arrangement you hadn't considered before, that it uncovers problems and insights you hadn't been aware of when you were merely talking. That's why writing is a valuable exercise for its own sake.

When you get to this stage, write your paper from beginning to end without looking at any of your sources or any of your notes. If you can't remember exact facts and figures, leave blank spaces and fill them in later. If you can't remember the exact words you want to quote, leave space and add them later.

After you have written the paper, then add the footnotes and quotations only where you need them. If you have followed the process outlined above, you should add quoted material only in a few special circumstances: when you are analyzing a text and you need to give the reader the exact words; when the source is an authority and you are relying on that authority to bolster a point you are making; when your source has expressed something in language that is so good that you want to preserve it. But if you have truly digested the material before you begin writing, quotations should be relatively rare. A paper with more than two or three quotations per page is suspect. It suggests that you have not really made the material your own.

Quotations, of course, must be footnoted, and the footnotes should tell the reader exactly where the quoted material came from (see Chapter Eleven for note form). Quotations also must represent the source accurately. Word for word. *Verbatim.* No changes. If for some reason you must add or leave out part of what you quote, look at pp. 399–400 for directions about how these alterations should be handled.

When do you use footnotes? As long as you are expressing yourself in your own words, you need footnotes to acknowledge only those ideas or bits of information that are not commonly available. This rule requires you to exercise some judgment. Ideas and information are considered commonly available even if only a few people know about them as long as they are recorded in a fairly large number of sources. Suppose, for example, you were writing a paper about Thomas Jefferson and you mention the fact that Jefferson was born in 1743. You may not have known that before you began writing. If you asked a hundred people when Jefferson was born, you probably would not get one correct answer, unless it was a lucky guess. And yet you would not have to footnote the year of Jefferson's birth because that is the sort of information that is commonly available in dictionaries, encyclopedias, and historical books and documents of various kinds.

Suppose, however, you discover from reading Jefferson's letters that he had corresponded with some Frenchman about the nature of rhythm in English poetry, and suppose you expressed Jefferson's theory in your own words. That is the sort of information that requires a footnote. Jefferson's theory of versification is not so commonly available that anyone could find it by looking in a few standard reference works.

Learning what to footnote and what not to footnote takes practice. And the rules change as you and your readers change. If you were a recognized authority on Jefferson's theory of versification and you were writing for readers who also had studied that theory, there would be less of a need to add a footnote, since the information would be commonly available *to those readers.*

Learning when to put quotation marks shouldn't require as much practice. *Whenever you are working with your sources so closely that you have to have them open before you as you take notes, use quotation marks and copy accurately.* Otherwise you will be playing the game of paraphrase and plagiarism.

Sorting It Out

Many student writers falter in this important step of the writing process. Instead of sorting their material out in a pattern that makes sense, they try to get it all in the paper, dropping footnotes along the way like bread crumbs to mark a path through a forest, hoping the teacher will be impressed by the sheer length of the trail.

Don't do it. If you have not discovered a viewpoint of your own as you read your material, look ahead to the chapter on organization. One of the standard patterns may help you to discover some simple relationships in your material, relationships that will give meaning to your work. Do not start writing the paper until you have at least a vague idea of the structure you want it to take, a plan for including certain information at certain stages. Above all, do not try to stuff all the information in your notes into the paper. Decide on a main point, choose information that supports it, and discard the rest, no matter how interesting or impressive it looks to you.

Remember, too, that using the library as a source does not cut you off from the other sources: observation and interviews. If at all possible, do not write a research paper in an ivory tower. Find some way of observing your topic and testing what you read against what you see and hear for yourself. Find an expert on your topic and ask for an interview. Test the expert's opinions against what you read, and test what you read against the expert's opinions. If you are writing a paper about literature, do not let the opinions of published critics take the place of firsthand observation on your own part: published critics can be wrong, and you can write a better paper by pointing out how their observations compare with your own.

Without your own observations, a paper is likely to be as dull and uninteresting to your readers as it is to you. Since writing is a way of thinking, keep thinking for yourself throughout the entire process.

EXERCISES

1. Read the following passage once or twice until you feel you understand it. Then close your book. Without looking at the passage, tell the student next to you what it says. Then listen to what that student thinks the passage says. When you think you both understand the passage, write the information down in your own words. Don't look at the passage again until you've finished writing.

Although the number of women working has doubled since 1950, the Census Bureau reports that in 1974 the median income for women was $6,957 or only 57% of the average take-home pay of the typical American male worker, $12,152. Just four years earlier, in 1970, the average working woman earned $5,440 or 59% of the median income for men, $9,184.

—Hana Umlauf, "Women in 1976: Progress (?) Report," *The World Almanac.*

After you have written your own version, discuss it with a class-mate or with your instructor. Would you have to add any specific figures to what you wrote? Would what you wrote require quotation marks or footnotes if it appeared in a research paper?

2. Repeat exercise 1, using the following text:

Last fall about 11% of M.S.U.'s 7700 freshmen were required to take a remedial course in English. Says English Instructor Mary Davis: "Even though they can talk to you as sophisticated and aware 19-year-olds, their voice on paper is that of a ten-year-old."

The same problem exists at scores of other colleges. Cornell, Stanford and Wisconsin have established special writing-improvement centers that students attend voluntarily. At Yale, for the first time since the late 1950's, "bonehead English" (basic composition) is being taught freshmen lacking the most rudi-mentary skills. . . .

—"Writing Wrongs," *Time*, 8 November 1976, p. 77.

3. Repeat exercise 1, using the following text:

Lynn Jordan of Virginia, a volunteer worker for consumers' rights, has proved again that when a woman takes up a cause she can get results. Lynn took legal action against an agency of her state—and won a far-reaching decision from the U.S. Su-preme Court. The issue was whether the Virginia Board of Pharmacy acted unconstitutionally in preventing pharmacists from advertising prescription-drug prices. The Supreme Court by a vote of seven to one ruled that it did. The full meaning of this historic decision is yet to come. It may mean that consumers will have a constitutional right to know competitive prices not only for drugs, but for *all* professional services. The Federal Trade Commission estimated that the invalidation of similar re-strictions against drug-price advertising in 34 states could save consumers more than $300 million yearly.

—"A Cure for Rx Prices," *Good Housekeeping*, November 1976, p. 82, by Glenn White.

WRITING ASSIGNMENT

With the help of your instructor, choose two or three topics you would like to know more about. Go to the library and conduct a preliminary search to determine if material on any of those topics is available. Read quickly through as much material as you can, searching for an approach to your topic. Make a set of note cards and bibliographic cards (see Chapter Eleven for bibliographic form). Return to class ready for the exercise described in the Checkpoint below at the end of Chapter Eleven.

Chapter Eleven

———◆———

Term Paper Form

1. A Variety of Style Manuals

Scholars and publishers seem unable to agree on the best form to follow in writing footnotes and bibliographies for documented papers. Each discipline and each press has its favorite authority on these matters. Writers in the social sciences and in some of the hard sciences generally prefer a book called the *Publication Manual of the American Psychological Association*, familiarly known as the APA style manual. Another popular guide is *A Manual for Writers of Term Papers, Theses, and Dissertations*, which is usually referred to as "Turabian," the name of its author. Turabian is based on a much larger book, *A Manual of Style*, which most people call the Chicago manual, because it is published by the University of Chicago Press. The Chicago manual is used mainly as a guide for preparing manuscripts that are going to appear in print. Departments of English and other modern languages use the *MLA Handbook for Writers of Research Papers, Theses, and Dissertations*, published by the Modern Language Association of America. This one is usually called the MLA handbook.

Because each one of these style manuals recommends different forms for footnotes and bibliographic entries, no one memorizes them all. If you use any one book often enough—as you are likely to do when you take advanced courses in your major field—you will soon memorize the correct form for the most common kind of sources; but you will still have to go back to the book on occasion to see how unusual publications should be handled. The forms explained below are based on the MLA handbook.

2. The Bibliography

A bibliography is an alphabetical list of works consulted in preparing a paper. It should include at least all the works that are mentioned in the paper and the footnotes. If it includes only the works referred to, it can be entitled "Works Cited" instead of "Bibliography." If it includes not only works cited, but other works consulted, the term "Bibliography" is more appropriate.

Although the bibliography is placed at the very end of a research paper, you should begin preparing it while you are doing your research. As soon as you discover a book or article that you are likely to rely on for your paper, copy down the bibliographic information in the correct form on a note card or note slip. If you will follow this procedure, preparing the bibliography for your final draft will be merely a matter of arranging your cards or slips in alphabetical order and typing them. If you do not follow this procedure, preparing the bibliography for your final draft will be a nightmare in which you wrestle with obscure forms, scurry back to the library for information you forgot to copy down, and perhaps fake information that you have lost, hoping that the instructor won't notice.

Although many writers do not realize it, there is a logic underlying bibliographic forms. If you can grasp this logic, you may find the forms easier to learn.

For example, the periods within the entries have a purpose. They mark off divisions between the several different kinds of information in the entry. In fact, you might think of the spaces between the periods as a series of five basic slots. The acronym ATTEP may help you remember them:

| author(s) | title | translator(s) | editor(s) | publication information |

Making a bibliographic entry is a matter of filling in these slots. If some of the slots are not appropriate for the work you are citing—if, for example, there is no translator, or no editor, or if the author is unnamed—then leave those slots vacant and fill in the others. In the examples below, none of the entries has an editor or a translator; therefore those slots are not represented. In the last item, the article in *Time*, even the author is unknown; the author slot therefore is left vacant, and the entry is filed alphabetically under *M*, the first letter in the title.

Examples

Defoe, Daniel. A Journal of the Plague Year. Ed. Louis Landa. London: Oxford University Press, 1969.

Frank, Robert Worth, Jr. Chaucer and The Legend of Good Women. Cambridge, Mass.: Harvard University Press, 1972.

"Making a Safer Microbe." Time, 18 Aug. 1977, p. 45.

The second line in a bibliographical entry is indented instead of the first for a good reason: because a bibliography is an alphabetical list, it makes sense to let the beginning of each entry stick out five spaces to the left, so that the alphabetical arrangement is more visible.

Similarly, it makes sense that authors are listed in a bibliography last name first; any alphabetical listing of people—a telephone book, for example—lists last names first, for reasons that will be obvious to you if you imagine a directory in which you had to look through all the Marys in town in order to find Mary Doe.

There are a few other conventions that you should take note of:

1. If there is more than one author, the additional names appear first name first. For example:

> Bennett, William and Joel Gurin. "Science that
> Frightens Scientists: The Great Debate over DNA."
> The Atlantic, Feb. 1977, p. 49.

2. Titles should be taken from the title page, not from the cover. For example, *The Journal of Basic Writing* (the title on the title page), not *Basic Writing* (the title on the cover).

3. Titles of poems, short stories, and articles are always enclosed in quotation marks. "The Red Wheel Barrow" (a poem), "Hills Like White Elephants" (a short story), "The New Alchemy" (a scholarly article).

4. Titles of plays, books, and journals are always underlined when typed and italicized when they appear in print. They are not enclosed in quotation marks. *The Wild Duck* (a play), *Happy Days* (a book), *Philological Quarterly* (a scholarly journal).

5. Publication information for books always includes the city (add the state or country if there is any chance of confusion—e.g., Cambridge, Mass. or Cambridge, England) followed by a colon, the publishing company followed by a comma, and the year of publication followed by a period. If more than one city is mentioned on the title page, there is no need to list them all; choose a major city and ignore the others.

One other convention is the distinction between magazines that begin with page one in each issue—like *Time, Newsweek, The New Yorker*—and periodicals that are numbered continuously through several issues, so that when all the issues are bound together into a single volume, the page numbers run from beginning to end, like the pages in a book. Most scholarly and professional journals have this second kind of pagination.

An entry for an article in a journal with continuous pagination includes the volume number, the year (in parentheses), and the pages, *without* "p." or "pp."

Example

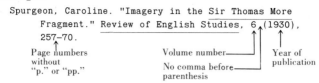

Spurgeon, Caroline. "Imagery in the Sir Thomas More
  Fragment." Review of English Studies, 6 (1930),
  257–70.

Page numbers   Volume number   Year of
without   publication
"p." or "pp."   No comma before
                     parenthesis

But a reference to a popular magazine omits the volume number, adds the precise date of the issue — without parentheses — and indicates the page numbers, preceded by "p." or "pp."

Example

Scheifelbein, Susan. "Teaching Poseidon to Turn a
  Profit." Saturday Review, 6 Jan. 1979, pp. 23–25.

Full date, no parentheses   Page numbers
                                   with
                                   "p." or "pp."

As a rule, don't use "p." or "pp." when you use a volume number.

You will find models of bibliographic entries for the most common sources on pp. 253–256. If you have a source that is not covered in these examples, consult the MLA handbook or ask your instructor for help.

3. Footnotes and Endnotes

In research papers, numbered notes are used to show the source of quotations or of some specific information that is not commonly available. Numbers are placed within the text of the paper, slightly raised, right after the quotation or the information to be documented.

Example

Marcus Klein claims further that it is the sheer weight of chaotic existence that first of all defines Bellow's heroes.[1] They are, then, first initiates in a conflict between "groping individuality and the darkness."[2]

The source of the information before the first number and the source of the quoted material before the second number could be indicated in one of two places: either in a footnote, which is a note that appears at the bottom of the page, or in an endnote, which would appear along with other notes listed in numerical order just after the end of the paper and just before the bibliography. Both forms are acceptable, but many students prefer endnotes, since they require considerably less typographic dexterity than footnotes. In either case, the notes take the same form.

Notes have the same five basic slots to fill as bibliographic entries:

‾‾‾‾‾‾	‾‾‾‾‾‾	‾‾‾‾‾‾‾‾	‾‾‾‾‾‾	‾‾‾‾‾‾‾
author(s)	title	translator(s)	editor(s)	publication information

But notes are arranged slightly differently. Most of the differences will seem logical to you if you can remember that a note is thought of as one continuous comment, as if it were a sentence just like other sentences in the text, whereas a bibliographic entry is thought of as several separate bits of information.

Because a note is thought of as a sentence, it has no period — except for abbreviations — until the end. And because notes are not arranged alphabetically, authors' names are given in their normal order, and the pattern of indentation is the same as it would be for the first sentence in an ordinary paragraph. Footnotes generally have one more specific bit of information: the exact page or pages from which the information or the quotation is taken.

Example

[3] Frank Bastian, "Defoe's Journal of the Plague Year Reconsidered." Review of English Studies, 16 (1965), 152.

[4] Susan Scheifelbein, "Teaching Poseidon to Turn a Profit," Saturday Review, 6 Jan. 1979, p. 24.

Notes differ from bibliographic entries in that in the former the pattern of indentation is normal, the author's name appears in normal order, the periods within a bibliographic entry are replaced by commas, and usually a reference to a specific page or to a few specific pages is added. Also, in a note, the publication information for a book is enclosed in parentheses.

Example

⁵Robert Worth Frank, Jr., Chaucer and The Legend of Good Women (Cambridge, Mass.: Harvard University Press, 1972), p. 132.

If an author's name is given in the text near the footnote number, there is no need to repeat the name in the footnote. For example, if the text looks like this —

Marcus Klein claims further that it is the sheer weight of chaotic existence that first of all defines Bellow's heroes.[1]

— the note may look like this:

¹"A Discipline of Nobility: Saul Bellow's Fiction," Kenyon Review, 24 (1962), 45.

The technique of mentioning the author's name in the text rather than in the note is worth considering, especially if the note refers to quoted material. Inexperienced writers often lace their research papers with quotations that have no persons attached to them, and the reader must look to the footnotes to determine whose voice is being heard.

Example

The effect of evaluating compositions while they are still in progress is threefold: it "helps the student to sharpen his skills as a critic of other writing, guides him as he revises, and demonstrates to him that, finally, evaluating his writing is *his* job."[6] But to write comments of any quality, the critic "must be able to analyze the student's writing and clearly communicate this analysis."[7]

This might be called the Hamlet's-father's-ghost syndrome, because it resembles those scenes in *Hamlet* when the dead king's voice rises mysteriously through the boards from an invisible source beneath the stage. To avoid this syndrome, make the source of your quotations visible by working the name of the author into the text near the quoted material.

Example

The value of having students criticize their work while it is in progress is summarized by Muriel Harris: it "helps the student to sharpen his skills as a critic of other writing, guides him as he revises, and demonstrates to him that, finally, evaluating his writing is *his* job."[6] But Catherine Lynch and Patricia Klemans have pointed out that to offer criticism that students will find useful, the critic "must be able to analyze the student's writing and clearly communicate this analysis."[7]

Because the authors are mentioned in the text, their names may be omitted in the notes.

Examples

[6] "Evaluation: The Process for Revision," Journal of Basic Writing, 1 (Spring/Summer 1978), p. 90.

[7] "Evaluating Our Evaluations," College English, 40 (1978), p. 180.

The habit of mentioning the authors' names within the text has fringe benefits. Inexperienced writers often have trouble leading into quoted material gracefully. If they mention a name, however, it is a relatively easy matter to write "Kleinsmith says" or "Peterson, on the other hand, argues that," or "Sagan proposed that." If the name you mention is not familiar to your readers, you might add an identifying phrase.

Examples

Kleinsmith, a public relations official with the NRC, says that . . .

Peterson, one of the mayor's advisors, argues that . . .

. . . ," said Sagan, who was in charge of the imaging team.

The second fringe benefit is that it makes inexperienced writers more aware of how much they are depending upon the words of other people. If you find yourself dropping more than four or five names and quotations per page, you should begin to suspect that you have not digested the material well enough to write about it in your own words. Go back to Chapter Ten and read the advice about putting your notes aside as you write a complete first draft (see especially pp. 239–240).

If you intend to make more than one reference to the same source, it is better to include the author's name in the note even though it appears in the text. If the first note for a particular source has full information, other references may be made simply by giving the author's name and the appropriate page numbers. For example, if you had two or more references to Klein's article about Bellow, only the first one would have to have the complete publication information.

Example

[1] Marcus Klein, " A Discipline of Nobility: Saul Bellow's Fiction," Kenyon Review, 24 (1962), 45.

[2] Klein, p. 46.

This method of making additional references is easier to handle than the old *ibid* and *op. cit.* method, which is no longer necessary. The author's name and the page number will serve as a reference even if the two notes are separated by notes referring to other sources. If you are using more than one work by the same author, however, you should add the title, or at least part of the title, to the short form to avoid confusion.

4. Sample Notes and Bibliographic Entries

Sample notes and bibliographic entries for the kinds of sources you are most likely to use in a paper for an introductory course are given below. If you run into a source that is not listed in the samples, consult the MLA handbook or ask your instructor for advice.

Article in a Popular Magazine

NOTE

[1] William Bennett and Joel Gurin, "Science that Frightens Scientists: The Great Debate over DNA," The Atlantic, Feb. 1977, p. 49.

BIBLIOGRAPHY

Bennett, William and Joel Gurin. "Science that Frightens
    Scientists: The Great Debate over DNA." The Atlantic,
    Feb. 1977, pp. 43–50, 55–62.

Article in a Scholarly Journal with Continuous Pagination

NOTE

[2] Peter E. Firchow, "Private Faces in Public Places:
Auden's The Orators," PMLA, 92 (1977), 254.

BIBLIOGRAPHY

Firchow, Peter E. "Private Faces in Public Places. Auden's
    The Orators." PMLA, 92 (1977), 253–72.

Article in a Scholarly Journal Without Continuous Pagination

NOTE

[3] Ann Petrie, "Teaching the Thinking Process in Essay
Writing," Journal of Basic Writing, 1 (Fall/Winter 1976), 61.

BIBLIOGRAPHY

Petrie, Ann. "Teaching the Thinking Process in Essay Writing."
    Journal of Basic Writing, 1 (Fall/Winter 1976), 60–67.

Article With More Than One Author

NOTE

[4] Catherine Lynch and Patricia Klemans, "Evaluating Our
Evaluations," College English, 40 (1978), 172.

BIBLIOGRAPHY

Lynch, Catherine and Patricia Klemans. "Evaluating Our
    Evaluations." College English, 40 (1978), 166–180.

Article in a Newspaper

NOTE

5

Bernard Gwertzmann, "State Dept. Says Israel Suspends Rights of Arabs in Some Areas," New York Times, City Ed., 8 Feb. 1979, Sec. A, p. 1, cols. 4 and 5; p. 9, col. 1.

BIBLIOGRAPHY

Gwertzmann, Bernard. "State Dept. Says Israel Suspends Rights of Arabs in Some Areas." New York Times, City Ed., 8 Feb. 1979, Sec. A, p. 1, cols 4 and 5; p. 9, col. 1.

Essay, Story, or Article in a Collection

NOTE

6 Mina P. Shaughnessy, "Basic Writing," in Teaching Composition: 10 Bibliographical Essays, ed. Gary Tate (Fort Worth: Texas Christian University Press, 1976), p. 151.

BIBLIOGRAPHY

Shaughnessy, Mina P. "Basic Writing." Teaching Composition: 10 Bibliographical Essays. Ed. Gary Tate. Fort Worth: Texas Christian University Press, 1976, pp. 137–167.

Book With One Author

NOTE

7 Christopher Jencks, Inequality (New York: Basic Books, 1972), p. 12.

BIBLIOGRAPHY

Jencks, Christopher. Inequality. New York: Basic Books, 1972.

Books With More Than One Author

NOTE

      8Herman A. Estrin and Donald V. Mehus, The American
Language in the 1970s (San Francisco: Boyd and Fraser, 1974),
p. 25.

BIBLIOGRAPHY

Estrin, Herman A., and Donald V. Mehus. The American Language
      in the 1970s. San Francisco: Boyd and Fraser, 1974.

Translations

NOTE

      9Homer, The Odyssey, trans. Albert Cook (New York: Norton,
1967), p. 256.

BIBLIOGRAPHY

Homer. The Odyssey. Trans. Albert Cook. New York: Norton,
      1967.

CHECKPOINT FOR RESEARCH PAPERS

Allow the instructor to select a few bibliographic cards from the
class and read them aloud—commas, periods, space, capitalization, and all. The class should interrupt the instructor whenever
the bibliographic form explained in this chapter is violated. If you
have a bibliographic card that you are unsure of, ask the instructor
to use it as an example.

After the instructor and the class have examined a few bibliographic cards together, swap cards with a student nearby and
check each other's work. Return the cards and ask whatever questions or offer whatever explanations you think might be necessary.

Read or reread Chapter Four for advice about choosing a rhetorical stance and a pattern of organization.

Next Checkpoint, p. 92 if you take a persuasive stance, p. 102
if you take an expository stance.

HANDBOOK

Chapter Twelve

Correctness, Dictionaries, and Spelling

1. Correctness

In the past, English teachers looked to grammarians for rules about correctness in language, and grammarians were sometimes fussy about what they considered correct English. If they heard a Cajun from Louisiana saying, "Hey, man, dat gumbo don't got no shrimps in it, no," they would either pull their hair out in despair or quietly regard the speaker as a barbarian for whom there was no hope. English, they would say, does not use double negatives (*"don't got no"*), much less triple negatives (*"don't got no* shrimps in it, *no"*), and they would object to the use of *got* for *have* and *shrimps* for *shrimp*.

But within the past fifty or sixty years, the emergence of a new field of study, linguistics, has changed the way grammarians look at language. Imitating scientists in other fields, linguists treat sentences like specimens in a laboratory. They observe, describe, analyze, and generalize about their specimens. Instead of telling us what the language should be, they tell us what it is. Linguists find out whether a given sentence is typical of the speaker's region, race, or age group, and they describe the grammar used by that group. Linguists, for example, might say that English speakers in southwest Louisiana use double negatives and an extra negative as an emphatic tag. They would not be likely to say anything about the rightness or wrongness of these structures, except, perhaps, that they are right for speakers in that region.

Linguistics has stirred up considerable controversy among teachers, writers, and editors. On the one hand, if all the varieties of English in America are considered correct, then English teachers — some of whom have made careers of telling the difference between good English and bad — would seem to have lost their usefulness. On the other hand, linguistics has confirmed something that many people already knew intuitively: the varieties of English spoken in this country are valuable and enjoyable in themselves.

The different kinds of English spoken in the United States and in other English-speaking countries are called dialects. A dialect is defined by those peculiar habits of pronunciation, vocabulary, or phraseology characteristic of any identifiable group. In Alabama, for example, many children say "nahce hwaht rahce" when they read "nice white rice." In Texas, many people grow up saying "fixin' to" instead of "going to" (e.g., "Ahm fixin' to go shoppin' in Dallas"). In New England, people use the word *pail* in ordinary conversation because *bucket* strikes them as poetical; in other parts of the country, *bucket* is considered the ordinary word and *pail* seems poetic. And the language of many black Americans has distinctive structural features, like "Ain' nobody gonna sell me no used car," and "Shirley asked her mother could she go out tonight." From a linguistic point of view, all of these varieties of English are equal.

Linguistics has pulled the rug from under people who think the variety of English they speak is better than the English spoken in other parts of the country or by other segments of the population. It makes these people seem like the waiter in New Jersey who told some Southern girls, "Youse guys sure talk funny." The fact is, we all talk funny. Since we all speak dialects, perhaps the most intelligent response to the diversity of the English language is to appreciate and enjoy it rather than to eradicate it.

This makes the English teacher's job more interesting and more difficult. In the old days, we could rely on books to make simple judgments about right and wrong usage; now we recognize that what's right in some contexts may be wrong in others. While it may be foolish for a reporter for the *New York Times* to write "They ain't gonna be no garbage pickup this week," it might be extremely effective for a Southern politician to put on her most Southern drawl and say in a campaign speech, "If the legislature gives us a good law, we flat ain' gonna mess with it in the courts." Politicians have known for a long time that imitating the language of their constituents is an effective device for winning their confidence. A senator in the Georgia legislature once summarized his opposition to a pending bill by saying, "It just ain't right." When reminded of the "correct" form he answered, "I know, but 'It *isn't* right' just doesn't have the same force as 'It *ain't* right.'"

Instead of telling students the difference between good and bad English, teachers now help them decide between effective and ineffective English in given contexts. Academic writing is one of those contexts.

The various dialects of American English have long had a place in print, but often as a way of identifying the regional, social, educational, or racial background of the persons using them. *Huckleberry Finn*, which many people regard as the greatest American novel, is written in seven different nineteenth-century dialects, all of which are different from the dialect normally used in newspapers and books at that time. But the dialects have a purpose, and they are used with a degree of control that is beyond all but the most gifted writers. Huckleberry's language is an important sign of the person he is, a boy largely untouched by school, who is for that reason innocent of the illusions as well as the sophistication of educated people. In more recent fiction, characters are still defined by the language they speak. When novelist John Cheever has a prisoner in *Falconer* say of his sons, "I know they won't stuff their wives or their kids into no rowboat and go down the river to wave to old Daddy," the language is intended to suggest something about the educational level of the speaker.

Sometimes the various dialects of English are used in situations in which they would not normally be expected, not only as an expression of pride in the writer's linguistic heritage, but as proof of the expressive power of these dialects. One of the most famous examples of this kind of writing is by a black language scholar, Geneva Smitherman, whose article "God Don't Never Change" is written entirely in what she calls "Black Idiom" (see *College English*, 34 [1973], 828–33). The article begins "Ain nothin in a long time lit up the English teaching profession like the current hassle over Black English."

Dialects associated with particular regions, races, or social classes are used in print when writers want to call attention to their regional, racial, or social background, or to the background of invented characters. When writers are not interested in calling attention to their background, they use another form of English, based upon the various dialects of spoken English but reflecting none of them completely. This is the dialect normally used in newspapers, magazines, and informative books. Ordinarily, the language in published work gives few if any cues about the writers' social, ethnic, or geographic background, even when their spoken language—if we heard it on a tape or telephone—might be rich with cues of this sort.

The importance of learning the conventional dialect of printed English has perhaps been greatly exaggerated in the past, since good writing is good in any dialect and bad writing is bad even if all its forms are standard. Nevertheless, it is useful for writers to know that "fixin' to" and "ain' nobody gonna" and "I seen it" call attention to themselves in print, and although these forms may have power and purpose in some contexts, they can undermine a writer's image and authority in others.

The conventional dialect of printed English differs from various spoken dialects in two ways—in its lexicon (i.e., its vocabulary) and in its syntax (i.e., the way in which words are put together). Because the words and structures of printed English often sound artificial to people who are accustomed to other words and structures, the conventions of printed English can be difficult to learn. To someone like Huckleberry Finn, the use of *without* for *unless* (see p. 9) would sound normal and correct, though for readers accustomed to printed English, it seems peculiar. To someone who knows a certain bird as an

"Indian hen," the term "pileated woodpecker" sounds rather awkward, even though that is the term normally used in books about birds.

The structures of printed English may also seem stilted to people who are accustomed to other structures. Louisiana Cajuns sometimes ask "What time it is?" and they would have to force themselves to ask "What time is it?" For people in many cities, *seen* is the normal past tense of *see*, and they feel better saying "I seen the ballgame last night" than "I saw the ballgame last night." Many people have trouble remembering to write the final *s* that is normal for the plural of nouns in print because in their speech they omit the *s*, especially when there is another signal, like a number, to indicate plurality. Thus, "The fire station is about three mile down this road" sounds as good to them or even better than "The fire station is about three miles down this road," which is the form that would be used in print.

Similarly, the final *d*'s, *ed*'s and *t*'s that signal past tense in English are often omitted in writing by people whose dialect omits them in speech. This is especially true when the past time is already indicated by some other word in the sentence (e.g., "Yesterday my older brother watch television all day") or when the past sense of the word is obscure (e.g., "I'm finish with this book now, so you can borrow it").

Some of these dialectal features have been associated with Black English, but in fact almost every one of them can be observed in the speech and writing of white students as well. One structure commonly mentioned in connection with the language of black Americans is what linguists call "copulative deletion," the omission of the verb *be* in sentences like "My brother sick today," or "This school good," which in conventional printed English would be "My brother is sick today" and "This school is good." But when a white city councilman in New Orleans phoned in a radio report from his Lakeview home during a recent hurricane, he said emphatically, "We dry," deleting the *are* that would have been required in printed English. And similarly, one of the more prominent Southern governors usually deleted the copulative more than he used it. Few dialectal features of American English observe racial boundaries.

Because everyone's speech is unique, the difference between each person's dialect (or idiolect) and the dialect of printed English is an individual matter. Students who are determined to master the dialect of printed English, therefore, might begin by discovering the characteristics of their own special language. One way to do this is to make two lists, one column for words and phrases used in ordinary conversation but not in printed English, the other column for equivalent expressions in printed English.

Good writing should never be thought of in terms of correctness alone: some of the most barbarous writing in America today—legal documents, sociological tracts, and even literary criticism—is impeccable in form. Correctness is merely the surface of a writer's skill: without economy, clarity, forcefulness, imagination, and, above all, good ideas, correctness is hardly worth pursuing. On the other hand, since most readers are not as dispassionate about conventions as linguists are, writers who flout the conventions are likely to alienate readers they might otherwise reach.

Concern for correctness should never slow a writer down in early stages of composition. Write or type as quickly as you can get your ideas on paper. Then go over your work very carefully and edit it. Of course you will not be able to remember all the rules; no one can. So return to these chapters whenever you have questions about punctuation or agreement, and consult a dictionary whenever you have questions about spelling or usage.

Meanwhile, a few exercises might help you remember some of what you may have recently learned.

EXERCISES

1. In a class discussion, make a list of words and phrases that are common in your language and in the language of your classmates but not common in printed English. Are any of these expressions limited to a particular region or group? Some examples of these expressions and words might include "make yourself to home," "please carry me home after the party," usages of *bring* and *take*, "like to have never," and so forth.

2. Dialects can be used by writers to establish characters or roles quite different from their real selves. In the following paper,

Janet Tomkins, a student, uses local dialect to describe a tent revival from the point of view of an eleven-year-old boy who did not
particularly want to be there. Identify the words and phrases that
would not normally be used in quite the same way in printed English. What effect do they have in this paper? Would the paper be
better or worse if it were written to conform entirely to the traditions of printed English?

It was the kind of steamy Alabama night that made you just want
to find the nearest creek and sink in up to your neck. Even the
mosquitoes were sweating. The big canvas tent was a faded
mustard color, and it smelled moldy and sour, like an old sneaker
that's been left out in the rain. Inside there were three sections
of seats made up of eight rows each. The seats were wooden
boards settin' on cement blocks. The bad thing about these
boards was that ever once an' a while a splinter got in your tail
end and kind of rubbed you the wrong way.

You could tell everybody was burning up. Some of the ladies
in the tent were fanning themselves with those fans that have the
wide popsicle sticks for handles and a picture of a little girl all
dressed up in her pink Easter dress, singing in the church. Some
people had fans with pictures of Jesus praying at Gethsemane,
and I think they came from the funeral home over at Putnam.
Nobody looked real happy.

Sarah Boone led the singing, and we sang four verses of
"Bringing in the Sheaves" and two verses of "Trust and Obey"
before she even let us stand up, and that was only because Mr.
Little suggested we sing "Stand Up, Stand Up for Jesus."

The visitin' preacher — I forgot his name — had on a white suit
with thin black stripes, and a tomato red shirt, with a red and
black and white flowerdy tie. He had black hair that was combed
to one side, but it was greasy lookin' and a little piece would
separate from the rest and fall down in his eye. He preached on
sinnin' of some kind, hollerin' and shakin' the Bible at us like he
didn't have no control over it. Then his voice would drop to a low
whisper and people'd sit on the edge of the benches, straining to
hear every word. Ever' now and then some man would say
"Amen," or some baby would cry, but for the most part people
just fanned and listened.

It kept gettin' hotter and hotter and my mouth started feeling
like cotton. I got this sick feeling like the time I'd smoked rabbit
tobacco and it made me wonder if God was getting back at me
for doing that. I wished that preacher would hurry up. My hands
were all sweaty, and things seemed kind of hazy for a while.

Then I felt Mama shakin' my shoulder. Everybody was singing "Just As I Am," and then the 10 o'clock whistle blew down at the convict camp, and I heart it start to rain.

3. Below are two passages written by the same student, Pat Banks. Both passages describe the same problem, juvenile crime; but one is written from the point of view and in the dialect of a person involved in the crime, while the other is written in the conventional dialect of printed English, several removes from the experience itself. After you have read both passages, discuss the specific ways in which the two dialects differ. Are some effects possible in each dialect that would be difficult or impossible to achieve in the other?

A. The gang tryin' to talk me into goin' wit' 'em. I tell Breeze, our main man, I don' wan' no part of it 'cos we ain' gon' do nothin' but get in trouble.

They think I'm scared—a chicken. I ain' no chicken. I ain' scared of nothin'. Hey, I wouldn' be no Black Fist if I was no chicken. I done prove myself just like the rest of them dudes. So I tell 'em what goin' down—I got to go meet the man 'bout a job tomorrow.

Now they think I'm crazy. Breeze say, "A job? You know ain' no jobs nowhere 'round here, man. Ain' we been lookin' since we got outta school? You already know what they gon' say tomorrow—they ain' got no openin's, but when they do, they gon' call you. And they ain', man. So what else you gon' do?"

I know he right. But s'poze somp'n happen. Breeze say can't nothin' go wrong 'cos they done plan this thing out to the max. It gon' be smooth as silk. Ain' none of us no fools.

"But . . ." I start to say, 'cos I still ain' sure.

Breeze cut me off; he was gettin' mad. He say, "But nothin'. Ain' no mo' 'buts', man. We wastin' time. Hey, either you in or you ain'.' Which one it gon' be?"

He right. Ain' nothin' else to do. So I say, "O.K., I'm in. Let's get it on."

B. The President's National Crime Commission today released the results of its newly completed study on juvenile crime in urban areas. The study, begun in May of this year, directly relates juvenile crime in our inner cities to the areas' increasing rate of teenage unemployment.

Commission figures indicate that unemployment among

inner city teenagers has risen from 11.2 percent to 17.3 percent within the last four months, a rise that is the result of large numbers of recent high school graduates flooding the job market. During this same four-month period, teenagers unable to find steady jobs or even part-time employment were reportedly involved in nearly 63 percent of neighborhood crimes.

Informed sources say plans are underway to form yet another committee, this one to investigate the Crime Commission's report and to offer feasible solutions for the juvenile crime problem.

2. Dictionaries

In the past, dictionaries were regarded as the ultimate authorities in correctness, and people referred to any dictionary at hand as "*the* dictionary," as if there were not enough differences among dictionaries to be worth taking note of. More recently, the development of linguistics has had a profound effect on the way dictionaries are made and the way people use them. Until 1961, *Webster's New International Dictionary* (2nd ed.) was regarded as the standard authority on American English. In 1961, however, the G. & C. Merriam Company published a third edition, called *Webster's Third New International Dictionary*, which reflected some of the attitudes toward language that linguists had been developing. In addition to citing established writers to illustrate definitions, the third edition quoted people like baseball superstar Willie Mays, former President Dwight Eisenhower, and entertainers Ethel Merman and Jimmy Durante. Many readers were horrified, since these celebrities were certainly not considered authorities on language. But the editors of *Webster's Third* had good reason for their practice: they had determined that the purpose of a dictionary was to indicate how a language is used by the people who speak it as well as how it is used by the relatively few people who use it in print. Even today many people find this broader concept of a dictionary difficult to accept.

In 1969 *The American Heritage Dictionary of the English Language* was published, partly in reaction to *Webster's Third*.

More traditional in its approach to language, the *American Heritage* relied upon a panel of professional writers and students of language to indicate preferences regarding more than six hundred debatable usages. A writer trying to decide whether to use *data* as a plural noun or as a singular collective noun would find this usage note in the *American Heritage:*

> *Data* is now used both as a plural and as a singular collective: *These data are inconclusive. This data is inconclusive.* The plural construction is more appropriate in formal usage. The singular is acceptable to 50 per cent of the Usage Panel.

Webster's Third is more cryptic in its discussion of usage:

> *data* pl but often sing in const: material serving as a basis for discussion, inference, or determination of policy < no general appraisal can be hazarded . . . until more data is available —*Publisher's Weekly.*

Which dictionary is better? Comparing them is like comparing apples and oranges. Both serve their purpose. *Webster's Third* is an unabridged dictionary, which means that it attempts to list all words current in America at the time of its publication. The *American Heritage* is a desk dictionary, which means that its coverage is deliberately selective. Being much larger, *Webster's Third* is much more expensive; but it is also considered the more accurate representation of modern American English in that it includes more words and a wider range of definitions. The *American Heritage*, on the other hand, is preferred by many people who are writing for publication and who seek clear guidance about the way English is used by professional writers.

There are several other excellent dictionaries on the market. Other unabridged dictionaries include *Funk & Wagnall's New Standard Dictionary* (1964) and *The Random House Dictionary of the English Language* (1966). The most comprehensive English dictionary is the *Oxford English Dictionary* (*OED*), originally published in twelve large volumes but now available in two volumes of small print. Modern desk dictionaries (besides the *American Heritage*) include *The Random House*

College Dictionary (1968), *Funk & Wagnall's Standard College Dictionary* (1963), *The Thorndike-Barnhart Comprehensive Desk Dictionary* (1962), *Webster's New Collegiate Dictionary* (8th ed., 1973, based on *Webster's Third*), and *Webster's New World Dictionary* (1970). This last dictionary, despite the "Webster" in its name, is not published by the company that produced *Webster's Third*, but rather by the World Publishing Company.

Students who are particularly interested in the English language might well spend some time comparing the introductions to different dictionaries and comparing entries for a number of words in each. They will discover that "the" dictionary —the single authoritative book on the English language—is nonexistent. Dictionaries differ in purpose, underlying philosophy, range of coverage, amount of information included in definitions, use of quotations to illustrate definitions, arrangement, and in a number of other ways that are important to serious students of language.

Questions about correctness in the use of words may be approached from two different points of view, which may be roughly described as the purist viewpoint and the pragmatic viewpoint. Purists in language are generally people who are expert in the English used by educated writers. They are uncomfortable with dialects other than their own, and they do not easily admit new words or new meanings into their language. They generally prefer the *American Heritage* and the second edition of *Webster's New International Dictionary*, and they tend to disapprove of *Webster's Third*. They think of changes in language as corruptions that, unchecked, will eventually make precise communication impossible.

The pragmatists, on the other hand, accept as a fact that language has changed throughout history and will continue to change despite the best efforts of the purists. They say that the same forces that made Shakespeare's language different from Chaucer's, and Faulkner's language different from Shakespeare's, are still at work, and that future writers of great English literature will be using a language much different from our own. They tend to prefer *Webster's Third*, but they regard any good dictionary as evidence of the way English is perceived by the people who use it.

Most people have a little of both viewpoints because both are reasonable in their own way. We differ only in our proportions. Few people today would agree with the extreme purism of John Witherspoon, an eighteenth-century Scotsman who was president of the College of New Jersey (Princeton). According to H. L. Mencken, Witherspoon objected to the American use of *notify* in a sentence like "The police were notified." Apparently Witherspoon was thinking of the Latin origins of the word — *notus* ("known") and *facere* ("to make") — and concluded that correct usage would require crimes and accidents to be notified (i.e., made known) to the police. There is some logic to that position; but even Mencken, who could be something of a snob at times, realized that centuries of use had irreversibly changed *notify* from its original Latin sense.

Within the past few years, however, it has been argued that the sentence "He convinced us to go" is incorrect because *convince* comes from Latin words meaning "to bind down with chains." Again, there is a certain logic to this argument, but it seems to suggest that only people with a thorough knowledge of the history of English would be able to use the language properly.

It is difficult to draw the line between pedantry and a healthy respect for useful shades of meaning. Recently, for example, a television announcer observed that an injured basketball player was "limping profusely," and a teacher of English described herself as a "prolific reader." Anyone who has studied Latin should know that *profusely* suggests the pouring or flowing of a liquid, and that *prolific* suggests a productive role rather than a passive one. It makes sense to bleed profusely or to become a prolific writer, but people can limp profusely and read prolifically only if these words have been reduced to mean nothing more than "a lot." And then it would make just as much sense to read profusely and to limp prolifically.

People who are sensitive to the meaning of words are distracted by phrases like "a very unique program." *Unique* means "one of a kind." If something is really the only one of its kind, it is hard to see how it might be "very" one of a kind. Similarly, people who are accustomed to a precise distinction between *infer* and *imply* do not like to see these words used interchangeably. And people who believe that the suffix *-ly* should be used only to form adverbs of a certain kind do not like to see *hopefully* used except when it means "in a hopeful manner."

Some writing problems stem from the fact that writers have more experience with the spoken form of the language than with the written form, and they have trouble transcribing what they say and hear onto paper. Many students, for example, write "use to" instead of "used to"; the final *d* that would be used in print to indicate the past tense of the phrase is omitted because it is inaudible in the speech they are accustomed to. Even more troublesome in writing is the conversion of phrases learned aurally into written phrases with completely different meanings. One student could find no library material on the topic of euthanasia because she had copied it down as "youth in Asia"; and another student baffled his philosophy professor by writing "for all intensive purposes," by which he meant "for all intents and purposes."

The list of troublesome words and phrases is almost endless, and entire books have been written about them. The "Do-It-Yourself Usage Guide" in Chapter Thirteen will help you learn how to deal with some of the more common puzzlers.

EXERCISES

1. Choose two different dictionaries. Study them closely and observe the particular ways in which they are different. Choose a few words from each and compare the definitions. What sort of information can you find in one dictionary that you cannot find in another? Can you find certain words in one but not in the other? Is there any difference in the way they arrange multiple definitions? Prepare a report of your observations and make some general comment about the different goals each dictionary tried to achieve. If you can, recommend one dictionary over the other and give reasons.

2. For each of the following words, compare the pronunciation indicated in two or more dictionaries.

advertisement	blackguard
ally (as verb and noun)	coupon
almond	flaccid
Arab	forehead
bayou	greasy

insurance	ribald
pall-mall	salmon
recuperate	strewn

3. The following words are among six hundred singled out by *The American Heritage Dictionary* for usage notes. Choose two dictionaries and compare and contrast their entries for any five of these words.

admittance	good
affinity	I
can (meaning "to be able")	most (adverb)
careen	O
each	so-called

3. Spelling

Another aspect of correctness in language is spelling. In the Middle Ages, scribes spelled by ear, using Latin vowels and consonants to indicate as well as they could the sounds of the English language. It was not uncommon for different scribes to use different spellings; indeed, in many manuscripts words are spelled first one way and then another by the same scribe. Even in the Renaissance spelling was to some extent a matter of individual judgment, and it should be of some comfort to students who have been penalized for misspelling Shakespeare's name to learn that Shakespeare himself spelled it more than one way. By 1650, however, spelling became relatively standardized; in subsequent centuries the standard forms took on an appearance of absolute correctness. Now people generally assume that words have only one correct spelling, and even misspellings that are more logical than the standard forms (*det*, for example, instead of *debt*) are regarded as errors.

Some students, even at the college level, have been so poorly prepared in spelling that they need to start from the beginning, learning the sounds of individual letters. There is no disgrace to this condition: it is often the fault of the school system rather than of the student. But there is no easy solution for it either. Students who are unable to spell even simple words need to spend many hours working with good tutors if they hope to become writers.

Other students need help with only a few dozen words they commonly misspell; for the rest, they need to keep a dictionary at hand whenever they write. Once they have made a list of words that give them trouble, they should memorize the correct spellings, perhaps with the help of a friend or roommate who is willing to give oral quizzes.

Mnemonic Devices*

One way to memorize difficult words is to invent mnemonic devices — tricks to aid the memory. The old standby about *i* before *e* except after *c* or when pronounced as an *a* as in *neighbor* and *weigh* is reliable enough for many words, though there are exceptions, like *either, foreign, seize,* and *weird,* among others.

In general, the more ridiculous the mnemonic device, the easier it will be to remember. Some people remember that *seperate* is an incorrect spelling because they know there is "a rat" in sepARATe. And one writer recommends SPEED as a device for remembering which words end in *-eed* and which end in *-ede.* The three words beginning with *s, p,* and *e* (*succeed, proceed,* and *exceed*) all end in *-eed.* There is one *p* word that does not follow this rule: *precede.* But if you remember that the phrase "full SPEed ahead" means *proceed,* you can remember which of the *p* words belongs in the SPEed group. Another exception is *supersede,* which not only ends in *-ede* but which has an *s* where the others have a *c.* This is because the other words are derived from Latin *cedere* ("to go, to yield") while *supersede* is derived from the Latin *sedēre* ("to sit"). To supersede someone means to sit in a higher (and therefore more honorable) position.

Vowels that are neutralized in pronunciation can cause spelling difficulties because they are impossible to hear. The final vowel in *neutr_l* and the vowel in the last syllable of *corpor_te* are both pronounced "uh." In some cases, a different form of the word will clarify the inaudible vowel: *neutrality, corporation.*

---

* **mnemonic,** pronounced nē-MON-ic, from Greek *mnemomikos,* meaning "of or related to memory." A mnemonic device is a device that helps you remember something.

Adding Suffixes

It helps to learn a few basic rules. When is the final consonant of a word doubled before adding a suffix (i.e., a syllable like *-ing*) beginning with a vowel? The final consonant is doubled when the suffix would otherwise change the quality of the vowel before it. Thus the final *r* in *refer* is doubled in *referring*, because if the word were spelled *refering*, readers would be tempted to rhyme it with *fearing*; and the final *n* in *begin* is doubled in *beginning*, because if the word were spelled *begining*, readers might be tempted to rhyme it with *dining*. But the final *n* in *retain* is not doubled in *retaining*, because the *ai* combination is not likely to change its quality even with a suffix added, and the final *r* in *order* is not·doubled in *ordering*, because there is no stress on the *e*, and readers are not likely to mispronounce it with the suffix added. *Becoming*, with one *m*, is an exception to this rule. And the double *ll* in *controlled*, which most dictionaries give as the preferred spelling, is unnecessary and illogical; but conventions are often that way. When suffixes beginning with a vowel are added to words like *picnic* and *panic*, the letter *k* is added to the *c* to prevent it from being pronounced like an *s*. The usual spelling, then, is *picnicking* and *panicking* rather than *picnicing* and *panicing*.

Silent *e* at the end of a word usually has a purpose: it signals the quality of the vowel two letters before it. To see how this works, compare *hat* with *hate*, *not* with *note*, *din* with *dine*, and *cut* with *cute*. When a suffix beginning with a vowel is added to a word with a final *e*, the vowel in the suffix takes the place of the *e*: this is why the *e* in *note* disappears in *notable* and the *e* in *dine* disappears in *dining*. If the suffix does not begin with a vowel, the final *e* must be retained to preserve the pronunciation of the word: thus *hateful* needs its *e*, for without it the word would become *hatful*.

The final *e* in words like *knowledge* and *notice* has a slightly different purpose: it indicates that the consonant before it has a soft sound (like the *g* in *George* or the *c* in *city*) rather than a hard sound (like the *g* in *go* or the *c* in *cat*). In combination with suffixes beginning with *i*, this *e* disappears (as it does in *noticing*) because the added vowel does the *e*'s job. In combination with suffixes beginning with a consonant or with a vowel other than *i*, this kind of *e* is usually retained. Thus *noticeable* is the usual form, because in *noticable* the *c* might be pronounced like a *k*. For some reason, however, dictionaries seem to prefer *judgment* to *judgement* — though they sometimes include this second spelling as a permissible alternative. This is simply another indication that the conventions of writing are not and probably never will be completely logical.

Adding s to Verbs That End in y

The rule for changing a final *y* after a consonant to *ie* before adding *s* to a verb also has something to do with the way spelling affects pronunciation. If *try* becomes *trys*, the *y* might be pronounced as it is in *tryst* (which rhymes with *kissed*). So *try* becomes *tries*. But final *y* preceded by a vowel (*a, e, i, o, u*) does not seem to be disturbed by the addition of an *s:* thus *play* can become *plays* and *destroy* can become *destroys* without suggesting mispronunciations.

Ordinary Plurals

Ordinarily, plural nouns are formed by the addition of *s* or *es* to the singular form.

Examples

Singular	Plural
book	books
typewriter	typewriters
musician	musicians
witch	witches
box	boxes
wish	wishes
boss	bosses

You can see from the examples above that the *es* ending is used when the plural form would be pronounced with one more syllable than the singular form. This normally occurs when the singular ends in *s, x, ch,* or *sh*.

The plural of a few ordinary nouns in English is formed by changing the interior of the singular form (man/men, mouse/mice) or by adding something other than *s* or *es* (child/children). Another small group of nouns has the same form in both singular and plural (fish/fish, moose/moose).

Adding s to Nouns That End in y

If a noun ends in *y*, add *s* to form the plural. If the *y* is preceded by a consonant (any letter except *a, e, i, o, u*), change the *y* to *ie* before adding *s*.

Examples

Singular	Plural
anomaly	anomalies
canopy	canopies
city	cities
remedy	remedies

Again, if these words were spelled *anomalys, canopys, citys,* and *remedys,* the *y* might be pronounced to rhyme with *miss* rather than with the long *e* sound represented by the *-ies* ending. When the final *y* is preceded by a vowel, however, there is no need to change the *y* to *ie* because the simple addition of *s* will not tempt readers to mispronounce the word.

Examples

Singular	Plural
bay	bays
convoy	convoys
guy	guys
journey	journeys

The *y* in these words does not form a separate syllable as it does in words like *city.*

Plurals of Nouns That End in f

Some nouns that end in *f* are made plural by changing the *f* to *v* and adding *es.*

Examples

Singular	Plural
calf	calves
half	halves
thief	thieves

Other nouns ending in *f* are made plural by the addition of *s*.

Examples

Singular	Plural
plaintiff	plaintiffs
motif	motifs
brief	briefs

A few nouns ending in *f* can be made plural by either method.

Examples

Singular	Plural
hoof	hoofs *or* hooves
roof	roofs *or* rooves

The only way to be sure about the normal plural of a noun end-ing in *f* is to check a dictionary. Remember, however, that some dictionaries will report spellings that others omit.

Plurals of Nouns That End in o

Most English nouns ending in *o* have been borrowed from one of the Romance languages—i.e., languages derived from Latin. In English, the plural of these words is usually formed by add-ing *s* or *es* to the singular form.

If the final *o* is preceded by a vowel, only *s* is added.

Examples

Singular	Plural
arpeggio	arpeggios
folio	folios
radio	radios
stereo	stereos

If you added *es* to these words, the result would be three vowels in a row (*arpeggioes, folioes, radioes, stereoes*), which is not normal for English words.

Among other words ending in *o*, the plurals of several that are frequently used are governed by rigid convention. They are formed by adding *es* to the singular.

Examples

Singular	Plural
hero	heroes
Negro	Negroes
potato	potatoes
tomato	tomatoes

The plurals of less frequently used words ending in *o* preceded by a consonant can be formed either by adding *es* or by adding *s* alone.

Examples

Singular	Plural
archipelago	archipelagoes *or* archipelagos
buffalo	buffaloes *or* buffalos (also buffalo)
crescendo	crescendoes *or* crescendos, (also crescendi)
zero	zeroes *or* zeros

Plural of Nouns Borrowed from Foreign Languages

Nouns borrowed from Latin, Greek, Italian, and French sometimes have the same plural forms that they have in their original languages.

Examples

Singular	Plural
index (Latin)	indices
libretto (Italian)	libretti
octopus (Latin fr. Greek)	octopi *or* octopodes
radius (Latin)	radii
tableau (French)	tableaux
thesis (Greek)	theses

Most of these nouns, however, also have plurals formed by the addition of *s* or *es.*

Examples

Singular	Plural
index	indexes
libretto	librettos
octopus	octopuses
radius	radiuses
tableau	tableaus

The plural of *thesis* is not formed this way, probably because a *th* followed by three *s*'s (thesises) would be something of a tongue twister.

All of these spelling rules in no way replace the most fundamental spelling rule of all: when you have the least doubt, use a dictionary.

EXERCISES

1. Add the suffixes *-s* and *-ing* to each of the following words. Consult a dictionary if you are uncertain.

annoy	expel	read
argue	glorify	reason
acknowledge	magnify	rebel
delay	play	ride
erase	pronounce	run

2. Write the plural form for each of the following nouns. Consult a dictionary if you need help.

arena	essay	press
avocado	fern	rose
bash	flambeau	sandwich
body	fur	saw
boy	imbroglio	stadium
calf	lynx	stay
country	money	story
crisis	nativity	symposium
donkey	peach	witch

Chapter Thirteen

A Do-It-Yourself Usage Guide

Writers often find themselves hesitating between two words or two forms of the same word. Should they write "beside" or "besides"? "In regard to" or "in regards to"? "Further" or "farther"? Does Light Beer have "less calories" or "fewer calories"? What is the difference between "which" and "that"? What preposition comes after a word like "knowledgeable"?

Some of these choices can be resolved by consulting a dictionary. Some are matters of personal preference. Most are discussed in books called usage guides, the best known of which are listed below:

Bernstein, Theodore M. *The Careful Writer: A Modern Guide to English Usage.* New York: Atheneum, 1973.

Bryant, Margaret M. *Current American Usage.* New York: Funk & Wagnalls, 1962.

Copperud, Roy H. *American Usage: The Consensus*. New York: Van Nostrand, 1970.

Evans, Bergen and Cornelia. *A Dictionary of Contemporary American Usage*. New York: Random House, 1957.

Follet, Wilson. *Modern American Usage: A Guide*. Edited and completed by Jacques Barzun. New York: Hill and Wang, 1966.

Fowler, H. W. A. *A Dictionary of Modern English Usage*. 2d ed., rev. by Sir Ernest Gowers. New York: Oxford University Press, 1965.

Hall, J. Lesslie. *English Usage: Studies in the History and Uses of English Words and Phrases*. Chicago: Scott, Foresman, 1917.

Morris, William and Mary Morris. *Harper Dictionary of Contemporary Usage*. New York: Harper & Row, 1975.

Shaw, Harry. *Dictionary of Problem Words and Expressions*. New York: McGraw-Hill, 1975.

Shostak, Jerome. *Concise Dictionary of Current American Usage*. New York: Washington Square Press, 1968.

Two of these books—Hall's and Bryant's—make an effort to record the facts of usage; they present evidence about how English is used, not merely the authors' opinions about how it should be used. The others rely more often on the opinion of the authors rather than on objective evidence. They are all useful, however, as guides to the word choices that are most likely to seem "right" to experienced readers.

One of the problems with usage guides is that writers who have problems with usage often don't know it. Consequently they don't know when to consult a usage guide and when to rely on their native intuitions. Another problem with usage guides is that the advice they give is often in language that student writers cannot understand or remember.

To solve some of these problems, construct your own usage guide. In all of the following sentences, there is a word that is either misspelled or misused. Identify the problem, and if it is a problem that you sometimes have in your own writing, make your own rule about how the word should be spelled or used. The examples are arranged so that you can construct an alphabetical guide to usage.

Don't try to go through all the examples at once; you will learn more if you limit yourself to ten at a time. Consult a dictionary or a usage guide whenever you need help. Keep a running glossary in your notebook.

1. No one trusts Nick's ability of thinking for himself.

2. The Sierra Club placed a full page add in the local paper.

3. The polar bear was unable to adopt to his new environment.

4. As it turns out, you were smart to ignore my advise.

5. The pesticide had unexpected side affects.

6. The plan was rejected all together.

7. For the first time in years, my family had dinner altogether.

8. Paul's dreams about a career in tennis are nothing but allusions.

9. The twins visted England, also Scotland and France.

10. Cindy and Julie divided the money among themselves.

11. Redwoods are larger than any trees.

12. Being as I like mathematics, I decided to major in it.

13. At the concert I found myself sitting besides the chief of police.

14. Marcus paid better than five thousand dollars for an old car.

15. When we arrived at the conference, we discovered that the three groups were divided between themselves.

16. Between you and I, the company is about to declare bankruptcy.

17. Because a pipe busted in his basement, Thompson died during the winter.

18. This university does not have but 15,000 students.

19. There is no doubt but what we will be attending a new school next year.

20. Her conscious would bother her if she ever cheated.

21. Pat found calculus considerable difficult.

22. Midnight seemed to be a very content cat.

23. Because of the good council he received from his minister, Charles is now leading a very productive and happy life.

24. In a recent meeting, the counsel voted to ban genetic research within the city.

25. Most of this data is incorrect.

26. Karl will debut as a soloist this evening.

27. According to the *Post*, our congressman's personal behavior was not discrete.

28. He was not invited to the play because everyone thought he was disinterested in theater.

29. His past behavior may have effected the jury's decision.

30. When the storm was eminent, we sought safety in the cellar.

31. Jeannie was impressed by the sheer enormity of the Rockies.

32. The press was enthused about the possibility of another trip abroad.

33. Nathaniel refused to engage in farther discussion.

34. Jackson was equally as good in speaking as he was in running an organization efficiently.

35. The Nelsons could not except our invitation tonight.

36. At the next meeting the board will finalize the offer.

37. No one who was not formerly dressed could be admitted to the ball.

38. Austin is further from El Paso than from Houston.

39. If the book is reviewed good, it will go into a second edition.

40. Sophie couldn't hardly be expected to do all the work herself.

41. The visiting team will headquarter in the Sheraton.

42. The resolution proposed by the finance committee can't help but start a controversy.

43. This here image is an allusion to the first chapter of Genesis.

44. Hopefully, my grades will improve next semester.

45. The research conducted by my colleague and I is described below.

46. I implied from your letter that you would not join the class.

47. The constable sauntered in the saloon and made three arrests.

48. My absence yesterday does not infer a lack of interest.

49. Irregardless of our performance today, the band will be invited to play on national television next week.

50. The public was unaccustomed to these kind of paintings.

51. Haydn, Mozart, and Beethoven are considered classical composers, but the latter was decidedly more romantic than the first two.

52. The chicken lay more than a dozen eggs last week.

53. After lunch, Grandfather will probably lay in his room for a short nap.

54. Leave the children have whatever they ask for.

55. The representative from Alaska is liable to filibuster to prevent the matter from being brought to a vote.

56. The senator behaved like he would never face election again.

57. Dr. Jones was mad about the answer he received from his office.

58. Our decision will be announced in all the news medias.

59. A more thoughtful diplomacy would greatly minimize the chances of war.

60. Henry and myself will be traveling to New York this fall.

61. He did not think he could negotiate a fifteen-hour course load this semester.

62. No one has published their thesis this year.

63. The officials asked for quiet, but the crowd continued to be noisome.

64. Despite our publicity, there was nowhere near the number of people we anticipated for our program.

65. Nowheres is it stated in the contract that the tenant must pay for routine repairs.

66. We could of spent an entire day in the Museum of Modern Art.

67. The librarian took the book off of the shelf and handed it to a student.

68. Alvin is one of those hunters who has their secret techniques.

69. He only expected a small raise.

70. The judge said our case was outside of his jurisdication.

71. Our energy reserve is over ten percent less than it was last year.

72. Only a small percentage of the children attends school regularly.

73. A large percent of our students pass the first course.

74. Interest rates continue to rise, plus the cost of fuel.

75. The engineers are presently developing a new technique.

76. The President had been persuaded that government spending was the principle cause of inflation.

77. Because of the general's prophesy of war, the President removed him from his post.

78. The essay begins with a quote from Shaw's play *Major Barbara*.

79. This last item refers back to a statement you made as governor.

80. In regards to your interest in antiques, please feel free to visit our collection.

81. Ray bought himself a new car, replete with bucket seats and power windows.

82. The bell rung and class was dismissed.

83. Jean wrote a poem and published same in the *Black Warrior Review*.

84. Dr. Davis's lectures are seldom ever boring.

85. A series of French films are going to be shown this summer.

86. This country is serviced by three general hospitals.

87. The hotel sets on a ridge overlooking the city.

88. The sight chosen for the new library was very expensive.

89. The professor was unable to locate the article she sited in her paper.

90. The pilot reported that he had sited the space capsule over Bermuda.

91. Traffic was moving slow because of the rain.

92. Some one has returned the book you lost.

93. Was the letter typed on official stationary?

94. The aircraft carrier was suppose to rescue the astronauts.

95. Thusly, the team established a new field for research.

96. Karen thinks she has discovered a new type butterfly.

97. Percival decided to try and join the debate team.

98. His manner of speaking was very unique.

99. Nikolai Podgorny use to be president of the Soviet Union.

100. Who's responsibility is it to find new oil fields?

Chapter Fourteen

———◆———

A Grammar for Writers

G1 *What Is Grammar?*

In the eighteenth century, when books on English grammar first became popular, they consisted mainly of rules to guide speakers and writers in the correct use of the language. In the twentieth century, grammarians are less concerned with prescribing rules of correctness than with describing the way a language is actually used by native speakers. The grammar in this chapter is more descriptive than the eighteenth-century grammars and more pragmatic than modern grammars. It is a working grammar for writers. It attempts to describe the surface structure of English as it normally appears in print at this time in the United States. "Normally" is used here in its statistical sense: the structures and conventions described are those that would most probably be encountered in a random sample of texts in a library or book store.

G2 *How Much Grammar Do Writers Need to Know?*

Theoretically, writers who read a great deal need to learn little, if any, formal grammar. If their objective is to write the sort of English they see in print, they can learn most of the conventions of printed English simply by constant exposure and practice—just as they learned the grammar of spoken English by listening and attempting to imitate what they heard.

Grammatical terms are useful, however, as a way of talking about language. Without grammatical terms, we would be limited to talking about each language problem in isolation, as if it had not occurred earlier and would not occur again. With grammatical terms, we can discuss particular problems in the light of general rules. In this way, we can learn to recognize problems when they occur in other contexts.

To use this chapter efficiently, glance over the headings and take time to study only those elements of grammar you have not already mastered. Return to appropriate sections when you are uncertain about a particular grammatical problem or when one of your readers suggests a grammatical revision.

G3 *Parts of Speech*

Grammarians traditionally divide all words into eight "parts of speech": nouns, pronouns, verbs, adverbs, adjectives, prepositions, conjunctions, and interjections. Each part of speech is discussed in some detail later in this chapter. Problems associated with each part are discussed immediately after the recognition exercises.

In general, remember that words can shift categories, changing from one part of speech to another depending upon their use in a given sentence. *Ring*, for example, can be a noun ("She gave her boyfriend a silver ring") or a verb ("If the bell does not ring, class cannot be dismissed") or even an adjective ("The ring collection was carefully guarded"). Although a dictionary is a good source for discovering how a given word is normally categorized, it is always necessary to consider the way the word is used in the particular sentence in which it appears.

The definitions given in this section are functional definitions. They would not satisfy the needs of a professional grammarian. They should, however, help nongrammarians acquire an adequate sense of the words they define. Technical definitions, which may be found in any good dictionary, would be less useful to most writers because technical definitions generally involve terms that themselves require definition.

G 4

G4 *Recognizing Verbs*

Verbs are words that will fit in the following slot:

She
He
It — constantly.
They

Examples
She runs constantly.

They tease constantly.

They trip constantly.

He thinks constantly.

She trained constantly.

He fought constantly.

A few verbs, however, express existence or appearance rather than action.

Examples
It is constant.

It seems constant.

They appear constant.

G4 Continued

EXERCISE

1. Use the test sentence

She
He
It   _____   constantly
They

to identify the verbs in the following list.

evening	pretend
restaurant	grows
builds	resisted
begin	competed
manage	next
throughout	large
destroys	perform
develop	survived
study	agree
cooperated	tough

G5 *Recognizing Verb Phrases*

In modern grammars the term "verb phrase" refers either to a one-word verb or to a group of verbs that work together as a single expression. Verbs often occur in combination with other verblike words called auxiliary, or helping, verbs. Words like *do, does, did, has, have, had, am, is, are, was, were, might, could, can,* and *should* are included among the auxiliary verbs. There is no need to memorize this list, but it is sometimes useful to be able to recognize these words and others like them as parts of verb phrases.

Examples
He has run beautifully in fifteen races.

Someone might trip on the broom in the doorway.

Jackson was training in Reno when he broke his nose.

The arrangements were being copied when the musicians arrived.

Notice that verb phrases can be interrupted by other words that are not auxiliaries. In identifying verb phrases, skip over all interrupting words except auxiliary verbs.

Examples

The arrangements were still being copied when the musicians arrived.

Mike had just returned when the phone rang.

In these examples, "were being copied" and "had returned" are verb phrases.

EXERCISES

1. Identify the verb phrases in the following passage. Remember that single-word verbs are considered verb phrases.

> As a matter of equilibrium, perhaps there ought to be some differences between the standards that are applied to TV about whites and TV about blacks. Is that an unfairness doctrine, a kind of reverse discrimination? Should shows about blacks be held to a higher standard of relevance, sensitivity and accuracy than those about whites? Though any hard and fast rules would be foolish, an effort to do just that might help correct some deep seated racial misunderstanding. Whites know about whites, and possess a built-in reality adjuster that makes all the necessary corrections and allowances for exaggeration and stupidity when whites are being portrayed. Blacks know something about whites too. But whites in the U.S. still do not know all that much about blacks; most whites possess no automatic focus mechanism to tell them what is nonsense and what is not. Whites receiving a brutalized, stupid or stereotyped image of blacks through TV are liable to tell themselves, "Why, yes, that's the way blacks are."
>
> —Lance Morrow "Blacks on TV:
> A Disturbing Image," *Time**

* Reprinted by permission of TIME, The Weekly Newsmagazine; Copyright Time Inc. 1978.

G5 Continued

   2. Copy a paragraph from a recent newspaper or magazine. Make a list of all the verbs and verb phrases in the paragraph. Swap paragraphs and lists with a classmate and check each other's work.

   3. Identify all the verbs and verb phrases in a paragraph you have recently written.

G6 *Splitting Verb Phrases*

Some writers believe that it is always improper to inter-rupt (or "split") verb phrases with modifiers. Split verb phrases are indeed sometimes awkward, particularly when they are split by more than a single word.

Examples
The club pro presented awards to those who had during the summer been losing every game they played.

For many years, Ross had without showing it suffered from a painful disease.

Often, however, modifiers within verb phrases seem perfectly natural and idiomatic.

Examples
Dr. Artemis was blithely jabbering with a friend while his patients waited for their examinations.

The citation had been properly issued and the offender had willingly acknowledged his guilt.

   Sometimes moving a modifier to avoid splitting a verb phrase is more awkward than the split. Because they know some readers object to all split verb phrases, many writers avoid them whenever they can gracefully do so without changing or obscuring their meaning. When style or meaning demands splitting a verb phrase, however, the split is perfectly justified. Split infinitives are another matter. See **G10.**

EXERCISE

Identify the split verb phrases in the following sentences and mend those that can be gracefully mended.

a. Jackson might, if no one runs against him, be elected to the finance committee.

b. We finally met Osborne, who was even at the age of eighty-three still running ten miles a day.

c. The sandwich had been reluctantly fixed by his wife.

d. The sandwich had been with considerable reluctance fixed by his wife.

e. Nobody likes spectators who are continually analyzing the game for the benefit of those around them.

f. Washington had unexpectedly been drafted in the first round.

g. The bill would be soundly defeated in the Senate.

h. The escapee had quietly been living in Minnesota for thirty-five years before her identity had been discovered.

i. The teacher should sternly have rebuked Jonathan for his failure to do his work.

j. In calling a press conference, the governor was ineffectively attempting to forestall criticism of his secret meetings.

G7 *Principal Parts and Troublesome Participles*

All verbs have basic forms, which are sometimes called "principal parts." Traditional grammars list three principal parts: the present, the past, and the past participle. Some modern dictionaries add two more forms to these three: the *-ing* form and the *-s* form.

The five basic forms will fit into the following slots:

Present	Right now I _____.
Past	Yesterday I _____.
Past Participle	Having been _____ too often,
	or
	Often I have _____.
-ing	I enjoy _____ing.
-s	He _____s.

G7 Continued

On occasion your ear will let you down, especially when you need to write a form that doesn't appear frequently in your reading or a form that requires some special rule of spelling. What is the past tense of *lend?* (Yesterday I *lent?* Yesterday I *loaned?*) What are the past participles of *swim* and *awaken?* (Often I have *swam/swum?* Often I have *awakened/awoke/awoken?*) How many *n*'s in the *-ing* form of *run?* How many *l*'s in the past tense of *travel?*

To discover how uncertain verb forms are likely to appear in printed English, consult a dictionary.

G 7

EXERCISES

1. Some verbs have irregular past and past participial forms. Often the form of the participle you would use when speaking carefully is the form that normally occurs in printed English. To find out which verbs you should be especially careful with in writing, indicate what you think would be the preferred past and past participial forms of the following verbs. Use the following test phrases as contexts. The answers appear on page 295.

Yesterday I _____.
Often I have _____.

arise	cut	grow	sink
bear	dig	hit	sit
beat	dive	know	slide
begin	do	lay	sneak
bite	drag	lead	speak
blow	draw	lend	steal
break	dream	loan	swim
bring	drink	lie	take
catch	eat	read	teach
choose	forget	run	throw
come	give	see	write

2. To make yourself familiar with the format of your dictionary, look up the five principal parts of the following verbs.

become	shake
freeze	tear
go	wear

3. The forms for each verb in the following list were taken from a modern dictionary and jumbled. Test your ability to recognize the various principal parts of each verb by arranging the words in the order in which they would appear in a dictionary (present, past, past participle, *-ing*, *-s*).

apprised, apprises, apprising, apprise
bites, biting, bitten, bit, bite
clutched, clutch, clutches, clutching
died, dying, dies, die
drives, driven, driving, drive, drove
flop, flopping, flopped, flops

Answers to *Exercise* 1: arise, arose, arisen; bear, bore, borne; beat, beat, beaten; begin, began, begun; bite, bit, bitten or bit; blow, blew, blown; break, broke, broken; bring, brought, brought; catch, caught, caught; choose, chose, chosen; come, came, come; cut, cut, cut; dig, dug, dug; dive, dived or dove, dived; do, did, done; drag, dragged, dragged; draw, drew, drawn; dream, dreamed or dreamt, dreamed or dreamt; drink, drank, drunk; eat, ate, eaten; forget, forgot, forgotten or forgot; give, gave, given; grow, grew, grown; hit, hit, hit; know, knew, known; lay, laid, laid; lead, led, led; lend, lent, lent; loan, loaned, loaned; lie, lay, lain; read, read (pronounced "red"), read (also pronounced "red"); run, ran, run; see, saw, seen; sink, sank or sunk, sunk; sit, sat, sat; slide, slid, slid; sneak, sneaked, sneaked; speak, spoke, spoken; steal, stole, stolen; swim, swam, swum; take, took, taken; teach, taught, taught; throw, threw, thrown; write, wrote, written.

G8 *Verbs: Problems with Past Tense and Past Participles*

In some varieties of spoken English, past tense and past participles sound exactly like the present tense.

Example
When I was hospitalize, I receive good treatment.

Normally, listeners can tell from context that the speaker is referring to events that occurred in the past. Printed English, however, relies less on context. It

G8 Continued

G 8

normally relies on a change in the verb form to signal past time.

Example
When I was hospitalized, I received good treatment.

To many speakers, the final *d* in "hospitalized" and "received" sounds not only unnecessary, but downright uppity. To people who read a lot, however, it is the absence of the *d*'s that calls attention to itself.

To learn to use these forms as they are normally used in printed English, first review the discussion of principal parts in the preceding section (**G7**). Then watch out for the following situations.

1. **Writing about actions in the past.** Use the past tense, which is signaled by the addition of -*d*, -*ed*, or -*t* in regular verbs (see **G7**).
2. **After have, has, had.** When *have*, *has*, or *had* is used in combination with another verb (e.g., "has received," "have taken"), the other verb should be a past participle (see **G7**).
3. **After forms of be.** When any form of the verb *be* (see **G12**) is used in combination with another verb (e.g., "is singing," "is sung," "was buying," "was bought"), the other verb will either have an -*ing* ending or it will be a past participle, depending on the sense you are trying to convey. Native speakers usually know when they want the -*ing* form. As a rule, when they *don't* want the -*ing* form, the past participle is appropriate.

If these situations seem too complicated to remember, you might prefer to learn verb forms by practice — which is how people usually learn them. Practice exercises like those below over and over until you can choose the form you want by ear.

EXERCISES

1. Write a paragraph that tells a story beginning as follows:

Let me tell you what registration in college was like for me. First I . . .

This story will probably include a number of occasions for using the past tense. Swap stories with a classmate and check each other's ability to use the past forms that would normally occur in printed English.

2. Repeat Exercise 1, using the following opening:

The most scared I have ever been in my life was when . . .

Then go on to tell about the events before and after the moment when you were most scared. Swap papers as in Exercise 1.

3. Repeat Exercise 1, making up sentences of your own as openers. The point is simply to tell a story about past events. The story will give you opportunities to use the past forms of the verb.

4. Below is a list of ordinary verbs in the present tense. Indicate what form they would take in printed English if they were used in combination with *have, has,* or *had*. Grammatically, the form you want is called the past participle. After you have attempted this exercise using your ear alone as a guide, check your results in a dictionary. In most dictionaries, the past participle is listed after the main entry for the verb, immediately before the *-ing* form.

a. talk
b. try
c. study
d. write   He has _____ more than he should have.
e. trust   We have _____ more than we should have.
f. pay   They had _____ more than they should have.
g. rest
h. plant
i. eat
j. dance

5. Make up a list of ten more verbs to put in the blanks in Exercise 4. Repeat this exercise, checking your own work or having someone else check it, until you consistently get nine out of ten forms right.

6. Indicate what form the verbs listed on the left below would take in the blanks to their right. Also, point out the form of the verb *be* in each sentence.

a. tackle   Tyson was finally _____ by the kicker.
b. touch   Ali was not _____ by his opponent.
c. kiss   At the reception, the bride is _____ by her friends.
d. send   This letter should be _____ first class.

G8 Continued

e. write   These documents were _____ on parchment.
f. teach   The younger children are _____ by their parents.
g. spell   My name had not been _____ correctly.
h. plan   The party was being _____ by creeps.
i. execute   He expects to be _____ by sundown.
j. annoy   I am most _____ by my own mistakes.

7. Anytime a form of the verb *be* appears in combination with the past participle of any other verb, the passive voice results. Practice your ability to form the past participle by converting each of the following sentences from active voice to passive voice.

Example

A baseball shattered the window. (Active voice)

The window was shattered by a baseball. (Passive voice)

a. The people elected Snodgrass. (Begin with "Snodgrass was . . .")
b. Mary was writing the letter. (Begin with "The letter was . . .")
c. The Smiths are obeying the rules. (Begin with "The rules are being . . .")
d. The Romans conquered the Gauls. (Begin with "The Gauls were . . .")
e. Loud noises bother me. (Begin with "I am . . .")

G9 *Finite/Nonfinite Verb Forms*

The terms *finite* and *nonfinite* come from Latin grammar, where they made more sense than they do in English grammar. Although the terms themselves are not ordinarily useful to writers, the concepts can be.

A finite verb form is one that can be used as the main verb in a sentence.

There are only three kinds of nonfinite verbs: verb phrases preceded by *to*; verb phrases beginning with an *-ing* form; and past participles (see above, p. 175) used as adjectives.

Examples

He claimed he did not intend to ruin the party.

His greatest achievement was to have been invited to the White House.

His mother left, taking the money with her.

Having been expelled from school, Marvin found plenty of activity in the streets.

He left the president's office encouraged by her promises.

Deeply moved by the sermon, Lee Ann cried silently.

G 9

Verb phrases that do not belong to one of these three categories are considered finite; they can be used as the main verb in a clause or sentence.

Examples

In the kitchen Marie was watching the steam rise from the boiling soup. (The *-ing* form is not the first or only word in the verb phrase; therefore this is a finite form.)

By breakfast time, Marcel had already chopped three rows of corn. (Although chopped is a past participle, it is used here as a main verb in combination with had — not as an adjective; had chopped, therefore, is a finite verb form.)

Verb phrases preceded by *to* are called infinitives. The *-ing* forms are called gerunds when they are used as nouns and present participles when they are used as adjectives.

Examples

She began to cry. (infinitive)

Studying was Tina's favorite pastime. (gerund)

In the library we found Tina studying for the final. (participle)

EXERCISE

Identify all the verb phrases in the following passage. Mark the finite forms with an *F* and the nonfinite forms with an *N*. The first sentence is marked as an example.

G9 Continued

In January, when the night air was [F] still, frosty and clean, Mercia was [F] brought to the track for her first official race. She was still a young bitch, a red brindle, whelped two springs earlier. Her training had gone well, but it was mostly in the daytime on a track she knew. The real track was different — smoother, softer under foot, lighted from above by what Mercia perceived as little low moons hovering over the rail as if they were waiting to watch the race. She smelled strange scents when she first stepped outside. She heard the murmuring of the crowd, whose presence along the rail made her uneasy. She stopped to empty her bladder on the grass, and then stepped nervously into the box indicated by her handler. Suddenly a bell rang, and Mercia crouched low, ready to leap forward, her ears pressed back along her head, her tail wound tightly between her legs. The gate flipped open and out sprang Mercia, sixth among eight hounds. The people along the rail shouted, and Mercia moved up to third as she passed the stands. Then she found herself boxed in, and two more hounds moved up on the outside. Halfway through the race Mercia was running fifth. In the far turn her luck began to change. The lead dog swung wide, the others following, and Mercia had room along the rail to move to second. In the stretch

she heard the crowd again, roaring louder and louder, and
Mercia, as if she were being pulled by the noise, glided to the
head of the pack, striding farther and farther away. She crossed
the finish line three lengths ahead of the others.

G10 *Split Infinitives*

Although infinitives occur in a number of different forms, they
can generally be recognized as verb phrases beginning with *to*.

Examples
Finally she began to study.

He claimed he was glad to pay his taxes.

Michael was said to have been annoyed by the results of the exam.

Maureen wanted to be dating an older man.

For reasons that are not entirely logical, many educated
readers believe that modifiers should never occur between *to*
and the first verb form in an infinitive phrase. **When *to* is
followed by a modifier, the infinitive is said to be split.**
Some split infinitives are in fact awkward.

Examples
The dog seemed to painfully walk on his injured paw.

The trees began to all of a sudden sway.

Mario realized that he would have to practice long hours if he
wanted to beautifully sing.

The budget was supposed to quickly have been approved by the
administration.

Other split infinitives seem perfectly natural and idiomatic
in English.

G10 Continued

Examples

Nancy seemed to sorely miss the clearer skies and sweet air of Boulder.

The attorney planned to gradually convince the jury that they would have behaved exactly as the defendant had behaved.

Before modern times, Bermudians knew when a hurricane was coming by the surf that would start pounding the reefs in otherwise calm weather, having travelled days ahead of the storm to ominously and relentlessly report on its course.

> —Suzannah Lessard "A Close Gathering"
> *The New Yorker* (April 16, 1979), p. 43.

G 10

Writers should be aware that many readers consider all split infinitives ungrammatical—even though there is no historical or grammatical basis for this belief. Rather than attempt to educate their readers, many writers simply avoid splitting infinitives whenever they can do so gracefully.

EXERCISE

Identify the split infinitives in the following sentences and mend those that can be gracefully mended.

a. Horace preferred to peacefully live on a farm rather than to riotously live in the city.

b. We expected to easily outdistance the newcomers, but we seem to sorely have been deceiving ourselves.

c. Marvin considered it his duty to steadfastly resist the compromises offered by the management.

d. No one seemed to really notice that the theater was half empty.

e. Eloise had forgotten to promptly let the cat out in the morning.

f. After a few years, Louise hated to continually be mistaken for the character she had played in an early movie.

g. As a teacher, Burleson was able to quickly dispel the anxieties of her students.

h. At an early age, Pearsall resolved to never marry.

i. The campaign was designed to slowly wear down the resolve of local environmentalists.

j. Even in public buildings, Jeanne-Marie seemed unable to effectively resist the urge to suddenly spin across the floor in a series of cartwheels.

G11 *Dangling and Squinting Modifiers*

When modifiers seem to describe the wrong word or no word at all, they are called dangling modifiers. When modifiers seem to be looking in two directions at once, they are called squinting modifiers.

Examples

Weighing all the evidence, the defendant was acquitted.

Exhausted from her travels, home was a welcome sight.

Ralph picked the lock using a paper clip.

Some subjects depend very much upon the judgment of the teacher like writing.

We decided reluctantly to demand an explanation.

Strakely pretended when the ceremony was over he would enlist in the Army.

In the first two examples above, "weighing" and "exhausted" are participles that do not refer to any noun or pronoun expressed in the sentence. These are dangling participles. In the next two examples, the modifying phrases seem to be attached to the wrong word. These are called misplaced modifiers. In the last two examples, the modifying phrases could be interpreted to modify what comes before them or what comes after them. These are squinting modifiers.

The remedy for a dangling or squinting modifier is to rephrase the sentence so that the modifier is attached to what it is intended to modify, or eliminated altogether.

Example

Weighing all the evidence, the jury acquitted the defendant.

Exhausted from her travels, she found home a welcome sight.

Using a paper clip, Ralph picked the lock.

Some subjects — like writing — depend very much upon the judgment of the teacher.

Reluctantly, we decided to demand an explanation.

When the ceremony was over, Strakely pretended he would enlist in the Army. (Or, depending on the intended meaning: Strakely pretended he would enlist in the Army when the ceremony was over.)

EXERCISE

Remedy the dangling and squinting modifiers in the following sentences.

a. Allen's anger was genuine, annoyed by his performance in the second set.

b. Sarah lost the election, freeing her to concentrate on sculpture.

c. The officer in charge said at three o'clock he would call the admiral.

d. Worn down by conflicting pressures, the decision was made arbitrarily.

e. Storing her furniture in a rented garage, the move to New York was complete.

f. The detective told us recently there was another robbery like ours.

g. Failing to understand the assignment, the paper was not counted toward the final grade.

h. The old houses increased in value, related to the sudden popularity of inner-city living.

i. My mother hoped while she was in town to do some shopping.

j. Based on the following reasons, I must reject your proposal.

k. Looking at the sky, it does not seem to be a good day for sailing.

l. The foundation agreed immediately to fund our project.

m. Relieved of her job, no one tried to cultivate her good will.

n. Fritz was instructed without delay to catch another plane.

o. Reeling in the line frantically, the fish jumped into my partner's net.

G12 *The Verb* Be

The most irregular verb in English is *be*. While most verbs have four or at most five basic forms (see Principal Parts, p. 293), the verb *be* has eight:

am, are, is
was, were
be, being, been

Memorize the list as if it were a jingle or a cheer. Notice that the first three forms start with vowels, the second two start with *w*, and the last three with *b*. If you recite the list rhythmically a few times, you will have no trouble memorizing it.

G 13

Good writers generally avoid the verb *be* when it is followed by an adjective or a noun that can be turned into a strong, economical verb. (See p. 150.)

G13 *Active Voice/Passive Voice**

The term *active voice* refers to sentences in which the subject performs the action. This is considered the normal pattern for English sentences.

Examples
The *manager* offered Roger a job.
   (subject) (active verb)

An *agency* of the federal government conducts inspections.
(subject)   (active verb)

In the first example, the "manager," the grammatical subject, is the one doing the offering, and Roger is the one receiving an offer. Similarly, in the second example, it is the "agency," the grammatical subject, that is conducting inspections.

In the passive voice, a past participle is combined with some form of the verb *be*, and the grammatical subject receives (becomes "passive" to) the action named in the verb.

* For advice about avoiding passive voice, see p. 151.

G13 Continued

Examples

Roger was offered a job by the manager.
(subject) (passive verb)

Inspections are conducted by an agency of the federal government.
   (subject)   (passive verb)

In the first example, "Roger," the grammatical subject, is not the one offering; he is the one receiving an offer. Similarly, the "inspections" are not conducting anything; someone or something is conducting the inspection.

Any verb phrase that includes a past participle and some form of *be* is in the passive voice. If you have trouble recognizing the forms of *be* in the examples below, see p. 305. If you have trouble recognizing past participles, see p. 293.

EXERCISE

Indicate which of the following sentences are in the active voice and which are in the passive. Remember that passive voice is always marked by some form of *be* plus a past participle.

a. Details about the contract will be sent by the Department of Defense.

b. Bulldozers had uprooted the trees in less than an hour.

c. The tax reform bill has not yet been approved by Congress.

d. Two policemen on motorcycles were escorting Jason and his wife to the hospital.

e. The sight of surgical instruments frightens many people.

f. Hot weather and frequent rain did not bother Jonathan.

g. The Peking duck was ordered four days in advance.

h. The city had cut down all the trees in our neighborhood.

i. Marty's canoe had been smashed against a rock by the rushing water and folded neatly in half.

j. Maria will be tapping the cymbal with a broken drumstick.

G14 *Nouns*

Nouns are words that fit in the following slot:

(A/An) _____ can be unforgettable.

Examples

Mozart can be unforgettable.

A policeman can be unforgettable.

Omaha can be unforgettable.

An ocelot can be unforgettable.

Style can be unforgettable.

Lectures can be unforgettable.

G 14

Nouns are name words. In fact, the word *noun* comes from the Latin word for "name" (*nomen*). Nouns are usually the names of persons (Mozart, Carter, mother, policeman), places (Omaha, kitchen, classroom), things (automobile, pliers, bottle), animals (ocelot, zebra, angelfish), abstractions (motherhood, beauty, truth, style), and even acts and activities (crime, punishment, pressure, insistence).

One way to find out whether a word can be a noun is to check a dictionary. In most dictionaries, nouns are identified by the single letter *n* after the entry. But remember, many words can be used as nouns in one sentence and as verbs or adjectives in others.

EXERCISES

1. Indicate which of the following words might be used as nouns. First see whether the word will fit in the slot: (A/An) _____ can be unforgettable. Check your answers in a dictionary.

of	in	assertion
because	horse	information
winter	August	happiness
pleasant	hostess	through
mountain	cat	frighten
worse	over	fright
never	index	

2. Each of the following words can be used as either a noun or a verb. First, insert each word into the slots for nouns (above) and for verbs (p. 289) and notice how context changes the meaning

G14 Continued

of the words. Then write two sentences with each word, using it as a noun in one sentence and as a verb in another.

mistake	rule
dance	train
increase	campaign
rest	book
cook	drink

**G
15**

3. Identify the nouns and verbs in the following sentences.

a. Foster and his friends often rent horses to ride along the mountain trails.

b. The stable is owned by a middle-aged couple with seven children.

c. The older children, three girls, groom the horses and give riding lessons.

d. Some horses want to be leaders; others are so easily spooked from behind that they must be placed at the end of the line.

e. The trail begins as a narrow path through the grass beside a busy two-lane highway.

f. After a few hundred yards, the trail veers away from the highway and becomes a stony path meandering between scrubby trees and tall underbrush.

g. As the noise of the highway becomes less audible, the terrain becomes more hilly and lush, covered with taller trees, teeming with wildlife.

h. Sometimes deer freeze and stare at passing riders, apparently surprised that the four-footed pace they hear brings with it a two-footed animal.

i. A waterfall spills noisily into a pool, which wanders off into a stream.

j. Tired and thirsty, some of the horses refuse to lift their heads from the stream; they buck and kick to test the authority of their riders before splashing across and scrambling up the rocky bank on the far side.

G15 *Problems with Nouns: Plurals*

Grammarians use the term *singular* to describe nouns that refer to only one person or thing and *plural* to describe nouns that refer to more than one person or thing. Thus *college* is a singular noun and *colleges* is a plural noun.

Ordinarily, plural nouns are formed by adding *s* or *es* to the singular form. Exceptions are discussed in the section on spelling, pp. 276–279.

In spoken English, there is sometimes a tendency to use the singular form after a number or after some other word that indicates plurality.

Examples

The fire station is three mile down this street.
We hope to spend several day in Montana.

**G
16**

Linguistically, this idiom is reasonable. If the plurality of *mile* and *day* is already indicated by the words immediately before them, the addition of the plural form seems unnecessary. In printed English, however, the plural marker is omitted only when the two words are joined by a hyphen and used as an adjective.

EXERCISE

Fill in the blank with the correct form of the word printed in parentheses.

a. All of the _____ (parent) were relieved when school began.
b. Last year we had a three-_____ (month) dry spell.
c. The police had blocked all seven _____ (exit).
d. A collection of twenty-three _____ (print) was on display at the Art Center.
e. Randal made a seven-_____ (dollar) profit on the books.

G16 *Pronouns and Their Referents*

The word *pronoun* literally means "in place of a noun." Pronouns—words like *I, me, you, he, him, she, her, it, we, us, they, who, which,* and sometimes *what, that, this, these,* and *those*—are used in place of a noun when we want to avoid using the noun itself.

Because pronouns depend upon other words for their specific meaning, it is important that they be

G16 Continued

placed in sentences in such a way that readers have no trouble understanding which words they refer to. Vague pronoun reference can make writing unintelligible.

Example

Peter told Justin that he would have to take him to the hospital.

In this sentence, it is impossible to determine whether Peter is taking Justin to the hospital or Justin is taking Peter.

Another kind of vagueness arises when a pronoun is used to refer to an idea implicit in its context but not expressed.

Example

If you drive your car to a second job, you can deduct it from your income tax.

In this example, "it" refers to the cost of driving, but there is no clear referent in the sentence.

Pronouns can also be used to refer to a group of words or to an entire statement rather than to a single noun only if the meaning of the pronoun is perfectly clear from its context.

Examples

Taiwan prospers within the political vacuum that history has put it in, and that does no one any harm.

> —Ross Terrill, *The Atlantic* (May 1978), p. 8.

For many, the best Hiss defense was the suggestion that Chambers and the FBI had forged the typed documents by which Alger Hiss was convicted. This was accomplished, the defense suggested, by getting access to the Hiss typewriter. . . .

> —John Kenneth Galbraith "Alger Hiss and
> Liberal Anxiety," *The Atlantic* (May 1978), p. 45.

Which is not to say that the contemporary world does not have its "heroes."

> —Paul Zweig, "The Hero in Literature,"
> *Saturday Review* (December 1978), p. 35.

In the third example, the "which" refers to the thesis implicit in the several paragraphs that precede it in the article.

Although the use of pronouns to refer to phrases and clauses is fairly common even in professional writing, some editors and writing teachers still object to this practice.

Another common problem is the use of pronouns to refer to nouns in the possessive case (that is, nouns followed by an apostrophe or an apostrophe *s*). This usage is perfectly clear and acceptable in speech and in informal writing.

G 16

Examples

After Van's tour of duty, he returned to Louisiana to settle down.

In Beethoven's Sixth Symphony, he depicts a country festival.

In Irving's novel, he writes about characters who are themselves writing books.

In Barbara Ward's essay "Triage," she examines two half-truths about the international food supply.

In formal writing, however, this structure is usually avoided by reversing the positions of the noun and the pronoun.

Examples

After his tour of duty, Van returned to Louisiana to settle down.

In his Sixth Symphony, Beethoven depicts a country festival.

In his novel, Irving writes about characters who are themselves writing books.

In her essay "Triage," Barbara Ward examines two half-truths about the international food supply.

EXERCISES

1. Identify the pronouns in the following list.

life	him	me
treason	manage	elf
they	rifle	them
we	you	series
artifice	special	us
it	she	even

G16 Continued

wolf	her	who
I	easy	towards
speech	prince	which
reason	person	when

2. Look for all the pronouns in an article in the newspaper you usually read. After marking the pronouns, discuss how they get their specific meaning from nearby nouns or groups of words.

3. Discuss and remedy the problems in pronoun reference in the following sentences.

a. Claudia asked Catherine if she could go with her to the supermarket.

b. These children are not good with animals because they are too easily excited.

c. Hamlet mistrusted the apparition, which caused him to delay his revenge.

d. When Tiresias proclaimed the murderer's name, it angered the king.

e. The government forced all the residents to sell their homes because they wanted to build a radar station there.

f. When she saw Jack in the role Robert had made famous, she knew why the audience preferred him.

g. In Fowles's new novel, he makes the protagonist a script writer.

h. If Lillian is as rich as she is rumored to be, she could use it to support our cause.

i. In Vernon's letter to the editor, he challenges the reporter's facts.

j. If we provide our friends with the help they need, it will benefit ourselves in the long run.

G17 *Pronouns: Agreement*

If a reader marks an agreement error in a pronoun, chances are you put a singular pronoun (*he, his, she, her,* or *it*) where you should have put a plural (*they, their*).

Examples
A woman should take pride in their work.

When I asked the nurse for an appointment, they told me to come at any time.

Pederson and Jones both brought his music.

To remedy the problem, make sure the pronoun is singular if it refers to a singular noun, and plural if it refers to a plural noun or to a combination of nouns.

Examples

A woman should take pride in her work.

When I asked the nurse for an appointment, she told me to come at any time.

Pederson and Jones both brought their music.

Ordinarily, native speakers of English have no trouble making pronouns agree with (i.e., match) the nouns they refer to. No one is tempted to write or to say, "My father cut herself while shaving this morning," or "My little sister can already tie their own shoes." In some sentences, however, the natural relationship between nouns and pronouns becomes obscured.

Examples

Was it Michael or Bryan who lost (his/their) temper?

Did Timmy and Mary Jane lose (his/her/their) temper?

Everyone enjoyed (himself/herself/himself or herself/themselves) at the party.

In printed English, a pronoun is ordinarily plural if it refers to two or more nouns joined by *and*.

Example

Did Timmy and Mary Jane lose their temper?

And a pronoun is ordinarily singular if it refers to two or more nouns joined by *or* or *nor*.

G17 Continued

Examples

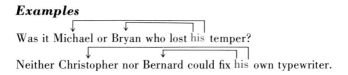

Was it Michael or Bryan who lost his temper?

Neither Christopher nor Bernard could fix his own typewriter.

This convention does not help, however, when the pronoun joined by *or* refers to a male and a female.

Example

Was it Timmy or Mary Jane who lost (his/her) temper?

In cases like this — and in all other situations in which you are faced with two unsatisfactory choices — the best solution is to avoid the problem by rewriting the sentence.

Example

Did Timmy lose his temper or did Mary Jane lose hers?

The convention governing references to words like *each*, *everybody*, *either*, etc., and to nouns of undetermined sex, has been complicated by the women's movement. Formerly, writers used *he* to include both males and females in this situation.

Examples

Everyone enjoyed himself at the party.

Every student should check his work carefully.

Nowadays many readers object to this use of *he* because it seems to slight the roles women play in the world. One solution is to employ the plural pronoun, as it is normally employed in conversational English.

Example

Everyone enjoyed themselves at the party.

This solution, however, will offend many readers who are convinced that words like *each*, *everyone*, *everybody*, and *either* are logically singular and should, therefore, be referred to by pronouns that are singular as well. It is possible that this grammatical objection will eventually give way to pressures from the women's movement and from the natural idiom of the language; for the time being, however, the "everyone . . . themselves" pattern is not normal in print, though a few intrepid writers have begun to use it.

Another solution is to use "he or she" and "his or her."

Examples

Everyone said he or she had a good time at the party.

Every student should check his or her work carefully.

But this solution is somewhat awkward, especially in extended passages requiring lots of pronouns. Other writers try to avoid charges of sexism by sprinkling *he* and *she* in equal proportions throughout a text.

Example

If an athlete wants to succeed, she should practice rigorously.

If a housekeeper wants to take pride in his work, he should perform his chores with diligence and care.

This solution probably distracts more readers than it satisfies, and, like the invention of sexually neuter pronouns (e.g., *co* and *cos*), it does not seem to be gaining much currency in printed English.

Perhaps the best solution to the problem is to avoid it altogether, either by rephrasing the sentence or by making both the noun and the pronoun plural.

Examples

Everyone said the party was a good one.

Students should check their work carefully.

If athletes want to succeed, they should practice rigorously.

If housekeepers want to take pride in their work, they should perform their chores with diligence and care.

G17 Continued

Collective nouns—nouns that are singular in form but plural in meaning—cause special problems in determining pronoun reference.

Examples
The orchestra packed (its/their) instruments and left the auditorium.

The basketball team returned to (its/their) classes.

The correct form in these situations is the one that expresses the writer's meaning. If the sentence portrays the orchestra or the team acting together as a unit, then *its* would be the appropriate pronoun; if it portrays the members of these groups acting individually, then *their* would be the appropriate pronoun. When the members of a group are acting as individuals, however, it is often better to rewrite the sentence.

Examples
The musicians packed their instruments and left the auditorium.

The players returned to their classes.

EXERCISES

1. Adjust any faulty pronoun agreement in the following sentences.

a. The jury had no trouble reaching their verdict.
b. Every voter should exercise their rights at election time.
c. To be successful, a secretary must have their desk cleared at the end of each day.
d. Either Terrence or Todd left their exam book in my office.
e. Neither Rufus nor his sister could control their laughter.
f. Language is important to a lawyer because he uses it to define and sanction the behaviors that separate civilization from chaos.
g. The army was defeated soon after their general was taken prisoner.
h. A cook can learn to flip omelets by practicing with a potholder approximately the size and shape of the eggs they will use.
i. Neither Pedro nor Raoul could be seen anywhere without a book in their hands.
j. Yesterday the Defense Department delivered their budget request to Congress.

2. Construct an exercise of your own like the one above. Swap exercises with a classmate and correct each other's work.

G18 *Pronouns: Use of* I/We

In academic writing there is a long-established tradition of avoiding the pronoun *I*. This tradition is based on the assumption that the intrusion of the author's persona makes the writing less objective, less scientific. Although many scholars and writing teachers still hold firm to this tradition, the use of *I* has become more widely accepted in journals and classrooms, partly because the attempt to avoid it often results in awkward and stilted prose.

If you are writing for readers who are interested in your impressions of the subject at hand, use *I* with confidence.

Examples
Although I was sympathetic with the female protagonist in the movie, I found the portrayal of men shallow and stereotypical — a fault which, I think, made the movie less a work of art, more a piece of propaganda.

At first, I was unable to see how Britton's theories added to what I had already learned from Vygotsky and Piaget.

Sometimes scholars will go to strange lengths to avoid saying "I," referring to themselves as "we" even when they are individually responsible for the work in question.

Example
In chapter three, we demonstrated that language not only expresses ideas, it actually shapes and limits the thoughts human beings can think.

The use of *we* to refer to one person may have been appropriate for kings, and it may still be useful for newspaper editors and occasionally for judges; but for individual writers it can seem stuffy and pretentious.

We is less objectionable when it is used to include the writer and the reader.

G18 Continued

Example

We have learned a great deal about rhetoric from Aristotle, but we should not ignore the contributions of more recent rhetoricians.

The use of *we* is offensive, however, when the writer tries to include the reader in company the reader objects to.

Example

Because we have come to recognize Freudian analysis as poetic and fanciful, we should limit our study of personality to observable behaviors.

Readers who disagree with this evaluation of Freudian analysis or with this emphasis on observable behavior will object to being included in this writer's "we."

G19 You/One

Some writers avoid *I* by using *one*, in the sense of "people in general."

Example

One notices a tendency among modern critics to regard fiction as an aesthetic construct, not as a means of shaping values.

Although this use of *one* is still fairly common in academic situations, many writers avoid it because it seems archaic and excessively formal. At the other extreme is the use of *you*, meaning "one," referring not to the reader in particular but to people in general.

Example

The murals of Rivera show you a side of Spanish colonialism that you may not have seen in your textbooks.

This use of *you* makes writing seem chatty and informal. If chatty informality is appropriate for the piece you are working on, use *you* with confidence. It is, however, possible to avoid both the informality of *you* and the stiffness of *one* by stating your observation without explicit references to people in general.

Examples

Modern critics tend to regard fiction as an aesthetic construct, not as a means of shaping values.

The murals of Rivera show a side of Spanish colonialism that is often ignored in textbooks.

**G
19**

Whichever pronoun you choose, stick to it. It is distracting to flit from one pronoun to another, as if the point of view were constantly shifting.

Example

When we arrived at the campsite, one could hear the wind whistling in the pine tops with a serenity you can find nowhere in any city I've ever visited.

EXERCISE

Discuss the effect of *I, we, you*, and *one* in the following sentences. If you cannot imagine a context in which the use of these pronouns would be appropriate and effective, revise the sentence.

a. One wishes that Rubenstein had played another encore.
b. To me, I think *The Magus* is a dangerous book, devoid of the horror one should feel toward a ruthless and arrogant manipulator like Maurice Conchis.
c. If you want to write well, you must learn to view your work with detachment.
d. We hold these truths to be self-evident.
e. In our first novel we wrote about man's bondage to landscape.
f. In Southeast Asia we learned costly lessons that we will not soon forget.
g. I think the sleigh driver in Frost's poem is Santa Claus.
h. In Tennyson's poem, you see the ocean from the eagle's point of view.
i. One has the impression that American voters distrust intelligence.
j. In our store on Fifteenth Street, one senses the indifference of the management.

G20 *Pronouns: Possessive Forms*

The possessive of definite pronouns (*I, you, he, she, it, we,* and *they*) is formed without an apostrophe and often without an *s*.

Examples

Nouns	Pronouns
Jack's mother	his mother
Mary's job	her job
The program's requirements	its requirements
The Joneses' house	their house
	your house
	our house
	my house

The possessive of indefinite pronouns (*anybody, anyone, one, somebody, someone,* and similar words) is formed by adding an apostrophe and an *s*.

Examples

anybody's house

anyone's house

one's house

somebody's house

someone's house

The apostrophe and *s* is also used with pronouns, not to form a possessive, but to indicate a contraction.

Examples

it's = it is *or* it has

he's = he is *or* he has

who's = who is *or* who has

Writers who confuse *its* with *it's*, *theirs* with *there's* and *who's* with *whose* may find it helpful to remember that definite pronouns never use an apostrophe to form a possessive. For exercises, see Exercises 3 and 4 in **G21** below.

G21 *Contractions*

In speech we often compress certain common phrases instead of pronouncing each word. "I will" becomes "I'll," "she is" becomes "she's," "we would" becomes "we'd," and so forth. These compressed forms are called contractions. In writing, contractions set an informal tone. If you are writing something formal — a proposal, a research paper, a letter of application — avoid contractions. If an informal tone is appropriate for the occasion, take advantage of contractions. But be careful: too many contractions can make your writing seem downright talky.

G 21

EXERCISES

1. Here are some common contractions. How would each one be written out in full? (Sometimes more than one answer is correct.)

weren't	it's	we're
couldn't	he'll	they're
we've	she's	can't
I'd	I'm	won't
who's	you're	I've
don't	doesn't	didn't

2. Cover up Exercise 1 above with a sheet of paper. How would you write the following verb phrases as contractions? (Check your answers against the forms in Exercise 1.)

were not	do not	does not
could not	it is	we are
we have	he will	they are
I would	she is	cannot
I had	she has	will not
who is	I am	I have
who has	you are	did not

3. As a review of **G19** and **G20**, choose the appropriate form in each of the following sentences.

G21 Continued

a. The bell is ringing; (its/it's) time for lunch.
b. The horse lost (its/it's) footing when it galloped into the mud.
c. Call the Thompsons; this book must be (theirs/there's).
d. Whenever (there's/theirs) doubt about the meaning of the Constitution, we construe it according to our political values.
e. No one knows (who's/whose) going to be in the White House next.
f. (Who's/Whose) words these are I think I know.
g. (It's/Its) not always easy to categorize units of language.
h. As long as (there's/theirs) an energy shortage, the eastern states will have expensive winters.

4. Construct an exercise of your own like the one above. Swap exercises with a classmate and correct each other's work.

G22 *Pronouns: Relative*

Relative pronouns are used to introduce a group of words that act as a noun or an adjective within a sentence. They include *that, what, whatever, which, whichever, who, whoever, whom, whomever.*

Examples

What *you see* is what you get.

Whoever *comes* will be welcomed by our committee.

The boss will hire whomever *you choose.*

I know that *you will be reliable.*

The manuscript, which *had been lost for years*, has been found.

The man who *lost this camera* has returned to claim it.

Jackson, whom *you recommended,* cannot be with us.

The fullback whose *name was in the paper* is a social worker.

For rules about punctuating groups of words introduced by relative pronouns, see **P7** and **P8**.

For the difference between *who* and *whom*, see **G34**.

EXERCISE

Identify the relative pronoun in each of the following sentences, and tell whether the group of words it introduces is acting like a noun or like an adjective.

a. We need to discover whose shoes these are.
b. You may choose whomever you like best.
c. They rejected Kleinsmith, whom the faculty had endorsed.
d. Whoever arrives earliest will get the best seats.
e. I know who you mean, but I can't think of his name.
f. The law, which should have been passed last year, has finally been sent out of committee.
g. It sometimes takes hard work to acquire the skills that you want.

G
23

G23 *Adjectives and Adverbs*

Most adjectives will fit in the following slot:

X didn't seem _____.

Adjectives are usually used to make the meaning of nouns and pronouns more specific. In the following examples, the adjectives make the meaning of the pronoun *it* more specific. In grammatical terms, the adjective "modifies" the pronoun.

Examples

It didn't seem warm.

It didn't seem expensive.

It didn't seem fast.

In other sentences, these same adjectives could be used to modify nouns — that is, to make the meaning of the nouns more specific.

Example

At Johnny's you can get fast service and warm food, but the desserts are very expensive.

G23 Continued

Although the term *adverb* technically includes a wide variety of words, the adverbs that writers need to identify are words that will fit in the following slot:

X will do it _____.

In general, adverbs are used to add information to the meaning of verbs — usually information about how, when or where the action takes place. In the following examples, the adverbs add information to the verb *do*. Adverbs modify verbs just as adjectives modify nouns. Many adverbs are formed by adding *-ly* to an adjective (but not all words ending in *-ly* are adverbs).

Examples

X will do it beautifully.   (how)

X will do it frequently.   (how often)

X will do it most.   (how much)

X will do it soon.   (when)

X will do it here.   (where)

Adverbs usually modify verbs.

Examples

Roosevelt sews beautifully.   (how)

Reid brought the old wreck here.   (where)

But words that modify adjectives or other adverbs are also considered adverbs.

Examples

The property was perfectly apt for a prison.

Alston walked through the room very quietly.

In the first example, "perfectly" is considered an adverb because it modifies the adjective "apt," which in turn modifies the noun "property." In the second example, "very" is considered an adverb because it modifies the adverb "quietly," which in turn modifies the verb "walked."

EXERCISES

1. Separate the following words into three categories: adjectives, adverbs, and neither. Some words can be used as an adjective in one sentence and an adverb in another; these words should be listed in both categories. Adjectives will fit in the slot: X didn't seem _____. Adverbs will fit in the slot: X will do it _____.

tie	oceans	jealous
wiry	there	envy
yellow	confidently	deeply
pertly	large	fuzzy
impartially	sorry	need
once	red	first
after	firm	fairly
afterwards	firmly	fair
organic	what	roof
with	somehow	awkward

2. Identify all the adjectives and adverbs in a passage of about five hundred words copied from a recent magazine or newspaper of high quality. In doing so, test this hypothesis: In good prose, adjectives outnumber adverbs by about fifty to one.

3. Identify the adverbs and adjectives in a piece you have recently written.

G24 *Using Adjectives for Adverbs*

In general, writers are careful to observe the distinction between adverbial and adjectival forms in writing whenever different forms are available.

Many adjectives can be converted to adverbs by the addition of *-ly*.

Examples

It didn't seem honest.   (Adjective)

G24 Continued

X will do it honestly.   (Adverb)

It didn't seem nice.   (Adjective)

X will do it nicely.   (Adverb)

X didn't seem quiet.   (Adjective)

X will do it quietly.   (Adverb)

In a few instances, the adjectival form can be used in place of the adverbial form.

Examples*
Shakespeare: "how slow time goes."   (Instead of "slowly.")

F. D. Roosevelt: "I would go pretty slow on that."   (Instead of "slowly.")

Let's get out of here quick!   (Instead of "quickly.")

But often the use of an adjectival form in place of an adverbial form seems colloquial and out of place in writing.

Examples
Myrna sings terrible.   (instead of "terribly")

Auden would sure have disagreed.   (instead of "surely")

The acting was real good.   (instead of "really")

Writers also use *well* as the adverbial form of *good*.

Examples
X didn't seem good.   (Adjective)

X will do it well.   (Adverb)

---

* The first two examples are cited in *Webster's Third New International Dictionary.*

Notice, though, that verbs like *appear, be, become, feel, look, seem, smell, sound,* and *taste* are normally followed by adjectives rather than by adverbs when the subject rather than the verb is being described or modified.

Examples

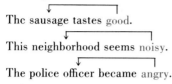

The sausage tastes good.

This neighborhood seems noisy.

The police officer became angry.

Sometimes, in an effort to produce schoolbook English, student writers will use hyper-correct forms that distort the meaning they intend.

Examples

That sausage tastes well.

This neighborhood seems noisily.

The police officer became angrily.

In these examples, the meaning is sacrificed to what the writer mistakenly considers good grammar.

EXERCISE

Choose the appropriate form in each of the following sentences.

a. At first, the band sounded (weak/weakly).

b. (Sudden/Suddenly) Larson appeared and snatched the ball away.

c. When we saw Exir, we ran (quick/quickly) to help her carry the cooler.

d. Your father seemed (angry/angrily) last night.

e. Edsel's behavior was (foolish/foolishly), but he admitted it.

f. Clyde is enthusiastic, but he doesn't play (good/well).

g. Except for Sharon, none of the candidates looks (good/well).

h. Doug could read (rapid/rapidly).

i. Eleanor seemed (confident/confidently) about her performance.

j. That chemical plant smells (awful/awfully).

G25 *Comparatives and Superlatives*

Most adjectives and adverbs have three different forms, which are traditionally called "positive," "comparative," and "superlative."

Examples

Positive	*Comparative*	*Superlative*
dedicated (adj.)	more dedicated	most dedicated
smart (adj.)	smarter	smartest
popular (adj.)	more popular	most popular
good (adj.)	better	best
well (adv.)	better	best
soon (adv.)	sooner	soonest
quickly (adv.)	more quickly	most quickly

Ordinarily, the comparative is used in normal printed English when two individuals, groups, or conditions are being compared, and the superlative is used when more than two individuals, groups, or conditions are involved in the comparison.

Examples

Comparative: Of the two, Dr. Johnson is the better qualified.

Superlative: Of the three, Dr. Johnson is the best qualified.

Superlative: Dr. Johnson is the best lecturer I have ever heard.

Comparative: Was Opal or her sister the better athlete?

Superlative: Was Opal the best athlete on the team?

Comparative: You are singing better today than you did yesterday.

Superlative: That was your best performance ever.

The comparative is also used along with the word *than* when more than two individuals, groups, or conditions are being compared.

Examples

Comparative: Opal was smarter than her sisters.

Comparative: Edward is more dedicated than the rest.

Comparative: Oscar was more popular than the other Jasons.

Except for *early,* adverbs that end in *-ly* are made comparative and superlative by the use of *more* and *most;* other adverbs either have irregular forms or are compared by the addition of *-er* and *-est.*

G 25

Examples

Positive	Comparative	Superlative
(early)	(earlier)	(earliest)
vaguely	more vaguely	most vaguely
grumpily	more grumpily	most grumpily
much	more	most
well	better	best
soon	sooner	soonest
fast	faster	fastest
loud	louder	loudest

Adjectives of one syllable are usually made comparative and superlative by the addition of *-er* and *-est.* Adjectives of three or more syllables are made comparative and superlative by the use of *more* and *most.* Many two-syllable adjectives can go either way.

Examples

Positive	Comparative	Superlative
blue	bluer	bluest
bright	brighter	brightest
turgid	more turgid	most turgid
restless	more restless	most restless
murky	murkier	murkiest
	or more murky	*or* most murky
subtle	subtler	subtlest
	or more subtle	*or* most subtle
inconvenient	more inconvenient	most inconvenient
purposeful	more purposeful	most purposeful

G25 Continued

G 25

When two forms are available, choose the one that sounds better in context.

Any doubts about the comparative and superlative forms can be resolved by consulting a dictionary. A good dictionary will list all irregular comparative and superlative forms after the entry for the positive form; it will also print *-er* and *-est* after adjectives and adverbs that use these suffixes for comparison. When no comparative or superlative forms are listed, use *more* and *most*.

Some adjectives have no logical comparison. *Unique*, for example, means "one of a kind." It is hard to imagine how something might be "more unique" (i.e., more one-of-a-kind) than something else. *Round, final, perfect*, and *dead* are also logically incomparable, though *rounder, more final, more perfect*, and *deader* are often found in print.

In Shakespeare's English, double comparatives and superlatives were used for emphasis, as when Mark Antony in *Julius Caesar* says, "This was the *most unkindest* cut of all." Because eighteenth-century grammarians thought that "most" merely duplicated the meaning of *-est* in "unkindest," written English is now devoid of an idiom that Shakespeare found useful.

Printed English generally avoids inexact comparisons.

Examples

Bill's talents were superior to Tina.

Catfish Hunter threw more strikes than any pitcher this year.

In the first example, Bill's talents should be compared with Tina's talents, not with Tina herself. In printed English, the comparison would probably read, "Bill's talents were superior to Tina's." In the second example, Catfish Hunter seems to be contrasted with pitchers, as if he himself were not a pitcher. The addition of *other* would make the comparison more exact: "Catfish Hunter threw more strikes than any *other* pitcher this year."

EXERCISES

1. Rewrite the following sentences as they would be likely to occur in print. Feel free to consult a dictionary.

a. After the dance, Warren felt more lonelier than ever.
b. Hemingway was more enamored of Spanish culture than any American novelist.
c. Johnston had hoped the troops would arrive more soon.
d. Reston chose the Pinto because it was more new.
e. Who spells best, you or your brother?
f. In the girls' group, Charlene was the more graceful of the eleven.
g. Choose the route that will get you to Cambridge most soonest.
h. Marston was the wellest writer in class.
i. The Vanity is one of the most unique dress shops in town.
j. Jean's financial condition was better than her husband.

2. Indicate the three degrees of comparison for each of the following words. Use a dictionary if you need help.

beautiful	supple	hot
noisome	clear	fit
reluctantly	deep	unfit
quick	reasonably	spry
loud	much	treasonous

G26 *Prepositions*

Prepositions are connecting words rather than content words. The meaning of prepositions—words like *to, by, for, in, through*—is so abstract as to be almost undefinable. These are clearly different from words like *cat, house, beauty, yellow, angrily,* and other words that we can act out, point to, or exemplify with reference to the world around us. Some people call prepositions relation words, because prepositions indicate relationships rather than objects or qualities.

Most prepositions indicate spatial relationships, and they generally fit in the following slot:

She walked _____ the ladders.

G26 Continued

Examples

above	into
along	near
among	over
around	to
by	toward
between	under
from	with

G 26

Other prepositions indicate relationships in time. These generally fit in the following slot:

It happened ——————— the war.

Examples
after
before
during
since
until

Sometimes two words work together as if they were a single preposition.

Examples
according to
together with
along with

And sometimes prepositions work as essential parts of verbs.

Examples
Amy has *come* up with a solution.
The wreck *was put* together and hauled to the junkyard.

To is not considered a preposition when it is used in a verb phrase to form an infinitive.

Examples
Suddenly it began to *rain*.

Steve seems to *have forgotten* his appointment.

Prepositions have objects. To find the object, ask *whom* or *what* after the preposition.

Examples

In "by the Senate," *Senate* is the object of by. (By what? The Senate.)

In "of the story," *story* is the object of of. (Of what? The story.)

In "for you," *you* is the object of for. (For whom? For you.)

In "to the Huntington Library," *Huntington Library* is the object of to. (To what? The Huntington Library.)

G 26

EXERCISES

1. Identify the prepositions and their objects in the following passage.

In the evenings, Evelyn used to sit alone on the window bench, watching the neighborhood men returning from work. She liked to pretend that one of them would walk up to her front door and enter, as they entered other doors, with the casual authority of a proprietor. She knew she was pretending, but pretense, she felt, was better than despair. One evening, when the street was still steaming from a summer shower and the black clouds had dissipated into gorgeous streaks across the western sky, Evelyn was surprised by footsteps climbing toward her own door. She watched, unafraid, as the knob inside the door was turned by an invisible hand, and the door itself sprung open, revealing a tall stranger dressed like a character in a Dickens novel—top hat, cape, and large umbrella, which he carried like a cane. Their eyes met for just a second; but before Evelyn could register fear or welcome or surprise, the stranger continued into the foyer, dropped his umbrella into an enameled milk can, removed his hat and cape and handed them to Evelyn as if she were supposed to know what to do with them.

And indeed she did.

2. Copy a one-hundred-word passage from any newspaper, magazine, or book. Underline all the prepositions and connect them to their objects with arrows. Swap papers in class and discuss your work.

G27 *Prepositions at the End of a Sentence or Clause*

In Latin, prepositions *always* come before the nouns that are their objects. Anyone who has studied even one year of Latin in high school knows that words like *ad, in, inter, per,* and *propter* would not make sense unless they were followed by nouns. When English grammars were first written, grammarians assumed that this characteristic of Latin ought to be imitated by good English writers. Hence, there is a longstanding tradition that prepositions come before their objects — which means that prepositions may not occur at the end of a sentence or at the end of a clause.

But English is different from Latin, and often the most natural place for a preposition in English is after its object, even at the end of a sentence or a clause.

Examples

Ethel Waters had a light, lissome voice that she could do anything with — growls, falsetto, mimicry, improvisation, parlando.
— Whitney Balliett, *The New Yorker*, May 22, 1978, p. 112.

Mr. Rothlisberger had constructed a large, deep, exciting set, one that could contain within it a variety of other scenes — some small, some large, some shallow, some deep — in a way that quite avoided the monotony of unit sets such as the Met "Prophete," "Aida," and "Rigoletto" are played in.
— Andrew Porter, *The New Yorker*, May 22, 1978, p. 119.

Loosely constructed as one more or less continuous dance suite broken by interludes of pantomime, slapstick, and exotic or fantastic spectacle, it needs space to sprawl in.
— Arlene Croce, *The New Yorker*, May 22, 1978, p. 127.

Pea-brained, which Reed is dimly harking back to, makes sense as a hyperbole meaning a brain the size of a pea; it does not mean the brain of a pea, which is inconceivable.
— John Simon, *Esquire*, May 23, 1978, p. 15.

Writing teachers are fond of Churchill's response to a press worker who had changed the Prime Minister's sentences ending with prepositions. Said Churchill: "That is the sort of impertinence up with which I will not put."

Churchill's point, of course, was that in many situations it is more graceful in English to end sentences with a preposition (". . . which I will not put up with.") than to twist the sentence unnaturally. The point is well taken. The sentences quoted in the examples above would not be stylistically improved with phrases like "with which she could do anything" or "unsuitable women with whom to go out."

Still, sentences with prepositions after their objects are relatively rare in good prose. Writers seem to avoid prepositions after objects whenever they can do so gracefully, but do not hesitate to violate this tradition whenever the natural idiom of English calls for a violation.

G 28

G28 *Conjunctions: Coordinating and Subordinating*

Conjunctions, like prepositions, are relation words. That is, they don't have the sort of meaning you can demonstrate by pointing or acting out. They just show different kinds of connections or relationships between other words or other groups of words.

Conjunctions that indicate logical relationships fit in the following slot:

Eat, drink, and be merry, _____ tomorrow you will die.

Examples
and	although	since
but	as if	unless
for	because	if

or (nor in negative sentences)

Conjunctions that indicate relationships in time fit in the following slot:

Let the trumpets play _____ the crowd arrives.

Examples
after	until
as	when
before	while

G28 Continued

Five of these conjunctions are considered *coordinating conjunctions:* and, but, for, or and, in negative sentences, nor. All the others are considered *subordinating conjunctions.*

EXERCISE

Pick up any printed material that is near at hand and select twelve sentences at random. Identify the conjunctions in those sentences and tell whether each is a coordinating conjunction or a subordinating conjunction. Discuss the results with classmates or with an instructor.

G
29

G29 *Coordinating Conjunctions at the Beginning of a Sentence*

Because conjunctions join two words or groups of words, prescriptive grammarians once made the rule that the word groups joined by conjunctions should not be interrupted by a period. More specifically, it has long been considered ungrammatical to begin a sentence with *and, or, but, for,* or *nor,* since these words make no sense unless other words come before them.

That tradition is no longer adhered to as strictly as it once was.

Examples

The State Department stressed Washington's "enduring and strong ties" with Israel. And Administration officials attempted to play down the threat posed by the Saudi F-15s.
—**Tom Gervasi,** *Esquire,* **May 1978, p. 20.**

For whereas historians who have touched upon literacy as a historical phenomenon have commonly mentioned its progress in terms of the history of writing, the actual conditions of literacy depend not upon the history of writing but of reading.
—**Eric A. Havelock,** *Origins of Western Literacy,* **p. 18.**

But let us suppose that somehow people would be able to get where they're supposed to go.
—**Norman Cousins,** *Saturday Review,* **3 Feb. 1979, p. 8.**

But the president then invokes executive privilege to withhold seventeen of the substitute documents, some of which bear his handwritten notations.

—Jack Egan, *New York*, 25 Dec. 1978/1 Jan. 1979, p. 16.

And one singer in Venice ate raw snails rolled in sugar to soothe his raspy throat.

—Eunice Fried, *Saturday Review*, 27 May 1978, p. 31.

Nor do we hesitate to enlarge this significance of the term to cover whole societies of men.

—Eric A. Havelock, *Origins of Western Literacy*, p. 3.

G 30

But because the old tradition is dying hard, many writers are careful not to begin sentences with *and, or, but, for,* and *nor* very often, unless they want their writing to seem casual and conversational in tone.

G30 *Conjunctive Adverbs*

Conjunctive adverbs are also connecting words. The difference between conjunctive adverbs and other conjunctions is that in speech we normally pause immediately after conjunctive adverbs if they occur at the beginning of a sentence. In writing this pause is represented by a comma.

Conjunctive adverbs are connecting words that will fit in the following slot:

_____ , we need you more than ever.

Examples

accordingly	instead
also	likewise
anyhow	meanwhile
besides	moreover
consequently	nevertheless
furthermore	otherwise
hence	still
henceforth	then
however	therefore
indeed	thus

G30 Continued

It is not unusual for a conjunctive adverb to occur at the beginning of a sentence and thus to connect its own sentence to the sentence before it.

Examples
Nevertheless, the CIA officially — if secretly — took the position that the LSD had "triggered" Olson's suicide.
> — **John Marks,** *Saturday Review,* **3 Feb. 1979, p. 12.**

However, the disappearance of the documents and the invocation of executive privilege have fed the prevalent but unsubstantiated suspicions. . . .
> — **Jack Egan,** *New York,* **23 Dec. 1978/1 Jan. 1979, p. 16.**

Moreover, no maintenance was carried on during the occupation, and, as a result, the Peninsula had to undergo extensive repairs in 1946.
> — **Richard Condon,** *Gourmet,* **Dec. 1978, p. 38.**

When a conjunctive adverb comes within a sentence, it is normally enclosed by a pair of commas.

Example
He has not, however, arrived at wisdom on any of these matters.
> — **Julian Moynahan,** *The New York Times Book Review,* **23 April 1978, p. 1.**

A conjunctive adverb by itself is not used to join two independent clauses within the same sentence. To join two independent clauses within the same sentence, a semicolon must be used along with the conjunctive adverb (see P13 for examples).

G31 *Prepositions and Conjunctions:* Like, As, As If, As Though

In casual English (and in ads for Winston cigarettes), *like* is sometimes used to join clauses of comparison as if it were a conjunction.

Examples

. . . impromptu program where they ask questions much like I do on the air.

> —Art Linkletter, cited in *Webster's*
> *New International Dictionary.*

. . . wore his clothes like he was . . . afraid of getting dirt on them.

> —St. Petersburg *Independent*, cited
> *Webster's Third New International Dictionary.*

There is considerable resistance to this use of *like* in printed English, because *like* has traditionally been perceived as a preposition rather than as a conjunction. In other words, *like* used in the conjunction slot (see **G28,** "Eat, drink, and be merry, _____ tomorrow you will die") is not a normal construction in printed English, except when writers are affecting a conversational tone.

The more usual word to occur in this situation would be *as:* ("much as I do on the air"), as if ("wore his clothes as if he . . ."), or as though.

Examples

. . . their eyes darted around the lobby as if they were looking for the handwriting on the wall that would warn them of their fate.

> —Landon Thorne, *Esquire*, May 23, 1978, p. 43.

. . . when he smiles, he looks as though he has been told a joke he doesn't understand.

> —Philip Terzain, *Harper's*, May 1978, p. 89.

G32 *Interjections*

Interjections are roughly equivalent to purring or growling. They are those parts of speech that do little more than express emotion. They include words like *oh*, *ow*, *ouch*, *shucks*, *hooray*, *wow*, and so on. They are usually separated from sentences by commas, or else followed by exclamation points. Interjections are not very common in college writing.

G33 *Case:* **I/Me, She/Her, He/Him, They/Them**

In many languages, nouns and pronouns take different forms according to their grammatical function in a sentence. These grammatical functions — for example, subject, direct object, indirect object — are called cases.

In English, an apostrophe or an apostrophe and *s* is added to nouns to indicate what is called possessive case (see **P25,** p. 404); otherwise, nouns have the same form, no matter what grammatical role they play in a sentence. In the following examples, notice that "Reston" and "car" remain unchanged, no matter what grammatical slot (i.e., subject, direct object, indirect object) they fill, except for the possessive.

Examples

Reston hit the car.

The car hit Reston.

Someone gave Reston a car.

Reston's car was stolen.

Several common pronouns, however, have one more form than nouns. Pronouns as objects are different from pronouns as subjects.

Subject forms	*Object forms*
I	me
he	him
she	her
they	them

Examples

I sued the Ajax Corporation. (*I* is the subject of the verb *sued*.)

The Ajax Corporation sued me. (*Me* is the object of the verb *sued*.)

The company sent a letter to me. (*Me* is the object of the preposition *to*.)

She saw the accident. (*She* is the subject of the verb *saw*.)

The car veered away from her. (*Her* is the object of the preposition *from*.)

The driver noticed her. (*Her* is the object of the verb *noticed.*)

To decide which of the two forms to use, first determine which of two relationships the pronoun will have with the rest of the sentence. If it is the subject of a verb (i.e., if it is the word that is the answer to the question "who" or "what" before the verb), use the subject form. If it is the object of a verb or of a preposition (i.e., if it is the word that is the answer to the question "whom" or "what" after a verb or preposition in the sentence), use the object form.

G 33

Examples

Between you and me, this movie stinks.
(Not "Between you and I." The pronoun is the object of the preposition *between.*)

Eleanor told me and my brother to type our own papers.
(Not "my brother and I." The pronoun is the object of the verb *told.*)

Terrence and I are going to pay for the party.
(Not "Terrence and me." The pronoun is the subject of the verb *are going.*)

She and Mary were under considerable stress.
(Not "Her and Mary." The pronoun is the subject of the verb *were.*)

EXERCISE

Choose the appropriate form of the pronoun in each of the following sentences.

a. The boss instructed (he/him) to slope the trench.
b. The boss instructed (he/him) and his brother to slope the trench.
c. Between you and (I/me), there is no hope of funding.
d. (We/Us) should unite.
e. (We/Us) and our colleagues should unite.
f. (He/Him) was bringing books to the jail.
g. (He/Him) and Mr. Mitchel were bringing books to the jail.
h. Coach praised (we/us).
i. Coach praised both (we/us) and our opponents.
j. (They/Them) and others like (they/them) should be richly rewarded.

G34 *Case:* **Who/Whom**

To decide whether to use *who* or *whom* in writing, first determine which of two possible relationships this pronoun will have with the words near it. If it is the object of a verb or of a preposition, use *whom*. Otherwise, use *who*.

Examples

Fred, whom we had hired as a replacement, is ill.
(*Whom* is the object of the verb *had hired*.)

Mona, with whom we normally sit, cannot attend tonight.
(*Whom* is the object of the preposition *with*.)

Michael, who is normally a starter, cannot play tonight.
(*Who* is the subject of the verb *is*.)

You may notice that *whom* as an object appears before the verb ("*whom* we had hired") rather than after it, as objects normally do. Partly because of this "abnormal" sequence — which requires speakers to plan ahead more carefully than usual — the distinction between *who* and *whom* is fast disappearing from spoken English. People generally use *who* when *whom* would be preferred by traditional grammarians. This is especially true when the pronoun occurs at the beginning of a question that ends in a preposition.

Example

Who should I send these books to?
(Instead of "To *whom* should I send these books?")

The choice between *who* and *whom* in writing is sometimes complicated by intervening words.

Examples

First we saw George, (who/whom) you thought could help us.

First we saw George, (who/whom) you thought another agency had hired.

To make the choice, delete the intervening words and decide whether the pronoun is a subject or an object in what remains.

Examples

First we saw George, who . . . could help us.
   (*Who* is the subject of the verb *could help*.)

First we saw George, whom . . . another agency had hired.
   (*Whom* is the object of *had hired*.)

Having chosen the appropriate form, restore the intervening words.

**G
34**

Examples

First we saw George, who you thought could help us.

First we saw George, whom you thought another agency had hired.

Sometimes, however, deleting the intervening phrase does not help.

Examples

This is a person (who/whom) the workers would like us to promote.

Norris called Tracy, (who/whom) he considered the best speech writer in Washington.

Unless you are willing to learn enough grammar to figure out why *whom* is the appropriate choice—because in the first example it is the object of an infinitive and in the second example, the object of an unexpressed infinitive—the best solution is to avoid this and similar structures altogether.

In fact, because *whom* is disappearing from spoken English, many writers simply avoid it by rephrasing their sentences completely.

Examples

The workers would like us to promote this person.

Norris called Tracy, who, in his opinion, was the best speech writer in Washington.

EXERCISE

Choose the appropriate form of the pronoun in each of the following sentences, or rewrite the sentence so that the choice is unnecessary.

a. It was Jones (who/whom) is credited with making the motion.
b. It was Jones (who/whom) the press blames for making the motion.
c. It was Jones (who/whom) the press believes made the motion.
d. Suzy is a woman (who/whom) everyone loves.
e. Suzy is a woman (who/whom) reads constantly.
f. He was a bright man (who/whom) the people thought they could trust.
g. He was a bright man (who/whom) won the trust of the people.
h. (Who/Whom) are we supposed to visit in New York?
i. (Who/Whom) are these costumes being sewn for?
j. Was it Mandy (who/whom) they considered the best president?

G 35

G35 *Identifying Subjects and Verbs*

One of the most basic relationships between words is the relationship between subjects and finite verbs. In a given sentence, the subject is the word or phrase that best answers the question "who" or "what" before the verb phrase.

Examples
Francis sold his house to a friend.
   S   V

The *captain told* Ron a new version of the story.
      S   V

The new *wing* of the museum *was designed* by Pei.
      S   V

In the first example, the verb is "sold." The subject is "Francis"; "Francis" is the answer to the question "Who sold?"

In the second example, the verb is "told." The subject is "the captain"; "the captain" is the answer to the question "Who told?"

In the third example, the verb is "was designed." The subject is "the new wing of the museum"; "the new wing of the museum" is the answer to the question "What was designed?"

Sometimes it is useful to distinguish between the simple subject and the complete subject. The simple subject is the main noun in the subject phrase without any of its modifiers. In the first example above, "Francis" is the simple subject; it has no modifiers. In the second example, "captain" is the simple subject; the modifier "the" would not be considered part of the simple subject. In the third example, "wing" is the simple subject; the modifiers "the new" and the prepositional phrase "of the museum" would not be considered part of the simple subject.

The simple subject of a sentence cannot also be the object of a verb or a preposition. For example, in the third example above, "museum" cannot possibly be the simple subject because it is the object of the preposition "of."

Sometimes entire phrases or clauses can be the subjects of sentences.

Example
What you see is what you get.

The main verb in this sentence is "is." If you ask "who or what is?" the answer is the entire clause, "what you see."

EXERCISES

1. Identify the verbs and simple subjects in the following sentences.

a. A new restaurant has opened on Pennsylvania Avenue.
b. The menu is written in French.
c. The hostess is a native of France.
d. Most of the waitresses speak French.
e. The chef specializes in seafood—shrimp, trout, mussels, and soft-shell crab.

G35 Continued

f. You can dine outside, beneath a canopy next to the sidewalk.

g. Most people prefer to dine inside, away from the turmoil of traffic.

h. To be served promptly, you must make reservations.

i. As an appetizer, the snails in mushroom caps are incomparable.

j. At the end of the meal, espresso coffee is served with a twist of lemon peel.

2. Copy a few paragraphs from a recent issue of a newspaper or magazine. Identify the subject and verb in each sentence. Discuss your analysis with a classmate.

G36 *Agreement: Subject-Verb*

If a reader marks an agreement error in a verb, chances are you forgot to put an *s* where one would normally occur in printed English, or you put one where you should not have.

Examples

In the next scene, Hamlet and his mother talks to each other.

The ring of gold coins sound____ good to me.

This battery of examinations prove____ nothing.

In these cases, put an *s* on the verb if the subject is singular; leave it off if the subject is plural.

Examples

In the next scene, Hamlet and his mother talk____ to each other.

The ring of gold coins sounds good to me.

This battery of examinations proves nothing.

In many languages, verbs have lots of different endings that have to match up with various subjects. In English, the verb system is much simpler than it is in those other languages.

Once you know what tense you want to use — past, present, future — the verb form stays the same for that tense no matter what the subject is.

Examples

Past tense	*Future tense*
I talked	I will talk
you talked	you will talk
he talked	she will talk
we talked	we will talk
they talked	they will talk

G 36

There is only one situation in which regular verbs require a special ending to match up with the subject: when the tense is present and the subject is a singular noun or pronoun other than the speaker or the person being addressed.

Examples
he talks
she talks
it talks
Mary talks

The technical description of this situation is "third person singular, present tense." Less technically, it is a present tense verb with a singular subject that is neither the writer nor the person addressed. Paradoxically, the verb is considered singular if it has an *s* on the end of it — the letter we normally associate with the plural form of nouns.

EXERCISES

1. Practice your ability to make subjects and verbs agree by adding the appropriate form of *work* to the following nouns. Try future tense first ("I will work," etc.), then past tense ("I worked," etc.), and then present ("I work, etc.).

I _____   it _____

you _____   she _____

Cheryl _____   carpenters _____

G36 Continued

Cheryl and George _____	a carpenter _____
we _____	Nellie _____
they _____	he _____

2. Choose six verbs at random and substitute them for *work* in Exercise 1 above.

G37 *Agreement Despite Intervening Nouns*

Sometimes writers are uncertain about whether to put a final *s* on a verb because the subject is separated from the verb by a noun that confuses matters.

Examples
The head of operations (call/calls) here every day.

The officers in charge of food (go/goes) to town frequently.

In situations like these, the writer has to identify the subject —the word that answers who or what before the verb—before choosing the appropriate verb form. In the first example, "head" is the subject, so the verb form should be *calls*. In the second example, "officers" is the subject, so the verb form should be *go*.

EXERCISE

Identify the subject of each of the following sentences and choose the appropriate verb form.

a. The bills at the first of the month (seem/seems) to bother her.
b. A train full of eggs (leave/leaves) Jackson at 4:00 A.M.
c. Morrison, more than any of his colleagues, (want/wants) to succeed as a teacher.
d. A detective assisted by ten policemen (guard/guards) this building.
e. The owners of the local franchise (pay/pays) little attention to the quality of the food.

f. The president of Multiplex Consolidated Industries (want/wants) to discuss your invention with you.

G38 *Agreement in the Verbs* Be *and* Have

If a reader marks an agreement problem with some form of *be* or *have*, chances are you have chosen the wrong form from one of the following pairs: *is/are*; *was/were*; *has/have*.

Examples

The psychosis are being treated.

Six pages was missing from the book.

A new round of hearings have been ordered.

In these cases, try the other member of the pair (*is* instead of *are*, *were* instead of *was*, *has* instead of *have*, or vice versa).

Examples

The psychosis is being treated.

Six pages were missing from the book.

A new round of hearings has been ordered.

If you have more than occasional trouble with the verb *be*, read on for a fuller explanation.

Of all the verbs in the English language, the verb *be* (see **G12**) is the most troublesome. Not only does it change its form to indicate different aspects of time (am → was/are → were), but it changes to match different kinds of subjects as well. You can discover how familiar you are with the conventions by mentally filling in the blanks in the examples below and comparing your answers with those at the bottom of page 350. For each of the following sentences, choose the form of the verb *be* (*am, are, is, was, were, be, being, been*) that would normally be used in printed English.

G38 Continued

**G
38**

1. I _____ frightened whenever I hear a siren.
2. _____ you a sophomore this year?
3. As soon as the bell rings, Justin _____ going to make an announcement.
4. Before we go to your party tonight, Louise and I _____ going to pay a visit to her mother.
5. Now that spring is here, baseball and pollen _____ in the air.
6. Yesterday I _____ homesick.
7. The last time I saw you, you _____ growing a beard.
8. Last night the radio _____ playing beautifully, even without an antenna.
9. When you called, Jack and I _____ already on our way to your house.
10. At that time, you and your husband _____ still planning to enroll in graduate school.
11. In the old days, crops _____ harvested by hand.

Chances are your ear guided you reliably in most of these examples. If you were confused by some of the sentences, however, don't try to memorize the entire list of verb forms. Instead, ask your teacher to help you identify those particular contexts for the verb *be* that may require your attention in writing.

EXERCISES

1. Sometimes the only way to gain control over the verb *be* is to practice by trial and error until you can "hear" the forms that normally occur in printed English. With the help of a tutor or a friend, practice filling out the following phrases with the appropriate form of the verb *be*. Do the exercise several times, perhaps once or twice a day for several days. After you feel confident about the forms in the present tense (I am, etc.), try working with the past tense (I was, etc.).

ANSWERS: 1. am 2. Are 3. is 4. are 5. are 6. was 7. were 8. was 9. were 10. were 11. were

I _____	we _____
you _____	you _____
he _____	they _____
she _____	the Smiths _____
it _____	the dogs _____
George _____	the machines _____
Fido _____	the kitchens _____
the machine _____	books _____
the kitchen _____	friends _____

G 39

2. For each of the following sentences, choose the verb form that would be most likely to appear in printed English.

a. Is it true that you (were/was) there?
b. The exits (was/were) poorly lighted.
c. The teacher (be/is) absent today.
d. The Pruit brothers (was/were) our best statisticians.
e. His troubles (is/are) mainly in his head.

G39 *Agreement: Verbs with Multiple Subjects*

Many writers, even professionals, have trouble with subject-verb agreement when multiple subjects are joined by certain kinds of relation words. Test yourself by choosing what you think would be the usual printed form in each of the examples below. Compare your choices with the explanations that follow.

Examples
1. Nancy and Sandra (like/likes) contemporary art.
2. Two and two (is/are) four.
3. A boar together with a sow (has/have) been spotted in these woods.
4. Either Joel or Mary (is/are) on duty tonight.
5. Joseph or his twin sisters (bring/brings) me my groceries.
6. Either you or your father (need/needs) to pay for the damage.

G39 Continued

7. Your pastor and friend (send/sends) his greetings.
8. Roofing and siding (is/are) a lucrative business.

Explanations

1. Two individual subjects joined by *and* are treated just as one plural subject would be: "*Nancy* and *Sandra like* contemporary art."

2. Editors disagree about this one, but in general both options are considered acceptable — "Two and two *is* four" and "Two and two *are* four" — as long as the writer sticks to one option within a given work.

3. Words preceded by phrases like "together with," "in addition to," "along with," and "including" are considered to be in the objective case grammatically, which means that they cannot be treated as subjects of the verb. The first part of the subject, then, determines the form of the verb. In printed English, "A *boar* together with a sow *has* been spotted" would be the normal form; but if more than one boar were involved, the normal form would be "Several *boars* together with a *sow* have been spotted. . . ."

4, 5, 6. Words like *or* and pairs of words like *not . . . but, either . . . or* and *neither . . . nor* suggest that one of the subjects is connected with the verb, but not both. The form of the verb, then, need match only one of the subjects. If both subjects are singular, the verb is treated as if it had one singular subject: "Either *Joel* or *Mary is* on duty tonight." If both subjects are plural, the verb is treated as if it had a plural subject: "Neither the *Falcons* nor the *Saints were* expected to be contenders this year." If the subjects seem to call for different verb forms, choose the form that matches the subject closest to the verb: "Joseph or his twin *sisters bring* me my groceries" and "Either you or your *father needs* to pay for the damage."

7, 8. Two or more subjects can be followed by a singular verb if the subjects are considered different aspects of the same person or thing. For example, if "pastor" and "friend" refer to one person, the verb should be singular: "Your pastor and friend send*s* his greetings." If "roofing" and "siding" are two aspects of the same business, the singular verb would be appropriate: "Roofing and siding is a lucrative business."

G
39

Try to avoid sentences that will seem wrong to some readers no matter how you handle agreement problems.

Examples
1. Neither the princesses nor their brother (talk/talks) very much in public.
2. The entire team, including (their/its) wives and families, (was/were) invited to dinner at the White House.

When you are faced with two choices either of which will be distracting to some readers, avoid them both by rephrasing the sentence.

G 40

Examples
1. The princesses do not talk very much in public, and neither does their brother.
2. All the players and their families were invited to dinner at the White House.

EXERCISE

Choose the appropriate verb form for each of the following sentences.

a. Either you or your husband (need/needs) to ask for a clarification of this bill.
b. Your father and friend (want/wants) you home again.
c. Tom and his daughter (enjoy/enjoys) watching ball games together.
d. Either Sid or the twins (is/are) babysitting for the Stoddards.
e. The sauce without any of the spices (taste/tastes) perfect in this recipe.
f. Spirit and determination (make/makes) a team what it is.
g. Bob and Mary (want/wants) to live in Idaho.
h. Either you or Tom (owe/owes) me five dollars.

G40 *Agreement: Verbs with Collective Nouns as Subjects*

Collective nouns are nouns that are singular in form even though they refer to a group of persons or things.

G40 Continued

Examples

army	crowd
assembly	faculty
athletics	family
audience	jury
band	majority
class	orchestra
committee	public

G 40

Normally, a collective noun is used with the singular form of the verb.

Examples

An army march es on its stomach.

The audience seem s to be enjoying the performance.

Remember, the distinction between singular and plural verb forms ordinarily occurs only in the present tense, and only when the subject is not the speaker or the person addressed. The singular of the verb form is signaled by a final *s*—the same letter, paradoxically, that signals the plural form of nouns. In the examples above, the s on *marche* s and on *seem* s indicates the singular form of the verb, which matches the singular subjects, "army" and "audience."

In other tenses, writers need not worry about subject-verb agreement. In the past, for example, *march* would become *marched*, whether one soldier marche d or a thousand soldiers marche d. The exception to this rule is *was* (singular) and *were* (plural).

Sometimes the writer is free to choose whether a collective noun is used in a singular or a plural sense.

Examples

The majority of the faculty *wants* to improve its teaching.

The majority of the faculty *want* to improve their teaching.

Both options are correct. In the first example, the writer is thinking of the majority as a unit acting together. Hence the singular form of the verb. In the second example, the writer is thinking of the majority acting independently as many individual faculty members. Hence the plural form of the verb.

Sometimes the choice is affected by other nouns that come between the subject and the verb.

Examples

The majority of our friends vote regularly.

The majority of our neighborhood votes regularly.

G 40

In these examples, the subject is the same "majority." But in one case, the plural noun *friends*, which is not the subject, would make a writer inclined to choose a plural verb form; while in the second case, the singular noun *neighborhood* seems to have the opposite effect. Grammatically, both the singular and the plural verb could be defended in either sentence.

As an unusual example of "writer's choice," consider these two sentences about Diane Keaton written by the British-born writer, Penelope Gilliatt, in a highly respected American magazine:

Her family are Methodists.

Her family were encouraging but were remote from the arts.
—Penelope Gilliatt, *The New Yorker*, 25 Dec, 1978, p. 38.

Gilliatt, following British usage, is clearly thinking of the family members acting as individuals rather than as a unit. Hence, the plural verbs "are" and "were." Normally in an American publication, the verbs would be singular: "Her family *is* Methodist"; "Her family *was* encouraging."

Even a noun that is plural in form can be treated like a collective noun—that is, it can be followed by a singular verb—if the noun is considered a single unit rather than a collection of individuals.

Examples

Physics relies on mathematics.

G40 Continued

Six million dollars was her only asset.

Five barrels was more than we had hoped for.

Better Homes and Gardens appears monthly.

The word *data* is sometimes treated as a plural and sometimes as a singular collective noun. In traditional scholarly and scientific writing, *data* is considered plural.

G 40

Example

These data come from a reliable source.

In this example, the plural demonstrative ("these") and the plural verb form ("come") indicate that "data" is considered as a collection of individual facts.

Sometimes, however, even in published writing, *data* is considered a collective noun and followed by the singular form of the verb.

Example

No general appraisal can be hazarded . . . until more data is available.

—*Publishers' Weekly*, cited in *Webster's Third New International Dictionary*

When you are in doubt about whether a given noun is treated as singular or plural, consult a good dictionary or usage guide (see p. 280).

EXERCISE

Choose the appropriate verb form for each of the following sentences, or rewrite the sentence to make the choice unnecessary.

a. Athletics (attract/attracts) large numbers of students to this campus.

b. Dumbarton Oaks (offer/offers) you more services than any other comparably priced apartment complex in town.

   c. The militia (practice/practices) marching every other week.

   d. The jury (need/needs) more time for its deliberation.

   e. The contents of this package (is/are) explosive.

   f. Measles (is/are) dangerous for pregnant women.

   g. Statistics (is/are) my favorite subject.

   h. Statistics (is/are) sometimes deceiving.

G41 Be *Between Singular and Plural Nouns*

G 41

When the verb *be* (see **G12**) has a singular noun on one side of it and a plural noun (or a pair of singular nouns) on the other, many editors prefer to make the verb agree with the noun or nouns before the verb.

Examples

The dessert was Mexican wedding cookies.

Mexican wedding cookies were the dessert.

Tom and Bob were the delegation from Caldwell Hall.

The delegation from Caldwell Hall was Tom and Bob.

Other editors prefer to see the problem avoided by rewriting the sentence.

Examples

Mexican wedding cookies were served for dessert.

Dessert consisted of Mexican wedding cookies.

Tom and Bob were the delegates from Caldwell Hall.

The delegates from Caldwell Hall were Tom and Bob.

Caldwell Hall was represented by Tom and Bob.

EXERCISE

Choose the appropriate verb form for each of the following sentences, or rewrite the sentence to make the choice unnecessary.

G41 Continued

 a. Three packages of cheese crackers (was/were) all the dinner we offered.
 b. Ham and eggs (is/are) a good breakfast.
 c. Our only alternative (was/were) the weather balloons.
 d. The committee (was/were) young people who had other things on their minds.
 e. Digging and planting (was/were) still his favorite pastime.

G
42

G42 *Agreement: Verb with* There *as Dummy Subject*

In expressions like "There is," "There are," "There goes," and "There go," *there* is considered a "dummy" subject—a mere substitute for the real subject, which in these expressions occurs after the verb. Identify the real subject before determining whether the verb should be singular or plural.

Examples

There were three senators in the conference room.

There was one senator in the conference room.

There goes a fool.

There sit three philosophers.

EXERCISE

Choose the appropriate verb for each of the following sentences.

 a. There (is/are) several good reasons for you to stay another year.
 b. There (is/are) another one of those sticky problems to be considered.
 c. There (was/were) more than a hundred letters demanding his resignation.
 d. There (was/were) a crowd at the station.
 e. There (is/are) no substitute for hard work.

f. There (come/comes) the new teachers.

g. There beside the bench (stand/stands) the men who could help us.

h. In Russia at that time there (was/were) few television sets.

G43 *Agreement:* **Each** *and* **Every**

Each and **every** are considered singular even when they refer to a number of individuals in a group.

Examples

Each of the tutors works long hours in the Writing Lab.

Every tutor works long hours in the Writing Lab.

Each and *every* signal individuality so strongly that they cause even compound subjects to be treated as singular.

Examples

Every man, woman, and child is expected to participate in the celebration.

Each man, woman, and child is expected to participate in the celebration.

EXERCISE

Choose the appropriate verb form for each of the following sentences.

a. Each group of parents (is/are) invited to the dinner.

b. Every bird, fish, and mammal on earth (is/are) threatened by this experiment.

c. Each of his closest friends (give/gives) him the same advice.

d. Every thousand years of recorded history (is/are) like an instant in the life of the universe.

e. Each of the sciences (reveal/reveals) a different facet of reality.

f. Each of the teams (has/have) been thoroughly prepared.

G44 *Agreement: "One of Those (Who/That) . . ."*

The "one . . . who" and the "one . . . that" constructions often result in a grammatical problem that might be easier to avoid than to solve.

Examples

She is one of those authors who (love/loves) to hear from (her/their) readers.

Detroit is one of those cities that (know/knows) how to deal with winter.

The sentence is grammatically ambiguous. Does "who" refer to "one" or to "authors"? Either answer is as good as the other. But if you answer "one," then the verb and the pronoun should be singular (*loves, her*). And if you answer "authors," then the verb and the pronoun should be plural (*love, their*).

The best solution is to avoid the problem.

Examples

She is an author who loves to hear from her readers.

Detroit is a city that knows how to deal with winter.

EXERCISE

Rewrite the following sentences to avoid the problem of choosing a verb form.

a. Howard is one of those administrators who (rely/relies) on the advice of experts.

b. The Pines is one of those hotels that (make/makes) its guests feel like intruders.

c. This is one of those situations that (give/gives) engineers trouble.

d. Sally is one of those teachers who (inspire/inspires) her students to learn.

e. We have one of those cases that (require/requires) the advice of a specialist.

G45 *Clauses: Dependent and Independent*

A clause is a group of closely related words including a subject and a finite verb.

Examples
Susan went wild in Atlanta,
which was her favorite southern city.

In the example above, "Susan went wild in Atlanta" is an independent clause (subject: "Susan"; finite verb: "went"); and "which was her favorite southern city" is a dependent clause (subject: "which"; finite verb: "was").

An independent clause is one that makes sense as a sentence in itself.

Example
Susan went wild in Atlanta.

A dependent clause is one that would be considered a sentence fragment in itself.

Example
. . . which was her favorite southern city.

Dependent clauses are usually introduced by relative pronouns **(G22)** or by subordinating conjunctions **(G28)**.

EXERCISE

Divide each of the following sentences into its clauses, and indicate which clauses are dependent and which are independent.

a. The Greek gods, Apollo and Dionysus, represent two opposite tendencies in human nature.

b. Our rational, orderly tendencies are represented by Apollo, who is associated with poetry, clear thinking, and medicine.

c. Dionysus, whose Latin name is Bacchus, represents our more impulsive, pleasure-loving instincts.

   d. The conflict between the two was dramatized in *The Bacchae*, a play that Euripides composed in the fifth century before Christ.

   e. The same conflict is the subject of a poem by W. H. Auden.

G46 *Fragments*

G 46

A fragment is a group of words that does not make sense as an assertion in itself.

   Sometimes fragments are intentional. They make writing seem clipped and informal. Consider, for example, this passage from *Time* magazine, in which only the first sentence is not a fragment.

Example

The symptoms are woefully familiar to college instructors everywhere. Nonsensical sentences. Disjointed paragraphs. Wandering structure. Recklessly dangling participles.

          —*Time,* 18 April 1977, p. 74.

At other times, however, fragments seem accidental and purposeless — half-formed sentences, or parts of sentences lying, like limbs blown off in a storm, near what they should be attached to.

Examples
The result being that the books were unavailable.

He introduced me to his brother. *Who lives in L.A.*

You can usually mend accidental fragments either by attaching them to a sentence nearby or by rewriting them as complete sentences in themselves.

Examples
He introduced me to his brother who lives in L.A.

The result was that the books were unavailable.

As a result, the books were unavailable.

If you often have trouble recognizing fragments in your work, read on for a fuller explanation.

Groups of words that make sense as assertions in themselves are called sentences.

Groups of words that do not make sense as assertions in themselves are called fragments.

One way to learn what a sentence is would be to learn its grammatical definition: a sentence is a group of words that includes a clause with a finite verb and at least an understood subject, not introduced by a subordinating conjunction. If you have a knack for grammar, you can learn the meanings of these terms and apply them to the exercises in this section.

For many writers, however, the grammatical definition is tougher than whistling underwater. In fact, most people learn the difference between sentences and fragments, not by definition, but exactly as they learned their colors as children—by examining example after example.

A sentence is a group of words that has a certain kind of completeness. Some kinds of *in*completeness are obvious to any speaker of English.

Examples
My piano teacher was a

Georgia is one of the

Miss Emily had

These statements are unstable; they leave the reader expecting more words.

In contrast, the following groups of words have an obvious completeness or stability.

Examples
My piano teacher was a genius.

Georgia is one of the fastest-growing states in the South.

Miss Emily had vanquished the aldermen.

This completeness or stability characterizes a sentence.

G 46

G46 Continued

Although none of these statements says everything there is to know about a particular subject — there are clearly other things to know about the piano teacher, the state of Georgia, and the character called Miss Emily — still the statements in themselves are perceived as having a certain stability.

But what about the following groups of words? Can they be punctuated as individual sentences or not?

Examples
Live television from the Met.

Simulcast on stereo FM in many cities.

Unique among the world's great cars.

What our two uncommon cars have in common.

The spirit of Marlboro in a low tar cigarette.

This is the most troublesome kind of completeness of all. Many students can tell that these word groups are more complete than those in the first group ("My piano teacher was a"), but they have trouble seeing that they are less complete than the statements in the second group ("My piano teacher was a genius"). These borderline statements are often used in informal writing and as captions to pictures in newspapers and magazines. The ability to distinguish between sentences and borderline sentences, like the ability to distinguish colors, is probably better acquired by practice than by definition.

EXERCISES

1. Cover the sentences below with a sheet of paper so you can reveal only one sentence at a time. Decide which are sentences (S) and which are fragments (F). The correct answer appears in the margin *below* each item, so you can check your work as you go.

    1. Blossoming earlier than the other flowers.

F

    2. Next to the garage.

F

    3. The great land war.

F

4. Forsythia blooms earlier than some other spring flowers.

S

5. The first book club for smart people who aren't rich.

F

6. How to get to the heart and soul of Britain.

F

7. World's most unique timepiece.

F

8. A calendar of romantic places.

F

9. Nothing good happens fast.

S

10. Gunfight at the Capitol Hill corral.

F

11. Nobody knows the trouble I've seen.

S

12. Jamaica's prime minister, Michael Manley.

F

13. Bring out the soda.

S

14. Tall, slender, and sophisticated.

F

15. An uncanny combination of grace and strength.

F

16. Powell's mother is a schoolteacher.

S

17. Carter was elected governor.

S

18. Carter at the victory celebration.

F

19. Questions are being asked about the new U.S. policy.

S

20. Vance in conference with Begin.

F

21. Concern for others.

F

22. Proctor could not afford a lawyer.

S

23. He did not want one.

S

24. As soon as the plane takes off, you may smoke again.

S

25. After the takeoff.

F

G
46

G46 Continued

26. Because of the authority in his voice, no one dared contradict him.

S

27. It's a satisfying decision.

S

28. One of the biggest gold strikes since Sutter's Mill.

F

29. The cure for America's health-care system.

F

30. Practice makes perfect.

S

31. Most of the players were tired.

S

32. Although most of the players were tired.

F

33. The mail was delivered later than usual.

S

34. Because the mail was delivered later than usual.

F

35. We were in New York.

S

36. While we were in New York.

F

37. Since we are proud of our heritage.

F

38. We are proud of our heritage.

S

39. Stopped the fight.

F

40. Martin stopped the fight.

S

41. After Martin stopped the fight.

F

42. Up the side of the mountain.

F

43. Scrambling up the side of the mountain.

F

44. She was scrambling up the side of the mountain.

S

45. While she was scrambling up the side of the mountain.

F

S

46. The Jets won last night.

F

47. If the Jets won last night.

S

48. We waited patiently.

F

49. While we waited patiently.

F

50. After we arrived.

S

51. The show began.

F

52. Until the show began.

G 46

F

53. Snowing.

S

54. It began to snow.

F

55. When it began to snow.

F

56. What ails you.

S

57. I know what ails you.

F

58. Who solved the problem.

S

59. The girl who solved the problem deserves the prize.

F

60. Whose book was stolen.

S

61. Irene, whose book was stolen, refused to come to school.

F

62. That I had started during the summer.

S

63. I forgot that I had started during the summer.

F

64. What caused the problem.

S

65. No one knows what caused the problem.

F

66. Which was reviewed in the *Times*.

G46 Continued

67. The book which was reviewed in the *Times*.

F

68. The book, which was reviewed in the *Times*, is his best novel.

S

69. Who invented the typewriter.

F

70. He invented the typewriter.

S

G 46

71. Whoever finds my ring.

F

72. Whoever finds my ring will be rewarded.

S

73. I will reward whoever finds my ring.

S

74. I hope whoever finds my ring.

F

75. Whom you met at my party.

F

76. My neighbor, whom you met at my party.

F

77. My neighbor, whom you met at my party, would like to join the club.

S

78. They were usually gentle with whomever they arrested.

S

79. They jailed whomever they arrested.

S

80. Whomever they arrested.

F

81. Whose nose was broken.

F

82. His nose was broken.

S

83. This is the end.

S

84. This winter, sunbathe on the most secluded beaches of France.

S

85. One of these men has a good job.

S

S
86. The price of looking it up just went down.

F
87. The greatest jazz collection ever issued.

S
88. Volkswagen does it again.

F
89. From him to her.

F
90. Getting stoned at the jewelers.

F
91. Bottled in Canada.

F
92. Perhaps the world's most unusual and convenient shopping cart.

F
93. The last word in fashion.

F
94. The most operatic of Shakespeare's plays.

F
95. Rick Devine, who is stoic.

F
96. He is more than a historian.

S
97. Now available in a new, expanded edition.

F
98. Twinkie was once too British.

S
99. What your home could have in common with the Met.

F
100. Crostics really obliterate stress.

S

2. Identify the fragment in each of the items below and attach it to the sentence nearby. Notice that sometimes a fragment will make better sense if it is attached to the beginning or to the middle of the sentence rather than to the end.

a. After sunset we returned home. Because we could no longer see the fish.
b. The child was standing alone in the corner. Crying real tears.
c. The chickens flew out of the barn. Squawking madly.
d. The fire went out. That had been keeping us warm.
e. Despite his wealth. He seemed unhappy.
f. They returned to their desks. Defeated and discouraged.

G
46

G46 Continued

g. She swayed peacefully in the hammock. Buried under a blanket of old *New Yorker*s.

h. He was a shy man. Almost annoyed with his fame.

i. He told the same story. That he always told to women he admired.

j. The beef was served on paper plates. Swimming in sauce that only Archibald himself knows how to make.

3. Examine an issue of any magazine, newspaper, or book and find examples of ten short sentences and ten fragments. Headlines and captions may be used. Mix the twenty items in a random list and swap lists with a classmate to see whether you agree on which you consider fragments and which sentences.

4. Write five short sentences and five fragments. Mix them together in a random list. Swap papers with a classmate to see whether you agree on which you consider fragments and which sentences.

5. Identify the sentence fragments in the following passage. What effect do the fragments have on the tone of the passage? Would the passage be improved or spoiled by changing the fragments to complete sentences?

Gustav made me go in while he stayed on watch outside. It was very dark. As bare as a monastic cell. A truckle bed. A rough table. A tin with a bundle of candles. The only concession to comfort, an old stove. There was no carpet, no curtain. The lived-in parts of the room were fairly clean. But the corners were full of refuse. Old leaves, dirt, spiders' webs. An odor of unwashed clothes. There was one book, on the table by the one small window. A huge black Bible, with enormous print.

—John Fowles, *The Magus*, p, 266.

G47 *Fused Sentences*

When two sentences are run together without any punctuation between them, the result is called a fused sentence.

Example
The ships set out to sea I knew they would never return.

To repair a fused sentence, locate the logical boundary between the two sentences and mark it with a period or semicolon. (If you use a period, you must, of course, capitalize the first word in the second sentence.) Another way to solve the problem is to join the two sentences by inserting a comma and a coordinating conjunction between them.

Examples

The ships set out to sea. I knew they would never return.

The ships set out to sea; I knew they would never return.

The ships set out to sea, and I knew they would never return.

For exercises, see **G48** below.

G48 *Comma Splice*

The use of a comma to join two sentences is called a comma splice.

Example

The ships set out to sea, I knew they would never return.

A comma splice is like splicing two pieces of rope together with Scotch tape. The tape won't hold; neither will the comma, unless the sentences are very short.

The remedy for a comma splice is just like the remedy for a fused sentence. Either change the comma to a period and start a new sentence, or change the comma to a semicolon, or add a coordinating conjunction.

Examples

The ships set out to sea. I knew they would never return.

The ships set out to sea; I knew they would never return.

The ships set out to sea, and I knew they would never return.

G48 Continued

Another remedy for the comma splice is to add a subordinating conjunction.

G
48

Example
When the ships set out to sea, I knew they would never return.

Conjunctive adverbs like *however* and *furthermore* (see **G30**) often cause a comma splice.

Example
"The Unknown Citizen" seems to be merely a listing of a working person's life, however, it gives a feeling of pity for the working class.

Remember that conjunctive adverbs in the second part of a sentence are normally preceded by a semicolon. See **P12.**

EXERCISES

1. Comma splices and fused sentences often result from a failure to recognize the boundaries between sentences. Before attempting this exercise, you may find it useful to review the discussion of sentences and fragments **(G45).**

Identify and remedy the fused sentences and comma splices in the following examples. Practice using two or three different remedies for each example. There may be more than one logical place to divide some of the sentences.

a. In recent years cooking has become something of an art for more and more American families cooking is no longer mere drudgery imposed upon wives and mothers.

b. Some men have willingly taken on the responsibility for outdoor cooking especially for cooking game now they are as interested in preparing quiches and soufflés as they once were in venison.

c. Julia Child is still recognized as the ultimate French cook her books and television shows have made her name a household word.

d. It is not uncommon for cooks to spend two or three days preparing a dinner party, the preparation is considered part of the fun.

e. Many couples cook as teams, dividing tasks and working on the whole meal at once, others prefer to divide the menu and make each partner entirely responsible for individual dishes.

f. In some families, one partner prepares good, healthful food for the children, who usually prefer ketchup to bearnaise, the other partner prepares fancier food to be eaten by those who care for it.

g. Sometimes cooking becomes part of the dinner party guests who enjoy working in the kitchen or who want to learn the art of cooking arrive early and work along with the hosts.

h. French cooking is hardly the only variety in fashion, many people specialize in international cuisine including national dishes from the Orient, Latin America, Africa, or the Middle East.

i. Health food cooking is a specialty of its own its appeal is the escape from the chemical additives in most processed foods.

j. In addition to the new interest in cooking there is a new interest in physical fitness, many people practice personal programs of dieting and exercise, others take advantage of the group support in commercial spas or weight-control clubs.

G 48

2. Compose five fused sentences and five comma splices and mix them in a random list. Swap lists with a classmate. Remedy the problems in the list you receive and discuss the remedies with the author of the list.

3. Punctuate each of the following passages and then compare your work with that of your classmates.

a. Idaho is famous for something else besides potatoes it is a state of great scenic beauty it has a number of mountains and mountain ranges in the northern part of the state are the Grand Tetons nearer to Boise are the Sawtooths in the winter these mountains are ideal for skiing in the summer they are perfect for camping.

b. Mexico City is one of the most interesting places in the world it is more than a mile and a half high it is surrounded by volcanic mountains the mountains are capped with deep snow even in the middle of summer the climate in Mexico City is pleasant throughout the year some of the buildings were constructed shortly after the arrival of the Spanish conquistadores others represent the most advanced designs of contemporary architecture one of the oldest structures within the city limits is a pre-Columbian pyramid discovered during the construction of a modern subway tunnel.

G49 *Questions: Direct and Indirect*

Direct questions are questions in the form you would actually use when asking them.

Examples
Who is playing the lead role?

Why are you crying?

Have you seen any games this year?

Indirect questions are questions that have been incorporated into statements indicating who asks the questions.

Examples
Her mother asked who was playing the lead role.

The teacher asked why he was crying.

Coach asked if you had seen any games this year.

There are two kinds of direct questions: those that begin with *who, what, when, where, why,* and *how* (the five *w*'s plus *how*); and those that begin with helping verbs—verbs like *have, has, would, could, is, are, was, were,* etc.

Direct questions beginning with the five *w*'s or *how* can be made parts of statements by using the first word of the question as a connecting word and changing the tense of the question so that it fits in with the tense of the statement. If there is a pronoun in the direct question, the pronoun, too, may have to be adjusted to express your meaning.

Examples
Direct: When will you come to see us?
Indirect: Missy asked when you would come to see us.

Direct: What sort of job do you have?
Indirect: The interviewer asked what sort of job I had.
Indirect: The interviewer will ask what sort of job I have.

Direct: Where was she living at the time?
Indirect: The judge asked where she was living at the time.
Indirect: The judge will ask where she was living at the time.

Direct questions that begin with a helping verb can be made parts of statements by making the same changes with the addition of a connecting word, usually *if* or *whether*.

Examples

Direct: Are you going anywhere this evening?
Indirect: I asked if you were going anywhere this evening.
Indirect: I will ask if she is going anywhere this evening.

Direct: Do you believe the results?
Indirect: The doctor asked if she believed the results.
Indirect: The doctor will ask whether she believes the results.

Direct: Have you seen any games this year?
Indirect: Coach will ask if you have seen any games this year.

G 49

Notice that in direct questions of this sort, the verb (or part of the verb) appears before the subject; but in the corresponding indirect questions, the subject comes before any part of the verb.

In some varieties of spoken English, direct questions beginning with a verb are converted to indirect questions without the addition of *if* or *whether*.

Examples

I asked were you going anywhere this evening.

The doctor asked did she believe the results.

Coach asked did you see any games this year.

But in printed English, the addition of *if* or *whether* is normal.

Of course, an easier way to incorporate direct questions into statements is to use quotation marks and to copy the direct question exactly as it was originally asked.

Examples

I asked, "Are you going anywhere this evening?"

The doctor asked, "Do you believe the results?"

Coach asked, "Did you see any games this year?"

G49 Continued

But sometimes this device will not fit what you are writing, and you will prefer to use the indirect form.

EXERCISE

Cover up the sentences below with a sheet of paper so that you can reveal them one at a time. Convert each of the direct questions to an indirect question beginning with the words suggested. Then move the paper down to check your answer.

a. Who were you studying with? She asked . . .
(She asked who you were studying with.)

b. What was the final score? The reporter asked . . .
(The reporter asked what the final score was.)

c. When will Jack be taking leave? The boss asked . . .
(The boss asked when Jack would be taking leave.)

d. When will Jack be taking leave? The boss will ask . . .
(The boss will ask when Jack will be taking leave.)

e. Where are you going to spend your vacation? The agent asked . . .
(The agent asked where you are going to spend your vacation.)

f. Why does he do these things? The public wants to know . . .
(The public wants to know why he does these things.)

g. How will she do in the election? We were wondering . . .
(We were wondering how she would do in the elections.)

h. Did Mike ever finish his degree? The governor will ask . . .
(The governor will ask if Mike ever finished his degree.)

i. Does the student senate accept his defense? Ask George . . .
(Ask George if the student senate accepts his defense.)

j. Were there more than two people involved? The D.A. asked . . .
(The D.A. asked if there were more than two people involved.)

G50 *Tense*

If a reader writes "tense" near a verb, you have probably made one of two errors. Either you have shifted from past tense to present (or vice versa) without good reason, or you have used an unconventional form of the past.

The first problem can be solved by keeping all verbs

in the same tense unless your meaning demands a change.

Examples

Unnecessary shift: At the beginning of the story, the old man seems gentle and serene. Later he turned into a monster.

Better: At the beginning of the story, the old man seems gentle and serene. Later he turns into a monster.

Notice that the present tense is normally used in writing about events in a story, play, or poem. The present tense is also used in discussing assertions in an essay. For example, "Middleton argues that . . ." rather than, "Middleton argued that. . . ." Events in a story and arguments in an essay are considered perpetually present; they exist every time the story or the essay is read, not just in the past when they were originally put on paper.

G 50

The second problem can be solved by looking up the conventional form of the past in a dictionary.

Examples

Because he had study for three hours each night, he manage to pass the exams.

In printed English these verbs would be *studied* and *managed*. For a fuller discussion of tense, see **G8.**

Chapter Fifteen

A Punctuation Guide

P1 *Punctuation: An Introduction*

Although the rules of punctuation are fairly easy to master and punctuation exercises are fairly easy to perform, the ability to punctuate your own writing requires practice. The purpose of punctuation is to arrange words in groups that are easily intelligible to a reader seeing them for the first time. But when writers punctuate their own work, they already understand which word groups belong together, so they have difficulty seeing their work with the eyes of readers unfamiliar with it. Writers do not need punctuation to make their work clear to themselves; it takes considerable practice to anticipate the cues that other readers will need.

This chapter will explain only the most common conventions in everyday writing. You probably already know many of them, so be prepared to skim over those sections you have no trouble with and to concentrate on those sections you recognize as problem areas. The conventions discussed here will cover most ordinary writing situations. For the special conventions practiced in academic writing, turn to Chapter Eleven. For problems in punctuation not discussed in this book, consult a good dictionary.

Punctuation is as unnatural as writing itself. It is one of the devices invented to translate words from a natural medium, the spoken language, to an artificial medium, writing. Even the spaces between words in writing are artificial, a kind of punctuation, for in speaking at a normal rate we often run words together asiftherewerenospacesbetweenthem. In some early forms of writing, words were in fact copied on the page without intervening spaces. In addition, scribes would write from left to right and right to left in alternate lines, like farmers turning around at the end of a furrow to plow another row in the opposite direction. From our point of view, it seems unthinkable that readers would learn to read the alternate lines backwards. But there was a certain logic to this method from the scribe's point of view: it was more efficient to begin each new line near the end of the old one, rather than to move the hand all the way over to the other side of the page and start anew. Our way of writing—from left to right at all times—would have seemed as inefficient to these early scribes as carrying a plow back across the field to begin each furrow in the same direction.

Printed this way, without spaces, capital letters, and other marks of division, the opening lines of Lincoln's Gettysburg Address would look like this:

fourscoreandsevenyearsagoourfathersbroughtforthon cideddnaytrebilnideviecnocnoitanwenatnenitnocsiht atedtothepropositionthatallmenarecreatedequal

The difference between this version of the Gettysburg Address and a modern version is nothing more than punctuation, the set of conventions developed by scribes and printers to make written language easier to read. The purpose of punctuation, then, is clarity. Modern students learn the conventions not because they are "right" in an absolute sense, but because they make reading clearer and easier. Even conventions like

P1 Continued

writing in the same direction on each line and putting spaces
between words are artificial developments, invented for the
convenience of readers. You can see how much easier Lincoln's words are to read when they are printed according to
just these two fundamental conventions:

> fourscore and seven years ago our fathers brought forth on
> this continent a new nation conceived in liberty and dedi-
> cated to the proposition that all men are created equal

Developments in the history of punctuation all have the
same purpose: to arrange the words on the pages in groups
easier for readers to comprehend. Sentences were eventually
marked off with an initial capital letter and a final period, or
with some other terminal mark. Related groups of words
within sentences were separated from the other words by
commas. And groups of sentences were arranged according to
relationships among them, first by the placement of an ornate
Greek *P* (¶) at the beginning of each group of related sentences, then by the indentation of the first sentence in each
group to signal what we now recognize as the beginning of a
new paragraph. All of these conventions together are designed
to make writing easier to read:

> Fourscore and seven years ago our fathers brought forth on this
> continent a new nation, conceived in liberty and dedicated to the
> proposition that all men are created equal.

Who makes these rules? It may surprise you to learn that the
rules are not made by grammarians or school teachers. Punctuation rules are not legislated by anyone at all; they are developed, very gradually, by the collective practice of the people who control writing and printing. For the most part these
people — scribes in the old days, publishers nowadays — think
of themselves as following precedents rather than establishing
them. For this reason, the development of punctuation has
been a slow process. Most scribes and most publishers have

been content to follow the practice of other scribes and publishers.

Still, like language itself, the conventions of punctuation are always changing, always developing. Old books often seem quaint to us now, not only because of their style and subject matter, but because of conventions in punctuation that we have long since ceased to observe. The *Leviathan* of Thomas Hobbes, for example, was generous in its use of capitals and, by modern standards, unusual in its use of semicolons and parentheses.

> Liberty, or Freedome, signifieth the absence of Opposition; (by Opposition, I mean externall Impediments of motion;) and may be applyed no lesse to irrationall, and Inanimate creatures, than to Rationall.

The *Leviathan* was published more than three hundred years ago; but even in books published a mere century ago, modern readers can detect differences in the conventions of punctuation. In this passage, for example, which is taken from the 1866 edition of *English Composition and Rhetoric* by Alexander Bain, capitals and semicolons are used in ways that they would not be used today:

> The subject of Description is perhaps the one that most signally attests the utility of Rhetorical precepts. In delineating any complicated object, there is a well-defined method; which being attended to, the most ordinary mind may attain success, and being neglected, the greatest genius will fail.

When writers of textbooks (like this one) set out "Rules" of punctuation, they are not establishing absolute laws. They are generalizing about the conventions they notice in material printed at a given point in history. The rules expressed in this book are only indications of what seems to be common practice among editors and printers today.

Once you realize how haphazard the history of punctuation has been, you should not be surprised to learn that even now some of the common conventions are more logical than others.

P1 Continued

Part of learning to punctuate is learning to tell the hard and fast rules from the rules that allow for editorial discretion.

P2 *Capital Letters*

Capital letters are used at the beginning of the first word in a sentence. We are, in fact, so accustomed to seeing capital letters at the beginning of a sentence that most editors recommend we never begin a sentence with a numeral or a figure that cannot be capitalized.

Examples
100,000 refugees swarmed into the city.

π may have been discovered by many civilizations independently.

To avoid beginning a sentence with a figure, which cannot be capitalized, either spell out the numeral or rearrange the sentence.

Examples
The concept of π may have been discovered by many civilizations independently.

One hundred thousand refugees swarmed into the city.

P 2

Capital letters are also used at the beginning of the names of individual persons (James Joyce), places (Reno, Nevada), or things (the Capitol, a Chevrolet, the local Sheraton), and they are used at the beginning of adjectives formed from capitalized names (e.g., Shakespearean tragedy, an American dream).

In titles, capital letters are generally used at the beginning of the first word and of all other words except short prepositions, conjunctions, and articles (i.e., *a, an, the*).

Examples
The Rise and Fall of a College Freshman

A Study of the Effect of Radiation on Termites

P3 *Question Marks, Exclamation Points, and Periods*

In printed English, sentences are marked off with a capital letter at the beginning and either a period, a question mark, or an exclamation point at the end.

Examples
David was in the back of the class, preparing a lecture.

Can you tell me when to expect the delivery?

Congratulations! You have just placed out of Freshman English!

A period, like the one in the first example, indicates the end of a statement or a command. A question mark, like the one in the second example, indicates the end of a question. And an exclamation point, like the one in the third example, indicates the end of a statement about which the writer or speaker expects the reader or listener to be excited.

Exclamation points are rarely used by good writers today. When they want their readers to be excited, they write exciting sentences.

Sometimes the choice of end punctuation depends upon the meaning the writer wants to convey.

Examples
You baked a cake.

You baked a cake?

You baked a cake!

Any of these marks would be correct, but each affects the meaning of the sentence.

P4 *Commas*

The comma has four major uses.

1. **It is used along with a conjunction to join independent clauses.**

P 4

P4 Continued

Examples

Guy had played in six tournaments this year, and he had won them all.

The subway had been operating for months, but Elsie had not yet learned how to use it.

2. It is used to set off items in a series of three or more.

Examples

The residue consisted of sodium, calcium, and iron.

The building was modest in size, sturdy in structure, delicate in design.

3. It is used in pairs, like parentheses, to set off nonessential material embedded within a sentence.

Examples

Abdul, a native of Algeria, was an excellent swimmer.

The ethics bill, which was recently approved by Congress, places strict limits on outside income earned by members.

4. And it is used to set off material at the beginning or at the end of a sentence.

Examples

Burrowing beneath the blanket, Misty pretended not to hear the alarm clock.

The riverbed was a patchwork of mud cakes, parched by the long summer drought.

Each of these four uses of the comma is treated more fully below.

P5 *Commas Before Coordinate Conjunctions*

A comma is normally used before a coordinate conjunction (e.g., *and, or, but, for*) joining independent clauses unless the clauses are very short.

Examples

He returned and she left. (Commas not needed since both clauses are very short.)

Airline prices were increased and more people considered riding trains. (Here the sentence is long enough to require judgment. Some writers would leave the comma out, but it would not be wrong to add it.)

The L-1011 was produced before the DC-10 and many travelers have developed a sense of loyalty to it. (Experienced writers would probably put a comma before *and* in this example.)

The use of a comma *without* a coordinate conjunction to join independent clauses is called a "comma splice." For more information about comma splices, see **G48.**

Notice that *and* is NOT preceded by a comma when it joins only two words or two groups of words, unless those groups of words happen to be independent clauses.

Examples

Jack and Jill went up the hill. (No comma before *and* since it joins only two words—the two names—which are not independent clauses.)

The blossoming of dogwoods and the return of robins are among the most welcome signs of spring. (No comma before *and* since it joins only two groups of words—"the blossoming of dogwoods"/ "the return of robins"—which are not independent clauses.)

The council approved the new zoning law and commended the people who proposed it. (Still no comma before *and* since the group of words after it—"commended the people who proposed it"—is not an independent clause.)

The judge entered the courtroom more than an hour late, and the members of the press were obviously annoyed by the delay. (Here the comma is needed since the groups of words on both sides of *and* could be complete sentences in themselves; they are independent clauses.)

P 6

P6 *Commas in a Series*

Commas are used to separate items in a coordinate series.

P6 Continued

Examples
The big, red, hairy setter jumped through the glass pane.

Her speech was long, boring, and inappropriate.

A series is considered coordinate if the word *and* would make sense between the items.

Writers disagree about the use of a comma before *and* joining the last two items in a series. Some writers believe that the commas between the other items in the series actually stand for *and,* so that a comma in addition to *and* would be superfluous.

Examples
The car was new, expensive and beautiful.

The weeds had grown up in the garden, on the lawn and even in the woods.

There is no linguistic evidence for this belief.

Other writers would insist on putting a comma before the *and* in each of these examples. Although either rule is defensible, many writers prefer to follow the practice of professional editors, who generally prefer the comma before *and* at the end of a series.

Examples
At such law schools as Yale, Harvard, and Columbia, it is not the students who are clamoring for jobs but the employers who are competing for students.

> —Marilyn Machlowitz, *Esquire*, May 23, 1978, pp. 86–87.

Their theological discussion allows them to avoid or postpone the temporal matters of race, poverty, crime, and justice.

> —Lewis H. Lapham, *Harper's*, May 1978, pp. 14–17.

P7 *Commas in Pairs*

Commas are used in pairs—just as parentheses are—to show that certain words are not essential to the meaning of the rest of the sentence.

Examples

The students, now numbering more than 45,000, **were courted by all the candidates.**

Francis's car, with its fancy wheels and custom grill, **was usually** parked near the library.

Arnie's dog, which everyone hates, came uninvited to the party.

Notice that in each of these examples, the meaning of the rest of the sentence would not be altered if the part enclosed by commas were omitted. In the following sentences, however, similar bits of information are needed to single out or identify a word elsewhere in the sentence. If that information were omitted, the rest of the sentence would lose an essential part of its meaning. This sort of information is not set off by commas.

Examples

Colleges with more than 45,000 students are rare.

The car with fancy wheels and a custom grill was stolen.

The course that everyone hates has been cancelled.

The technical names for these two kinds of information are "restrictive" and "nonrestrictive." Restrictive information is essential information; it restricts (or limits or identifies) the meaning of a word nearby. Restrictive information is *not* set off by commas. Nonrestrictive information is information that is not essential, and for that reason it is enclosed by commas.

Instead of memorizing rules and definitions, some students find it helpful to read a few pairs of sentences out loud, pausing deliberately at the commas and noticing how punctuation affects meaning.

Examples

My roommate George owns a complete set of James's novels.
My roommate, George, owns a complete set of James's novels.

Jim's wife Ginny accompanied him to San Francisco.
Jim's wife, Ginny, accompanied him to San Francisco.

Students who work hard generally succeed.
Students, who work hard, generally succeed.

P7 Continued

> Composition, which is a required course, is not popular.
> Any course that is required will not be popular.

If you read the examples aloud and listen carefully, you will notice that in the first pair, the first version suggests that the speaker has more than one roommate, while the second version suggests that the speaker has only one roommate. In the second pair, the first version suggests that Jim has more than one wife, the second that he has only one. In the third pair, the first version suggests that only those students who work hard are likely to succeed; the second version seems to imply that all students work hard. And in the last pair, the *which* clause is set off by commas because it is not needed as an identification of composition, but the *that* clause is not set off by commas because without it we would not know which course the writer was referring to.

The difference between *which* and *that* is worth noting: *which* is normally used when commas are required, and *that* is normally used when commas are not required.

Perhaps the most common mistake in this situation is to put in one of the commas but not the other—which makes about as much sense as putting one parenthesis.

P 8

Example

George Gaskins, a lawyer with considerable experience in publications instructed us about recent developments in copyright laws. (Writers who omit one of the commas usually hear one of the pauses more clearly than they hear the other.)

P8 *Commas to Set Off Material at the Beginning or End of a Sentence*

In general, a comma is placed after an introductory clause or phrase of more than a few words.

Example

At midnight Jack heard a scream.

Two words — "at midnight" — are hardly "more than a few." Most editors would not put a comma after "midnight" in this sentence.

Example
At the stroke of midnight Jack heard a scream.

Here the introductory material — "at the stroke of midnight" — is four words. Is four "a few" or "more than a few"? Should there be a comma after "midnight"? This is a matter for editorial judgment. If you are in an editorial position, punctuate according to your preference. If you are a writer, subject, like most writers, to the whims of editors or teachers, conform to their preference unless you have good reason for insisting on your own. A handy rule to solve doubts: if the introductory words include more than one preposition, use a comma.

Example
In the middle of a dark and stormy night, Jack heard a scream.

Eight words are more than a few; use a comma.

Some material at the beginning of a sentence needs to be followed by a comma even though the material consists of only a word or two.

Examples
Defeated, the team shuffled sadly into the dressing room.

Incidentally, this is the finest paper you have written.

Without warning, the defendant stood up in the witness box and rebuked the judge herself.

Put commas wherever they are needed for clarity.

In the three examples above, the omission of the comma would cause words to run together that should be kept separate. When in doubt, try writing the sentence both ways, with commas and without, and choose the version that best indicates the way you would read the sentence aloud.

P 8

P8 Continued

Judgment is also necessary in deciding whether to put a comma before words added at the end of a sentence. The rule is to use the comma if the added information is not essential to the meaning of what goes before it.

Examples

Studs grew up during the Depression, when no one could find a job.

The vacation was pleasant, although I wish you had been with me.

If the added information is essential, the comma is omitted.

Examples

There was a time when no one could find a job.

The vacation was dull because you were not there.

The difference between "essential" and "nonessential" information is often a matter of judgment.

P9 *Comma Before* But

The word *but* is often preceded by a comma even when it is not joining independent clauses. Exception: *but* meaning "except" is not preceded by a comma.

Examples

Jack accepted the invitation, but then failed to show up at the party.

Irma left, but returned within five minutes.

No one but Horace insisted upon an honorarium.

In the first example, as in most occurrences of *but*, the comma is conventional. In the second example, a writer might get away without the comma because the first part of the sentence is very short. Putting it in, however, as the rule suggests, would not be incorrect. In the third example the comma is omitted because in that sentence *but* means "except."

P10 *Dates and Addresses*

Dates and addresses are conventionally set apart from the rest of a sentence by commas, even when these commas do not correspond to pauses in oral reading.

Example
On January 10, 1943, a star was born.

Many writers forget to put the comma after the year. The commas on *both* sides of the year are generally preferred by editors; the year is treated as if it were just a bit of added information.

Example
My address is 4627 Hillsdale Road, Northport, Georgia 50135.

Notice that the individual elements in an address are set off by commas — the street address, the city, and the state. The ZIP code, however — a relatively recent invention — is not generally set off by commas.

P11 *Colons and Semicolons*

Many writers are confused by the difference between the colon (:) and the semicolon (;). The easiest way to master their use is to remember what they mean.

The colon (:) usually means something like "namely" or "for example." What comes after a colon is not necessarily an independent clause.

Example
Each camper will be expected to bring the following items: a canteen, a sleeping bag, a pocket knife, and one complete change of clothes.

Here the colon means "namely"; the list of items after the colon does not happen to be an independent clause.

P11 Continued

Example
She had good reason to cry: her little brother had broken her favorite figurine.

Again, the colon means "namely," but this time the words after the colon happen to be an independent clause.

The semicolon can be used by itself to join independent clauses. It often means "and," "and therefore," or "rather," and it is frequently used between two independent clauses that are balanced or antithetical.

Examples
The election was not just close; it was virtually a tie.

He returned; she left.

Travis flicked a switch; the lights went out.

The semicolon is normally followed or preceded only by a group of words that would make sense as a separate sentence.

Examples
wrong: The attitudes toward honor that the poets adopt; provide sharp contrast between the two poems.

wrong: Poisonous gas shells explode; leaving a man unable to get his mask on.

In the first of these examples, the semicolon has been inserted where no punctuation at all is necessary. In the second example, the semicolon is used where a comma would have been appropriate.

P12 *Semicolons Before Coordinate Conjunctions*

The comma that normally comes before coordinate conjunctions (*and, or, but, for*) joining two inde-

pendent clauses may be promoted to a semicolon when one of the independent clauses has commas within it or is unusually long.

Examples

Finally, at the very end of the concert, a trio composed by Charles Ives was performed with unforgettable delicacy; but by that time, most of the audience had left.

The sergeant, who was a brave man with a prodigious mustache, had asked for Natalie's hand; but Natalie had already made different plans for her future.

The quality we most admire in a politician is wisdom; for wisdom, unlike ideology, is capable of adjusting to circumstances that cannot be foreseen at election time.

A comma before the conjunction in sentences like these would get lost among the other commas, and the grammatical center of the sentences would not be clearly marked.

P13 *Semicolons with Conjunctive Adverbs*

The semicolon is used together with conjunctive adverbs to join independent clauses. Conjunctive adverbs are words and phrases like *however, moreover, furthermore, nevertheless, on the other hand,* and *therefore.*

Examples

Jasper was inordinately proud of his house plants; however, it was his wife who actually took care of them.

As a public speaker, Torres was unusually eloquent; moreover, he was effective in private negotiations between labor and management.

Older textbooks, following the style of Latin writers, insist that words like these should be buried within the clause they belong to.

P13 Continued

Examples

Jasper was inordinately proud of his house plants; it was his wife, however, who actually took care of them.

As a public speaker, Torres was unusually eloquent; he was, moreover, effective in private negotiations between labor and management.

The older way of treating conjunctive adverbs is perhaps more graceful stylistically; the newer way is perhaps clearer. In your own writing, choose the form that best expresses what you want to express. In either case, notice how these words are punctuated. If the conjunctive adverb comes at the beginning of what it introduces, it is sandwiched between a semicolon and a comma. If it occurs within the clause, it is sandwiched between two commas—but don't forget that a semicolon is still needed to join the two clauses. Conjunctive adverbs, even if they are preceded by a comma, cannot join independent clauses; they need the help of a semicolon.

P14 *Commas and Semicolons in Series*

Because the colon means "namely" or "to be specific," it is often used to introduce items in a list. If each of the items consists of a single word or only a few words, the items are usually separated by commas.

Example

Jeanne-Marie loves all sorts of human movement: ballet, modern dance, gymnastics, basketball, tennis—anything that requires coordination and grace.

If the items in the list consist of several words, however, and especially if there are commas within some of the items in the list, then the items are normally separated by semicolons.

Example

There were plenty of signs that Leslie was at home: soggy toast on the floor; a trail of crumbs from the kitchen to the nursery; and a profusion of small toys scattered throughout almost every room as if they had been distributed by a benign windstorm.

Modern editors also allow the use of semicolons to separate items in a list even though the list is not preceded by a colon.

Examples

There were red and green crepepaper decorations on the flourescent ceiling fixtures; a bar; a buffet with veal and peppers, steak and mushrooms, and a giant clamshell full of shrimp salad; and, in one corner, a five-piece Sanman band.

> — *The New Yorker*, May 22, 1978, p. 28.

There is a mounting fear of engaging in extraparliamentary political activity; hesitation about signing even liberal petitions for groups like Amnesty International; anxiety about associating with the "wrong" people; isolated instances in which wives up for promotion have been asked to dissociate themselves from their husbands' political convictions (and vice versa); and what political theorist Wolf-Dieter Narr refers to as a "general uncertainty as to what may or may not be articulated, written, learned, or even taught."

> — David Zane Mairowitz *Harper's*, May 1978, p. 28.

In these examples, the semicolon is used as a more forceful comma to mark the divisions between long items in a series.

P15 *Open Quotation Marks and Commas*

P 15

Quoted material is not preceded by a comma when the quotation seems to be a grammatical continuation of the sentence to which it is attached.

Examples

What he uncovered instead was evidence that led him to write that jurors "made no mistake in finding Alger Hiss guilty as charged."

> — Richard Rovere, *The New Yorker*, May 22, 1978, p. 133.

Everywhere you looked there was the "heartbreaking flatness of the steppe."

> — Alfred Kazin, *Esquire*, May 23, 1978, p. 74.

P15 Continued

If the quoted material within a sentence is itself a sentence, the first word is capitalized and the first quotation mark is normally preceded by a comma.

Examples

One piece begins, "Bob has just died. Does that make him less dead than Peter, who's been dead for sixty years?"
—Jeffrey Burke, Harper's, May 1978, p. 75.

I jokingly said to Tom Victor as he was changing film, "Who *are* all these people?" To which he replied, "I wish I didn't know."
—William Cole, Saturday Review, April 15, 1978, p. 89.

A colon is sometimes used as a formal introduction to quoted material.

Example

When it became a Dover favorite, he admitted one of his few errors: "My former decision was, of course, not justified."
—Time, March 27, 1978, p. 97.

For the use of a colon before long quotations, see **P18.**
   Sometimes quoted material is woven into a writer's text, interrupted with comments or attributions.

Examples

"I've known Alger Hiss for years," Lippmann once told a friend. "It's absurd to think that he ever committed treason."
—Richard Rovere, The New Yorker, May 22, 1978, p. 133.

"In the space of two months," he points out, "we abandoned very nearly one third of our population to the enemy."
—Alfred Kazin, Esquire, May 23, 1978, p. 74.

P16 *Quotations in Dialogue*

Usually, when a conversation is reported in writing, a new paragraph is begun with each change in speaker—

even if this results in paragraphs of one sentence or one word.

Example

"Let's invite X," says the wife.

"We'd better not," replies hubby. "He thinks Heinrich Boll is a good writer."

"What about Y?"

"No. He once said 'Baader-Meinhof *group*' instead of 'gang.' But we could always ask Z."

"It's too risky. He is thought to 'sympathize' with a suspected sympathizer of a suspected terrorist."
> —Quoted by David Zane Mairowitz, *Harper's*, May 1978, p. 28.

P17 *Quotes Within Quotes: Single Quotes and Double Quotes*

If the material you are quoting includes quoted material, change the double quotation marks (") in your source to single quotation marks (').

For example, if your source looks like this—

Jones uses the encompassing "us," not the more personal, more particular "me."

—you might quote it in your own work like this—

As Tim O'Brien points out in a recent review, "Jones uses the encompassing 'us,' not the more personal, more particular 'me.'"

Notice that what you are quoting—O'Brien's observation—is enclosed in double quotation marks, while the words O'Brien had enclosed in double quotation marks are, in your version, changed to single quotation marks.

P 17

P18 *Quotations More Than Four Lines Long*

The longer quoted material is, the more difficult it will be for readers to remember that they are reading quoted material, not the author's original voice. To avoid this confusion, writers normally set off quotations more than four lines long by giving them wider margins and perhaps a different typeface.

In academic writing, long quotes are usually introduced with a comma or a colon and indented.

Example

In *The Philosophy of Composition*, p. 7, E. D. Hirsch argues that mass literacy and universal schooling have slowed the rate of change in the English Language:

> Some linguists have too flatly asserted that all languages change, and while this was indeed true of written English through the mid-eighteenth century, it has not been true of English since that time. Because of the conservatism of literacy, Standard English is unlikely ever again to change significantly in grammar or phonology, as long as universal schooling persists.

If the material quoted is one paragraph or less, there is no paragraph indention for the first line (see example above). If the quotation is two or more paragraphs long, the first line of each paragraph is indented.

Since readers know that material presented in this format is a quotation, there is no need to add quotation marks. If the material contains quotation marks within it, these quotation marks should be reproduced exactly as they are in the source.

Students — and some teachers — are often unnecessarily anxious about whether quotations a few words longer or shorter than the four lines mentioned in the rule should be indented. In cases like this, remember the purpose of the rule — to make the boundaries of the quoted material visually clear to your readers — and use your judgment.

P19 *Altering Quoted Material*

In general, whatever you represent as a quotation should be word for word what appears in your source. There are, however, some conventions for indicating additions or deletions in what you quote.

If you add to or change any part of the quoted material, put the additions or changes in brackets.

If your typewriter does not have brackets, you can either draw them in by hand or make them with a combination of a slash and the underscore key.

Example
"Some [new words] are found used a few times and then forgotten."

In the source, *A History of the English Language* by Albert C. Baugh and Thomas Cable, "new words" does not appear in the sentence quoted. Brackets are used to add clarification that would have been provided by context in the original sentence.

Sometimes writers draw attention to certain words or phrases in quoted material by underlining them when typing or italicizing them in print. If you do this, add the phrase "emphasis added" in parentheses after the quotation to indicate that the words or phrases were not underlined in your source.

Example
"In and out of the profession, *law and order involves emotions,* as we well know today" (emphasis added).

Notice the conventional sequence: end quotation mark, open parenthesis, parenthetical comment, close parenthesis, period.

When you leave words out of quoted material, indicate the omission by placing three spaced dots where the omitted words would be.

Example
As Montaigne tells us in his essay on solitude, "In husbandry . . . men are to proceed to the utmost limits of pleasure. . . ."

P19 Continued

In this example, Montaigne's original sentence actually goes on for a few more words. The omission of those last few words is indicated by four dots — the first of which stands for the omitted period and is placed as a period would be, without a space between it and the word before it. Four dots would also be used to indicate the omission of a sentence or the last part of a sentence within a quoted passage.

Example
As Montaigne observes, "In husbandry . . . men are to proceed to the utmost limits of pleasure. . . . We are to reserve so much employment only as is necessary to keep us in breath and defend us from the inconveniences that the other extreme of a dull and stupid laziness brings along with it."

If you notice an error or what might appear to be an error in material you intend to quote, you may add the word "sic" (Latin for "thus" or "so") in brackets to indicate that you are merely copying your source exactly.

Example
According to Bogardus, "When Bach died in 1950 [sic] his fame was already eclipsed by the popularity of two of his sons."

In the case of obvious errors in printing or typography, it is probably better to paraphrase the material and correct it in the process rather than call undue attention to it with *sic*.

P20 *Quoting Poetry*

Because line endings and the lengths of lines are important in poetry, the ends of lines must be indicated when poetry is quoted. If you are quoting only a line or two of poetry, you can work it into your text, using slash marks (/) to indicate the ends of lines. Leave a space on both sides of the slash.

Example

When Marvel refers to a certain love affair as "the conjunction of the Mind, / And opposition of the Stars," he is depending upon the reader to bring a knowledge of astrology to the poem.

If you are quoting more than one or two lines of poetry, introduce the quoted material with a sentence ending in a colon.

Example

In the first stanza of "The Definition of Love," Marvel personifies Love as the daughter of Despair and Impossibility:

> My Love is of a birth as rare
> As 'tis for object strange and high:
> It was begotten by Despair
> Upon Impossibility.

P21 *Titles*

In academic writing, references to titles of longer works are generally italicized (underlined in typescripts). Books, plays, magazines, and journals are considered longer works.

Examples

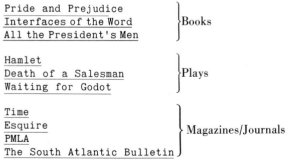

Pride and Prejudice	
Interfaces of the Word	Books
All the President's Men	
Hamlet	
Death of a Salesman	Plays
Waiting for Godot	
Time	
Esquire	
PMLA	Magazines/Journals
The South Atlantic Bulletin	

P 21

Titles of shorter works are generally put in quotation marks. Short stories, poems, and articles in a journal or magazine are generally considered shorter works.

P21 Continued

Examples

```
"The Secret Life of Walter Mitty"
"Barn Burning"                        } Short Stories
"The Eighty-Yard Run"

"Richard Cory"
"The Death of the Ball Turret Gunner" } Poems
"Because I Could Not Stop for Death"

"The Writer's Audience Is Always a Fiction"
"Isabella and the House of Esmond"     } Articles
"Key West, the Living End"
```

P22 *Question Marks and Exclamation Points with End Quotation Marks*

If the question mark or exclamation point applies to the quoted material, then it belongs *within* the end quotation mark.

Example
The article asks the question, "Is solar energy practical?"

Here the question is entirely within the quotation marks, so the question mark belongs before the end quote.

Example
She shouted, "Good heavens, my house is burning!"

Here the exclamation point applies to the words that were said excitedly, the words within the quotation marks; hence the exclamation point comes before the final quotation mark.

If the question mark or exclamation point applies to the entire sentence and not just to the quoted material, then it should come *after* the end quotation mark.

Example
Did she say, "Open the door yourself"?

Here the material within quotes is not a question, but the entire sentence is. Therefore the question mark is placed after the end quotation mark.

Example

Good grief, George, she called me "a perfect zero"!

In this example the writer of the entire sentence is the one who seems excited; the speaker of the quoted material seems to have been comparatively bored. The exclamation point, then, belongs to the sentence as a whole, not to the quoted material, and it should be placed after the end quotation mark.

P23 *Colons and Semicolons with End Quotation Marks*

Colons (:) and semicolons (;) are always placed after end quotation marks.

Examples

The announcer said, "This is a tornado warning"; a warning means that a tornado has actually been sighted.

Everyone knew why Bryant was called "the other end": as a college player he was overshadowed by his teammate, All-American Don Hutson.

P24 *Periods and Commas with End Quotation Marks*

The relationship between commas, periods, and end quotation marks is rigorously consistent in most American publications. Commas and periods next to end quotation marks are placed before the quotation mark, even if the quoted material consists of a single word.

P24 Continued

Examples

At present it is maneuvering to rid itself of this unprofitable piece of "varnish."

—Tracy Kidder, *Atlantic,* June 1978, p. 20.

The U.S. Constitutional notion of "separation of powers," borrowed by the Founding Fathers from the eighteenth-century French philosopher Montesquieu, has become a trap.

—Kevin Phillips, *Harper's,* May 1978, p. 44.

Some people say the reason for this convention is that linotype operators in America have simply refused to type the sequence". or the sequence", because these sequences are more difficult to finger than the reverse sequence. Now American readers are so accustomed to seeing periods and commas before end quotation marks that the reverse sequence seems wrong. In Great Britain, however, and in American publications that follow the style manual of the Government Printing Office, the comma and period often follow the end quotation mark.

P25 *The Apostrophe to Mark the Possessive*

P 25

The apostrophe (') or the apostrophe followed by an *s* is used to mark the form of nouns that grammarians call possessive. Frequently, the possessive form indicates that a noun "owns" or "possesses" what comes after it.

Examples

John's book

The policeman's uniform

The rules that describe the convention for forming the possessive are fairly simple. If you need the possessive form of a noun, first make sure that the noun is singular or plural, according to the meaning you intend.

Examples

Singular	Plural
car	cars
man	men
child	children
radio	radios
party	parties
James	Jameses

**If the noun is singular, form the possessive by adding
'*s* no matter what letter the noun ends in. (Some books
allow the apostrophe alone after ancient names—e.g.,
Jesus' cross or Xerxes' mother; but these might be
better written as "the cross of Jesus" or "the mother
of Xerxes.)**

Examples

car's
man's
child's
radio's
party's
James's

**If the noun is plural, there are two possibilities: either
the plural form ends in *s* or it doesn't. To form the possessive, add only an apostrophe to a plural form that
already ends in *s*; but add '*s* to a plural form that ends
in anything else.**

**P
25**

Examples

Plural	Plural Possessive
cars	cars'
men	men's
children	children's
radios	radios'
parties	parties'
Jameses	Jameses'

The most common mistake writers make in this matter is to
try to form the plural and the possessive at once. They know

P25 Continued

that they need an apostrophe and probably an *s* as well, but they are never sure which order they belong in. Solve this problem by attacking it one step at a time: first decide whether you want a singular noun or a plural noun and write down that form; then you can decide what needs to be added to form the possessive. If the noun is singular, there is no choice: add *'s* no matter what the noun ends in. If the noun is plural, an apostrophe alone will work if the plural form already ends in *s*; if the plural form ends in some other letter, add *'s*.

Writers sometimes get themselves tangled in nearly impossible situations with the possessive form of plural nouns. What if, for example, Scones was a person's last name, and there were several Scones brothers living in the same neighborhood, and one night all of their houses caught on fire. How would you say the Sconeses' houses burned down? Answer: try to avoid the situation altogether. "The Sconeses' houses" could be defended according to one set of conventions, and "The Scones' houses" could be defended according to another set. But when you have to choose between one awkward situation and another, the best thing to do is to rephrase what you want to say so that it does not attract attention to itself on the page: "The houses of all the Scones brothers burned down."

P26 *The Apostrophe to Mark Plurals*

The apostrophe and the apostrophe followed by *s* are never used to mark the plural of nouns.

The apostrophe followed by *s* is, however, used to mark the plural of numerals and letters.

Examples
On her report card she received three A's and two B's.

The error was caused by a defective printout on which all the 8's looked like 6's.

The plural of acronyms and initials is often marked by the addition of *s* without an apostrophe.

Examples

The Army requested funds for modernization of its tactical nuclear weapons without, however, including ERWs.

> —George B. Kistiakowsky, *Atlantic*, June 1978, p. 6.

Sen. Daniel P. Moynihan said he was confident that Congress would "disapprove the sale of the F-15s to Saudi Arabia."

> —Tom Gervasi, *Harper's*, May 1978, p. 19.

P27 It's/Its

The difference between *it's* and *its* is confusing to many writers.

Example

The dog was wagging its tail.

Notice that "its" is a possessive form here, but, unlike the possessive forms of nouns, it does not have an apostrophe before the *s*.

Example

It's going to be a long, rainy weekend.

Here the apostrophe does not signal a possessive form; it signals a missing letter. "It's" is really a contracted form of *it is*.

Although the distinction between *its* and *it's* is not especially logical, it is firmly established. The failure to observe the distinction is regarded by many readers as a minor distraction, and by many other readers as a sign of sloppy thinking. It's a minor rule, but its violation can mar the writer's image. (See also Pronouns: Possessive Forms, p. 320.)

P28 *Dashes and Parentheses*

In many situations dashes and parentheses are interchangeable with commas.

P 28

P28 Continued

Examples
```
Jack--Susan's brother--has been accepted by
Georgetown University.

Jack (Susan's brother) has been accepted by
Georgetown University.

Jack, Susan's brother, has been accepted by
Georgetown University.
```

Which version is correct? All of them. This is a matter of editorial preference. Dashes and parentheses, however, are stronger than commas, and they emphasize the break in thought more than a pair of commas would. In your writing, choose the marks that best fit the context and the intended meaning.

There are some situations in which commas are not strong enough to prevent confusion, so stronger marks—dashes or parentheses—have to be used. Why, for example, were dashes used in the previous sentence instead of commas or parentheses? Because, of the three options, dashes seemed to make the meaning clearest.

Example
```
A better diet, more proteins and fruit, was pre-
scribed by the physician.
```

Commas are not strong enough. For a moment, the reader might read the sentence as if it were about a series of three items—diet, proteins, and fruit.

Example
```
A better diet (more proteins and fruit) was pre-
scribed by the physician.
```

Parentheses are satisfactory here.

Example
```
A better diet--more proteins and fruit--was pre-
scribed by the physician.
```

The use of dashes here would be a matter of editorial preference.

In general, dashes are much more common in journalism than in academic writing, and they are regarded as informal marks of punctuation. Many academic writers prefer parentheses to dashes whenever they have a choice, simply because parentheses seem more formal.

Dashes and parentheses can be used to separate an entire sentence within a sentence; commas would be inadequate in this situation.

Examples

```
Samuel Robert Williams--his friends call him Wizzard
--runs the most progressive newspaper in Wisconsin.
```

```
Samuel Robert Williams (his friends call him Wizzard)
runs the most progressive newspaper in Wisconsin.
```

Notice that parentheses are never preceded by commas.

A single dash can be used to set off added material at the end of a sentence.

Example

```
I'll be happy to take you to the train station--
unless, of course, I can persuade you to spend the
weekend here.
```

And a single dash can be used to lead from a list of specific items to a more general statement.

Example

```
Tornadoes, hurricanes, blizzards, and earthquakes--
these disasters generally confine themselves to
different parts of the country.
```

P 29

P29 *Dashes vs. Hyphens*

Perhaps the most common problem regarding dashes in student writing is the typographical convention itself. In printed material and in handwritten material, the dash is a single line about twice as long as a hyphen.

P29 Continued

Examples
Hyphen:-

Dash: —

In typewritten manuscripts, the dash is usually represented by two hyphens with no spaces between them and the words next to them. The common mistake is to use only one hyphen, which looks, as you might expect, like a hyphen.

Examples
```
He said he was in Denver--a likely story. (Correct)

He said he was in Denver-a likely story. (Confusing)
```

Some people consider it fashionable to represent a dash in typed papers by a single hyphen separated by spaces from the words next to it.

Example
```
He said he was in Denver - a likely story.
```

This fashion is certainly less confusing than the practice of using a single hyphen without spaces. In academic writing, however, the double hyphen with no spaces is still the most common form.

P30 *Hyphens in Compound Words*

In general, two or more words that work together as a single adjective before a noun are hyphenated.

Examples
blue-eyed baby

vote-getting speech

all-out war

twelve-mile walk

If the first word of the pair ends in -*ly* however, the hyphen is omitted.

Examples
highly strategic airbase

tightly organized team

Compound nouns are usually hyphenated when they are made up of nouns of equal rank.

Examples
She prepared the brief in her office-home in Newport.

Quentin, a doctor-poet was the first to speak in favor of the new regulation.

They were speaking about Chardin, a priest-scientist whose books were popular in the early sixties.

For guidance in the use of hyphens, consult an unabridged dictionary. If the dictionary does not help, consult *A Manual for Writers* by Kate Turabian (Chicago: The University of Chicago Press, fourth edition, 1973) for further principles.

P31 *Hyphenated Words at the End of a Line*

In deciding where to divide a word at the end of a line, use the following general rules:

1. **Divide the word according to the way it is pronounced.**
   Correct: bi-cycle *or* bicy-cle
   Wrong: bic-ycle *or* bicyc-le

2. **Divide between double consonants.**
   Correct: recom-mend
   Wrong: reco-mmend *or* recomm-end

3. **Do not leave a single letter stranded on either line.**
   Wrong: a-bout
   Wrong: rhyth-m

P31 Continued

4. Do not hyphenate one-syllable words.
Wrong: thr-ough
Wrong: fi-ght

5. Names of persons are not usually hyphenated in manuscripts.
Wrong: Samuel John-son

It is also considered good form in typing or writing to avoid hyphenating the last word in a paragraph and the last word on a page.

If you have any doubt about where to divide a word, do what professional writers do: consult a dictionary.

EXERCISES

1. After punctuating each of the following sentences, write a sentence of your own that requires the same pattern of punctuation.

a. His three favorite authors were Hemingway Heller and an obscure columnist in a Terrytown newspaper. **(P6)**

b. He picked up the check and started walking toward the cashier but she refused to let him pay. **(P5)**

c. He would not listen to any composer but Bach. **(P9)**

d. Because he was an hour late he had to begin the tournament without warming up. **(P8)**

e. After listening to his mother complain about everything she hated in her new apartment Crowder decided that it was time for him to go. **(P8)**

f. The temperature had plummeted to thirty degrees below zero and everyone was hoping that the maneuvers would be canceled. **(P5)**

g. The sky was faintly lit and Venus was still visible but the sun had not yet begun to climb out of the ocean in the East. **(P5, P12)**

h. Nothing pleased him more than searching through stacks of old books and discovering a rare first edition or an autographed copy of one of James novels. **(P25)**

i. A policeman patrolling the subway station found my wallet. (Indicate with punctuation that the "patrolling the subway station" is necessary to identify the policeman.) **(P7)**

j. A policeman dressed in plain clothes was patrolling the entrance to the subway station. (Indicate with punctuation that "dressed in plain clothes" is not necessary identification but added information.) **(P7)**

k. Yuri Johnson a lifeguard on Vincent Beach found a dozen Spanish coins buried in the sand. **(P7)**

l. Would you please have a seat in the office and wait for the President **(P3)**

m. The Hotel Caledonia 23 West 26th Street New York New York was O. Henry's last address. **(P10)**

n. On May 23 1836 John C. Calhoun argued for the admission of Texas into the Union. **(P10)**

o. Disgusted with his performance Kodolsky stormed into the wings and vented his anger on his manager. **(P8)**

p. The House had passed the bill the Senate was still discussing it. **(P11)**

q. Goldsmith was confident he could win the election his opponent however had a different opinion. **(P13)**

r. Everyone expected Victor to appear at the party it was moreover his own intention to arrive before anyone else. **(P13)**

s. He had published six books however none of them achieved the success the critics thought they deserved. **(P13)**

t. Joe Venutti the famous jazz violinist made a recording of some of Jelly Roll Mortin's most famous songs and his solos apparently improvised on the spot were as ingenious as any he had played as a younger man. **(P7, P12)**

2. Indicate which sentence in each of the following pairs is correctly punctuated.

Gene called the movie "pretty," which meant he didn't like it.
Gene called the movie "pretty", which meant he didn't like it.

The policeman said, "Show me your license," and I reached for my wallet.
The policeman said "Show me your license," and I reached for my wallet.

Tricia decided to name her poem "Rotten".
Tricia decided to name her poem "Rotten."

Who said, "Damn the torpedoes, full speed ahead?"
Who said, "Damn the torpedoes, full speed ahead"?

The crowd shouted, "Kill the umpire"; they had been patient long enough.

The crowd shouted, "Kill the umpire;" they had been patient long enough.

3. Indicate the possessive form for the first noun in each of the following phrases.

a. The boy___ father
b. Seven boys___ report cards
c. Travis___ new fishing boat
d. Louise___ new drawing board
e. Harold___ home town
f. The men___ locker room
g, The women___ locker room
h. The fish___ fins

Appendix

───◆───

Two Advanced Discovery Procedures

1. Burke's Pentad: Questions for Understanding Human Behavior

There is an important difference between knowing and understanding. If you could answer the five journalistic questions about some human act (a robbery, for example), you would know something about the act. But would you really understand it? How deeply could you answer the question *why?* Suppose the robbery was committed to support a drug habit. Is the robber's purpose all we need to know to understand why the act was committed?

According to Kenneth Burke, a philosopher and critic, we do not really understand any human act unless we consider its five essential components *in relation to one another:* the act itself, the scene of the action, the instrument or means used, the character of the person doing the act, and the goal or benefit that person has in mind.

To use these five components as Burke uses them would require a course in philosophy. A simpler way to use them, however, is to ask five questions about any human act and to see how the answers are related to one another.

1. What is the act?
2. What is the personality or character of the person doing it?
3. What instruments or means are used?
4. What is the scene of the act?
5. What purpose or benefit does the actor have in mind.

In Burke's terms, these questions refer to the **act,** the **actor,** the **agency,** the **scene,** and the **purpose.**

At first it might seem that to understand why an act is committed, you would need to answer only the fifth question — what purpose did the actor have in mind? In the hypothetical case of a robbery, the actor's purpose was to get money to buy drugs.

From Burke's perspective, this would be a very shallow answer to the question *why*. Burke sees conscious goals as only one ingredient in any human act. Unless we understand how the act results from a complex web of causes in which purpose is only a single strand, we do not understand the act at all.

The robbery is a case in point. Suppose, for example, you were a judge whose duty it was to sentence the robber. How would your understanding of the robbery be affected if you knew that the robber was the son of a wealthy doctor? The son of a poor man? A teenager who had no idea who his parents were? How would your understanding be affected if you knew that the robber was weak and frightened, afraid of the gun in his hand? What if he was a cynical killer who actually hoped for an excuse to shoot a bystander? An intelligent and well-educated person? A mentally retarded person? A veteran who had been tortured in a prison camp? These are the kinds of considerations that should emerge when we examine an act in relation to the character or personality of the actor. Once we begin this line of questioning, we quickly realize how little we understood the act when all we knew was that the robber had a habit to support.

Relationships among the answers can be equally illuminating. How was the scene related to the act? An address does not really answer the question. What sort of place was it? What sort of neighborhood was it in? How did the place and the neighborhood influence the robber's behavior? What means did the robber use? Is a robbery committed with an ax the same as a robbery committed with a pistol? Where did the weapon come from? Was its accessibility in any way partly responsible for the act itself? What other means did the robber use? Masks? Accomplices? A getaway car?

Underlying Burke's discovery procedure is the assumption that human beings are to a large extent creatures of their environment. We do not fully understand human behavior, then, unless we take its environment and its instruments into account. Character and intention play important roles too, sometimes the most important roles, but not by any means the only roles. People we know would have had different personalities with different needs if they had grown up in different settings. Had the robber—whoever he was—been swapped with another infant in the hospital and raised by different parents in a different setting, is it likely that he would have committed the same robbery? If another child had been given to the robber's parents, would that child have developed a motive for stealing? These considerations do not excuse the robber, but without them we have only a limited understanding of the robbery.

In all there are ten possible relationships—Burke calls them ratios—that you could examine by pairing off the five terms in Burke's pentad. How is the act related to the person, to the scene, to the means, to the purpose? How is the character of the person related to the scene, the means, and the purpose? How is the scene related to the means and the purpose? And how are the means and the purpose related to each other? In Burke's terms, the ten ratios are: (1) act to actor, (2) act to scene, (3) act to agency, (4) act to purpose, (5) actor to scene, (6) actor to agency, (7) actor to purpose, (8) scene to agency, (9) scene to purpose, and (10) agency to purpose.

To see what sort of understanding Burke's pentad should produce, apply it to a subject you know well: your decision to attend the school you are now attending. The ten ratios are expressed in the following questions.

1. **Act to actor.** To what extent did you choose your school because of some aspect of your character or personality (e.g., your ambitiousness, your self-confidence, your standards, other values and convictions)?

2. **Act to scene.** To what extent was the choice affected by the scene around you (by other people, by conditions at home, by conditions at the school you chose and at the schools you did not choose)?

3. **Act to agency.** To what extent was your choice affected by the means at your disposal (i.e., by how much money you had available)?

4. **Act to purpose.** What was your purpose in making the choice? What benefits did you expect to occur that would not have occurred with other choices?

5. **Actor to scene.** To what extent was your personality at that time a reflection of your home setting? How does your personality fit in the school you chose? How would it have fit in other schools?

6. **Actor to agency.** How are your means affected by your personality? Would you have more or less money to spend on education if you were a different sort of person?

7. **Actor to purpose.** How do the benefits you expect reflect something about your character or personality? About your values?

8. **Scene to agency.** To what extent did the means at your disposal depend upon your being in a certain place at a certain time?

9. **Scene to purpose.** To what extent are your conscious goals affected by your environment at home and at school?

10. **Agency to purpose.** How was your purpose affected by your means? Would you have had other purposes if you had had other means?

Some of these relationships will be more revealing than others. Some of them play major roles in some human acts and minor roles in others. But if you explored your choice of schools with this discovery procedure, you can see why people consider it more powerful than the journalist's questions in understanding human acts. You could satisfy the journalist's questions with fairly superficial information:

> I, Jane Doe, while sitting on my back porch one Monday afternoon in May, chose Terpsichore U. because it has a good dance program.

That tells us who, what, when, where and why. But it gives the impression that Jane Doe's choice was based solely on a rational motive, as if Jane were not a flesh-and-blood person conditioned by her upbringing, influenced by her environment, and limited or liberated by the means at her disposal. Instead, she seems more like a disembodied free will that is drawn to rational decisions because they are rational. If she were to examine her choice with Burke's pentad, as you examined yours, she would become aware of how much her free will is limited and conditioned by matters entirely beyond her control.

Burke's pentad is especially useful in studying human behavior that is unusual in some way—either unusually good (e.g., an act of heroism, an act of artistic excellence) or unusually bad (e.g., crime, drug dependency, child abuse). It can be helpful in understanding a single act (e.g., a wedding, a political decision, an important failure) or in understanding the accumulated acts that constitute a career (e.g., Chris Evert's career as a tennis player or Fidel Castro's rise to power in Cuba).

Castro will serve as an example. If you asked a journalist's questions about Castro's rise to power, you would come up with the sort of information you might find in an almanac or in a biographical dictionary: Fidel Castro Ruz. Cuban. Born in 1927. Leader of dissident students. Lawyer. Leader of opposition to dictator Fulgencio Batista from 1956 to 1959. Conducted guerrilla warfare from bases in jungle. Became premier of Cuba after the collapse of Batista's government in 1959.

Asked repeatedly, the journalist's questions could lead to mountains of information. But by examining the information through the relationships in Burke's pentad, we would be able to develop a deeper understanding of what made Castro's rise to power what it was.

1. **Act to actor.** What personal traits of character made Castro, rather than one of the other revolutionaries, the leader?

2. **Act to scene.** Would Castro's rise to power have been possible in another country or another time? To what extent was his career made possible by the political corruption of the Batista regime?

3. **Act to agency.** To what extent did his rise depend upon means (food, weapons, personnel, tactics) that were at his disposal?

4. **Act to purpose.** To what extent did Castro's rise spring from a conscious desire to win benefits either for himself or for others?

5. **Actor to scene.** To what extent was Castro's personality at that time the product of his upbringing, his education, his political and geographical environment?

6. **Actor to agency.** How were the means he used (e.g., guerrilla warfare) related to his character or personality? Can just any sort of person use means of this sort? Would a different sort of person have looked for different means?

7. **Actor to purpose.** In what way were Castro's conscious motives related to the sort of character or personality he was at that time? To his values?

8. **Scene to agency.** To what extent did the means (e.g., guerrilla warfare) depend upon the scene (e.g., the Cuban terrain) and the times?

9. **Scene to purpose.** To what extent were Castro's conscious purposes and goals created by political and geographical conditions in Cuba?

10. **Agency to purpose.** How were Castro's purposes affected by the means at his disposal? Would he have had other purposes if he had had other means?

Unless you happen already to be thoroughly familiar with Castro's career, these questions are likely to lead to lines of investigation rather than to definite answers. But having asked the questions, you would know what to look for in your research. You would also know the difference between the historical information — names, dates, places — that is produced by the journalistic pentad, and the more thorough understanding of human behavior that should result from using Burke's pentad. When you examine Castro's rise to power with this discovery procedure, you begin to realize that Castro did not descend from heaven into Havana, swathed in army fatigues and smoking a cigar. Like any of us, he is as much a creature of his own career as he is a creator of it.

If you use Burke's pentad as a way of investigating human behavior, remember that it should not become a rigid, mechanical device. Don't be too concerned if the answers you get do not precisely fit the questions. Like other discovery procedures, this one is intended to stimulate ideas, insights, intuitions, and to suggest lines of investigation that might not have occured to you otherwise.

Don't let the terminology of the pentad frighten you. Instead of dealing with the terms themselves — act, actor, agency, scene, and purpose — you might find it easier to look at the list of questions about Castro (p. 420) or about your choice of college (p. 418) and ask yourself similar questions about the human act you are investigating.

As you study some aspect of human behavior, keep in mind the traditional angles that you might use in your writing — cause and effect, definition, comparison and contrast, and so on (see p. 26 above). Since Burke's pentad gets at the *why* of human behavior, you might want to write a paper about the causes of some specific acts or kinds of acts. You will discover that Burke's terms have varying degrees of application to any particular act. After you have analyzed the act (e.g., Castro's rise to power), you could arrange the answers to your questions in order from most important to least important. Then you could write a paper explaining the act by one or several of its most important causes, or a paper arguing that one or several causes were in fact essential to the act.

You might also use Burke's pentad as a way of defining a particular act or behavior. Or you might think of one kind of behavior as a problem and study it in hopes of finding a solution. Or you might use the pentad to find points of comparison and contrast between two different acts or the behaviors of two different people with something in common (e.g., Fidel Castro and Che Guevera, Shakespeare and Marlowe, Jesse Jackson and Martin Luther King, George Washington and Thomas Jefferson).

Keep these options in mind as you do your prewriting exercises. If you need more information about your topic, turn to the section on interviewing in Chapter Two or to Chapter Ten, on library research. Then turn to Chapter Four for some advice about choosing a rhetorical stance and a pattern of organization.

EXERCISES

1. Look through a recent issue of a newspaper and analyze the information given in one of the lead stories on the front page. Does the reporter answer the questions who, what, when, where, why, and how within the first few lines? After you've read the story, examine the central human action in it from the ten ratios suggested by Burke's pentad. Do these questions suggest lines of investigation that are not covered in the story?

2. Choose one example of unusual human behavior (a murder, an act of heroism, a recent act of some world figure, the career of a celebrity) and with the help of your classmates examine this behavior as thoroughly as you can by asking the questions suggested by Burke's pentad. Do the questions lead to information that you could turn into a paper? If not, how could you supplement the questions or increase your knowledge so that you could write a paper?

WRITING ASSIGNMENTS

1. Choose one instance of human behavior that you know a lot about — either an incident in your own life, in the life of one of your friends, or in the life of someone you have read about. Examine that incident by jotting as many answers as you can to the three sets of questions you have studied in this chapter and in Chapter Two. After you have thoroughly examined the incident, write a paper in which you both describe and explain it. Turn to Chapter Four for advice about choosing a rhetorical stance and developing a pattern of organization.

2. With the help of your instructor, choose an instance or a pattern of human behavior that you know little about. Then prepare yourself to do some research by examining this behavior through the questions discussed in this chapter and in Chapter Two. After you have discovered questions you would like to know the answer to, turn to the section on interviewing in Chapter Two or to Chapter Ten, on library research, to see how you might find answers to those questions. When you have gathered your information, sort it out and turn it into a paper. You may either report on your findings without trying to support some specific point of view, or you may choose to formulate a thesis and defend it. Turn to Chapter Four for advice about choosing a rhetorical stance and developing a pattern of organization.

2. Tagmemics: Questions for Analyzing Systems

Burke's pentad is useful for analyzing human acts, even the collective human acts of large groups of people. But there is another set of questions that is useful for exploring the activities of systems or institutions, whether human or nonhuman. Anything that is alive or in motion can be considered a system. Any organization can be considered an institution.

The questions were developed by three professors of rhetoric and linguistics, Richard Young, Alton Becker, and Kenneth Pike. Their approach consists of two sets of three questions each. The first three questions were developed by Pike to study grammatical units that he called *tagmemes.* Hence, this procedure is called tagmemic. You need not worry about learning what tagmemes are. The point is that the questions Pike used to ask about tagmemes turn out to be good questions to ask about any system or institution.

1. How is it different from other things of its kind?
2. How many different forms can it take without losing its identity?
3. In what contexts does it occur?

In Pike's terms, these questions refer to **contrast, variation,** and **distribution.**

Consider the Mississippi River as an example of a system. *How is it different from other things of its kind?* The Mississippi is longer than any other river in the world except for the Nile. *How many different forms can it take without losing its identity?* It can vary considerably in its depth from time to time. It can vary considerably in its content. It can be warm and muddy or, at least in some places, covered with ice. It can even change its course at times and still be the same river—though its abandoned beds often become lakes or bogs, no longer part of the Mississippi. *In what contexts does it occur?* It divides the United States into East and West. It fits in with local landscape in different ways, sometimes flowing beside high bluffs, sometimes through flat farmland, sometimes through marshes and swamps.

To the first three questions, Pike, Becker, and Young added the physicist's notion that things can be viewed as particle, wave, or field. In simpler terms, this means that you can study something by considering it as a single unit (the particle approach), or by considering its activity (the wave approach), or by considering the way its various internal parts are related to one another (the field approach). Particle, wave, and field may be expressed as three questions:

4. What is it at a given instant?
5. What does it do?
6. What is its internal structure?

Apply these questions to the Mississippi River. *What is it at a given instant?* You could either define it as a dictionary would, by giving its length, and location, and direction of flow. Or you could describe the way it appears to the senses of an observer. *What does it do?* It flows south. Rises. Falls. Drains land. Irrigates land. *What is its internal structure?* The river is composed not only of its bed and its water, but of plant life, which needs the water for survival, and marine life, which needs both the water and the plants for its survival.

These six questions suggest even more lines of study when they are worked together in pairs, somewhat like the paired items in Burke's pentad.

In this system, however, the questions from each set are paired not with one another, but with each of the questions in the other set. As a result, there are nine possible combinations, which are illustrated in the following chart.

	How is it different from others?	*How many forms can it take?*	*In what contexts does it occur?*
What is it at a given instant?	1	4	7
What does it do?	2	5	8
What is its internal structure?	3	6	9

The combination of questions represented by each of the squares in the chart suggests new lines of investigation that are not quite contained in the six original questions. For example, the three questions represented by squares in the first column, under "How is it different from others?" suggest three different ideas for comparison and contrast analysis. The combined questions can be expressed as follows:

1. **Define or describe it in relation to other things of its kind.** (You could compare and contrast descriptions of the Mississippi with descriptions of some other river—the Nile, for example, or the Amazon.)
2. **Compare and contrast its activity with the activity of other things of its kind.** (You could compare and contrast the direction and volume of the Mississippi's flow, the acreage of land it drains, and its seasonal fluctuation with similar activities of other rivers.)
3. **Compare and contrast its internal structure with the internal structure of other things of its kind.**

(You could compare and contrast relationships among the quality of the water, the composition and shape of the river bed, and the kinds of plant life and marine life in the Mississippi with corresponding features of another river.)

The question at the top of the second column, "How many forms can it take?" might be answered with a specific number. Once you have identified the forms, you can analyze each of them as particle, wave, or field. For the sake of simplicity, we will say that the Mississippi has two major forms — high in some seasons, low in others. The combined questions represented by squares in the second column could be expressed as follows:

4. **Define or describe each of its forms.** (When the Mississippi is high, it reaches to the top of the levees that contain it in the South, and tops of ships become visible for miles around. When it is low, the banks are muddy and the water traffic is invisible to people beyond the levee.)
5. **What does it do in each of its forms?** (When it is high, it floods down to the Gulf of Mexico, pushing logs and debris along with it. Sometimes it floods over its banks, threatening lives and damaging property, altering the ecology of nearby lakes. When it is low, it is sluggish, peaceful, but never quite motionless.)
6. **What is the internal structure of each of its forms?** (Obviously, the relationship between the water and the banks changes at each stage. Less obviously, the internal ecology of the river is much more turbulent when the water is high than when it is low.)

The three questions represented by the squares in the third column, under "In what contexts does it occur?", lead to an analysis of how the subject is a part of larger systems. The combined questions could be expressed as follows:

7. **How would you define or describe it in its various contexts?** (How does the river look at its point of origin in Minnesota? Where is it joined by the Missouri? As it flows through Louisiana farmland? What does it look like in New

Orleans? In the marshes to the south of New Orleans? What is the delta and what does it look like?)

8. **What does it do in its various contexts?** (In some places it merely drains the land. In others, it irrigates it. It provides fish and drinking water. It acts as sewer for urban and industrial wastes. It is a port or a passageway for ships of various sizes.)

9. **How is its internal structure affected by its various contexts?** (Near its source, the internal structure of the river is relatively pure, because its context supplies clean water along with food for the fish. As it travels southward, the river is increasingly polluted by its contexts, carrying off insecticides from farmlands and wastes from cities and factories. Plant and animal life are threatened by the pollutants.)

Like any other discovery procedure, tagmemics itself will not provide you with new knowledge. If you apply these questions to a subject you know, you will be reminded of things that might be worth writing about. If you apply the questions to a subject you know little about, you will discover lines of investigation that you might want to explore in interviews, experimentation, or library research.

Do not be alarmed if you cannot remember the six original questions and the nine combined questions. Instead of memorizing these questions, keep the list before you as you explore a system or institution of your choice. As an example, consider your family, an organization you belong to, a branch of the military service, a division of government, a religious denomination, or a business organization. After choosing a subject, see if you can get answers similar to those in the list above, in which the Mississippi served as an example. Don't be concerned if some of your answers overlap. Discovery is a creative process, and creative processes are not necessarily neat.

If you have asked these questions about a subject of your own choice, you have discovered that some questions produced more interesting lines of investigation than others. Stick with the interesting questions as you develop material for a paper. There is no need to find the answers to all the questions once you have at least a few answers that you consider worthy of development. Nor is there any need to include all the answers in your paper, if some of the answers are uninteresting or irrelevant.

You should also have discovered either that you know enough about your topic to be writing immediately, or that you need to supplement your knowledge by interviewing an expert. making firsthand observations of your own, or researching in the library. If you need more information, the questions should at least help you identify what sort of knowledge you need.

Tagmemics, like any other discovery procedure, may lead you to information and lines of investigation, but it does not lead you directly to the sort of purpose that you need in order to bring the information to life. After all, if you have answered the nine questions, what can you do with the answers?

Perhaps the best way to bring the information to life is to view it from one of the angles discussed in Chapter Two.

EXERCISE

In class choose a system or an institution that is worth knowing more about. Anything that is alive or in motion can be considered a system. Any organization can be considered an institution. Ask the questions on pp. 425–427 about the subject and answer as many as you can. Discuss how you could find the information you need for the questions that the class cannot answer. After you have explored as many lines of investigation as you can, look over the answers and try to find a potential angle for writing about some of them. The traditional angles, discussed in Chapter Two, are definition, division and classification, cause and effect, comparison and contrast, and process analysis.

WRITING ASSIGNMENT

Choose what you consider the most interesting line of investigation developed in the discussion generated by the exercise above. Choose a strategy for increasing your knowledge about the subject matter: observation, aided by the discovery procedures discussed here and in Chapter Two; an interview or a series of interviews; library research; or some combination of these sources. Investigate the topic as thoroughly as you can and put your findings in the form of a formal report — like a research paper — to be shared with your classmates.

Index

Boldface indicates sections in the handbook that can be located with the help of the marginal tabs. Other numbers refer to pages. Exercises and writing assignments are related to the material immediately preceding them.

ability of/ability to, 282

absolute
  as stylistic device, 180–181 (exercise, 181–182)
  defined, 180

accept/except, 283

act, 416
  see also pentad, Kenneth Burke's

active voice, 165
  defined, 305 (**G13**; exercise, 306)

actor, 416
  see also pentad, Kenneth Burke's

ad/add, 282

adapt/adopt, 282

addresses, punctuation of, 391 (**P10**)

adjectives
  after verbs of being and perception, 327
  comparative and superlative, 328–330 (**G25**; exercises, 331)
  defined, 323 (**G23**; exercises, 325)
  distinguished from adverbs, 325–327 (**G24**; exercise, 327)

adverbs
  comparative and superlative, 328–330 (**G25**; exercises, 331)
  conjunctive. *See* conjunctive adverbs
  defined, 324 (**G23**; exercise, 325)
  distinguished from adjectives, 325–327 (**G24**; exercise, 327)

advice/advise, 282

affect/effect, 282, 283

agency, 426

   see also pentad, Kenneth Burke's

agreement of pronouns with ante-
cedents, 312–316 (**G17**; exercises, 316–317)

agreement of verbs with subjects,
346–347 (**G36**; exercises, 348)

   collective nouns as subject, 353–
356 (**G40**; exercise, 356–357)

   despite intervening nouns, 348
(**G37**; exercise, 348–349)

   each and *every* as subject, 359
(**G43**; exercise, 359)

   one of those who . . ., 360 (**G44**;
exercise, 344)

   with multiple subjects, 351–353
(**G39**; exercise, 353)

   with *there* as dummy subject, 358
(**G42**; exercise, 358–359)

   with verb "to be," 349–350 (**G38**;
exercise, 350–351); 357 (**G41**;
exercise, 357–358)

all together/altogether, 282

allusion/illusion, 282

also, 282

among/between, 282

analogy, as evidence, 72

angles, five traditional, 26–43

   see also cause and effect; comparison and contrast; definition; division and classification; process analysis

angry/mad, 284

APA Publication Manual, 245

apostrophe

   in contractions, 321 (**G21**; exercises, 321–322)

   to mark plurals, 406–407 (**P26**)

   to mark possessive, 404–406
(**P25**)

appeal

   emotional, 63–65

   ethical, 60–62

   logical. *See* assertions and evidence

appositive

   as stylistic device, 178–179 (exercise, 179–180)

   defined, 178

argumentation. *See* rhetorical stance

   see also critical reading

argument from circumstance, 59

arranging, 83–100

   see also outlines; paragraphs;
plural-noun formula

articles, citation of

   from newspaper, 255

   from popular magazines, 253–254

   from scholarly journals with continuous pagination, 254

   from scholarly journals without
continuous pagination, 254

   in bibliography, 247–249, 253–255

   in notes, 249–255

   reprinted in a collection, 255

   titles, 248

   with more than one author, 254

as, as if, like, 284, 338 (**G31**)

assertions and evidence, 52–60,
68–69, 75

assignments. *See* writing assignments

associative pattern in description,
127

audience, implied, 60, 62–63, 69–70,
71, 76

author

   implied, 60–62, 69, 76

   unknown, 247

authority

   as source of definition, 35–36

   as proof, 56

authors, multiple

   in bibliography, 248–254

   in footnotes, 254

balanced sentence, 188–189 (exercise, 193)

be. *See* verb "to be"

being as, 282

beside/besides, 282

better than/more than, 282

between you and I/me, 282
bibliography
  defined, 246
  form, 246–249
  notes on cards, 237
  sample entries, 224–225, 253–256
Black English, 261–263
books, citation of
  in bibliography, 247–248, 255–256
  in footnotes, 250, 255–256
  titles, 248
  with more than one author, 256
  with one author, 255
brackets in quoted material, 49,
  399–400 **(P19)**
bust/burst, 282
but, commas before, 390 **(P9)**
but what, 282

can't help but, 283
capital letters
  for first word in sentence, 382
  (P2)
  for proper nouns and adjectives,
  382 **(P1)**
  in titles, 382 **(P1)**
card catalog, in library, 230–231
case
  of nouns and pronouns, 340–341
  (G33)
  who/whom, 342–343 **(G34;** exercise, 344)
cause and effect
  as invention, 39–43 (exercise, 43;
  writing assignment, 43–44)
  in critical reading, 57–58, 59
charged language, 63–65
checkpoint
  final for all papers, 160–162
  for descriptive papers, 130
  for expository outlines, 102
  for narrative and process papers,
  125
  for overall organization, 136
  for persuasive outlines, 92
  for research paper form, 256
Chicago Style Manual, 245

circumstance, argument from, 59
cite, site, sight, 286
city, as place of publication, 248
classification and division, 29–30
  (exercise, 30–31; writing assignment, 31)
clauses, dependent and independent, 361 **(G45;** exercise, 361–
  362)
cliché, 147–148 (exercise, 148)
coherence. *See* paragraphs
  see also outlines; arranging
colloquial diction, 142–143, (exercise, 144)
colons
  before quoted material, 396
  distinguished from semicolons,
  391–392 **(P11)**
  next to quotation marks, 403
  (P23)
combination as stylistic device, 182–
  183 (exercise, 183–184)
commas
  before *but*, 390 **(P9)**
  before coordinating conjunctions,
  384–385 **(P5)**
  before open quotation marks,
  395–396 **(P15)**
  for clarity, 389
  four major uses of, 383–384 **(P4)**
  in dates and addresses, 391 **(P10)**
  in pairs, 386–388 **(P7)**
  series, 385–386 **(P6)**
  to set off material at beginning or
  at end of sentence, 388–390
  (P8)
  within end quotation marks, 403–
  404 **(P24)**
  within series after colon, 394–395
  (P14)
comma splice, 371–372 **(G48;** exercises, 372–373)
comparison, degrees of
  for adjectives, 328–330 **(G25;** exercises, 331)
  for adverbs, 328–330 **(G25;** exercises, 331)

comparison and contrast, 32–34 (exercise, 34; writing assignment, 34)

outlines, 94–96

complete/replete, 285

compound words, hyphens in, 410–411 **(P30)**

conclusions. *See* paragraphs, concluding

conjunctions, coordinating

at beginning of a sentence, 336–337 **(G29)**

comma before, 384–385 **(P5)**

defined, 335–336 **(G28; exercise, 336)**

semicolon before, 392–393 **(P12)**

conjunctions, subordinating, 335–336 **(G28; exercise, 336)**

conjunctive adverbs

defined, 337 **(G30)**

position of, 338

punctuation required with, 338, 393–394 **(P13)**

connotation, 63

conscience/conscious, 283

considerable/considerably, 283

content/contented, 283

contractions, 321 **(G21; exercises, 321–322)**

contrast, 423

see also tagmemics

contrast and comparison. *See* comparison and contrast

control sentence, 92–100 (exercises, 100–101)

coordinating conjunctions. *See* conjunctions, coordinating

correctness, 259–267

see also dictionaries; grammar; punctuation; spelling; usage

couldn't hardly, 283

could of/could have, 285

council/counsel, 283

critical reading, 51–78 (exercises, 78–79; writing assignments, 79–82)

cumulative sentences, 191–192 (exercises, 194)

dangling modifiers, 303–304 **(G11; exercise, 304)**

dashes, 407–409 **(P28)**

distinguished from hyphens, 409–410 **(P29)**

data is /data are, 268, 283

dates, punctuation of, 391 **(P10)**

debut (as a verb), 283

definition, as invention, 35–37 (exercise, 37; writing assignment, 38)

in critical reading, 58–59

description

associative patterns in, 127

invention for, 16–18 (exercise, 19; writing assignments, 19–20, 129)

organization of, 125–128 (exercise, 129)

dialects, 249–264 (exercises, 264–266)

dialogue

as invention, 24 (exercise, 25; writing assignment, 25–26)

paragraphing of, 396–397 **(P16)**

diction, colloquial, 142–143 (exercise, 144)

pretentious, 144–146 (exercise, 146)

dictionaries, 267–271 (exercises, 271–272)

direct questions, 374–376 **(G49; exercise, 376)**

discreet/discrete, 283

disinterested/uninterested, 283

distribution, 423

see also tagmemics

division and classification, 29–30 (exercise, 30–31; writing assignment, 31)

each

as singular antecedent, 314–315

as subject, 359 **(G43; exercise, 359)**

editor, citation of, 247–250

-eed/-ede, in spelling, 273

effect. *See* cause and effect

effect/affect, 282, 283

either, as singular antecedent, 314–315

ellipsis in quoted material, 49, 399–400 **(P19)**

eminent/imminent, 283

encyclopedias, 232–233

endnotes. *See* footnotes

Engfish, 5–7

enormity/enormousness, 283

enthuse, 283

enthymeme as evidence, 71

equally as, 283

essay in collection, citation of, 255

every, as subject, 359 **(G43;** exercise, 359)

everybody, as singular antecedent, 314–315

everyone, as singular antecedent, 314–315

evidence, 52–60

   sufficient, relevant, and random, 42

except/accept, 283

exclamation points

   as terminal punctuation, 383 **(P3)**

   next to quotation marks, 402–403 **(P22)**

exposition. *See* rhetorical stance, expository

fact, 55–56

farther/further, 283

faulty parallelism, 154–156 (exercise, 156–157)

faulty predication, 153–154 (exercise, 154)

field, 424

   see also tagmemics

finalize, 283

finite and nonfinite verb forms, 298–299 **(G9;** exercise, 299–300)

footnotes, 249–253

   for second reference, 253

   sample entries, 222–223, 253–256

   when needed, 240–241

   see also articles, citation of; books, citation of

formally/formerly, 283

fragments, 362–364 **(G46;** exercises, 364–370)

fused sentence, 370–371 **(G47;** exercises, 372–373)

garbles, 158–159 (exercise, 159–160)

gerunds, defined, 299 **(G9;** exercise, 299–300)

good/well, 283, 326

grammar, 287–377

   defined, 287 **(G1)**

   usefulness for writers, 288 **(G2)**

Hamlet's-father's-ghost syndrome, 251–252

headquarter, as a verb, 283

he/him, 340–341 **(G33;** exercise, 341)

hopefully, 271, 283

Humanities Index, 207

hyphens

   at end of a line, 411–412 **(P31)**

   distinguished from dashes, 409–410 **(P29)**

   in compound words, 410–411 **(P30)**

I, authorial, 317 **(G18;** exercise, 319)

idiolect, 264

idiom, tangled 141–142 (exercise, 142)

images, 19

I/me, 282, 284, 340–341 **(G33;** exercise, 341)

imminent/eminent, 283

imply/infer, 270, 284

I/myself, 284

indirect questions, 374–376 **(G49;** exercise, 376)

inductive leap, 42

infer/imply, 270, 284

infinitives

   defined, 299 **(G9;** exercise, 299–300)

   split, 301–302 **(G10;** exercise, 302)

in regards to/in regard to, 285
interjections, 339 **(G32)**
International Index, 207
interviewing, 44–50 (exercise, 50; writing assignment, 50)
introductions. *See* paragraphs, first
invention
    Burke's pentad as, 415–422
    cause and effect as, 39–43
    comparison and contrast as, 32–34
    critical reading as, 51–78
    definition as, 35–37
    dialogue as, 22–25
    division and classification as, 29–30
    for descriptive writing, 16–18
    for narrative writing, 20–21
    interview as, 44–50
    library research as, 228–242
    process analysis as, 27–28
    tagmemics as, 423–428
    see also writing assignments
irony, 73–78
irregardless, 284
its/it's, 320–321

jargon, 144–146 (exercise, 146)
journals, citation of. *See* articles, citation of
judgments, 55, 60

latter, referring to last of three, 284
lay/lie, 284
leave/let, 284
length, rhythm, and variety in sentences, 167–171 (exercises, 171–173)
liable/likely, 284
like, as, as if, 284, 339 **(G31)**
linguistics and dialectal variety, 259–264

mad/angry, 284
magazines. *See* articles, citation of
A Manual for Writers of Term Papers, Theses, and Dissertations, 245

A Manual of Style, 245
MLA Handbook for Writers of Research Papers, Theses, and Dissertations, 208, 245–246, 249
modifiers
    dangling, 303–304 **(G11;** exercise, 304)
    squinting, 303–304 **(G11;** exercise, 304)
myself/I, 284

narration
    invention for, 20–21 (exercises, 20–22; writing assignments, 22, 124–125)
    organization of, 122–124 (exercise, 124)
negotiate/cope with, 284
noisome/noisy, 284
nominative absolute. *See* absolute
nonfinite verb forms, 298–299 **(G9;** exercise, 299–300)
not . . . but, 282
notes. *See* footnotes
note-taking
    in interviews, 47–48
    in library research, 236–238
notify, 270
nouns
    collective, 353–356 **(G40;** exercise, 356)
    defined, 306–307 **(G14;** exercises, 307–308)
    omission of plural marker, 308–309 **(G15;** exercise, 309)
nowhere near, 285
nowhere/nowheres, 285

objective case, 340–341 **(G33)**
object of preposition, 333
off/off of, 285
one, generic, 318–319 **(G19;** exercise, 219)
one who, 285, 360, **(G44;** exercise, 360)
only, 285

organization. *See* arranging
outlines
  beyond basic, 96–100
  for comparison and contrast,
    94–96
  for expository papers, 92–100
    (checkpoint, 102)
  for persuasive papers, 87–89
    (checkpoint, 92)
  plural-noun formula, 93–94
outside/outside of, 285
over . . . less, 285

paragraphs
  basic pattern, 111–116 (exercises,
    116–117)
  beyond the basic pattern, 117–121
    (exercises, 121–122)
  concluding, 130–135 (exercises,
    135)
  descriptive, 125–128 (exercise,
    129)
  first, 104–111 (exercises, 111)
  narrative, 122–124 (exercise, 124)
parallelism, faulty, 154–156 (exercise, 156–157)
paraphrase, distinguished from plagiarism, 238–242 (exercises,
  242–243)
parentheses, 407–409 **(P28)**
participle, past
  as stylistic device, 175–177 (exer-
    cise, 177–178)
  defined, 175, 293–294 **(G7;** exer-
    cises, 294–295)
  irregular, 294 **(G7;** exercises,
    294–295)
  problems with form, 295–296
    (G8; exercises, 296–298)
participle, present
  as stylistic device, 173–174 (exer-
    cise, 174–175)
  defined, 173
  distinguished from gerund, 299
    (G9; exercise, 299–300)
particle, 424
  see also tagmemics
  parts of speech, 288–289 **(G4)**

passive voice, 165
  avoiding, 151–152 (exercise, 153)
  defined, 305–306 **(G13;** exercise,
    306)
past tense and past participles,
  problems with forms, 295–296
  (G8; exercises, 296–298)
  see also participle, past
pentad, Kenneth Burke's, 415–422
  (exercises, 422; writing assignment, 422–423)
percent, 285
percentage, 285
periodicals. *See* articles, citation of
periodic sentence, 189–191 (exercise, 194)
periods
  as terminal punctuation, 383 **(P3)**
  within end quotation marks, 403–
    404 **(P24)**
persuasion. *See* rhetorical stance,
  persuasive
plagiarism, distinguished from paraphrase, 238–242 (exercises,
  242–243)
plays, titles in citation, 248
  see also titles, capitalization of
plural form of nouns (exercise, 279)
  nouns ending in *f*, 276
  nouns ending in *o*, 277–278
  nouns ending in *y*, 276
  nouns from other languages, 278
  omitted marker, 308–309 **(G15;**
    exercise, 309)
  regular, 275
plural-noun formula, 93–94
plurals marked by apostrophe, 406–
  407 **(P26)**
poems, titles in citation, 248
  see also titles, capitalization of
poetry, quoting from, 400–401 **(P20)**
possessive
  marked by apostrophe, 404–406
    (P25)
  of pronouns, 320–321 **(G20;** ex-
    ercises, 321–322)
post hoc fallacy, 40–41
precedent, as evidence, 72

predicate, defined, 153

predication, faulty, 153–154 (exercise, 154)

prepositions

  at end of sentence or clause, 334–335 **(G27)**

  defined, 331–333 **(G26;** exercises, 333)

  distinguished from conjunctions, 338–339 **(G31)**

  object of, 333

presently/currently, 285

present participle. *See* participle, present

pretentious diction, 144–146 (exercise, 146)

prewriting. *See* invention

principal parts of verbs, 293–294 **(G7;** exercises, 294–295)

principal/principle, 285

process analysis, as invention, 27–28 (exercise, 28; writing assignments, 28–29, 124–125)

profuse, 271

prolific, 270

pronoun reference, 309–311 **(G16;** exercises, 311–312)

  to phrases and clauses, 310–311

  to possessive nouns, 311

pronouns

  agreement, 312–316 **(G17;** exercises, 316–317)

  defined, 309 **(G16;** exercise, 311–312)

  possessive forms, 320–321 **(G20;** exercises, 321–322)

  relative, 322 **(G22;** exercise, 323)

  sexism in use of, 315

prophecy/prophesy, 285

Publication Manual of the American Psychological Association, 245

punctuation, 378–412 (exercise, 412–413)

  an introduction to, 378–882 **(P1)**

purpose, 416

  see also pentad, Kenneth Burke's

question marks

  as terminal punctuation, 383 **(P3)**

  next to end quotation marks, 402–403 **(P22)**

questions

  an open set, 22–25 (exercises, 25; writing assignment, 25–26)

  as invention for library research, 234–236

  direct and indirect, 374–376 **(G49;** exercise, 376)

  five senses as, 16–18 (exercise, 19)

  journalistic, 20–21 (exercise, 21–22)

quick/quickly, 326

quotation marks

  double and single, 397 **(P17)**

quotation marks, closed

  next to colons, 403 **(P23)**

  next to commas, 403–404 **(P24)**

  next to exclamation points, 402–403 **(P22)**

  next to periods, 403–404 **(P24)**

  next to question marks, 402–403 **(P22)**

  next to semicolons, 403 **(P23)**

quotation marks, open

  commas before, 395–396 **(P15)**

quotation/quote, 285

quotations

  accuracy, 48

  alterations in brackets, 49, 399–400 **(P19)**

  ellipsis in, 49, 399–400 **(P19)**

  footnoting, 240–241, 249–253

  from poetry, 400–402 **(P20)**

  in dialogue, 396–397 **(P16)**

  more than four lines, 398 **(P18)**

  preceded by colon, 396

  within quotations, 397 **(P17)**

quoted material, errors in, 400 **(P19)**

rang/rung, 285

Reader's Guide to Periodical Literature, 203, 204, 231–232

reading. *See* critical reading

real/really, 326
reductio ad absurdum, 75
reference, in pronouns, 309–311 **(G16;** exercises, 311–312)
refer/refer back, 285
repetition, 157 (exercise, 157–158)
replete/complete, 285
research, in the library, 228–242
research paper. *See* term paper
rhetorical stance, 84–85
    expository, 92–100 (exercises, 100–101; writing assignment, 101)
    persuasive, 90 (exercises, 90–92; writing assignment, 92)
rhythm, variety, and length in sentences, 167–171 (exercises, 171–173)

same, 285
scene, 416
    see also pentad, Kenneth Burke's
seldom/seldom ever, 286
selecting and arranging. *See* arranging
semicolons
    before coordinating conjunctions, 392–393 **(P12)**
    distinguished from colons, 391–392 **(P11)**
    in series after colon, 394–395 **(P14)**
    next to end quotation marks, 403 **(P23)**
    with conjunctive adverbs, 393–394 **(P13)**
sentence combining and generating exercises, 166–167, 174–175, 177–178, 179–180, 181–182, 183–184, 185–187, 193–194
sentence fragments, 362–364 **(G46;** exercises, 364–370)
sentences
    balanced, 188–189 (exercise, 193)
    control, 92–100 (exercises, 100–101)

cumulative, 191–192 (exercise, 194)
    fused, 370–371 **(G47;** exercises, 372–373)
    periodic, 189–191 (exercise, 194)
separate, 273
series
    as stylistic device, 184–185 (exercises, 185–187)
    commas and semicolons within, 394–395 **(P14)**
    defined, 184
series comma, 385–386 **(P6)**
series is/series are, 286
served/serviced, 286
-s/-es
    in spelling, 275–278 (exercise, 279)
    omitted in plural of nouns, 308–309)
set/sit, 286
sexist usage in pronouns, 315
she/her, 340–341 **(G33;** exercise, 341)
SHLC, 229
short stories
    citation of, 248
    see also titles, capitalization of
sic, 400 **(P19)**
site/sight/cite, 286
slow/slowly, 286, 326
Social Sciences and Humanities Index, 207
Social Sciences Index, 203, 204, 207
some one/someone, 286
spelling, 3, 272–279 (exercises, 279)
split infinitives, 301–302 **(G10;** exercise, 302)
squinting modifiers, 303–304 **(G11;** exercise, 304)
stance, rhetorical. *See* rhetorical stance
stationary/stationery, 286
statistics, 59
story in a collection, citation of, 255
structure, 65–66, 70
    see also arranging

style, 163–196 (writing assignment, 196–197)
  as the person, 195–196
  defined, 163
  see also sentence combining and generating exercises
style manuals, 245–246
subject, defined, 153, 344–345 (**G35;** exercises, 345–346)
Subject Headings Used in the Dictionary Catalog of the Library of Congress, 299
subject-verb agreement. *See* agreement of verbs with subjects
subordinating conjunctions. *See* conjunctions, subordinating
suffixes, 274–275
superlative
  of adjectives, 328–330 (**G25;** exercise, 331)
  of adverbs, 328–330 (**G25;** exercises, 331)
supposed to/suppose to, 28
sure/surely, 326
synonymy, 164–166 (exercises, 166–167)

tagmemics, 423–428 (exercise, 428; writing assignment, 428)
taking notes. *See* note-taking
tangled idiom, 141–142 (exercise, 142)
tense, past
  problems with forms, 295–296 (**G8;** exercises, 296–298)
tense, unnecessary shifts, 376–377 (**G50**)
term paper, 201–256 (writing assignment, 244)
  diary of, 201–210
  sample, 211–225
terrible/terribly, 326
than . . . any other, 282
their, agreement, 284
theirs/there's, 320–321
there is/there are, 358 (**G42;** exercise, 358–359)

these kind, 284
thesis, 85–87 (exercises, 90–91)
they/them, 340–341 (**G33;** exercise, 341)
this here, 284
thus/thusly, 286
titles
  capitalization of 382 **(P2)**
  form in citation, 248, 401–402 **(P21)**
tone, 63–65, 69–70, 76
topic sentence, 113–116 (exercises, 116–117)
  in descriptive paragraphs, 128
transitions, 118–121 (exercises, 121–122)
translator, citation of, 247–250, 256
try and/try to, 286
T-units, 172–174
"Turabian," 245
type, 286

uninterested/disinterested, 283
unique, compared, 286
usage, 3, 280–286
  reference books for, 280–281
use to/used to, 271, 286

variation, 423
  see also tagmemics
variety, length, and rhythm in sentences, 167–171 (exercises, 171–173)
verb
  defined, 289 (**G4;** exercise, 290)
  finite and nonfinite forms, 298–299 (**G9;** exercise, 299–300)
  of being and perception with adjectives, 327
  principal parts, 293–294 (**G7;** exercises, 294–295)
  problems with past and past participles, 295–296 (**G8;** exercises, 296–298)
verb phrase
  defined, 290–291 (**G5;** exercise, 291–292)
  split, 292 (**G6;** exercise, 293)

verb "to be"
   agreement in, 349–350 (**G38;** exercise, 350–351)
   avoiding, 150 (exercise, 150–151)
   defined, 305 **(G13)**
vocabulary, 4–5, 163
voice, active. *See* active voice
voice, passive. *See* passive voice
voice as style, 196

wave, 424
   see also tagmemics
we, authorial, 317–318 (**G19;** exercise, 319)
well/good, 283, 326
who's/whose, 286
who/whom, 342–344 (**G34;** exercise, 344)
wordiness, 138–139 (exercise, 139)
writing
   as an unnatural form of speech, 3–5 (exercises, 9–11; writing assignments, 11)
   as a way of thinking, 2
   as hard work, 7–9
writing assignments
   based on Burke's pentad, 422–423
   based on tagmemics, 428
   cause and effect, 43–44
   comparison and contrast, 34
   definition, 38
   description, 19–20, 129
   division and classification, 31
   expository, 101
   from critical reading, 79–82
   from interview, 50
   from observation, 25–26
   narrative, 22, 124–125
   persuasive, 92
   preliminary, 11
   process analysis, 28–29, 124–125
   research paper, 244
   stylistic variation, 196–197
wrong word, 140 (exercise, 140–141)

you, generic, 318–319 (**G19;** exercise, 319)

Twelve Problems in Style

Problem	Symbol	Page
1. Wordiness		138
2. Wrong Word	*WW*	140
3. Tangled Idiom	*ID*	141
4. Colloquial Diction	*D↓*	142
5. Pretentious Diction (Jargon)	*D↑*	144
6. Cliché	*cliché*	147
7. The Verb *Be*	*BE*	150
8. Passive Voice	*PV*	151
9. Faulty Predication	*FP*	153
10. Faulty Parallelism	*X*	154
11. Repetition	*rep.*	157
12. Garbles	*?*	158